Best Wishes

Jim Speight

FORK-TAIL DEVIL

The Biography of
First Lieutenant Robert Carl Milliken
(US Army Air Corps, 1942–46)
World War II Fighter Ace
and
Husband, Father, Grandfather, Great-Grandfather

James G. Speight

authorHOUSE®

AuthorHouse™
1663 Liberty Drive
Bloomington, IN 47403
www.authorhouse.com
Phone: 1 (800) 839-8640

Published by AuthorHouse 01/15/2015

ISBN: 978-1-4969-6423-6 (sc)
ISBN: 978-1-4969-6415-1 (e)

Library of Congress Control Number: 2015900551

Tribute

To fallen comrades—gone but never forgotten
and to all men and women who have fought for the United States

A nation reveals itself not only by the men it produces
but also by the men it honors, the men it remembers.
—John F. Kennedy, 1963

Contents

FORK-TAIL DEVIL

This is an American story as told to me during many conversations that I had over a four-year period with Robert (Bob) Carl Milliken. The book is the result of the urgings of many colleagues and friends. They have wanted to know—in specific terms—how a boy from Hanna rose to become a fighter pilot in the United States Army Air Corps. There is interest in those critical growing-up years during which Bob's yearning to fly developed from a dream and became a reality. Then followed the years when his aircraft—the Lockheed P-38 Lightning—became his weapon of destruction as his flying skills took him to the level of fighter ace. So this is Bob's story. It is being told so that the reader can have a better understanding of the mortal combat known as World War II.

The account of Bob's life is important because it tells of men and women who stood up to be counted when their country called—people whose deeds are fading into history and soon may be forgotten. This is not the first book to tell of the full life experience of a man from the High Plains, and I hope it will not be the last. Bob grew up as most boys did on the High Plains, learning to hunt, herding sheep, and attending school as the family managed to cope with day-to-day living. This is significant, as this type of life makes a man such as Bob. But typical of Bob, all he had done (he continued to remind me) was to serve his country as many other American men and women had done.

I have chosen to start with the arrival of Bob's family in the Wyoming Territory before statehood was conferred on it, and I follow the events which led Bob to his actions as a World War II fighter ace and then as husband, father, grandfather, and great-grandfather. For the reader, I have also placed Bob's life in the perspective of the parallel actions that occurred in the Western United States and then during World War II in the European and Pacific Theaters.

Bob was seventy years old when I was first introduced to him at a meeting of the local Rotary Club. Now he is approaching ninety-two, one of the few men remaining who enlisted within days of the Japanese attack on Pearl Harbor. Because of his quiet manner, it is difficult to picture him in the heat of an airplane dogfight. Instead, I can easily imagine him as a boy living in Hanna on the High Plains of Wyoming. I see the vast expanses of the High Plains with Bob, a diminutive figure, in the sunbaked windy landscape with sagebrush in abundance.

When Bob and I first met, I had heard (via the whispered grapevine of the Rotary Club) that he had been christened a fighter ace—having secured five confirmed kills of enemy aircraft. At that time, we did not know that we'd create this book, and I had to decline to write the story of his life. I had several contracts to write technical books as well as several visits to teach at various places throughout the world. I did suggest that he make contacts and invite someone to write a *memoir* of his life

As a person who was born in a mining village in northeastern England at the beginning of World War II, and being a child of the World War II years, I am familiar through experience and reading with many of the actions described in this book. I also found that we had much in common as a result of Bob being initially stationed in England prior to the D-Day landings of Allied forces on the beaches of Normandy (Operation Overlord) and my fascination with history. We talked and talked and talked. But talking with Bob was not enough. Stories of that cruel war have always caught my attention. Then, hearing of Bob's childhood on the High Plains took me into another area of the interest—the history of the western United States in the immediate aftermath of the Civil War. Then everything began to fit together. Bob still requested that I compile a full history of his family and his service to his country, and so almost four years ago I was honored to undertake the task.

Early in the project, Bob did express some concerns. He was uncertain that his memory would be true to the events that he described to me. If his memories seem to diverge from accepted history, his memories take precedence. This is an accurate depiction of the wealth of information that Bob remembers and passed to me. He also worried about failing to remember something important—an incident, the survival or death of a colleague—or whether or not he would remember something incorrectly, or if readers would find his story to be unexciting. There are some things that Bob remembers that do not (and cannot) match completely with history as written in a textbook—which is to be expected, especially concerning the wartime events experienced by military personnel. Soon such memories will be the stuff of legends as they pass into unwritten history.

In the book, the reader is introduced to a close look at Bob's childhood, after surviving a close call with death on the birthing table and with appendicitis during boyhood years. This is a childhood that, generally speaking, represents the formative years of generations of children from the High Plains. It examines the courage and fortitude that that imbued many flyers, foot soldiers, and naval personnel in World War II who fought against tyranny and oppression.

As my weekly conversations with Bob progressed, I began to write. His calm, modest voice remained strong as he told me his multifaceted story. His manner also reminded me that traditionally, World War II warriors are private people. They do not seek praise or applause when they have simply done their duty. In the telling of his story, Bob's request is simple and unassuming—he hopes that those readers who are not familiar with the events of World War II will appreciate and understand something outside their own experience, and that those who are the families of World War II veterans will remember with pride the men and women who answered the call of their country.

The story recounts the beginnings of Bob's passion for flying, and of the men he trained and flew with during World War II. Most of them were still in their teens when, on December 7, 1941, bombs rained down on Pearl Harbor, destroying part of the US Pacific Fleet and changing the world that America knew. The tragic events of that violent Sunday morning and the days that followed are difficult to comprehend or even imagine.

Overnight, high school dances and homecoming events were pushed aside by recruiting posters and nightly radio newscasts reporting Axis advances and Allied defeats. In the days following that fateful Sunday, men and women of Bob's generation across America stepped forward without hesitation to fight for their country and turn the tide of Axis domination in Europe. They flocked to the recruiting offices, and there was no question of their motives—the United

States had been attacked and the young men and young women of America were willing and ready to volunteer to stand up and defend their country.

Bob flew sixty-eight combat missions, and the reader is able to follow his (and the squadron's) flights into combat. This not only adds realism to the narrative but also allows the readers to see the depth of penetration of the squadron into Nazi-occupied Europe. Bob also has the distinction of being the last pilot to achieve *ace status* with the P-38 Lightning in northern Europe.

Bob and his colleagues were not only true Americans, but they were extraordinary individuals who volunteered, even before the call to arms was made. They were part of a generation who fought—through a long, painstaking process—and stood, determined to remove the concepts and beliefs of a National Socialist regime from Europe and the world. All parts of the process were news in their day, but as the years have moved on and the surviving veterans died, there has been a tendency for their brave actions to be forgotten as they fade into the mists of history.

The actions and sacrifices made by the men and women of Bob's generation must never be forgotten. Each is an individual story that *must* be told, and we owe a debt of gratitude to all men and women who answered the call to arms. The few remaining survivors of those men and women who fought World War II are now aging veterans who make the sentimental journeys to stand reverently at the side of the graves of their fallen comrades and remember them as they were on the day that they fell—young men and women who had just emerged from their teen years.

And there is the other side of war for the pilot and aircrew. It is always a traumatic experience to see colleagues go down in burning aircraft, knowing that they were gone forever. Even when a pilot escaped from a stricken aircraft, he would still be in danger from enemy pilots shooting at him as he hung in his parachute and also, if he survived and was captured on landing, in danger from the dreaded SS and Gestapo. These are the devastating memories of war that stay in mind for many decades.

Tribute is also due to all armed forces personnel and their supporters who fought during the war and also to people such as Mademoiselle Suzanne Schneider—a citizen of France, despite the German-sounding name—and her colleagues, who resisted the efforts of the occupying German forces and put themselves in the path of the hated Gestapo. Their efforts must also be continuously remembered, not forgotten in the mists of time.

I am also thankful to Scott Frederick, son of First Lieutenant James S. Frederick, a P-38 pilot in the 428th Fighter Squadron, 474th Fighter Group, for providing his father's story and also for the translation of the original version of the journal of Mademoiselle Suzanne Schneider, which was a notebook written during the time (July 6, 1944, to August 1, 1944) that the Allied forces were gaining a foothold in fortress Europe and pushing the German forces back into Germany.

And last but definitely not least, there is also Zella's story—the young woman who Bob married on August 25, 1946, and who bore four children, three daughters and one son. Zella's family history is also interesting. The family can be traced back to 1617 in England, and she is a descendent of one of the two *regicide judges* who authorized the execution of King Charles I of England after he was deposed by the forces of Oliver Cromwell during the English Civil War (1642–49). Furthermore, this book is not only a tribute to Bob and Zella but also to Zella's brother Bobby (Master Sergeant Robert Lewis Bell), who saw action on many missions as the belly gunner in a B-24 bomber and who researched the history of the Bell family in considerable detail.

For the person who may not be familiar with this subject, I have tried to avoid technical jargon and elaborate footnotes. In the text I have provided helpful background explanations, because I believe that they are relevant to the story and important to a wide circle of readers. I have also been able to make use of publications that are listed in the section headlined as *Information Sources*. Those who are interested in learning more after reading this book can turn to these sources.

I want to express my gratitude to the members of the Laramie Writers' Group (who wish to remain anonymous as individuals). Being accomplished and published writers, their comments were constructive, meaningful, helpful, and always welcome.

Finally, throughout the writing of this book, it has been my pleasure and privilege to get to know Bob and Zella on a more personal basis, and I also thank them for giving me unrestricted access to their family archives.

I also give grateful thanks to Mr. James David of Worland, Wyoming, who allowed me to use his portrait of Bob and the P-38 Lightning to use as cover art for the book.

Dr. James G. Speight, PhD, DSc, PhD
Laramie, Wyoming, USA

Chapter 1: The Beginnings

For one hundred years commencing in the mid-to-late nineteenth century, the primary form of transcontinental travel in the United States was by rail. The railroad ran on steam which was generated by the coal-fired boiler, making the various towns in Wyoming, which were separated by a network of six thousand miles of dirt roads, more accessible.

Towns such as Hanna could provide coal for rail transport. The trains of the Union Pacific Railroad ran east to west and west to east, and all stopped in Hanna for coal and water. Coal was mined in Hanna, and water was piped into Hanna from the hills near Elk Mountain, where it was stored in the Hanna reservoir. The importance of Hanna grew as coal became essential for other sources of energy, such as electricity, and the city became a prime target for men seeking work and also provided opportunities for those with entrepreneurial skills.

Hanna was a typical western town—the Wyoming breeze (a twenty-five-mile-per-hour wind) blew almost every day. Dust, tumbleweed, dogs, horses, the occasional feral cats, rats, mice, and sundry other animals from the nearby plains could be seen in the streets. The Ford Hotel (owned and operated by Mrs. Mary Ford, the widowed and later remarried mother of Dr. Stebner, the dentist) supplied comfortable accommodation for visitors, especially for schoolteachers who were brought in from other parts of the country to work in the local school. However, the schoolteachers were responsible for the costs of their own accommodation.

But this was not always the case, and the quality could vary, as a segment from the journal of Anna Doggett (who became Mother Anna) illustrates:

Before marrying Robert Milliken (Father Robert) I was a country school teacher when I first started to teach. My wages were from thirty five to fifty dollars per month over the period that I taught. Many of the small towns where I taught could not afford hotel accommodation so we were boarded in the town or the district around the town and usually fared fairly well. But it was anything but modern in terms of toilet facilities and comfort.

Sleeping accommodation did not always have any privacy—I once shared my bed with a nine year old girl. Another time I shared my room with the two children in the home—there was a curtain on a taught wire between my bed and the twin cots of the children.

The houses for the miners were simple and for the most part were owned by the Union Pacific Coal Company, and taxes on businesses were unknown. Virtually all businesses (with, it seems, the exception of the Ford Hotel) were owned by the coal company. Most of the houses had only cold water. Water was piped to each house, but the occupants were responsible for their own water heating, usually on the stove. The town water supply came courtesy of the Union Pacific Railroad from a dam in the nearby mountains that fed water into two reservoirs.

The company store provided most of the supplies and goods required by the families. The miners were paid in tokens (with an occasional cash payout) for use in the company store. The railroad also provided an ice house that was available to the Hanna populace. Ice was taken from a nearby frozen lake during the winter months.

A deputy sheriff lived in a house that sat on a hill overlooking the town, from where he could see most of the happenings in the town, some of which might be of concern to him. Any legal matters and differences in opinion, whatever the nature and cause, were first attended to by a lawyer whose name is lost in the mists of history, but he lived in Hanna and owned his own house. More serious cases were adjudicated by a judge in the law court at Rawlins.

It was into this environment that Robert Carl Milliken was born on June 6, 1922, at the Milliken home in Hanna. The birth was not easy for mother and baby. Fortunately, a doctor was present, and both mother and son survived.

But perhaps first things first…

***

The records of the Milliken name show an ancient origin (pre-1100 AD), and the name was first used by the ancient Strathclyde-Briton people of the Scottish-English border country. The first Milliken family lived in Wigtown, a former royal burgh in the Machars of Galloway (the Plains of Galloway) in the southwest of Scotland. This burgh was first mentioned in an indenture of 1292, and the sheriff of the area was in existence in 1263.

The saga of the Milliken family in the United States began in the mid-nineteenth century when William Milliken, a native of Scotland and Bob's paternal great-grandfather, moved to Ireland to live in the city of Newtownards, County Down, just a short distance from Dublin. He was a weaver by trade, and he, with his wife Mary, moved to Ireland to serve as a Presbyterian missionary. His zeal for expansion of the church was almost unmatched.

At that time there were several hundred Presbyterians living in the area, and Great-Grandfather William was trying to organize them into a distinct church group that was to follow the Presbyterian way of life. To this end, in 1853 he sent a note to the Presbyterian inhabitants of Newtownards with the following message:

It is now upward of a year since a number of individuals impressed with the spiritual destitution of the humbler classes of the Town, established the Newtownards Town Mission. The actual amount of destitution was brought out in the Report read at the public meeting, held in August last, from which it appeared that upward of 400 Presbyterian Families were wholly unconnected with any House of Worship. The readiness with which these families have availed themselves of the agency established for their benefit has been manifested in the large attendance at the various meetings held in connection with the Mission. The result has been that a large number of those families, having gradually become anxious for the enjoyment of more extended spiritual privileges than a Town Mission is able to afford, have originated a movement of the attainment of this object and already attached their names to a document declaring their desire to be formed into a Congregation in which all ordnances of the

Gospel may be administered to them. Their aim is simply to procure the enjoyment of all the means of grace for themselves, without interfering in the slightest degree with an existing Congregational interest. As a considerable interval must elapse before a meeting of the Presbytery occurs, at which their case could be laid before it—to prevent the families who have subscribed their names being scattered, and what they conceive to be a good work temporary checked; they have requested the Town Missionary to continue his labors amongst them, till they shall be regularly organized by the Presbytery, with which request he has complied.

They desire the sympathy of all who are in the enjoyment of those spiritual privileges which they wish to obtain for themselves, and in due time may call upon them for their assistance in carrying out the proposed object.

Signed on behalf of the Committee of the above Families,
William Milliken.
Newtownards, 15th February, 1853

However, Great-Grandfather William's efforts were often interrupted by religious (often sectarian) violence. During one demonstration he was dragged through the street by his beard. He was a very stern individual and even such treatment—his injuries were not recorded or mentioned by him to anyone—did not deter him from his task.

His missionary activities and thoughts were at a high peak, and his stern nature, embedded in him by his Scottish Presbyterian upbringing, caused his son—John Milliken, born in 1854, eventually known as Grandfather John—to be dissatisfied with that style of living, so he left Ireland in 1869 at the ripe old age of fifteen to *go it alone* and make a life for himself elsewhere. Initially, John had just wanted to live elsewhere with his brother Robert, a mine superintendent living and working in Scotland, in the area of Blair castle, the ancient seat of the Dukes and Earls of Atholl. But John's feelings for elsewhere ran deep, and his thoughts were for open plains and grasslands. The United States was trying to recover from the costly Civil War that had decimated the available manpower—immigrants either with education or a strong work ethic were more than welcome.

Robert was an engineering graduate of the University of Edinburgh who came to Pennsylvania to run a coal mine in Shenandoah, Schuylkill County. He was to be a victim of the group known as the Molly Maguires—a nineteenth-century secret society of mainly Irish and Irish American coal miners who were active in the anthracite coal fields of Pennsylvania between the time of the Civil War until a series of sensational arrests and trials from 1876–78.

Robert was warned by the priest's sister that he was in imminent danger—the reason for this is not known—and left town with a young family to go to Rock Springs, Wyoming. He later went to Coal Creek, Colorado, where he died in 1898 at the age of about fifty-two as the result of a mine accident where he was the superintendent of the Rockvale Mines. He, his wife Jean Tait Milliken, and his son George Washington Milliken are buried in a family plot in the Highland Union Cemetery, Florence, Colorado. Rockvale and Coal Creek were mining towns near Florence. Robert's eldest sons, William Boyd Milliken and John Tait Milliken, graduated from the Colorado School of Mines in 1893 and 1894, respectively. William Boyd's grandson, W.B. Milliken III, also graduated from the School of Mines.

***

After a sojourn with his brother, who had moved on to the United States, Grandfather John decided to seek his fortune elsewhere. He moved further afield and followed Robert to the United States, where opportunities were available to the ordinary working men that were not available in Great Britain (now called the United Kingdom). His first stop was Pennsylvania, followed in 1875 by the move to Carbon, and thereafter to Hanna—both mining towns in the High Plains of Wyoming. He had heard of the coal being mined in the area and knew that there would be work.

Ignoring the risk, he traveled to the High Plains, intrigued by outcroppings in the mountains that ranged around the area, seeing the occasional prospector who still believed that a fortune was to be made from gold and silver, especially silver that had been discovered in bounteous veins to the south in the Arizona Territory. But precious metals were never discovered in great quantities in Wyoming, although a small amount of gold was discovered near South Pass—the lowest point (7,412 feet elevation) on the Continental Divide in the western part of the state—prompting a small rush in the 1860s. The vast majority of prospectors were misinformed, as coal was the black gold of the future.

These were difficult times, and the life was not smooth. One year after John Milliken's arrival in Hanna, on June 25, 1876, General George Armstrong Custer and his ill-fated Seventh Cavalry were annihilated at the Little Big Horn.

To give this story more perspective—at about this same time, John Henry Holliday (aka Doc Holliday) was in Cheyenne (Wyoming territory). He had realized that gambling at cards was more to his liking than dentistry, and was making his way by this roundabout route south to Arizona Territory where he would eventually meet with the Earp brothers and join them in the infamous gunfight at the OK

Corral on October 26, 1881. Holiday had the misfortune to have his wallet and its monetary contents removed or commandeered from his person by an unfriendly highwayman just outside of Cheyenne.

Needless to say, Doc Holiday was not amused—which did nothing to improve Holiday's somewhat poor disposition toward others. So much for the brief sojourn by Doc Holiday on the High Plains of Wyoming. After the gunfight, his deteriorating health finally led him to settle in the high-altitude town of Leadville, Colorado, for many years, along with many other well-known names of that era. He died of tuberculosis at age 36 on November 8, 1887, in Glenwood Springs, Colorado.

***

The *High Plains* are a subregion of the *Great Plains* in the central United States, generally encompassing the western part of the Great Plains on the east side of the Rocky Mountains.

The eastern boundary of the High Plains is often cited as the 100th meridian or the 1,968-foot contour or elevation line. But prairie vegetation boundaries are flexible, advancing or retreating in response to the weather. Located in the rain shadow of the Rocky Mountains, the High Plains of southeastern Wyoming rise in elevation to over 6,000 feet and are semiarid, receiving between ten and twenty inches of precipitation annually. Prairie short-grass, prickly pear cacti, and scrub vegetation (mostly sagebrush) cover the region, with occasional buttes or other rocky outcrops. The arid nature of the region necessitates either dry-land farming methods or irrigation, taking water from the underlying aquifers. The High Plains of Wyoming have significant coal deposits as well as petroleum and natural gas reservoirs.

In contrast to the states and territories to the south, which in the mid-to-late nineteenth century were rich sources of silver, the High

Plains of Wyoming are a major source of coal, oil, gas, and uranium for the nation. For example, the Powder River Basin in northeastern Wyoming and southeastern Montana is home to the largest low-sulfur coal reserves in the United States. Low-sulfur coal burns cleaner than the high-sulfur coal found in the eastern United States. The coal in the Powder River Basin is found in thick seams—horizontal layers of solid coal running for miles beneath the earth's surface. Some of these seams are a hundred feet thick and close to the surface, so the coal can be mined without going far underground. As a result, huge quantities of low-cost, high-quality coal can be shipped by rail to more than twenty states to generate electricity.

***

Mining was a difficult way to survive, both at work, which occupied most of a miner's waking hours, and at home, where family life was restricted to a few hours of waking time each day. Because of the long hours, lack of family life, and harsh working conditions (not necessarily in that order), the miners became increasingly militant. Hence unionization was born, and there was a strong tendency to view all mine owners and superintendents as enemies of the miners. The mine owners (on both sides of the Atlantic) refused to acknowledge the simple equations:

Dissatisfied miners = no miners
No miners = no coal production
No coal production = no sales of coal
No sales of coal = no profits
No profits = close the mine

Because of the attitudes of industry owners toward workers, the workers were entering a new phase in which they began to realize that these equations were indeed true. In this sense, workers in the United States were probably fifty years ahead of workers in other parts of the world. There were troublesome times, as workers banded together to make claims for fair pay and reasonable working hours with release from the deplorable conditions prevalent in many industries. Workers' unions were formed to represent workers' claims to industry owners. However, all was not well, and the problems were not solved to a high degree of satisfaction.

Because of this attitude by the mine owners and the differences of opinion with them, Robert, while living in Pennsylvania, somehow became embroiled in the various arguments—or "discussions" as they might be called. One might say that Robert was quite outspoken about the activities of the union, and he learned (via the miner's grapevine) that his name was on the union's do-him-grievous-bodily-harm-or-death list. The forewarning led to Robert's somewhat hasty but timely decision to move west. It was not surprising that Grandfather John followed his brother out west.

John worked his way as a miner through Colorado to the then-thriving town (now the ghost town) of Carbon, Wyoming. The town was so named (the French *charbon* means coal) because of the coal mining activities in the area.

There wasn't much in the area (now called Carbon County) in 1868 other than a small number of trappers and Native Americans, who were often hostile. Then coal was found north of Elk Mountain, and Thomas Wardell of Bevier, Missouri, brought a crew of miners from his coal properties in Missouri. Wardell leased Union Pacific lands at Carbon for a period of fifteen years. He contracted to sell coal for six dollars per ton for the first two years, five dollars a ton for the next three, four dollars per ton for the next four, and three dollars a ton for the next six years. Wardell was joined in this venture by Michael Quealy, William Hinton, and other unknown associates under the company name of Wyoming Coal & Mining Company, but the Union Pacific Railway's coal department took charge in 1874.

It was during these years that the territory of Wyoming recognized that there were inhabitants other than the mountain men, trappers, and Native Americans—all of whom gave to the territory as much as the men. Thus, in 1869, the people of Wyoming Territory recognized the contribution of women by enacting legislation that gave them the right to vote, making Wyoming Territory the first state or territory within the United States that was willing to recognize the natural rights of women. In fact, Wyoming was also the home of many other firsts for US women in politics. For the first time, women served on a jury in Wyoming (Laramie in 1870). Wyoming had the first female court bailiff (Mary Atkinson, Laramie, in 1870) and the first female justice of the peace in the country (Esther Hobart Morris, South Pass City, in 1870). Later, Wyoming became the first state in the Union to elect a female governor, Nellie Tayloe Ross, who was elected in 1924 and took office in January 1925.

In the meantime, from 1868 onward, the miners needed a place to set up housekeeping, which they did in Carbon, the first mining town to be established along the Union Pacific rail line. Houses in Carbon sprang up immediately, as miners dug caves into the side of the nearby ravine and covered the fronts with boards and earth, with a stovepipe poked thru a hole in the top of each roof. More substantial houses and buildings were later constructed using twelve-inch planks, but living conditions were primitive during most of the town's short life.

Seven mines were opened at Carbon, and during its heyday, six hundred men were employed there. They may have taken out as much as two hundred tons of coal each day. Early-day Carbon has been described as resembling a prairie dog village surrounded by sagebrush against the sage slopes. The *shoddies* (shacks) in which the miners lived were fashioned of stone slab gathered from nearby knolls, or of twelve-foot boards bought by the railroad and used upright, packed with sod to close gaps, and roofed with mortared earth or flattened tin cans.

And to make life really interesting, the area around Carbon had long been Native American hunting ground, and hostilities frequently broke out between miners and Indians. During those times it was not uncommon for Carbon's women and children to stay in the mines at night, while guards kept watch for *local hostiles* on the surface.

Furthermore, the mines themselves were not free from trouble, without any interference from the Indians. Troubles broke out in 1874 when four men were killed by cave-ins. That year also saw the burning of the No. 1 Mine shaft in which the mules Sage and Pete were trapped. The miners were not about to give up on the mules, and with the aid of rope and windlass, one man went down the shaft and secured ropes around the animals. Sage was hoisted to the surface without incident, but Pete, being of a somewhat feisty nature, began to struggle halfway up the shaft. The rope slipped around his neck, and when he was finally brought to the surface, he seemed to be dead. But Pete was a sturdy animal, and much to the delight (or relief) of the rescuers, he revived and went back to work, along with Sage, pulling coal cars through the mine tunnels.

Shortly after Sage and Pete had been hauled up the No. 1 shaft, an Italian (whose name is unknown) was hired to fill in the mine. When he was about midway through the job, he fell down the shaft and was killed. Another incident occurred in the No. 1 Mine when the shaft was being flooded by water entering through surface caves. The women of Carbon sewed sacking together to be filled with sand and used as levees for diverting the water flow away from the mine.

The No. 2 Mine had an interesting ventilation system—boys aged ten or so were the so-called *trappers*, who would pull strings that opened and shut doors to the mine tunnels. The door facing the prevailing wind was opened, and fresh air was forced through the mine. While young boys operated the ventilation system, older boys (possibly aged twelve and older) were used as *spraggers*, whose job it was to shove pointed wooden poles (*sprags*) approximately twelve inches in length into the spokes of the ore cars. This would decelerate the cars as gravity sped them toward the mine entrance. Other boys were stationed along the path to pull out the sprags when the ore cars needed to pick up speed. This alternate slowing down and speeding up of the ore cars required skill, and *spragging* was considered a dangerous (indeed, a very dangerous) occupation—loss of whole or parts of fingers were commonplace among spraggers.

It was into this OSHA-less society that Grandfather John arrived to find work and build a future. At that same time, Brother Robert was working as a mine superintendent in Rock Springs, a hundred or so miles west on the main line of the Union Pacific Railroad. Brother Robert was fortunate not to be working in Rock Springs in 1885, when one of the worst race riots in American history (the Rock Springs massacre) occurred among miners working near Rock Springs on September 2, 1885.

In those days, miners continued to be exploited to the fullest. They worked long and dangerous hours underground, receiving only meager pay to house and feed their families. Life was a true struggle for existence. The miner toiled twelve or more hours each day for less than one dollar, which may seem a lot of money by the standards of the day, but put realistically, the miner had to free nine tons of coal from the seam to collect a paycheck based on product mined, not hours worked. That amounted to approximately ten cents per ton, with each ton equivalent to three cans of soup at the company store—owned and operated by the Union Pacific Railroad. There was also the persistent threat that if the miner did not fill his allotted number of coal cars during a shift, he could be fired upon reporting for work the next day.

In keeping with the times and deplorable working conditions, the miners working in the mine as employees of the Union Pacific Coal Company had been struggling to unionize and strike for better working conditions for years. But fortune was not on the side of the miners, and the coal company had been prepared for every move of the miners.

Recognizing that the Chinese coal miners were hard workers, the Union Pacific Coal Company had initially brought many of them to Rock Springs as strikebreakers, and they (the Chinese workers) showed no interest in the mineworkers' union. Angry emotions were high, and the miners seeking the reasons for their plight blamed the Chinese immigrants. Thus angered and feeling betrayed by a company decision to allow Chinese miners to work the richest coal seams, a mob of white miners impulsively decided to strike back by attacking the Chinatown area of Rock Springs. The sight of a group of angry miners carrying pickaxes, pickaxe handles, and sundry other makeshift weapons was not a pleasant experience. Seeing the armed mob approaching, most of the Chinese abandoned their homes and businesses and literally fled for the hills. Those who failed to escape in time were brutally beaten and killed without mercy. A week later, on September 9, federal soldiers escorted the surviving Chinese back into the town where many of them returned to work. Eventually the Union Pacific Coal Company fired forty-five of the white miners for their roles in the massacre, but no effective legal action was ever taken against any of the participants.

The white mob—on the order of one hundred to one hundred and fifty persons, some of whom were women—killed twenty-eight Chinese coal miners, seriously wounded at least fifteen, and looted and burned the Chinatown district. The massacre was symptomatic of the anti-Chinese feelings shared by many white Americans at that time. The Chinese immigrants had fled famine and political upheaval in their own country to become victims of prejudice and violence from the time they first began to come to the western United States in the mid-nineteenth century but fell into a situation where they were blamed for all manner of social ills. They were also singled out for attack by some national politicians who popularized strident slogans such as "the Chinese must go" and an 1882 law that closed the United States to any further Chinese immigration. In this climate of racial hatred, violent attacks against the Chinese in the West became all too common, though the Rock Springs massacre was notable both for its size and savage brutality.

Brother Robert was fortunate enough not to be involved in the moves against the Chinese in Rock Springs, having moved on to Colorado. Sadly, after avoiding such trials and tribulations, Robert was killed in a mine accident in Colorado.

In the beginning, Grandfather John lived alone for a short period in what may seem today to be a primitive shelter—a dugout—while working in the mine at Carbon. As a result, he was underground most of the time, whether sleeping in the dugout or during his waking hours in the mine. He saw very little of the daylight hours and the long hours in the mine made social life a minimal part of his existence.

A Wyoming Dugout Home

***

A dugout, also known as a pit house, earth lodge, or mud hut, was a form of home for early prairie dwellers. It was based on a hole or depression dug into the ground or into the side of a hill and is one of the most ancient types of human housing known to modern archeologists. Dugouts can be fully recessed into the earth, with a flat roof covered by sod, or dug into a hillside. They can also be semi-recessed, with a sod roof that extends from the walls to guide rainwater and melted snow away from the dugout. An individual dugout was typically occupied for less than fifteen years.

By more current housing standards, these dwellings were cramped and dark, and the centralized hearth created a smoky, cold environment during the winter. Most dugouts were associated with an open air plaza or rooftop, where inhabitants carried out most of their daily activities during good weather. In areas suitable for intensive agriculture and other occupations, groups of dugouts clustered to create communities of varying sizes. One might suggest (with some degree of peril) that the dugouts of major league baseball are based on this principle—but the working hours and the pay is much better than ever dreamed of by Grandfather John and his subterranean colleagues!

Grandfather John Milliken

***

Hanna Coal Miners, 1892

As for many workers in those times, the miner had no security. There was no form of health insurance during a miner's working life, and the concept of social security to assure retirement with some form of income was unknown. Labor laws were non-existent—children younger than age twelve worked in many mines pulling coal wagons. In fact, the only form of security for the miner was a canary in a cage.

These bright yellow birds were an early coal miner's life insurance policy. Carried below ground in cages, the canary, with its highly sensitive metabolism, can detect methane and carbon monoxide gases in trace amounts that miners could not detect until it was too late. The presence of these gases signaled potential explosions, poisoned air, or both. Canaries were preferred over mice to alert coal miners to the presence of carbon monoxide underground because, when influenced by the effects of methane or carbon monoxide, a canary will sway noticeably on its perch before falling. For the miner observing the actions of the bird, timing was everything.

Methane and carbon monoxide are poisonous, but once the concentration of methane in air reaches 5 to 18 percent by volume, an explosion can occur without warning, leading to a flame front that will shoot along the mine tunnel, killing everyone in its path.

Deciding that living in a dugout and that the dangers of working in the mine were not to be his lifelong residence and occupation, Grandfather John worked to establish his own business. His desire for independence was indomitable and moved him to action. Grandfather John purchased a stable and a combined saloon and billiard hall and staked claim to a homestead approximately one mile south of Carbon.

***

Working to further his businesses during the winter of 1874–75, Grandfather John became involved in a partnership that comprised

William Richardson, Jobie Nixson, Pap Amous, and himself. The idea of the partnership was to purchase cattle and horses.

John Milliken, Bill Richardson, and Jobie Nixson (left to right)

In all, Grandfather John made five trips to purchase horses from the Nez Perce Indians and sold the horses along the trail on the way home. Particularly noteworthy is the first such trip. Grandfather John and his companions left Carbon for Utah in the spring of 1875, each riding a horse, leading his packhorse, and carrying his bedroll and cooking equipment. It was really a spring vacation until they came to the North Platte, where much discussion took place as to who should swim the river first. Once that was settled—the name of the *volunteer* is unknown—they made this crossing without any difficulty and journeyed on.

However, when the partners came to the Green River, they nearly came to grief as they forded just above a canyon and were almost washed into it. From there, they followed the Overland Trail through the Wasatch Range and on into Utah, going into the country of the Ute Indians to a place called Camas Prairie, so called because of the abundance of wild cammis growing there, which the Indians ate.

They dug up the cammis roots or bulbs, then dug a hole in the ground some two feet deep and shoveled in a lot of live coals from their camp fire. They placed the cammis roots on these coals, covered them with more live coals, and then buried all with wood ashes and left the roots there cooking for two days. When they were taken out and eaten, Grandfather John and Richardson became very fond of them, so they would buy them from the Indians when possible.

The Indians were suspicious and distant for a long time and would not sell horses to them. Finally Grandfather John and his partners came into contact with a mixed-race man called Half Moon, from whom they bought horses. Half Moon also accompanied the partners and helped them buy more horses. From that point on, the partners could buy all the horses that they wanted. The Indians would not accept paper money and preferred silver coin, but it was quite a problem to obtain silver coins in large amounts and to pack the heavy metal. Later on, when the partners bought some more horses from Half Moon, he agreed to accept paper money, which for a time he concealed in his braided hair.

Once back in Carbon, the horses were turned loose to graze the sand creeks nearby. In the autumn they divided the horses between them. Grandfather John and William Richardson took their horses to Nebraska and began to sell them at Ogallala, then continued eastward until they had successfully sold off the rest of them.

During the winter of 1876–77, Grandfather John Milliken, William Richardson, Charles Vagner, Robert Jackson, and Edward L. Swazey formed another livestock partnership. Entertaining visions of being cattle barons someday, they started for Utah again with all their trail equipment. The journey took them through the Uintah Mountains and across Uintah Basin, where they started to buy cattle, after which they went into Strawberry Valley to buy more cattle, and then camped at Stinking Springs, also buying cattle there and swelling the size of the herd. When they had amassed approximately 1200 head of cattle, they were ready to start on the return journey home. At this time they met Tom McCarty, who happened to ride into their camp. It was a fortuitous meeting, since McCarty had guided them over the Wasatch Mountains with their horse herd in a previous year. McCarty offered his services to see them safely out of the region. The partners had not realized they were in dangerous territory until McCarty's arrival.

On the way back, they stopped again at Stinking Springs, where— to his delight, since one of the great joys of his life was to play a prank on someone—Grandfather John found out that Bob Jackson was afraid of Indians.

Without wasting any time, Grandfather John talked an Indian into walking up behind Jackson when he was on his knees around the campfire peeling potatoes. The Indian caught Jackson by the hair from behind, and when Jackson looked up and saw him with his dagger drawn to scalp him, he dropped both spuds and knife and sang out, "Oh, Lord, save me!"

This was too much for the solemn-faced Indian, who laughed and ran. Jackson, who had a high temper, flew into a rage and gave everyone around a very loud piece of his mind, but never knew who was responsible for the joke on him. Then they left that camp but soon met some Indians. They recognized McCarty and began talking to him, finally telling him they had some bronco cows on Deep Creek and they did not want him to touch them when they passed.

***

Back in Hanna, Grandfather John worked to build up his businesses. In time, he met, courted, and married Hannah Sutton in 1881. Hannah was born in Warwickshire, England. That same year, Grandfather John took advantage of the provisions of the Homestead Act. He applied for and was granted land in the Hanna area.

The Homestead Acts were several federal laws that gave an applicant ownership of land, typically called a *homestead*, at little cost—this consisted of 160 acres (65 hectares, or one-fourth of a section) of unappropriated federal land within the boundaries of the public land states. The first of the acts, the Homestead Act of 1862, was signed into law by President Abraham Lincoln on May 20, 1862. Anyone who was age twenty-one or older (including freed slaves and women) or the head of a family, and who had never taken up arms against the government of the United States could file an application to claim a federal land grant. There was also a residency requirement. An amendment to the Homestead Act of 1862, the Enlarged Homestead Act, was passed in 1909 that increased the allotted acreage to 320 acres. Another amended act, the Stock-Raising

Homestead Act, was passed in 1916 that again increased the amount of land that could be homesteaded, this time to 640 acres.

Just prior to his marriage to Hannah, Grandfather John recorded in two letters (that still exist in the collection of the American Heritage Center, University of Wyoming) indications of life in the western United States. One is autobiographical and the other a description of the killing of Sheriff Bob Widdowfield and the hanging of "Dutch Charlie" Clark in 1879 and George "Big Nose" Parrott (also known as Big Nose George, Big Beak Parrott, George Manuse, George Curry, and George Warden) in Rawlins in 1881.

Whether or not Grandfather John attended the hanging of Dutch Charlie is unknown, but it was reported that he did attend the hanging of Big Nose George.

***

The execution of Big Nose George on March 22, 1881, represented the third and final time that Carbon County law enforcement officials had tied a noose around George Parrott's neck in less than a year. The hanging took place near Front and Third streets in Rawlins. George had confessed to the shooting of the Carbon County sheriff Robert Widdowfield and an unnamed deputy sheriff—the two reasons for which he was executed.

The outlaw gang that George was a member of may have included either of the infamous James Brothers. During a pretrial interview, some accounts said that Parrott named the outlaw Frank James as one of his fellow coconspirators in the crime. It is possible that the James Brothers could have been in Wyoming at the time. Parrott also may have used aliases including George Manuse and George Curry prior to his death, complicating historical documents still further.

Most accounts of the story begin in August of 1878, when Parrott and a gang of about eight other ne'er-do-wells attempted to derail and rob a westbound train east of Medicine Bow. A Union Pacific Railroad section crew discovered the missing spikes and telegraph wire with which the gang intended to pull the tracks at the last minute. The crew repaired the rails and alerted authorities. The gang headed for Elk Mountain and camped in Rattlesnake Canyon.

Sheriff Widdowfield, Henry H. "Tip" Vincent (a Union Pacific detective), and the deputy sheriff pursued them and found an apparently deserted campsite where the gang was waiting in the brush. Widdowfield was shot in the neck and died very soon thereafter. The deputy was also wounded by the gunfire and was shot dead as he attempted to flee. The outlaws looted the corpses and dispersed. A reward for the arrest of the outlaws was set at the royal sum of $10,000, which was later doubled to $20,000.

Bob Widdowfield was a popular individual in Carbon County, and there was a lot of anger at his death.

The outlaw "Dutch Charlie" Clark, through a haze of frontier whiskey, boasted of having committed or at least been in on the murders and was arrested. En route to Rawlins, a mob stopped his train near Carbon. Clark was taken unceremoniously from the boxcar where he had been held and, without any thoughts of gentle conduct by the abductors, he was hanged with a rope from a telegraph pole.

George Parrott was heard at some distant place to make a similar drunken boast and was arrested. He was transported from Miles City, Montana, in July 1880. He almost did not make it to Carbon—a railroad incident similar to that which led to the demise of Dutch Charlie was enacted outside of Carbon. At the last minute, Parrott swore he would tell everything he knew about the murders if the mob would let him go—he was cut down and jailed in Rawlins.

Once jailed, Parrott initially pleaded the charge of murder. Four days later he changed his plea to *not guilty*. On November 8, 1880, the first day of trial, he argued for a change of venue on the grounds of a prejudiced jury and landed the associate justice William Ware Peck of the Wyoming Supreme Court as the justice of record. He later changed his plea back to *guilty*. On December 15, 1880, he was sentenced to be hanged on April 2, 1881. George is reported to have wept at the sentence, but little did he know that he would never see the dawn or any part of the day of April 2. Had he known what lay in store, he may have wept even harder.

On March 22, 1881, Parrott attempted a prison break. He freed himself by filing his seven-to-eight-pound shackles, struck jailer Robert Rankin from behind, fracturing his skull—Rankin is reported to have survived—and almost made it out of the jail. Rankin's wife Rosa, being a frontier woman and made of stern stuff, appeared with a pistol in hand. Showing herself ready to use it, she persuaded Parrott (it didn't seem to take much persuasion) to return to his cell.

But it was not over; March 22, 1881, seems to have been ordained to be George's unlucky day.

At about ten o'clock that night, presumably when Parrott was ready to sleep for eight hours and not for eternity, a gang of masked men with guns stormed the jail and took George from his cell—not to freedom, but with the purpose of justice in mind—to the site of his lynching. Whether it was prearranged or not—word does travel quickly in small towns, especially frontier towns—a crowd of about two hundred amassed at the site of the gallows, which just happened to be a sturdy telegraph pole that obviously had other uses than passing electrically generated messages. The crowd was eager for justice, for revenge for the death of the three law enforcement officers, or for both.

Whether or not George was able to believe his luck, the rope broke on the first hanging attempt. He begged for mercy, and seeing none coming, he pleaded for someone to shoot him. If a man was to be hanged, he would be hanged and not pardoned because of a faulty rope, as had been rumored to be the outcome of such incidents in some jurisdictions. To George, shooting must have seemed to be preferable to strangling at the end of a rope. The clean neck break and instant death of the victim was not in vogue in those days.

Not having the wish to die by any means, Parrott had at some point managed to partially free himself of his hand restraints, and when he climbed the ladder to be hanged the second time and, after the ladder was pulled from under him, he managed to hold onto the telegraph pole. But justice was evident that night, much to the delight of the onlookers. The weight of Parrott's shackles pulled him down and he slowly suffocated.

Thus ended the life of "Big Nose George" Parrott—outlaw and murderer—a man who would never terrorize local citizens again.

***

Hannah Sutton was the daughter of William Sutton, a one-time railroad agent for the Union Pacific Railroad, and Ann Mowe Sutton.

Hannah arrived in the United States and thence in Wyoming as an infant during the 1860s. The Sutton family originated in the area of England known as Ascot and had interests in horses—which seemed natural, being from an area close by the now famous Ascot Downs, one of the premier race tracks in Europe.

It was Queen Anne who first saw the potential for a racecourse at Ascot, which in those days was called East Cote. While out riding in 1711, she came upon an area of open heath not far from Windsor

Castle that looked an ideal place for "horses to gallop at full stretch." The first race meeting ever held at Ascot took place on Saturday, August 11, 1711.

The Suttons fared well in the United States and owned land in western Wyoming. William Sutton's land was a registered homestead, and his patent was registered on September 28, 1894, with water rights registered in 1888. Ann Sutton's patent was registered on June 22, 1895.

William and Ann Sutton came with their family to the Hamsfork Ranch in 1885 from Twin Creek, where they had operated a hotel or rooming house. Mr. Sutton worked in connection with the coal mines for the Union Pacific Railroad. One of Mr. Sutton's tasks was to carry the mine payroll. Having to sleep out overnight, he would pitch his tent, then crawl out of the tent in the dark and bury the money in the sagebrush so no one could steal it from him in the night.

William and Ann Mowe Sutton had nine children: seven daughters and two sons. In order of birth they were: Hannah Milliken, Sarah Ann Wood, William Sutton (who died within one year of birth), Mary Wright, Eliza Sutton (who died within five years of birth), Caroline Rich, Elizabeth Miller, Edward Sutton, and Agnes Clementson.

Ann Mowe was born in Warwickshire, England, on October 9, 1841, and William Sutton was born in Alderman Green, England, on September 9, 1841. They were married in England on June 19, 1862. William came to the United States in 1863, at a time when the states were not quite united because of the Civil War; but Ann did not come to the US until 1865. They located in Pennsylvania, where Mr. Sutton was engaged in mining and where they built their home. Later they moved to Bellville, Illinois, where they lived until 1877, and then they came to Wyoming, making their home first in Carbon before moving to Uinta County, and locating at Twin Creek before the Oregon Short Line was built. Then they moved to Hamsfork in 1885, and in 1890 they again moved, this time to Daniel, Wyoming, where they built another ranch near to the Green River.

Ann Mowe Sutton died at the Green River Ranch on March 27, 1909. Her son-in-law, Thomas Clementson, built her casket. Mrs. P.J. Quealy and Mrs. Paul Kenyon made her burial robe.

The following paragraph, taken from her obituary in the Kemmerer Camera, April 8, 1909, shows the hardships the people had in those days:

After a short service read by Reverend J.W. Naylor at Daniel, she left the ranch home for the last journey to Kemmerer, the family leaving about 11 o'clock on Monday morning of last week, reaching Big Piney about 4 o'clock and resting at the Budd home until the next morning, except Tom Clementson who drove with the remains to the Spur ranch arriving at 4 a.m. Tuesday, where a change of horses awaited him, and after a two hour rest, drove on reaching Opal on Tuesday night at 9 o'clock, where L.D. Tanner met him and kindly assisted him by driving to Kemmerer, reaching Kemmerer on Wednesday morning about 3 o'clock, after a two days and two nights drive. The family followed on and reached Fontenelle, where they remained over night at the Holden ranch, and left next morning for Opal, reaching there in time to catch No. 1 for Kemmerer, Wednesday. They met with the greatest kindness all along their journey here, fresh horses awaited them, when their own were exhausted from wading thru the deep snow and mud, and nothing was left undone that willing hearts could do, for it was the saddest journey they had ever been called upon to make.

William Sutton married a second time, in 1911, to Mrs. Ella Evans of Diamondville, Wyoming. He sold his ranch at Daniel to G.F. Whitman and D. Baum on December 22, 1916. The ranch included 1,280 acres. He had shipped six carloads of cattle to Omaha October 13, 1916. They then moved to Erie, Colorado. Mr. Sutton's second wife preceded him in death by eleven days and was buried in Erie, Colorado. William Sutton died May 23, 1919, and his remains were brought back to Kemmerer for burial beside his first wife in the Kemmerer City Cemetery. His survivors included forty-two grandchildren and twenty-seven great-grandchildren.

The Sutton name lives on even today, not only because of descendants, but also by the fact that the name is etched on Register Cliff, currently listed as a historic site in the state of Wyoming.

Register Cliff is a sandstone precipice rising one hundred feet from the valley floor of the North Platte River. Despite erosion by wind and water, it remains very much as travelers on the Oregon Trail saw it more than 150 years ago. Immigrants traveling along the Oregon Trail camped at the site on the banks of the North Platte River and etched their names into the soft sandstone cliff. The beginnings of carving names into the cliff go as far back as 1829, when trappers and traders passing through did it. This habit continued during the 1840s and 1850s—the peak years of travel on the Oregon Trail—during which time a trading post was located near the cliff. In 1861, the trading post was turned into a Pony Express stop, and later it became a stage station.

Register Cliff, one of the three main sites along the Oregon Trail where emigrants left inscriptions, is the closest to any towns and currently lies on the northern edge of the town of Guernsey, to the east of Hanna, and a day's travel by wagon train to the west of Fort

Laramie. The city of Guernsey did not exist when William Sutton moved west.

***

Grandfather John and Grandmother Hannah took up residence in the house on Grandfather John's homestead. Having a place to live that they could call their own immediately after marriage was considered a boon in those days (and perhaps still is). Approximately one year after they were married, further good fortune was visited upon them. They were able to move to a house on a hill. In spite of overlooking the cemetery—a constant reminder of human mortality—the view was one of the better views in Carbon.

It was at about this time that Grandfather John sold the homestead to provide money to invest in his business ventures. He and Grandmother Hannah acquired what had formerly been a Union Pacific Railroad store, and the converted two-story white structure where they served meals became the focal point of social life in Carbon. It was given the grandiose name of the Opera House. This went through various iterations, and later it became known as the Finnish Opera House.

During this time, Grandmother Hannah proved to be made of stern stuff. Whereas the Mormon Church had failed to influence Grandfather John in his religious leanings—he had remained a staunch Presbyterian—he was strongly influenced by his new bride, a devout Episcopalian, and John left the Presbyterian Church to become an Episcopalian.

It is rumored that the true reason for Grandfather John's move to the Episcopal Church, other than Grandmother Hannah's means of persuasion, was that the Episcopal Church of Carbon was only a short walk from the front door of their home.

Grandfather John and Grandmother Hannah raised nine children in Carbon. The children were born in groups of three. Three children were born close together, then there was a break of approximately two years, then three more children were born, then another break of approximately two years, and then the final three children were born.

Providing food for a large family was no mean task. One of Grandmother Hannah's habits was to feed sage chickens that came close to the house, even within a step or two of the door. In addition, pronghorn antelope and other wild game were never far away. The hunting took place whenever food was needed and was, of course, more often than not out of season.

The sage chicken is actually the greater sage-grouse (*Centrocercus urophasianus*), also known as the sage-hen. It is the largest of the North American grouse; the male is twenty-five to thirty inches in length and may weigh up to seven pounds. The female is smaller, averaging twenty inches in length and slightly less than three pounds, but overall providing plenty of meat per bird.

Sage-grouse are less abundant today than they were in in pioneer times. Sagebrush eradication and intensive use of lands by domestic livestock have reduced their numbers. These birds inhabited areas where sagebrush is the predominant plant, and the High Plains of Wyoming offer a plentiful supply of food for the birds. During summer, the fruiting heads of sagebrush, leaves and flower heads of clovers, dandelions, grasses and other plants, and insects are taken by the birds. Their principal winter food item is sagebrush leaves. The equation of life for the birds is simple: if there is no sagebrush, there are no sage-grouse.

Grandmother Hannah's kindness to the fowl of the air and the animals of the forest had its rewards. The meat of many a sage chicken, antelope, or deer adorned the meal table of the Milliken family on weekends.

***

In the winter of 1885–86, Grandfather John, William Richardson, and several others decided to get some more horses. Mrs. Richardson tried to talk them into getting more cows from Utah, which would have been the wisest, but she was overruled, and in January they left old Carbon by train and went to San Francisco. Here they were met by Coffee Johnson, who took the time to show them San Francisco, with its beautiful gardens and parks. The night before they left, he treated them to a Chinese dinner in Chinatown. When asked how he liked the Chinese dinner, Richardson would pronounce the dinner good, but complained that there were too many small bones in it that made him think he was eating mice!

From here they left by boat, went up the coast to Portland, Oregon, and then took a smaller boat up to The Dalles, Oregon. Grandfather John always talked of the beauty of the Columbia River.

The Dalles was first brought to notice when Meriwether Lewis and William Clark camped there in 1806 and named it Rockfort Camp, after which it became the site of Fort Dalles, established in 1850 to protect immigrants from local hostile tribes. It was the only military post between the Pacific Coast and Wyoming.

Richardson, Milliken, and the others soon became acquainted with the Nez Perce Indians and purchased two thousand Indian ponies from them.

While they were buying horses from the Nez Perce Indian tribe, an Indian agent went the rounds with them. If they went into remote valleys, they would bargain for the horses to be delivered at a specified location, pay the money to the agent, and leave for safer territory. Usually ponies would be there the next morning. The agent paid each Indian for the horses he had sold. This continued daily, going out during the day and coming back at night, and the Indians never failed to show the next morning with the horses.

After they had purchased all of the horses that they could handle, the partners followed the west bank of the Snake River to a place called Harper's Ferry, where they tried to encourage their horses to swim across the river but without success. The men had had no previous experience with such a large river. Thoroughly discouraged, they stopped on the bank of the river and wondered how it could be done. Finally, with shouts of encouragement they were able to get the horses into the river. From there on, it was each horse and man for himself all the way to the opposite bank.

It was at about this time, when the horses were being driven over the Little Lost River in Idaho, that Grandfather John had an accident that almost cost him his life. One member of the party, Bill Richardson, borrowed Grandfather John's Colt 45 revolver to shoot at wild pigs that were invading the camp and eating anything that looked like food. The shooter had replaced the gun in the holster with a round left in the chamber. The gun should have been set with the hammer on an empty chamber and the safety catch left on. This was not done, hence the unfortunate, but preventable, accident.

Grandfather John was driving his own horse with his quirt—a forked type of stock whip—when he inadvertently caught the tail of the quirt on the hammer of his Colt 45. The gun discharged and the bullet injured his leg, fortunately missing the femoral artery. Had the bullet hit the artery, Grandfather John would have bled out and died within fifteen minutes, but that was not to be the case.

He had to ride horseback for almost two hundred miles—a harrowing journey even for an unwounded man—to the nearest stagecoach stop, where his leg was given emergency treatment. The only medicaments were water and Castile soap, a soap made from fat of purely vegetable origin and which had (supposedly) antiseptic properties. After that he was taken to the nearest doctor by stagecoach, with his leg painfully suspended from the interior roof of the stagecoach. After more official medical treatment and rest for several days (probably less than one week), he was allowed to proceed with his partners on the horse drive, but he was not able to play any further active part in the horse drive other than the role of observer.

From there they travelled up the north side of the Snake River, thence to the south, and once more into Carbon.

It was an adventure—some might call it an experience in pain and terror—driving the horses back all the way from Oregon to Carbon and then selling the horses.

This third drive to bring horses back was the most important and final drive. In spite of the inherent dangers, all three drives helped Grandfather John get onto a sound financial footing.

***

One interesting story that remains is the manner in which Grandfather John handled a liquor thief.

The story starts when Grandfather John, an observant business owner and not a drinker himself, noticed that some of his liquor was disappearing after the closing hour. Determined to find out who, why, when, and where, Grandfather John waited in a concealed spot after closure. He had the foresight to place a chair in a strategic position close to the trapdoor that led to the cellar —which he left open. The would-be thief emerged from a closet where he had been hiding, felt his way past the chair in the darkness, and fell into the cellar. The injuries received by the thief as a result of the fall or from the wrath of Grandfather John or both are not recorded. But the theft of the liquor ceased.

It was also at the height of the town's popularity that Grandfather John had a very unusual but welcome visitor to his bar. The young woman walked purposefully into the bar and ordered a drink—it was unusual in those days for a woman to enter a bar alone—but this was the West. It took Grandfather John only moments after they started chatting to realize that his customer was none other than Calamity Jane.

***

Calamity Jane (born Martha Jane Cannary on May 1, 1856; died August 1, 1903) emigrated with her family in 1865 by the Overland Route (believed to be the older name for the Overland Trail) from Princeton, Missouri, to Virginia City, Montana. After the death of her mother and father and as head of the household, Jane took her siblings back to Wyoming, arriving at Fort Bridger on May 1, 1868. Taking whatever job that was available in order to provide for the family, she worked as a cook, a nurse, a dishwasher, a waitress, an ox team driver and a dance hall girl, which (according to some tales) introduced her to the world of prostitution.

In 1870, she joined General George Armstrong Custer as a scout at Fort Russell, Wyoming, during which time she wore the uniform of a cavalry soldier—the beginning of her habit of dressing like a man. In 1872, she returned to Fort Sanders, Wyoming, where she was involved in several campaigns in the long-running military conflicts with Indians.

Her unconfirmed claim was that she acquired the name Calamity Jane when she lived in Goose Creek, Wyoming, the town that eventually became Sheridan. Later she returned to Fort Sanders, Wyoming, approximately one mile south of Laramie. While there she made several visits to Rawlins and at least one visit to Carbon. It was believed that she had a boyfriend or companion or lover there, and she remained in the area for several years before she became acquainted with James Butler Hickok (aka Wild Bill Hickok) only weeks before he was murdered.

In 1883, Calamity Jane, who was occupied with freighting contracts in the area, stopped frequently at Carbon, joining the men in the saloon bar, ostensibly to drown her quarrels with her lover, believed to be a gentleman by the name of Bill Steers. For some time, it seems that Steers had been acting in the capacity of the husband of Calamity Jane. Apparently the women of Carbon were not amused at Jane's lack of a dress. She wore a buckskin blouse and trousers that were not the cleanest garments in the land. Nor did they care for her frequent appearance in a saloon bar, where she took her whiskey neat, with more whiskey instead of the usual beer, as a chaser. The comments of Grandfather John and the menfolk of Carbon related to Jane's antics are not recorded and have been lost in history.

Further research led to confirmation of this story. There is no reason to doubt that Calamity Jane frequented Carbon for a period of time during the 1880s and that she did indeed visit Grandfather John's saloon.

***

It will be no surprise to learn that in 1908 Grandfather John and the family abandoned their home and moved to Hanna. They were among the last of the residents to leave Carbon, and after their departure the town fell into disuse. Seven coal mines had seen decreased production, causing the Union Pacific Railroad to move the main line to run through Hanna. Consequently, Carbon became a ghost town. Only remnants of some buildings remain today.

The population of Carbon decreased, businesses closed, and the residents followed the mines to Hanna. Father Robert was able to salvage the top of the bar, which was an unusually fine piece of work, and sold it later at a nice profit. Very little remains of the town other than the base course of stone walls and various metal artifacts that can be found with the use of a metal detector.

Hanna, named after Mark A. Hanna, a Union Pacific Railroad director, is a small town located in the High Plains of Wyoming, lying just north of Interstate 80. It started life as a stage station and mining town in the years after the Civil War, when the western part of the United States was being colonized and rediscovered. Laramie (formerly Fort Saunders in the years immediately after the Civil War) is approximately sixty miles to the east of Hanna. Rawlins lies a few miles to the west of Hanna and is the largest city in the area.

When General Grenville Dodge's crew discovered a clear, alkali-free spring, General John A. Rawlins made the comment, "If anything is ever named after me, I hope it will be a spring of water." Shortly after that, Dodge named this tiny oasis Rawlins Springs. In time, after service as an early frontier post, that oasis became a division point for the railroad, and the division point eventually became a town. Somewhere along the way, the town of Rawlins Springs became simply Rawlins.

In 1886, while Wyoming was still a territory, the legislature voted to construct a territorial prison and chose a site outside of Laramie. Poor funding slowed construction, and the prison did not accept its first prisoner until thirteen years later. By that time, not only had Rawlins grown to completely surround the prison, Wyoming had also become a state. This oppressive, medieval-looking stone building was Wyoming's only state prison for eighty years, until a new, more modern facility was built outside of Rawlins. The Old Frontier Prison, as it is best known, was closed in 1981.

***

Coal was discovered in Wyoming by the Fremont Expedition of 1843. Commercial mining began with the arrival of the railroad. The first mines were located in Carbon and Rock Springs and were owned by the Wyoming Coal and Mining Company.

Prior to the emergence of Hanna as a mining town, Carbon was the center of activity. The community was named for its coal deposits and is in the Mountain Standard time zone at an elevation of 6,831 feet above sea level.

Carbon, which saw its heyday in the period from 1868 to 1902 as a mining and railroad town, was the first coal camp on the line of the Union Pacific Railroad. An 1888 map shows carbon lying just to the east of Rawlins. The Carbon Cemetery holds a record of the Union Pacific coal miners and their families.

At its peak, Carbon had seven coal mines being worked by *Lankies* (miners so named because several of them came from Lancashire, England) as well as by men from Ireland, Scotland, Denmark, and Finland. Approximately 3,000 residents lived at Carbon. There was a General Store, two or three saloons, Carbon State Bank, Slack

Diamond Newspaper, a school, Miners Hall, two churches, and the large Finn Hall.

However, the future of Carbon was cut short by Simpson Hill, a steep grade to the west of Carbon that required helper engines for about six miles to the top. In 1899, Union Pacific Railroad surveyors found an easier grade through present day Hanna. This happened at about the same time the Carbon mines were playing out. In 1902, the town of Carbon was abandoned and exists now only as a ghost town just south of Hanna. All that remains of carbon is the cemetery, which lies to the north of the original town site, a few partial foundations, and sandstone walls.

***

With the Town of Carbon abandoned, Hanna became a major hub of the emerging transportation industry. The Overland Trail and the Union Pacific Railroad all passed through Hanna. The first transcontinental airmail planes flew over Hanna. The Lincoln Highway passed through Carbon a few miles south of Hanna. As of 2008, Hanna had a population of 866 persons, a slight reduction from the 873 residents reported in the 2000 census.

The history of Hanna is intertwined with the history of the town of Carbon. Hanna is a town with a rich history of hard luck coal miners and the Union Pacific Coal Company. Hanna is an old coal camp, founded in the late 1800s by the Union Pacific Coal Company to house the families of workers that were mining coal for the Union Pacific Railroad steam locomotives. Life was hard for the coal miners who lived in and around Hanna, but they always had time for a company-sponsored baseball team. It is rumored that more than one unqualified coal miner was hired for his baseball skills.

Carbon County, the county in which Carbon and Hanna are located, was organized in 1868. Prior to that, an area of about 3,400 square miles in the center of Carbon County was once part of the Republic of Texas (1835–45) and part of the state of Texas until 1852, when the northernmost part of that state was ceded to the US government.

Carbon County owes much of its early history to the Union Pacific Railroad. The railroad gave names to unnamed places as it laid tracks westward over the Rocky Mountains that would eventually become the Transcontinental Railroad. Well ahead of those tracks were army surveyors laying out the route and marking the waterholes the great steam locomotives would need to fill their empty tanks.

Commercial mining in Carbon County came with the arrival of the railroad. The first coal camp on the original line on the Union Pacific Railway was Carbon (1868–1902). These were the days of picks, powder, and mule power. In 1889—on May 17 of that year, Grandfather John became a US citizen—most mining activity and much of Carbon's population shifted to nearby Hanna, an exemplary company town, controlled by the Union Pacific Coal Company.

At first, the coal mines were held by the Wyoming Coal and Mining Company, with the first mines at Carbon, west of Medicine Bow, and at Rock Springs. The first dwellings at Carbon consisted of little more than dugouts and *shoddies* consisting of upright boards— the gaps between the boards were closed with sod—and with sod roofs. Carbon, now a ghost town, grew to a population of about 3,000 residents, with a state bank, newspaper, and seven active mines.

Hanna has a total area of 2.0 square miles, all of it land. It's called the town that refused to die. Lying as it does in the center of one of Wyoming's largest and richest coalfields, Hanna has an equally rich past and present. Mining has been the mainstay in this part of the county since coal was discovered here in the late 1800s. A massive old dragline system still stands as a backdrop to the town, a reminder of days gone by.

***

Once settled in Hanna, Grandfather John, son John, and Father Robert started a horse-drawn construction business—given the appropriate name of Milliken and Sons—even though the internal combustion engine already was changing the West. Grandfather John never really accepted the reality that the era of horses was coming to an end. Although he did buy two or three vehicles from a dealer in Rawlins that he planned to incorporate in his freight and taxi enterprises, true to his lifestyle, he never got used to the idea of driving a vehicle that was not drawn by a horse! He even tried driving—just once—but he somehow managed to run off the road and he never drove again.

***

Hanna, Wyoming, was in all senses of the words a *company town*. The dirt streets were straight and orderly, and the small houses were constructed on a basic pattern—four rooms and a privy out back. The streets ran up the low hills away from the railroad and into the sagebrush. And the majority of the houses were owned by the Union Pacific Railroad.

The main street, aptly named Front Street, ran along the north side of the railroad tracks. It consisted of a row of small stores and a boarding house. Even though it was a small town, Hanna was divided into sections—One Town, Two Town, Three Town, Four Town, and

The Hill, also known as Tipperary, obviously after the namesake county in Ireland.

The divisions of the town were made according to where the miners worked. The houses built on the south side of the railroad tracks in Number One Town, more often just called One Town, were populated by miners who worked in the company's Number One Mine (No. 1 Mine). Two Town was composed of the houses on the north side of the tracks, behind Front Street, and in keeping with the number designations, miners in Two Town all worked in the company's Number Two Mine (No. 2 Mine). This was also true of Three Town and Four Town.

The residents of the area were a mixed group of immigrants. At the time the mine in Carbon opened in 1868, the miners were mostly immigrants from the British Isles and were collectively referred to as *Lankies* after the English county of Lancashire from which they came. Later, when the English miners went on strike, the company brought Chinese miners to Rock Springs, and Finnish miners to Carbon. Members of both groups of immigrants ended up in Hanna after the opening of the mine there. So it is not surprising that other divisions of Hanna residents were made along ethnic lines. Most of the Finnish immigrants lived in a section of Hanna that was, for obvious reasons, called Finn Town. Japanese immigrants congregated in four or five houses at the west end of Hanna, often referred to as Jap Town. On the east end of Hanna, in One Town, there were quite a few Italian and Greek immigrants.

Another demographic shows simply and without further description, leaving much to the imagination, that more than half the miners in Hanna were married and had families; the rest were unmarried.

All the coal mines in Hanna sat on a hill to the west of town. The main one then operating was Number Four Mine. It had a powerhouse to provide the power to operate the hoists that raised and lowered miners to the various underground levels, and it also generated electricity for the community. The hoists also pulled the coal cars to the top of the tipple, where the coal was dumped onto conveyor belts that carried the coal to the chutes and eventually to the railroad cars.

The mines in Hanna were underground. The main tunnels, called slopes, descended to side tunnels, called entries, which led off either side of them. The entries led to rooms underground, where it was a stygian darkness all of the time. Each miner carried his own light, a small lamp on the front of his hat. The light came from the battery and provided the miner with the means to see what he was doing. As already mentioned, the canary in a cage was the sole protection for the miners.

The mine was divided into rooms, a forerunner of the current room and pillar system of mining, in which coal was extracted (leaving the rooms) and pillars of coal to support the mine roof. If a mining company decided to extract more coal by taking it from the pillars, the remaining pillars were often not strong enough to support the weight above, and timbers were used to hold up the roof. These often deteriorated with time and, unless replaced frequently, would lead to roof collapse.

The work itself was very dangerous, and the early mines had few safety features. Extra airshafts for ventilation, extra exits in case of cave-ins, and timbers strong enough to hold up the roofs in the tunnels and rooms were all lacking.

Holding a hand-cranked steel drill at shoulder height, one miner drilled a hole into the coal. At the same time, his partner, on the ground with a pick, worked to undercut the coal face. The miners would fill the hole with blasting powder, light a fuse, and leave the room. The blast brought the face down. The loose coal was loaded into small cars that ran on tracks that led out through the entries. Some of the cars were pulled by mules, while others were hauled up the slopes by cables connected to steam engines located on the surface.

Even though the work was dangerous and life-threatening, and knowing full well of the ever-present danger, the men kept going back down underground. The rationale was simple. Many of the men had families to support, and those without families needed to earn enough money to marry someday and raise a family.

The sheer difficulty of the work made them proud—made them feel like real men. And the shared danger made them close comrades. These feelings combined into what the Finnish miners called *sisu*—a mix of courage, endurance, fierce will, and burning energy. But all the ethnic groups shared something similar. The women kept their minds on their immediate tasks, careful not to worry too far beyond them. They were careful, too, never to let a miner leave the house in anger. Anger could distract a man underground, where the slightest carelessness could get him killed.

The 1939 movie *How Green Was My Valley* was based on the novel by Richard Llewellyn and told the story of a miner and his family and the mining community of the Rhondda Valley in Wales. The facts behind the story were gathered from the author's conversations with mining families.

In my experience, being raised in a mining village, mining in the years just after World War II in the Durham coalfield was always an extremely hazardous occupation. Every time we heard the mine siren signaling an accident—which happened frequently—families of those miners on-shift and even families of miners off-shift and the off-shift miners themselves would gather at the mine gate, hoping and praying fervently that a loved one or friend would emerge unscathed from the mine shaft entrance.

And there were always those miners for whom the siren had sounded for the last time.

***

On Bob's mother's side of the family, Grandfather Newton Doggett relocated to Wyoming. The area he settled became known as Doggett, later becoming known as the town of Riverside, which eventually became the town of Encampment.

Prior to the Riverside to Encampment name change, the earliest town along the Encampment River, Swan, gave way in 1895 to Doggett, a community located about a mile upstream. Started by Johnson and Newton Doggett, the town served ranchers in the region as the primary gathering place until the formation of a townsite.

The town of Swan was originally a ranch headquarters for the Swan Land and Cattle Company, and the Swan brothers established regular mail service in 1881, along with building a school and opening a general store. So it was only natural for the town to be called Swan. Prior to that, Newton Doggett and his brothers had established a weigh station, and the Swan site was eventually sold to the Doggett brothers, who erected a store and cabins where travelers could spend the night. The town was then named Doggett.

In 1887, Henry P. Cullerton acquired a 157,650-acre homestead around the town of Doggett. The homestead was sold in 1900 and then subdivided into lots, which were called the Riverside addition to the town of Doggett, Wyoming. Doggett served as a social center for the area, with dances common, but in 1900 the local newspaper announced the sale of the Doggett townsite. The new owner was a company organized under the name of Riverside Town Company, which intended to block out more territory. They changed the name from Doggett to Riverside in 1902. It is also believed that the name was changed from Doggett to Riverside to escape the town's unflattering nickname of Dogtown.

Various members of the Doggett family were merchants and ranchers, but equally adept at carpentry. They moved to Saratoga, Wyoming, where they built a store and a house. The house in Saratoga and a house they built in Riverside are still standing.

In any event, Grandfather Doggett had to be institutionalized, and he died at the state hospital in Evanston. As a result of his death, Grandmother Mathilda Naumann Doggett, who had arrived in the United States from Germany as a governess, was left to run their Saratoga ranch on her own and raise eight children. One died at an early age, one was drowned, and another had a severe case of diabetes. The strain of coping led her to move into Saratoga, then to Denver, Colorado. She endured a hard-working, tragic life before losing a battle to throat cancer.

Anna Valeria Doggett and her sister, Nora Elizabeth Doggett, became schoolteachers while still in their teens, at about the age of sixteen. Anna met Robert Milliken when she moved to Hanna to teach. Nora Doggett stayed in Saratoga, where she married a forest ranger, Ray Riggs. They did not have any children, and Bob spent many summers with them at various ranger stations, where he was free to roam the countryside and fish to his heart's content.

***

Hanna was the site of the worst mining disaster in the history of the state of Wyoming. On June 30, 1903, an explosion occurred in the Union Pacific's Hanna No. 1 Mine, and 169 miners were killed. Six hundred children were rendered fatherless. The list of casualties included many Finnish names.

This was not the first mining disaster in the state, and it was not the last, but it was certainly the worst. Earlier, disasters had occurred in 1886 at the Almy No. 4 Mine, which killed thirteen miners. In 1895, at Red Canyon near Evanston, sixty miners were killed. In 1901, at Diamondville, two disasters occurred, one on February 15, with twenty-six miners killed, and another on October 26, in which twenty-two miners were killed.

Another disaster occurred in Hanna in 1908, with fifty-eight miners killed; Kemmerer No. 4 Mine in 1912, with six miners killed; Cumberland No. 2 Mine with five miners killed; the Frontier No. 1 Mine near Kemmerer in 1923, with ninety-nine miners killed; and Sublet No. 5 Mine in 1924, with thirty-nine miners killed.

The explosion at Hanna happened suddenly, as is often the case with methane-derived mine explosions. It even took six gas watchmen by surprise. Gas watchmen wore a special type of helmet for detecting methane gas and carried safety lamps—all to no avail. They perished with their comrades in the explosion.

The disasters at mines other than those at Hanna are believed to have followed the same track as the Hanna disasters. Flames, fumes, and cave-ins claimed the lives of the miners. There is one monument to the victims of the No. 1 Mine disasters of 1903 and 1908, and two monuments to all those who died in the Carbon and Hanna mines.

***

At age fourteen, Father Robert started working in the family drayage and construction business—Milliken and Sons—which had been started by Grandfather John Milliken. Some of the work involved road construction work on Highway 30 using horse-drawn construction equipment. The men used a two-handled scoop and a four-horse grader with a Fresno scraper.

Highway 30 (US Route 30) is the east-west main route of the system of numbered highways, with the highway traveling across the northern tier of the country. The western end of the highway is at Astoria, Oregon, and the eastern end at Atlantic City, New Jersey. Over the years, the highway has managed to avoid the decommissioning that has happened to other long haul routes. In Wyoming, Highway 30 remains with the Interstate for most of its path and is often referred to as the Lincoln Highway.

The design of the Fresno scraper included the basic features of most modern earthmoving scrapers, having the ability not only to scrape and move a quantity of road dirt, but also to discharge it at a controlled depth as the horses pulled the equipment, thus quadrupling the volume that could be handled manually. The blade scooped up the soil instead of merely pushing it along and ran along a C-shaped bowl, which could be adjusted in order to alter the angle of the bucket to the ground, so that the dirt could be deposited in low spots. This design was so revolutionary and economical that it has influenced the design of modern bulldozer blades and earthmovers.

Unfortunately, the construction business failed, and Grandfather John was not receptive to change. On top of that, he was not a very good businessman. He had taken Father Robert and Uncle John out of school in the eighth grade to put them to work in the family business.

After several years of working in the family business, Father Robert went to work in the coal mines. He detested working as an underground miner, but he had a family to support, so every day he went off to the mine, with hours of darkness, danger, and hard work ahead of him. He carried a lunch bucket, really a two-part pail with a handle. The bottom of the pail held water, and the upper part, which was a separate container, held his lunch.

When Father Robert came home at the end of his mine shift, his children would run to meet him and see if he had left anything in the lunch pail. There was always some little treat waiting for them.

CHAPTER 2: GROWING UP

In the early twentieth century, the Union Pacific Coal Company provided the jobs in Hanna and had its tracks in the southern part of the town, parallel to Stink Creek, along with the coal chutes. The railroad ran on coal and needed a steady supply if it was to keep on running. So it was not surprising that by the time of Bob's birth, Hanna had grown from a few original houses to a busy town of approximately 1,500 people, consisting of about five hundred families, and it was a close-knit, stable community. It was a company town; most of the houses were owned by the Union Pacific Coal Company. The company store was also owned and operated by the coal company.

Hanna's bank was the hub of the Hanna business community. The bank was owned and operated by C.D. Williamson, who also had banking business in Laramie and was one of the few people in Hanna who owned his own house. His curriculum vitae also included an unsuccessful run for governor of the state.

***

Carlyle Dougan Williamson (1886–1959) was born in Leadville, Colorado. He became a cashier at Carbon State Bank in Hanna, Wyoming, in 1909 and was president of that bank from 1930–55. The bank was reorganized into the First National Bank of Hanna in 1920 and again in 1927 to the Hanna State & Savings Bank.

In 1916 Williamson became affiliated with P.J. Quealy, the receiver of the Carbon Timber Company, which conducted logging and tie-cutting operations in Carbon and Albany Counties, Wyoming, and was often Wyoming's sole producer of ties for the Union Pacific Railroad.

Construction of the Union Pacific Railroad stimulated the growth of the timber industry in southern Wyoming. Two companies began supplying ties to the railroad in 1868, but the firm of Coe and Carter was the leading supplier to the Fort Fred Steele collection yards until 1896. The Fort was located thirteen miles east of Rawlins, where the site can be visited to this day. Cut and shaped in the Medicine Bow Mountains to the south, ties were floated downriver during spring run-off and were gathered behind a boom here. Coe and Carter also supplied timbers for coal mines at Carbon and Hanna as well as lumber for buildings at Fort Fred Steele and the surrounding area. The Carbon Timber Company, successor to Coe and Carter, floated over 1.5 million pieces of timber down the North Platte in 1909.

***

Fort Frederick Steele (Fort Fred Steele, Fort Steele, or Fort Fred) was established on June 30, 1868, by Major Richard I. Dodge, 30th US Infantry and was named for Colonel Frederick Steele, 20th US

Infantry. The fort was charged with guarding the railroad from hostile Indians from 1868–86. The Native American threat was judged to be non-existent in 1886, and the fort was abandoned on November 3 of that year, after being transferred to the Interior Department on August 9, 1886. It came under the jurisdiction of the Department of the Interior in 1887. In 1892 and 1893, most of the buildings were sold at public auction, and in 1897 the land, opened to homesteading, was patented by the Union Pacific Railroad.

The Fort Steele cemetery served as a graveyard for soldiers, their dependents, and civilians during army occupation of the fort (1868–86). Although some soldiers died during the Indian Wars of the 1860s and 1870s, most of the military deaths at the fort were the result of accidents and disease. Civilians and travelers who expired in the vicinity of Fort Steele were interred in the cemetery, too.

The Fort Steele hospital provided medical services to military personnel and their dependents. The lack of refined medical techniques often resulted in death from infection and diseases like pneumonia and tuberculosis. The infant mortality rate was particularly high; 25 percent of the graves in the cemetery were of children. However, not all the men, women, and children who died at Fort Steele were buried in the post cemetery. Rather than surrender their loved ones to an eternity on this windswept riverbank, some chose to ship the deceased by rail to other final resting places. Military families occasionally requested official assistance with the shipments. Officers reported civilian requests for coffins and embalming materials, complaining that supplying them was not a military responsibility.

When the fort was decommissioned in 1886, the secretary of the interior declared the cemetery exempt from sale or transfer to public property because of the military burials. In 1892 the graves of the soldiers, their dependents, and some civilians were moved to Fort

McPherson National Cemetery near Maxwell, Nebraska. Civilians continued to use the cemetery after the departure of the military, and the last documented burial took place during the 1920s. The land occupied by the cemetery is still owned by the government of the United States.

Primary industries in the town of Fort Steele at the beginning of the twentieth century were sheep ranching and tie processing. The latter was the best-paying job but more dangerous because of the cancer-forming coal tar used to spray on the ties for preservation and longer in-service life. With sheepherding being a lesser popular occupation—because of the lower pay—there was a demand for shepherds, most of whom were Basque immigrants who lived in or around the town of Rock Springs, and their accommodation was a horse-drawn sheep wagon.

Sheep wagons are an American West style. They have curved, heavy-duty cloth roofs supported by hoops, and they look more like covered (Conestoga) wagons. Typically, a sheep wagon was approximately seven to eight feet wide and approximately twelve to sixteen feet long. Inside the wagon there is usually room for one bed or bunks; a small stove, sink, and cooking area; storage for clothes; and an eating area. As might be expected, sheep wagons do not have bathrooms or showers.

It was the habit of the sheepherders to drive their flocks past Hanna as they moved from summer-to-winter or winter-to-summer pasture. On occasion, as might be expected, a lamb or two would go astray, get hopelessly lost, and appear at some later date as the well-prepared lip-smacking-delicious centerpiece on a local dinner table.

As an example of a lamb going astray, on one particular day during or after a sheep drive, Father Robert and Bob were surprised—perhaps pleased—to hear the bleating of a lamb from close by the house. Upon further investigation they discovered that the lamb had entered the outhouse and, young animals being what they are, fallen into the hole. A noose was fashioned at the end of a rope, and they managed to place it around the lamb's neck. Moments later, without being strangled, the lamb was hauled out of the hole—smelling less than sweet—hosed down, and kept for later use.

The death knell for the town that existed close to the fort came when the Lincoln Highway (later to become Interstate 80 under President Eisenhower's interstate construction initiative) was the first transcontinental highway in the United States and passed through the town adjacent to—some would say even part of—Fort Steele, and boosted the economy between 1920 and 1939. Changes in the placement of the highway in 1939 caused an end to most commercial activity with a rapid decline in the number of residents leaving the deserted townsite.

***

Meanwhile, it was in the early years of the twentieth century—after the decommissioning of Fort Steele—that Williamson and Quealy were busy supplying timber to nearby towns such as Carbon and Hanna for building, as well as to the Union Pacific Railroad for railroad ties, and to the mines for posts to support roofs. Williamson and Quealy then decided to reorganize the company into the Wyoming Timber Company, with Williamson serving as president.

In addition, Williamson had other business interests. He was closely associated with the Quealy Land and Livestock Company, which was owned by Quealy; and he helped to found the Intermountain Telephone Company of Hanna in 1912. The Wyoming Timber Company held interest in the Wyoming Timber Lands Company and the Megeath Coal Company, both of Hanna, Wyoming. In addition, Williamson had a hand in the banking business in Laramie.

The Laramie banks founded by Williamson were preceded by the bank founded by Edward Ivinson, who arrived by rail with his heavy secure safe. The safe, which reportedly was never breached, and Ivinson's reputation as an honest business man led to his entering the banking profession. In 1870, he purchased the local bank, which became the First National Bank and is now part of the First Interstate Bank chain. He served as a contractor and lent the money to build the first courthouse, which was at the same location as the present one. His many other interests included a partnership in the Buckeye Ranch in Centennial Valley and a large share in the Laramie, North Park and Union Pacific Railroads, which he promoted with great enthusiasm.

In Hanna, Williamson's bank was located on Front Street. At that time it was the only building in town with a sidewalk in front. Other businesses strung along Front Street were the Hanna Hotel, the post office, the barber shop, and a boarding house that was adapted for various uses over the years. Grandfather John and family moved into this boarding house. Rounding out the business district was the Union Pacific Coal Company store and the local theater. A Methodist church lay to the east side of the town. The company store had a monopoly in Hanna. The only competition was in Elmo, a small town approximately one mile east of Hanna.

For the entertainment and social activities of the citizens of Hanna, the Opera House—a large building on a hill overlooking the town—became the center of all social functions but was destroyed by fire a few days before Christmas 1927. As far as the records indicate, the Opera House was never the venue for any operas but was more for any type of social function that required space for a dozen persons or more. It was superseded by Finn Hall, which was relocated from

Carbon to Hanna. As was the custom, the building was removed from its foundations and carried on a flatbed wagon, which was the old fashioned building-moving style of those days, and is still in vogue in modern Wyoming and other parts of the United States.

The coming of movies to Hanna was a major move toward keeping the citizens entertained. A movie theater was built to provide humor and tragedy (depending on the film being shown) most nights of the week. The theater was situated across the road from the Milliken and Sons business, and since Grandfather John also took on the role of the ad hoc blacksmith, he was available to anyone with a spare moment to strike up a conversation while he watched Father John shoe the horses.

As is always the case when life seems to be going well, some form of tragedy always seems to strike to dampen the human spirit. In this case, the casualty was the movie theater, which, unfortunately, like the Opera House, was destroyed by fire in 1941. But this did not stop some of residents attending the Christmas Eve program in the burned-out remains. As soon as possible thereafter, efforts were made by the stalwart citizens of Hanna to replace the theater.

On the more personal side of life in Hanna, the town, including the utilities, was owned by the Union Pacific Coal Company, and it was the duty of the company to cater to the sanitation issues of the population through the building of outhouses. Every home had an adjunct outhouse out back, and it was possible to look up and down the alleys and watch the comings and goings of the neighbors as they walked well-worn paths from the back doors of the houses to their respective outhouses. Whoever built the outhouses seemed to have social activities in mind—the two-hole outhouses would often be centers of social chatting when used by two occupants at the same time.

As part of the sanitation duties of the company, the outhouses had to have the waste pumped out periodically, and the outhouses had to be changed every five years. (It seems that the worthy citizens of Hanna could do nothing without their actions being monitored by the Union Pacific Railroad.) And the outhouses also served other purposes. In such close living accommodation, it was not unusual after the birth of a child to see the father figure of a family carry the placental expulsion—known more commonly as *the afterbirth*, which appears just after the baby is expelled from the mother—to the outhouse for collection with the other waste and eventual disposal.

In addition, every alley between the houses, where the outhouses were located, had several round waste bins for other garbage. Being of an entrepreneurial spirit, Uncle John Milliken obtained the contract from the railroad to haul the garbage to a waste dump.

***

Robert Carl Milliken arrived into the world of Hanna kicking and screaming in the late evening of June 6, 1922. The kitchen table was the birthing table, and it was fortunate that a doctor, R.A. Smith, MD, was in attendance. It was a breech birth—Bob's feet appeared first—and was a very difficult delivery for Mother Anna and baby Bob, but both mother and son survived, thanks to the ministration of the doctor and the strength of mother and child!

At the time of Bob's birth, the soon-to-be Father Robert and soon-to-be Mother Anna lived in a cold-water flat—an apartment which had running cold water but no running hot water—which was part of a larger building on Front Street, less than two hundred yards from the Union Pacific Railroad main line and across the line from Stink Creek. As a boy in the fourth grade, Father Robert had acquired the name "Swat" because of his interest in baseball, especially Swat Mulligan, who is considered by Grandfather John to be the greatest baseball player of all time. Swat's team—the Mighty Mulligans—won more than one thousand consecutive games. They had won so many games that no one would let them join any of the baseball leagues and their manager, Stump Mulligan (Swat's uncle) was always looking for a team for the Mulligans to play. He never had to look too hard because there was always some team that thought they could beat the Mighty Mulligans. It did not happen very often. Two later well-known players, Gabby Kraveth and Babe Ruth, both of whom were strong hitters of the ball, helped Father Robert's acquired name Swat to stick, and he eventually had the name added as a legal name on his birth certificate.

In 1923, the Milliken family, comprised of Father Robert, Mother Anna, and Bob—moved from the cold-water flat on Front Street to a home in a row of three houses. The house on the north side was occupied by Bob's grandparents and their family, and the Stebner family occupied the middle house. The Milliken house was on the south end of the row, and the family lived in that house from 1923 to 1929. It will not be surprising to anyone, Hanna being a Union Pacific Coal Company town, that the house was company-owned and, on occasion, was shared with another couple by the name of Hapgood. In the meantime, Father Robert and Mother Anna had also produced two daughters. Frances LuCeil was born in the Hanna Hospital on January 24, 1927. The kitchen table was no longer required as the birthing table as it had been for Bob, because modern medicine and medical services had moved into Hanna since Bob's birth, a provision from the Union Pacific Coal Company. Carol was also born in the Hanna Hospital, on June 1, 1928.

When Bob started kindergarten at age five in 1927, he had fifteen classmates who would continue as a group to high school graduation. The Hanna school was just a short walk from his home—three blocks. In fact, everything in Hanna was just a short walk away from anywhere else, and anything other than a short walk would take a person out of town.

The Hanna elementary school was a one-story frame construction building in which grades one through three were taught. There was a separate gymnasium to the north, then a stone building for grades four through twelve. It was at the elementary school that Bob was introduced to his first public urinal, a trough flushed by an overhead pierced pipe with streams of water trickling down. At least there were separate toilets for boys and girls.

One of Bob's classmates was Dean Ryder. They had started school together in Kindergarten and continued though the grades together. Dean was a rebel whose ethics pushed the envelope. He was classed as a troublemaker with low moral standards. Dean was the one who climbed out the window to escape kindergarten. He also challenged the ironbound rules of the schoolyard and tempted his classmates to stray from the paths of righteousness. Dean's outlook and approach to life impacted Bob and caused him not to follow Dean's lead through university and well into the war years.

With elementary school also came girls. Bob was in the first grade when he kissed one of the girls on the school porch. Like Dean, that kiss changed his life. He definitely knew then that there was a difference between the boys, who were his friends, and the girls he was just beginning to meet.

Most of the teachers lived up on the Tipperary hill, just as Mother Anna had done when she first started teaching in Hanna. Some of Bob's relatives also lived there—Uncle Bill and his large family, and some of the in-laws that came along as Uncle Bill's children married and started families of their own.

Hank Jones was Uncle Bill's brother-in-law (married to Hank's sister Rachel). He worked with the mine superintendent at the mine offices in the area south of town. Hank was also the mayor of Hanna and, as such, was responsible for all housing assignments. Whether or not he was elected to office is unclear, but one thing was certain: if anyone wanted to do something or needed something done in Hanna, they started with Hank.

***

If a year was to be assigned to the time that Bob showed an interest in flying, it would be 1927. It was in that year that Father Robert paid five dollars—a handsome sum in those days—for Bob to sit on the lap of a passenger in a two-seat biplane. This was an experience that Bob remembers with excitement to this day. He was so enthralled by the event that he became determined to learn to fly.

It was also the year that Babe Ruth (the Sultan of Swat) hit sixty home runs, Al Jolson was filming the first talking picture, and Al Capone was tightening his vice-like grip on crime. More pertinent to Bob's future, 1927 was the year that Lindbergh made his solo flight across the Atlantic Ocean in the *Spirit of St. Louis* and then made his flight across the United States using the *iron compass* as his guide—the lines of the Union Pacific railroad, which ran from east to west. More than anything else in that notable year, it was the year that Bob decided—as young as he was—that he wanted to be a flyer.

As he crossed the United States, Lindbergh's location and progress were easy to follow. At that time telegraph stations were approximately twenty miles apart along the railroad, so his progress could be followed through them, and each telegrapher would send out a signal when Lindbergh was passing over. The mine whistle also sounded, marking the special event, and the people of Hanna—including Bob, who would not miss such an occasion—turned out to see the new American hero. Lindberg didn't land in Hanna but received the usual cheering welcome as the *Spirit of St. Louis* passed by, following the line of the Union Pacific railroad.

The mine whistle was steam-powered and, as in many mines, was used to signal the start and end of shifts, but there was also a sequence of whistles for emergencies. When the Hanna telegrapher was alerted that Lindbergh was close, the mine whistle sounded the alert, and the townspeople left their homes to watch the sky. As if to oblige the reception, Lindbergh flew over Hanna at an elevation of approximately five hundred feet, which put the aircraft at approximately 7,318 feet above sea level (Hanna is 6,818 feet above sea level). In a sense, this occasion reaffirmed Bob's decision that he was going to be a flyer. He thought of flying as a joy, not knowing that he would be flying in a wartime situation.

Lindbergh's three-month nationwide tour was sponsored by the Daniel Guggenheim Fund. Flying the *Spirit of St. Louis*, Lindbergh visited 92 cities, gave 147 speeches, and rode 1,290 miles in parades, after which he returned to New York.

On April 28, 1927, Lindbergh and the *Spirit of St. Louis* flew together for the final time while making a hop from St. Louis to Bolling Field, located in southeast Washington, DC, on April 30, 1928. There he presented his monoplane to the Smithsonian Institution, where for more than eight decades it has been on display. Today it hangs in the atrium of the National Air and Space Museum.

At the time of its retirement, the *Spirit* had made 174 flights for a total of 489 hours flying time. As a final note to this event, the last fixed-wing flight out of Bolling Air Force Base was in 1962. Bolling Field is now Bolling Air Force Base, and the only aeronautical facility at the base is a 100-foot by 100-foot helipad.

While Bob was thrilled by the Lindberg flyover, it merely confirmed that aviation was in Bob's blood. Father Robert was drafted into the army during World War I at the age of eighteen, where he was trained as an aviation mechanic. The flying machines of yesteryear were relatively complex pieces of equipment that required strict maintenance and service. They were not, as many myths would have us believe, maintained with bailing wire and the early nineteenth century equivalent of duct tape.

In late 1918, Father Robert was doing duty at Kelly Field in Texas and had been there for only a few weeks when the Armistice was declared and the guns fell silent on the eleventh hour of the eleventh day of the eleventh month in 1918. There was no guarantee that the guns would remain silent, but the signing of the Treaty of Versailles by Allied representatives and by German representatives on June 28, 1919, brought an end to World War I. The war had started on June 28, 1918, and had cost millions of lives on both sides. Father Robert was demobilized and he came home to Hanna, but he had picked up a love for aviation. Whether advertently or inadvertently, he passed that passion on to Bob.

Father Robert (second from left) and Unnamed Colleagues
Just Prior to Cessation of World War I Hostilities

Even as a youngster, Bob's interest in flying never waned. He read as many books as he could on the subject. As a fourth grader, he even took it upon himself, with permission from Mother and Father, to write to a company that sold kits for constructing model airplanes. He explained his circumstances as a short-of-money farm and ranch boy and requested a complimentary model. He did not receive a model kit but the company sent him the next best thing—a book about flying. Bob was happy.

Bob's memories from the late 1920s and early 1930s include coming home one day from attending Sunday school at the Episcopal Church. His mother walked out of the house to meet him, and he was carrying a card with stamps on it that showed perfect attendance at the Sunday school. Each stamp had a candle on it that represented a Sunday attendance. It was one of the proudest moments of his young life.

***

Father Robert and family moved out of town in 1929. It was a move that changed Bob's school life in many ways. Any hesitancy he had about leaving town life was overruled by Father Robert's unhappiness and uneasiness with the lack of safety precautions in the mine. He was also unhappy working for others and wanted to own his own place, to be self-employed. But most of all, he wanted to work above ground where risks to life and limb were much reduced.

The new property, which cost $1,500—the mortgage took many years to pay off—was an 80-acre homestead located approximately one mile north and west of the town of Hanna, with a hill between the town and the homestead. There already was a house on the property, along with a barn and a smaller rectangular building.

The tar paper-covered house was small: a kitchen, living room, two bedrooms, and a small closet area. The closet became Bob's bedroom. When Bob saw it for the first time and looked in through the window, he saw a rocking horse that the previous owners had left behind. He remembers thinking, *Well, at least I'll have a rocking horse!*

Moving day came during the summer of 1929, shortly after Bob's seventh birthday, and soon the family was settled on what they called The Ranch—actually an eighty-acre homestead northwest of Hanna with a plentiful and colorful growth of the Indian paintbrush plant that is now the state flower. Shortly after the move, the Great Depression hit the United States, but the Milliken family survived, and for the next forty-two years, the address for the Robert Milliken family was P.O. Box 72, Hanna, Wyoming, USA.

The survival of the family was due in no small part to Mother Anna, an intelligent, refined, and extremely talented woman who was always able to make the best of whatever situation she found herself in. She was a wonderful seamstress. Bob remembers standing beside her as she worked her sewing machine and used the various threads to teach him the different colors as well as the color variations.

Ranch living conditions were isolated and primitive. Water was pumped using windmill power from a well into a cistern, thence into the house, and heated on a stove. Lanterns that burned kerosene (sometimes called coal oil) afforded the only light. Originally, water was brought from Hanna by wagon and loaded into the cistern. If there were no incidents that required excessive use of water, the full cistern could supply the family's water needs for a month or more. However, Father Robert, not wishing to rely on others for delivery of a valuable commodity such as water, made certain of their own supply of water by drilling a fifteen-foot-deep well that provided water into the cistern on an as-needed basis, with no reliance on others. The well was fed from the water that arose from the confluence of two streams where the drainage from the nearby high ground made sure that the well had plentiful amounts of water.

Electric power was provided to the Ranch by the Rural Electric Company (REA) in the late 1940s. Upon moving onto the Ranch in 1929, Father Robert had made them self-sufficient by using kerosene as the source of fuel. Installation of a wind charger to generate electric power added another dimension and level of comfort to their ranch-style living.

There was no telephone and only a basic radio that captured more static than real programming. The house had a small cellar under it that served as a storage area for items that were too valuable to leave in a barn or outer storage area. Mother Anna coped by concentrating on her family as well as applying her skills to dressmaking, wallpapering, writing poetry and articles, and creating small works of art to brighten their little house on the prairie.

Family entertainment came in the form a Victrola—a Victor phonograph that was originally made by the Victor Talking Machine Company. In 1929, RCA purchased the Victor Talking Machine Company, and the new company was called RCA Victor. By this time, the popularity of the phonograph was quickly diminishing in favor of the louder and more flexible electronic combination systems, and only cheap portables and children's phonographs continued to use acoustic reproduction. In October 1929, the onset of the Depression killed the sales of all non-essential commodities, and Victrolas were to be had for bargain prices— probably less than $25 for a machine originally costing $250.

History records that Father Robert did not purchase the table model Victrola but that he won it as the prize for the raffle at an American Legion meeting. He was a member of the American Legion by virtue of his military service at the end of World War I. Acquiring the machine added much fine entertainment to the Milliken family evenings though the purchase of a variety of records.

Father Robert also put family first—he loved his children and all of his relatives. Dad and Bob were comfortable together hunting, fishing, and just observing the wildlife surrounding in the area. These were important times of camaraderie for father and son—they could drive for miles with no need for conversation.

***

Horses were a big part of Bob's early years. Hanging around Grandfather John Milliken's stable had its advantages, one being that Bob learned to ride horses at a young age. But he was ten years old before he was allowed to ride alone. Father Robert inherited ten horses from Grandfather John when the horse drayage business closed down. At about that time, Father Robert started to look around for another business, and he became the proud owner of a taxi service that operated from Hanna to Elmo, the small town approximately one mile east of Hanna. Between runs he also did mechanical work.

That same year, Bob had a close call with a mountain lion, a rather large cat that still roams Wyoming and can be ferocious when hungry or protecting cubs.

Bob was out and about with his homemade bow and arrows, which he carried in a quiver made by Mother Anna. He spotted the cat in the near (in fact, too close) vicinity—a matter of several yards. Bob froze and didn't move or even blink. Whether or not the big cat saw him and decided that he was too small to make a good-sized meal only the mountain lion knows. It is believed that a mountain lion prefers to attack from the rear so that it can paralyze the victim with a bite to the spinal column. Some hunters recommend that if a mountain lion is close, the potential victim should always turn to face the cat. I wouldn't recommend that this strategy be attempted by anyone reading this book. Given the opportunity, the best course of action is to remove oneself as quickly as possible from the vicinity of the animal. Maybe no one explained the rules of attack to the lion! As it happened, Bob's immobility and the fact that he was facing the animal may have saved his life. It walked past him without even breaking stride. Bob was relieved, and much to his relief, he never saw or encountered the big cat again.

Mother Anna's and Father Robert's comments about the incident have not been recorded, but I imagine that they were pertinent and to the point!

***

In the early years of Bob's life, there was no school bus service, so when the weather was bad, Father took Bob to school. The means of transport was an old blue Chevrolet pickup truck. Father Robert had made arrangements for the gasoline fuel to be delivered and stored in a 250-gallon pedestal tank at the Ranch. The truck had only a small piece of one fender still attached. The remainder of the fender had succumbed to rust and dropped off during the truck's long service.

When the weather was favorable, Bob would ride to school on a horse that once belonged to the failed Milliken and Son business. When the family business turned sour, many of the horses were turned out to range, but Father and Bob rounded up about a half dozen horses for the ranch. They also acquired a mule called Quesix, and Bob usually rode to school on Quesix or on a gelding called Prince or on the dependable mare Sally.

He usually rode bareback, so getting aboard either horse or the mule was a challenge. He had help at home, but if he fell off along the way, which sometimes happened, Bob had to walk the animal to a big rock and convince it to stand still long enough for him to get up on the rock and then pull himself back up to where he should have stayed in the first place. Upon arriving in town, Bob would tie up his mount at Grandfather John Milliken's house and walk the short distance to the schoolhouse. While he was in school, Uncle John Milliken would tend to the mount and leave it hitched to a power pole so that Bob could be assured of a ride back home.

***

Moving to the Ranch had its advantages, but there were also the disadvantages. Being out of town, Bob was not as free to participate in all the town activities, because he had to factor in the process of getting into town, which involved walking or riding. But another form of transport also came into Bob's life.

When he was twelve years old, Bob woke on Christmas morning to find a pair of strap-on skis under the fir tree. It was a real tree cut by Bob and his father; there were no artificial trees then.

Bob quickly learned the art of skiing the hard way. He would go out and climb the hills, then ski back down the slopes, often falling into the cold snow. Although Bob enjoyed this form of travel, there was a disadvantage. When he skied to school, he usually got wet, and his pants and underwear would be frozen stiff by the time he arrived at the schoolhouse.

Later on, when Bob was still twelve, there was a school bus, and the route took the bus past the Ranch. This was ideal for getting to and from school and removed the falling-off-the-horse-or-mule-and-sitting-in-school-in-wet-clothes episodes from his life. However, he still could not participate in many of the school activities.

He did try out for the basketball team, but with no success. The coach, seemingly with a mere glance and not even taking a breath, had come straight to the point.

"Bob," he said, finally looking Bob up and down, "you're too short."

In today's politically correct world, the expression would be that he was *vertically challenged*, but at five feet seven inches as an adult, Bob indisputably lacked vertical height. His height coupled with the problems of getting to and from practice during harsh winters ruled out basketball.

Not being one to give up on sport, and under the watchful eye of Uncle John Milliken, who had encouraged him to try for the team (the Hanna Miners), Bob did go out for football in his junior year of high school. Upon being accepted, Bob felt a modicum of success.

Team members were allowed to have three personal items: shoes, socks, and an athletic supporter (referred to as a *jock strap* in the modern idiom), but everything else was provided by the school—which was a financial relief. But other equipment had been worn by previous generations of players.

What was generously and with a touch of pride referred to as the football field was a plowed and harrowed piece of ground that froze into clumps when the weather was cold. That didn't matter to Bob at first, since he was warming the bench. Bob had one or two practice sessions as a quarterback, but when game time rolled around, he was always classed as being too small to see much action.

When he first suited up, Bob weighed 125 pounds. He had not grown to his mature height of five feet seven inches. He did make a lot of trips with the team, and the travel and team camaraderie made it an important time of his life.

***

There was little else in the way of sport or activities for young people in Hanna in the 1920s and 1930s.

Recognizing this, the local Episcopalian minister, Father Kellam, went to a union meeting and tried to get the miners' union to sponsor a tennis court, but such a venture did not fit into the agenda of the union, and it was considered that tennis was not a sport for hard-working miners or their sons and daughters. Naturally, the proposal was voted down.

As a result, Hanna remained a two-sport school—basketball and football—and Bob did not have the build and physical stature for either! Fortunately, there were other extracurricular activities such as the junior and senior class plays, and he participated in both with gusto.

It was always Bob's wish that there should be a swimming pool in Hanna, but that was wishful thinking, and swimming was not a school sport either. The nearest water that was anything more than knee-deep was twenty miles away. The town youngsters used to swim a little in the overflow from the town reservoir, but that was never very deep and seldom lasted long. Swimming definitely was not a major activity in Hanna.

Living out on the Ranch, much of Bob's entertainment was solo. Often he would put on a pair of basketball trunks, lace up his pre-Nike gym shoes, and run through the countryside. He would run for miles and miles with the sun beating down and the dry Wyoming grassland passing under his feet. He got himself into a high level of fitness and acquired a deep, enduring tan.

For a short time, when he was about fifteen, Bob had his own saddle horse and frequently rode him to town to see friends.

The horse was called Ginger, and he had been purchased from a ranch west of Hanna, on Highway 30. Father Robert took Bob to the purchase in his truck. After the sale, not having the saddle or other trappings of horse leather, Father Robert drove slowly while Bob walked the horse back to their home, a distance of about twelve miles.

Ginger was obstinate—*a little ornery* in the language of the area. Given the slightest chance, the animal would try to throw Bob or roll on him or both. Bob finally taught the horse who was boss by biting the animal's ear. Then he would twist the horse's head, as they do to cattle during a rodeo, get him down flat on the ground, and sit on his head. The horse did not try to roll on Bob much after that discipline. Bob now admits that he wasn't a very good horse, and being a useless horse, he finally ended up as horse meat, which made excellent protein fodder for the foxes. This was the fate of most useless horses.

Horses, firearms, flying, and outdoor sports were the main interests that carried through Bob's life. He was looking over the sight of a gun as soon as he was old enough to hold a gun to his shoulder, and he started hunting when he was twelve, going out with Father Robert and his friends. For many years Bob hunted deer and antelope. He learned patience from Father Robert, who was always there to guide him, such as when Bob was gun-sighting a game animal or bird and father Robert's whispered voice told him: "Steady, Bob, steady.... Lead the animal [or the bird] so that your shot arrives at a place the same time as the animal [or the bird]."

Uncle Bill's son, Rob, had a 410 shotgun, which Bob borrowed on occasion to hunt sage chickens. During this time, he learned the principle of leading the target, a technique in which the prey moves into the bullet or hail of shotgun pellets.

This technique was to stand Bob in good stead in later life when he was in the cockpit of a P-38, pursuing and shooting at enemy aircraft.

Both Father Robert and Mother Anna were excellent shots. Many sage grouse and antelope or deer who strayed within shooting distance of the Ranch house could attest to that, and they taught Bob well. Uncle Newt gave Bob a .22-caliber single-shot rifle when he was fifteen, which became one of Bob's prized possessions. But accidents happen, and Bob was devastated when he lost the rifle bolt on a pasture on the UL Ranch. He searched endlessly for the bolt but never found it. Without the bolt, the treasured rifle was just a piece of iron with some hunks of wood attached.

Rabbit was another dinner delicacy, as it is in many parts of Europe to this day. Bob went rabbit hunting as soon as he could and often hunted alone, just he and whatever .22-caliber rifle he could use. In the winter, the snow-covered ground was covered with rabbit tracks, so it was no problem finding lots of targets, and they were welcome additions to the family's Depression-era menu. Sage chickens also were staples of the Milliken table, and Bob got to be a good shot with a 410 shotgun borrowed from Cousin Rob, with which he would bring down coveys of game birds during his school years.

Father Robert hoped to improve the Ranch property by putting in some irrigation. With Bob's help he was able to dam up some water and dig ditches, but the attempts at irrigation didn't work out. It was a hit-or-miss proposition, with more misses than hits. But they were successful in cultivating a large garden and four potato fields.

They used a one-horse plow. Bob drove the horse while Father Robert guided the plough to cut the furrows. Before planting, they had to take the seed potatoes out of storage and cut them, making sure there was an eye in every cut section. If a section didn't have an eye, it couldn't sprout. Once the cutting was done, they planted the sections on the furrows, covered them, and waited for the crop to come in.

***

After four seasons, the potato venture proved to be financially disastrous, so Father Robert turned his attention to chickens. He started the chicken enterprise in 1930–31. He had about a hundred chickens, which he used to establish an egg and chicken business. He also added a cow to the list of livestock that made the Ranch their home. That added a milk route to his activities. Goods were delivered and customers were served from Father Robert's prized possession—an open-bed truck with no cab. Father Robert—assisted at times by Bob when he was of age, and with permission from Mother Anna—would drive the truck rigged up for milk and chicken deliveries, summer and winter, twenty miles to Walcott and twenty miles from Saratoga, to pick up milk, return to Hanna to bottle the milk, and deliver it to customers. It was a forty-mile round trip in a truck with no cab over roads that were little more than ruts over the prairie. Father Robert would also deliver chickens and whatever eggs could be gathered. Mother Anna would candle the eggs and package them.

The cow turned out to have quite a character. She was an escape artist, perhaps the Henrietta Houdini of the bovine world. On one occasion she decided to make her escape and had disappeared before her absence was noticed. Father Robert, Uncle John, and Bob, in the manner of Native American trackers, went after her using the only form of transportation available to them—an ancient Oldsmobile that had been reconditioned and rebuilt by Father Robert. They ran her to earth five miles away from the Ranch, where she was grazing peacefully with not a care in the world. But alas—the once-luxury car could not accommodate the cow.

There was nothing left to do. Father Robert lifted Bob onto the back of the cow and told him to follow with care. The cow obliged, but the weather did not. The sudden onset of a thunder and lightning storm gave the cow some moments of eye-rolling fear, and Bob some moments of terror as the cow moved uneasily after the car. Finally the journey was complete, and Madame Cow was returned to her pasture.

As a reward for his efforts in the adventure of the cow, Father Robert decided that Bob, as a nine-year-old, was sufficiently mature to learn the basics of driving. All went well (Bob was quick learner) until they took the Oldsmobile through a rough-terrain gulley—a deep channel that the regular and prolonged downpour during summer months had cut in the earth, and that was big enough to accommodate the car. Unfortunately, the Oldsmobile was not built for that type of terrain. Bob managed to strip the gears. The car was not repaired. They sent it to the car graveyard from which it never returned.

Bob remembers that Father did not get angry. He was very patient but he did read Bob a little bit of the riot act. Then, as in other times of his life, it was Mother Anna who meted out the punishment. In fact, Bob recalls being physically struck by his father. That was after Bob had pulled LuCeil's hair and, as girls are prone to do when hair is pulled, she had let out a yelp that bought Bob's deed to the attention of Father Robert. Punishment was dispensed accordingly.

It was shortly after this, in 1931, that on a joyful but sad note the milk business came to an abrupt end. In that year Bob developed appendicitis that almost took his life, but thanks to the ministrations of Dr. McDermott, his life was saved. However, payment had to be made, part of which was a large and very noticeable scar. The inner membranes of his lower abdomen had not been sewn correctly and would remain on Bob's abdomen for the rest of his life and would also affect his future.

Dr. McDermott, the attending physician surgeon who operated on Bob at the Hanna hospital (a Union Pacific Railroad property) and saved his life, worked for the Union Pacific Railroad, and his duties were to minister health and happiness to the Union Pacific employees as part of the benefits that the company provided to all employees.

Bob recovered, but there being no health care or benefits outside the Union Pacific Railroad—at the time Father Robert was not a UPRR employee—the doctor had to be paid, so the other part of the payment, in addition to the scar, took the form of the cow and several turkeys. This brought a halt to the milk business and cost Father

Robert part of the Ranch's income. Such was life in the absence of health care benefits.

***

Following the transfer of the cow to another life, the major occupation at the Ranch became chicken processing, which was an art. Small chicks would be ordered from a Montgomery Ward poultry farm, and they would arrive by rail. Bob and Dad would pick them up at the depot, raise them on the Ranch, sell what eggs they could gather along the way, and then kill the adult birds for fryers or roasting chickens.

Each egg would be checked before sale by the processing known as *candling*. Using a coal oil lamp for light, the egg would be held in front of the light for any with double yolks or blood spots, which appeared as shadows within the shape of the egg. The eggs would also be given the water test using a large dish of cold water—if the egg floated, it was doomed for rejection, but if it sank, it was deemed to be all right for sale. The eggs that floated had too much in the way of gas inside the shell due to decomposition of the yolk and egg white (albumen).

Dad and Bob found that the best way to process chicken was to tie each bird's legs together, hang the chicken over a clothesline, then insert a specially-made curved knife into the bird's brain. If it was done correctly, the chicken would die without fuss, and the feathers could be stripped without first scalding the bird. After cleaning the chickens in a big tub of hot water, any remaining feathers would be plucked thoroughly before selling the birds.

During the 1880s, the railroad companies divided the tracks into sections between ten and thirty miles long and assigned a foreman and crew to tend each section. The railroad provided a two-room building (section house) as dwelling for a railroad section crew or for storing and maintenance of equipment for a section of railroad.

The Union Pacific Railroad had homes called *section houses* along the track. When the railroad consolidated various services, they disposed of many houses. Father Robert purchased three such houses and moved them to the top of a small hill about one mile from the Milliken home. Several cables were used to haul the houses to the top of the hill.

One night there was quite a thunderstorm. The family was awakened by the thunder, and lightning was flashing everywhere. Some of the haulage cables were left strung near the section houses, so Father and Bob took them down and left them on the ground nearby, but the discarded cables attracted the lightning. Lightning struck the cables, and the current jumped from the cables to one wooden section house, which was hungrily consumed by the flames of the ensuing fire. It was a setback, just one of those things that happened, but it didn't stop Father Robert and Bob.

One of the remaining section houses was moved to the Ranch without incident, but moving the second house caused a minor but surmountable problem. While they were working on the second house, Bob stepped on a nail that went through the sole of his shoe, through his foot, and out the top of the shoe. Father Robert pulled the nail out, removed the shoe, plastered some chewing tobacco over both holes, top and bottom, put the shoe back on, and they went back to work.

The two section houses led Father Robert and Bob to construct a two-story chicken house. This was a grandiose two-story building as opposed to the original single-story section house, and they got on with the business of chicken farming.

In time, the cow and the daily production of milk were no longer Ranch assets, and Father Robert also gave up chickens to concentrate on a silver fox farm. Fox furs were all the fashion at that time, so people were raising foxes for their pelts. Father purchased his initial breeding stock from Laramie, and he and Bob had to build a large enclosure of chicken wire with an overhang so that if foxes got out of their individual pens, they would have difficulty getting away. Each pen was a solidly built kennel, with two partitions covered by a heavy lid. The lid could be lifted so that the fox could go through an enclosed chute and bed down in a warm space.

Father Robert carefully monitored the behavior of each vixen to determine when she was ready for mating. At the right time, a male fox would be introduced, and nature would take it from there. In time the foxes grew in number to about five hundred animals, which had to be fed. Father and Bob hunted rabbits to feed the foxes. The rabbit carcasses were cleaned and run through a grinder driven by a Model T engine, and the meat was served to the foxes. Fortunately, the rabbit population of the area never seemed to decrease, rabbits being prolific animals in terms of their breeding habits, and rabbit meat was not in short supply.

However, the Depression hit the family hard. About the time that they had numerous beautiful foxes ready for pelting, the market for their fur collapsed, so Father decided to go to work in the Hanna mine. It was a two-mile walk from the Ranch to where the mine had opened a new portal, the L Plane. Summer and winter, Father Robert would walk two miles over one hill, through a little valley, and up another hill. He usually worked the night shift, adding to the stress and difficulty of his on-foot commute.

Later on, when the Monolith Mining Company started open-pit mining, the Milliken family became acquainted with the Heinemann family. Their son, Buck, became one of Bob's best friends.

Mr. Heinemann arranged for Father Robert to get a job as hostler, which meant that he would get up in the morning, fire up the steam shovel, and make sure it was operational for the day. In the evening he would go back and stoke it up for the night shift. Father Robert was able to go to work, then return home during the day. He held that job until his retirement at age sixty-five.

***

While in high school, Bob and a friend, Don Park, who lived on a ranch near the reservoir, cooperated in operating the high school print shop. The printer had a big circular plate on a long handle to apply pressure to the type as the plate moved back and forth, reminiscent of the press used by Gutenberg some five hundred years earlier. They had to set the type by hand, insert the letters and words in a form, level it so the impressions would be consistent, then start working on the handle to move the plate back and forth as ink was applied from rollers. They put in a single sheet of paper each time the plate passed under rollers, then removed the printed piece and inserted a new blank page.

Bob and Don built up quite a business printing special notices and other things for the local people. All of the money went to the school, but they got the experience of commercial work.

Bob also enjoyed being in plays at Love's Theater. There was a popular radio program at the time—*Major Bowes Amateur Hour*—which gave one of the men in Hanna, Mark Jackson, the idea to sponsor a local amateur hour. Bob emerged as the winner, not because he was particularly talented, but because he could answer all the various questions that were asked of the contestants leading up to the competition.

In addition, the Methodist minister sponsored three-round boxing matches. Father Robert and Uncle John were both good boxers. They coached Bob, practiced with him, and loaned him some lightweight boxing shoes. There were posters all over town promoting the matches, including the match for Bob against Fog Norris—so named because he was a little foggy and cloudy in his judgment of others. Bob was listed as *Swat* Milliken and when a friend of Father Robert saw that Swat Milliken was to fight Fog Norris, they accused him of picking on children. Most of them were there when the young Swat won the bout.

One of Bob's most interesting high school classes was woodworking, where he was able to build some very good furniture. A desk that he built was charred in an apartment fire, but the drawers fit so closely that the contents came through intact.

Unlike multi-car families of today, the Milliken family had only one vehicle, a blue pickup truck of uncertain vintage. When Father Robert was on a shift, Bob would take him to work at the mine so he (Bob) could use the truck while Father Robert was working. Then Bob would return to the mine, park, and sleep in the truck until Father Robert came off shift.

Boy Scouts were important in the upper grades and high school, and Bob has fond memories of many camping trips and of climbing Elk Mountain for the first time. Bob's membership lasted approximately one year. He had trouble attending the meetings during the winter, when bad weather set in and made the journey from the Ranch to Hanna difficult. It was during this time in the Boy Scouts that Elk

Mountain, a towering peak dominating the local landscape, almost became Bob's tombstone.

Buck Heinemann and Bob decided they were old enough, strong enough, and smart enough to climb Elk Mountain alone in February. They started out on skis, which lasted for about a hundred yards, just far enough for them to conclude that going uphill with boards strapped on their feet was not going to work out. They stuck their skis in the snow and started climbing. They struggled through deep snowdrifts and worked their way along bare rocky ridges to within fifty yards of the peak. The wind was blowing so hard that Bob and Buck had to crawl on their hands and knees. Snow was whipping all around, nearly blinding them and freezing any exposed skin. In spite of the adverse weather conditions, they made it all the way to the top. Somehow, by default and good luck, they were able to make their way back down the mountain, retrieve the skis, and return home to thaw out, proud of themselves for their achievement, but knowing deep inside that what they had done was not the smartest thing in the world!

***

As a young boy, Bob experienced the pain and sorrow of the death of close friends. One friend was Billy Pickup, and the other was Nick Zakis.

The Pickup family lived next to the house where Bob was born, so it was natural that he became close friends with Billy, a boy of Bob's age.

Summer was much better for outdoor activities, and Bob spent much of his time fishing with the Pickup family. Billy Pickup's dad chewed tobacco. It was necessary to be constantly on guard driving to and from the fishing spots because when Pickup senior spit out the front window, the back window had to be rolled up or you might find yourself covered with tobacco leftovers.

Bob's final memory of Billy Pickup is of them sharing a two-hole outhouse that was behind his house. This brought on a Halloween prank. Bob and Billy pushed over one of the outhouses. This was not a major crime by any stretch of the imagination—but it was occupied at the time by one of the ladies who lived in that street. She was not amused!

Billy died early in his life—at age six, in 1928. The precise cause of Billy's death is lost in the mists of time, but it was believed to be through blockage of the bowel. Billy's death was the first time that Bob had experienced death of a friend. Deaths among mining families are still a hazard of the job and are felt by everyone in a small community. Bob was one of the casket bearers for Billy and he can clearly remember standing in the American Methodist Church, the casket in the aisle during the service. Then followed the journey to the cemetery, where Bob watched as the casket was lowered into the grave. Over the years, when visiting Hanna, Bob would visit Billy's grave.

In 1932, when he was in the fourth grade, another classmate, Nick Zakis, also died. Like Billy's death, the precise cause of Nick's death is also lost to history. All of Nick's classmates attended the funeral, after which the casket was placed into a pickup and the classmates followed in a school bus. The cemetery lay one mile west of town, across a bridge and up a hill with a stop at the railroad crossing just prior to reaching the cemetery. After the stop at the crossing, the pickup truck driver, who had forgotten that the tailgate of the pickup was down, started to move the pickup too quickly. As a result, the casket slid out of the back of the truck, and Nick was ejected from the casket. All of Nick's classmates were in the school bus behind the pickup and viewed the whole incident. Nick's body was quickly replaced in his casket, the casket was put back in the pickup, the tailgate was secured, and the entourage proceeded to the cemetery without any further delay or incident.

Chapter 3: The Teen Years

Bob's early teen years were years of thinking about and searching for his future. He was going through a metamorphosis, walking from the Ranch to town and back again, pondering what he was going to do in life, what he was going to be, who he wanted to become. Even at that not-so-tender age, he knew that decisions had to be made and that those decisions would shape his life for all the years to come. The adventures that lay ahead were unknowns, and he could not imagine what events and forces would transform not only his life but the lives of all men and women in his generation.

And then a change, in fact a milestone came to Bob's life— for the first time he became the proud owner of a one-speed bicycle. His home—The Ranch—was approximately two miles from town, and he had few-to-no opportunities to do jobs for townspeople and earn money. Being determined to change this prognosis, Bob saved as much as he could until he finally had enough money—thirty dollars, a princely sum at the time—to purchase his very own almost-new bike.

This magnificent machine had big balloon tires—possibly almost equivalent to the ties on a modern mountain bicycle—and was a variable-speed machine insofar as the speed of the bicycle depended on how fast Bob pedaled. Owning such a machine gave Bob a sense of liberty, and he no longer had to depend on Father Robert, or riding a horse, or riding a mule, or the school bus (which did not come into service until 1936, when Bob was an eighth-grader), or walking. Bob now had an alternative and independent form of transportation to take him wherever he wished to go.

However, there were rules to follow and be obeyed—Father Robert and Mother Anna demanded a promise, which Bob gave, that he would not ride on the highway. It was left to Bob to use any off-highway road into and out of Hanna.

The two miles of rough, bumpy, and unpredictable country roads—some of these thoroughfares could only be called tracks at best—from the Ranch and the town were passable and relatively but not completely safe for a young cyclist. In times of inclement weather, it was possible to ride the bicycle on the back roads, but mud would build up under the bicycle fenders. This required scraping the mud off the fenders or carrying the bike the rest of the way. Bob opted for the former solution to the problem. And country roads are always a challenge, especially after sunset. All he had to guide him on his way was a small battery-operated night light attached to the handlebars.

However, on one occasion after sunset, Bob decided that he would prefer a smoother ride from Hanna to the Ranch, so and he ventured onto the highway. As bad luck would have it, a local man with his girlfriend was driving a truck on the highway and—not surprisingly—he was paying more attention to his girlfriend than to the controls of his vehicle. The man did not see Bob, the bicycle, or the night light, and Bob was bumped and forced off the road. The driver, realizing that something had happened, stopped to help. Fortunately, Bob was not hurt, and there was no damage to the bicycle. But the thoughts of *what if* and *what could have been* scared everyone, especially Bob's parents. He was given a stern lecture and made to renew his promise not to ride the highway, and he never again broke that promise.

Early on in his high school career, Bob's Aunt Mary taught him how to dance so that he would not be left on the sidelines at the junior or senior proms. Mother Anna and the mother of one of his classmates conspired to arrange Bob's first date. As he remembers, she was a lovely girl, but it was not an evening for the scrapbook. They both knew they were there because of their mothers, but they made the best of it by pretending to have a good time—and perhaps they did.

Often on weekends Bob would go to Elk Mountain to a dance that was held at the Garden Spot Pavilion. Sometimes the music was provided by a local band, while at other times the dancers reveled to the sounds of big-name bands willing to make an extra stop on their coast-to-coast tours. During the dancing, the floor moved up and down in a bouncing motion, and the word spread that the floor was supported on railroad springs for the benefit of the dancers. Alas, the truth was that the floor had been so well used by so many dancing feet, with the accompanying weight of the dancers, that the underlying timbers had lost their rigidity, giving the floor a life of its own.

Off the dance floor, the consumption of alcoholic beverages was a big part of the evening, and being underage didn't always prevent drinking. The boys who aspired to be older than their years would fill Coke bottles with whatever spirits they could get from their elders, and then strut around boasting of, and toasting, their amazing ingenuity. Two saloons were located within a hundred yards of the dance venue, and during intermissions, quick visits to one of the saloons was a means of securing refills of the Coke bottles.

However, Bob's premature forays into adulthood had repercussions. On one occasion—there had been no alcoholic consumption—he took it upon himself to drive Father Robert's Model T truck to the house from the Ranch gate. Seeing the truck moving, Father Robert ran to catch up, and Bob had to circle the house before his father was able to climb on board. Bob knew how to steer the truck but he had never learned to stop the vehicle. Father Robert was not amused!

On another occasion, after Bob had been sufficiently schooled in truck driving and the art of stopping the Model T truck, he was driving it with three friends squeezed with him on the front seat and several more friends sitting on the open truck bed behind the cab. One of the boys had been sipping a little too much of the exuberating liquid from his Coke bottle. He fell out of the open truck bed and was knocked unconscious, but fortunately had no injuries other than a bruise or two.

When Father Robert found out about the incident, Bob received a stern and poignant lecture from his father. Bob knew that he was lucky to get off with only the lecture. The incident could have resulted in the death of his friend, or he could have been seriously injured.

***

The Union Pacific Railroad, through the needs of the Union Pacific Coal Company, was the main force in the character and development of Hanna.

Because of the needs of the coal company, Hanna became a mule-powered town. The mule barns were ubiquitous. Mules pulled the mine carts to the surface and moved equipment whenever and to wherever it needed moving. The barns where the mules were fed and housed were cleaned between shifts. There are no records of the disposal of the matter that was shoveled out of the barns.

The mules were not allowed much in the way of exercise—the continuous work in the darkness of the mine caused many of the mules to go blind. When the working days of a mule were over, the animal may have been assigned to live out its life in the barns.

The dangers of mining dictated that *first aid* was a critical component of life in Hanna and, as a result, the Union Pacific Coal Company sponsored a five-member first aid team. Bob was a proud member of the team. As part of the training exercise, four team members would practice on the fifth member, and since Bob was the smallest of the group, he was usually elected by acclamation as the patient. In spite of this military style of volunteering, he still managed to learn and practice all of the first aid procedures.

However, it was not all work. The city of Rock Springs scheduled a first aid team competition every summer in conjunction with Old Timers' Day.

The Union Pacific Coal Company's Old Timers' Association held its first reunion at Rock Springs on June 13, 1925, and the attendees represented a cross section of the various ethnic groups in Rock Springs. The coal company wanted the people to enjoy life and have a community spirit and participation. The company and residents were integrated to try to make life as enjoyable as possible. A Community Council was formed with the aim of promoting all aspects of neighborhood work, including recreational, social, musical, civic, and charitable. Old Timers' Day has not been celebrated for several years. Instead International Day is celebrated on July 13, which may be a date close to the date of last celebrations of Old Timers' Day.

Naturally, the Hanna First Aid Team would be entered in the competition at the Old Timers' Day festival. Bob and the co-members of the team took the train to Rock Springs to show their capabilities against teams from other mining towns of the region. To his joy, the Hanna First Aid Team won first prize both of the times Bob competed, but he was uncertain if the win resulted from his ability to be a good practice patient or the ability of his team to respond quickly and efficiency to the emergencies that were a planned part of the competition.

***

Once Bob was involved in an accident that almost ended with his unplanned but permanent residency in a cemetery plot.

As is typical in western towns and townships, Bob's family attended many rodeos. Grandfather John even judged at the Frontier Days Rodeo in Cheyenne—then, as now, the capital city of Wyoming. Billed as *The Daddy of Them All*, the Cheyenne Rodeo has been held annually since the first Frontier Days held on Thursday, September 23, 1897. Currently, Frontier Days are held during the last ten days in July, and the event still attracts the top cowboys and cowgirls from across the United States, Canada, and Mexico and is one of the largest, rodeo events, possibly the largest, in the world.

Thus it came to pass that on Bob's sixteenth birthday, June 6, 1938 (about six weeks before the start of rodeo festivities), Father Robert and Mother Anna agreed that he was old enough to attend Frontier Days without the benefits (or restrictions) of direct adult supervision. Accordingly, arrangements were made for Bob to stay with Uncle Harry and Aunt Agnes, Father Robert's sister, who lived in Cheyenne. Harry Challendar, Agnes's husband, was a pleasant man and a veteran of World War I, and they welcomed Bob into their home.

Harry had survived the mud and death of the war and returned to take a degree at Stanford University, then opted for the teaching profession, eventually rising to the position of School Superintendent for the Hanna area. During that time he met, courted, and married Agnes.

Harry had been gassed in 1918, and as the years passed this had an effect on his health, usually resulting in an asthmatic condition. He also had hearing problems that developed from having his ears pounded by the sound of many exploding shells. He had been allowed to retire on the basis of disability, and he and Agnes moved to Cheyenne, where they were able to live comfortably on Harry's disability pension.

Looking forward to this unsupervised (or chaperoned) opportunity, Bob sought means of transportation to Cheyenne. With the assistance of a Union Pacific Railroad clerk who worked out of the Hanna depot, Bob was put into contact with a driver who regularly drove to and from Cheyenne to deliver beverages, driving a truck that pulled a smaller trailer loaded with the full and empty glass beverage bottles.

The journey to Cheyenne started on July 8, 1938, and Bob was on his way to the *big one*—the Cheyenne Rodeo. They were only a few miles out of Hanna on Highway 30 when the driver stopped to give a ride to a roadside hitchhiker. There was no room for all of them in the cab of the truck, but the hitchhiker, being desperate for the ride, agreed to ride in the trailer to the rhythmic musical sound of the bottles clinking against one another.

As is customary on such a sunny day in Wyoming—air conditioning in vehicles was still an unknown fact of the future—the driver had rolled down the window and drove with his left arm resting on the window frame. Not to be outdone, and in need of fresh air, Bob took up a similar position with his right arm resting on the passenger-side window ledge and his elbow sticking out the open right window. All seemed to be well with the world. The rhythmic sounds of the tires on the asphalted highway and the rhythmic clinking of the bottles were music to the driver's ears. He lost his concentration and, unknown to Bob, was in the early stages of sleep.

About fifteen miles east of Hanna, the truck moved slowly to the left, where the roadside was fairly level and even. Bob assumed the driver was pulling over, but this was not the case. The almost-sleeping driver awoke with a start and jerked the wheel sharply to the right, but his attempts to save the truck from an incident were not successful—the truck rolled over once and, surprisingly, came to rest upright on its wheels. Seat belts, a vehicular item of the future, were unknown. Bob was partially thrown out, his face had a painful collision with the ground, and then—perhaps miraculously—he was tossed back into the cab. Luckily, all Bob had to show for it was a big bruise on his temple.

The hitchhiker was more severely injured. He survived the rollover, but the bottles in the trailer did not. The broken shards of glass cut his left earlobe, which was hanging by a thread and bleeding profusely. Bob's first aid training sprang to the fore, and he took control. He applied a compression dressing to the almost-separated ear. As is the case even now, when an accident happens, it is always the fault of someone else. The truck driver reprimanded Bob for not keeping him awake. Bob responded accordingly. The colorful language is not described, but the color blue might spring to mind! Fortunately, a passing motorist stopped to offer help, and he took the hitchhiker back to Hanna and the nearest hospital. With cooler attitudes prevailing and the attention on him lessening, Bob decided to continue on to Cheyenne using s different conveyance. The truck was still operational, but the cleanup of the broken bottles was a sight to behold and would require time. Bob recognized that he and the driver were no longer compatible.

The accident had occurred in a nowhere place, fifteen miles east of Hanna, sixty miles west of Laramie, and 130 miles west of Cheyenne. As luck would have it, seeing that an accident had occurred, a truck stopped at the scene. It was going to Laramie, and Bob was able to get a ride to continue on his way, with three cowboys in the cab of the truck and Bob, the lone hitchhiker, riding in the truck bed.

No matter what happens in the Wyoming wilderness, word of an incident can spread quickly. The news of the accident got back to Hanna. The truck driver and hitchhiker had been accounted for as survivors, but Bob's whereabouts was unknown, and it was rumored and feared that he had wandered off into the sagebrush dazed or wounded or dying. Meanwhile, back at the Ranch, Father Robert and Mother Anna had heard the news and were very worried. The Ranch did not have a telephone hookup, so Father Robert quickly drove into Hanna where a telephone was available at the Hanna Café, and he started his search by making calls to Cheyenne.

And so the saga continues.

When Bob arrived in Laramie, the Cheyenne-bound bus was just about to leave, but was full. Listening to Bob's tale of woe with the obvious evidence showing that Bob's face had made contact with the ground, the driver allowed Bob to sit on the jump seat, close to the driver. Before the bus left, Bob quickly bought a postcard, one on which the message could be streamlined by checking various boxes such as "How are you?" "Wish you were here," and "The weather is fine." He checked two of the boxes: "Flying high," and "Things are exciting," mailed it to Father Robert and Mother Anna, and boarded the bus. He was on the last leg of his journey to the rodeo.

Bob arrived in Cheyenne somewhat behind his original schedule and a little worse for the journey. Aunt Agnes was waiting at the front door, anxious for any news of his whereabouts, and was relieved when he appeared. Bob did attend the Frontier Days Rodeo. The journey home from Cheyenne was almost as quick as the mail carrying the postcard that he mailed days before from Laramie. His parents saved that postcard, and it is still in Bob's possession some eight decades later.

***

Bob's real approach to manhood started in 1938. In the summer of that year, Bob, along with friends Dean Ryder and Bryan Bailey, got a summer job weeding the garden at the UL Ranch in the Elk Mountain area, approximately sixty-five miles west of Laramie. The ranch was owned by his uncle and aunt.

The garden covered at least an acre and had long rows stretching toward the horizon. Unfortunately, Dean and Bryan found greater pleasure lying down between the rows, looking up at the blue Wyoming sky and talking of their futures as they watched the clouds roll by. Eventually Bob gave into temptation and joined them. It came as no surprise when they were fired.

This was an embarrassing situation, not only for Bob but for his family, and it was one of the few times that Father Robert expressed disappointment in his son. He gave the three boys quite a lecture, with particular emphasis on Bob's involvement.

During the summer of 1940, Bob worked in the hay fields, driving a two-horse team of gray mares—Biscuit and Raisin. He drove the hay rake, a boring task, because it involved riding in endless circles, sweeping up loose hay, and then tripping the rake to dump the hay in windrows that later would be collected and stacked. Horses were used to push the heavy sections of hay up a wooden frame to the top of the haystack.

There is no typical size for a haystack. The size depends upon the farmer's projected needs of hay for his animals. Building haystacks from the ground up was quite an art. It took engineering artistry, talent, and understanding to dump each load of hay so that the stack stood straight from all sides and did not bow outward, leading to collapse of the stack. If the stack leaned even a little, the Wyoming winds and winter weather would topple it and the loose hay would be scattered—and constructing medieval-style cathedral-type flying buttresses to support the sides of the haystack and prevent destruction of the stack was not an option! In addition, the stack was made waterproof as it was built and the hay would compress under its own weight and cure by the release of heat from the residual moisture inside and from the compression forces. The stack was fenced from the rest of the paddock and often thatched or sheeted to keep it dry. When slices of hay were needed, they would be cut using a hay knife and fed out to animals each day.

Safety issues were also involved, because hay baled or stacked before it is fully dry can produce enough heat to start a fire. Being dry is the key to preserving hay—a wet stack will rot from the inside, or ferment, generating heat and resulting in a fire. The production of such heat and the ensuing fire requires farmers to be careful about moisture levels to avoid the spontaneous combustion—the leading cause of haystack fires.

Haystacks are no longer a common sight on the landscape of the High Plains of Wyoming. Technology has made harvesting hay a one-man-and-a-tractor operation, in which the grass goes straight to the bale, skipping the stacking stage.

During that time, Bob lived in the ranch bunkhouse. This was the beginning of his other-world experiences. Most of the hired hands were older; many were even older than Father Robert. As might be surmised, the hired hands were a *little* rough around the edges, had extensive four-letter-word vocabularies, and they were generous in sharing stories—real or imagined—of their romps with the opposite sex. Bob found that living among them was more than a liberal arts education!

He was paid a dollar a day plus room and board. An additional perk was a sack of Bull Durham tobacco once a week—none of those tailor-made cigarettes for these fine fellows. In the bunkhouse they rolled their own cigarettes. This involved whipping out the sack of Bull Durham, holding a piece of cigarette paper just so, filling it with loose tobacco, rolling the paper over, sealing it with a quick lick of the tongue, then striking a wood match on the seat of their Levis and lighting up. There were no designer Levis in those days, and the coarse material was ideal for lighting a match. A boy was not classed as a man until he could roll a cigarette and light it one-handed in a Wyoming breeze. Even today to non-Wyomingites such a breeze would be classed as a high wind, with speeds on the order of fifteen to twenty-five miles per hour.

In the summer of 1939, Bob spent more time working at the UL Ranch. His job was that of sheepherder. His home for the summer was a sheep wagon of the type described earlier. Grandfather John and father Robert had decided that the outdoor life and the fresh prairie and mountain air would be good for Bob. It is not recorded if Mother Anna made any contribution to the decision. Nevertheless,

Bob became a student (albeit a summer student but still a student) of nature.

***

As Bob's high school days neared their end, he was looking ahead, and on May 16, 1940, he graduated from the Hanna High school, one in a class of fifteen, most of whom had been classmates since kindergarten in 1927.

With commencement, the classmates were splintered from a cohesive whole, and each one headed in a different direction. For Bob, Hanna was in his rearview mirror, as a new, exciting life in a big city loomed on his horizon. He had his sights set on the University of Wyoming (UW) in Laramie, a booming metropolis of some ten to twelve thousand people, including all the students, faculty, staff, townspeople, and assorted dogs and cats, and the occasional antelope that lost its way and wandered down the main street.

One of Bob's first actions at the University of Wyoming was to enroll in the ROTC (Reserve Officers' Training Corps).

The concept of ROTC in the United States began with the Morrill Act of 1862, which established land-grant colleges. The University of Wyoming was that state's land-grant college. Part of the federal government's requirement for these schools was that they include military tactics as part of their curriculum, forming what became known as ROTC. Enrollment in ROTC was compulsory for all male freshmen and continued until the 1960s. However, because of the protests that culminated in the opposition to involvement by the United States in the Vietnam War, compulsory ROTC was dropped in favor of voluntary programs. In some universities, ROTC was expelled from campus altogether, although it was always possible to participate in off-campus ROTC.

In a world far away there was war. Events in Europe were in turmoil. Although Bob didn't realize the seriousness of these events, they would eventually shape his life.

***

World War II is generally accepted to have begun on September 1, 1939, when the dogs of war were turned loose and Germany invaded Poland. On September 3, 1939, Germany had failed to respond to a diplomatic ultimatum by the governments of England and France to withdraw from Poland. On that same day, both governments declared that a state of war existed, with Germany on one side and England (and the Commonwealth countries) and France on the other.

Many historians consider that the preliminary moves to World War II started when Adolf Hitler became Chancellor of Germany in 1933. This was followed in 1935 by the legal reunification of the Territory of the Saar Basin with Germany followed by Hitler's repudiation of the Treaty of Versailles, acceleration of Germany's rearmament program, and the introduction of conscription. Further steps toward war were taken in March 1936 when Hitler defied the Versailles Treaty by remilitarizing the Rhineland. The so-called European powers did nothing but turn a blind eye or mutter a ho-hum to the event.

In March 1938, Germany annexed Austria, again with little or no response from other European powers. As a result, Hitler laid claim to the Sudetenland, an area of Czechoslovakia with a predominantly ethnic German population. Without much debate or protest, England and France conceded this territory to Germany against the wishes of the Czechoslovakian government, but Germany promised to make no further territorial demands. In March 1939, Germany invaded the non-Sudetenland part of Czechoslovakia and subsequently split it into the German protectorate of Bohemia and Moravia and the pro-German state of the Slovak Republic.

It was only when Hitler made further demands on Danzig (Gdansk) that England and France seemed to become aware of what was going on and decided to guarantee their support for Polish independence. But Hitler had not been inactive. In August 1939, Germany and the Soviet Union signed the Molotov-Ribbentrop Pact—a non-aggression treaty with a secret protocol in which the two parties (Germany and Russia) gave each other rights in the event of a territorial and political rearrangement to spheres of influence (Western Poland and Lithuania for Germany, and Eastern Poland, Finland, Estonia, Latvia, and Bessarabia for Russia).

Polish independence and the independence of aforementioned small Republics were doomed.

***

At the time of Bob's graduation on May 16, 1940, Germany had invaded France Belgium, Netherlands, and Luxembourg by May 10. In June, during the last days of the Battle of France, Germany was making plans for the invasion of England but decided instead to enter into what became known as the Battle of Britain—an air battle that ran from mid-July until late September of 1940.

It was in the late summer of 1940, when the skies above England were filled with German bombers and the RAF Spitfires and Hurricanes, that Bob left Hanna and set off for university, specifically, the University of Wyoming. At that time the student population was approximately nine hundred young men and women, a far cry from the modern enrollment of approximately 11,000 students at the Laramie Campus. Currently the University of Wyoming consists of seven colleges: Agriculture, Arts and Sciences, Business, Education, Engineering, Health Sciences, and Law. The university offers a variety of bachelor's, master's, and doctoral degrees. The present campus covers several square miles, with dozens of buildings, hundreds of faculty members, thousands of students, and an annual budget that exceeds $200 million.

But it was not always like this, and in the summer of 1940 when Bob arrived bearing the signs of a fresh-faced student, the university was still young. His goal was to study for a degree in civil engineering, and he dutifully registered for the required courses.

***

The University of Wyoming is situated on Wyoming's High Plains, at an elevation of 7,160 feet, between the Laramie Mountains to the east and the Snowy Range Mountains to the west. It is known as UW (often pronounced "U-Dub") to people close to the university.

The University of Wyoming was established as a land grant university in 1886, when Wyoming was still a Territory.

Land-grant universities (also called *land-grant colleges* or *land-grant institutions*) are institutions of higher education in the United States designated by each state to receive the benefits of the Morrill Acts of 1862 and 1890, which funded educational institutions by granting federally controlled land to the states to develop or sell to raise funds to establish and endow *land grant colleges*. The mission of these institutions as set forth in the 1862 act is to focus on the teaching of agriculture, science, and engineering as a response to the industrial revolution and changing social class rather than the typical core of classical studies seen at then-current institutes of higher education.

The new campus of the fledgling University of Wyoming was located on ten acres of land that had served as Laramie's City Park, deeded to the town by the Union Pacific Railroad when Laramie City was first laid out. The park was then the terminus of Center Street (later renamed University Avenue), which was designed to be the town's main avenue. The first university building, now called Old Main, was erected in the center of the former park. There were five faculty members and forty-two students. The initial budget, which included construction costs, was $50,000, paid for by raising bonds.

The university was officially begun on September 27, 1886, when the cornerstone of Old Main was laid. The stone is inscribed *Domi Habuit Unde Disceret*, often translated as "He need not go away from home for instruction." The following year, the first class of forty-two men and women began their college education. For the next decade, the Old Main building housed classrooms, a library, and administration offices. This building *was* the University of Wyoming when it opened in 1897.

In the early years, every function was housed in Old Main, then known as the Main Building. When Dr. Grace Raymond Hebard accepted the job as university librarian, she presided over a collection of some 3,000 volumes stacked in the library on the second floor. The *assembly room* held not only morning assemblies for the entire university, but also served as a primary lecture hall for visiting dignitaries. Even though the room was large enough to accommodate the entire student body and faculty well into the early 1900s, it was not large enough to hold the huge crowd that came to hear President Theodore Roosevelt on his visit to Laramie in 1903. Instead, he spoke from the front (west) porch prior to mounting a horse and riding fifty miles over the summit to Cheyenne. Major renovations of the structure were made in 1949 and again in the middle 1970s.

The summer of 1939, Bob worked in the hayfields of the UL Ranch, owned by Uncle Hank and Aunt Dorothy Cheeseborough (Dorothy was Father Robert's sister) to try to save enough money to go to the university.

It was into this idyllic academic setting of the University of Wyoming that Bob arrived in the late summer of 1940 to further his education through courses and passing the exams that would allow him to become a qualified engineer.

Father Robert and Mother Anna had started a college fund for Bob in 1925, but the Great Depression wiped that out, and there was no spare cash to finance his higher education. Uncle Hank Cheeseborough and Aunt Dorothy, owners the UL Ranch, gave Bob $100 that they had saved—a princely sum in those days—and the rest was up to Bob. He still needed a job to supplement the money that he had when he arrived in Laramie.

The fees at the University of Wyoming, although cheap by modern standards, were a considerable sum of money by the standards of 1940, sufficient to eat up the $100 gift that he had been given by his uncle and aunt.

***

All fees and laboratory deposits had to be paid to the cashier each quarter as a part of the student's registration. Students were not allowed to enter classes until their respective fees had been paid. Parents or guardians wishing to remit directly to the university in payment of fees for room and board had to give written authority to the cashier at least ten days prior to the first registration day for which this arrangement was desired.

The assessment of university fees all students, including graduates, considered whether they were registrants or part-time registrants, defined as follows: A full-time registrant was any student enrolled for eight and a half credit hours or more, regardless of the outside employment status of that student, and a part-time registrant was any student enrolled for less than eight and a half credit hours and holding in addition, full-time employment of not less than forty work hours per week. Part-time registrants were not required to take military or physical education, but these two requirements had to be satisfied by candidates for graduation.

Although the actual fee data for 1940 are no longer available and have been lost in the archives of time, studies of total cost estimates have been made from surveys for a number of years up to and including 1941–42, and it is these studies that give an indication of the fees Bob paid for the 1940–1941 academic year:

Fees to the University:	$100
Books and supplies:	$75
Room and board:	$375
Fraternities and clubs (fees):	$45
Laundry and cleaning:	$30
Miscellaneous expense:	$100
Total:	$740

Meals were available at the university cafeteria and the Wyoming Union at about $1.20 per day, approximately $35.00 per month. The residence halls and cafeteria were operated on a non-profit basis, and costs were "kept at the lowest level consistent with maintenance of proper standards of living." Since the costs were based on existing economic conditions and price levels, the university did reserve "the right to adjust prices charged for room and board at any time, should changing conditions warrant such action."

The university also pointed out to students that voluntary Christian influences make one of the helpful factors in maintaining a high moral standard in the university. The different churches of the city gladly encouraged students to attend their meetings, including Sunday church services of the denomination to which they belonged. At the time, the churches in Laramie were Episcopal, Roman Catholic, Methodist-Presbyterian, Baptist, St. Paul's Evangelical Lutheran, First Covenant, Trinity Evangelical Lutheran, Latter Day Saints, Christian, Christian Science, Zion Evangelical Lutheran, Church of the Nazarene, and Pentecostal.

Organizations sponsored by church denominations also existed to foster the interests of students of their respective faiths. They are listed with the other student organizations in this catalogue. To further the religious interests of the students, university faculty committees included one on religious education. This committee represented the University in accrediting relationships with church groups affiliated under the Laramie School of Religion.

Finally, the university had a Health Service, which was established in 1928 and had remained under the direction of a nurse until early in 1939, when the service was expanded and placed under the supervision of a physician. The services were provided for all students who had paid the regular fees, and because of the rapid growth of the department and increased demands from the student body, a second physician was employed in June 1940, shortly before Bob arrived on the campus. This Health Service was later expanded for the 1941–42 academic year to consist of two physicians, a registered nurse, and a secretary.

***

Bob knew he had to find work, so he applied for work at the Connor Hotel. To his surprise, he was hired as the night janitor. The job was seven days per week, and the hours were amenable to his schedule as a student.

Although he was hired as the night janitor, he also filled in at times in other jobs. His work started as soon as the kitchen closed. As a night janitor he could work any time after the dining room and restaurant were closed and before the kitchen opened in the morning.

The work was not helpful to his wardrobe. At that time, he had a sport coat, a sport shirt, and some good slacks, but he did not have a suit or tie. In addition, he had a pair of high-top shoes, an old pair of ski boots, a pair of black shoes, and a pair of moccasin type shoes that were a little too small for him, causing the development of corns. He finally had to wear his black dress shoes for work, and it didn't take long for them to deteriorate. The barber, Mr. Jackson, made an acceptable contribution in the form of a suit—an excellent gift. There was also the problem of sleep time, which he managed to fit into his twenty-four-hour-per-day schedule. Also, he was on duty seven days a week and started work as soon as the hotel kitchen closed for the night, remaining at the hotel until all that needed doing had been done.

Bob's job at the hotel paid him barely enough for survival. Had it not been for the free meals, money would have been scarce, but he did manage to earn extra money by taking on the additional task of dishwasher at the hotel. Spending money was a thing of dreams. He could barely afford the bare necessities; social events were out of his vision. But he did manage to find free time to fill in at other jobs in the hotel dining room and the kitchen as needs dictated.

Bob lived with a friend, Bob Cooper, in a basement apartment at what is now 1310 Custer Street. It was owned by Mom and Pop Squires, who also had a grocery store. Bob's mother and father helped him with the rent, and he was only a short walk from the Connor Hotel where work and meals awaited him.

Mr. Hanson, the manager who, in the manner of hotel managers, was always well dressed in his dark business suit, clean shirt, and tie, was quite a taskmaster, but he was always ready to hire college students (for which Bob was grateful) and would come and inspect the work frequently. He would also test Bob by placing a dining utensil—a spoon fork, or knife—in an out-of-the-way place. Then he would check to see if it was still there after Bob had cleaned the area. So it didn't take long for Bob to learn that his cleaning efforts had to be thorough.

When he finished in the kitchen, Bob would go down to the basement, which was at the other end of the hotel, where it was his to job to mop the male and female toilets. In between these times, Bob would have sack of potatoes or onions or both to peel. Once Bob had to peel a sack of onions, but didn't have time to change his clothes before his eight o'clock morning class. He became the source of a powerful odor, to the great discomfort of many of his classmates.

There were times when he found it difficult to get to an early class after working at night, and he found it hard to stay awake. A few minutes of sleep could be a benefit or a bust—he would wake up feeling refreshed or groggy depending upon the night work he had done. However, he did find that an eight o'clock morning class often helped him to be ready for the day. If he had later classes, it took him longer to get started. In addition, he had to spend a great deal of time at the library, so the walking back and forth to his room on Custer Street to the university contributed to his general feeling of tiredness.

There was one occasion when the chef Bob reported to in the kitchen gave him the job of cleaning the ubiquitous grease off the window wells where the exhaust fan was located. Bob worked all morning for the promise of a dollar additional pay. The grease was so thick that it took no effort to leave a highly observable hand-print in it! So he spent his Labor Day working, and it took hours to clean the window wells. In the meantime, the chef left the job and didn't pay Bob the promised dollar. But not being a person to give up, Bob had quite a time following Mr. Hanson the hotel manager around, whom he reminded repeatedly that the hotel owed him a dollar. Persistence does tend to pay off. Mr. Hanson finally took out a silver dollar from his pocket and Bob was paid in full!

There were days when he had not eaten for some time and he would arrive at work after the kitchen was closed. There were two things Bob could get. There was always a loaf of bread available and the inevitable large jar of peanut butter. In the cooler there would be a large can full of milk that was used for cooking. Bob would often hide a little bottle of milk to drink after he had eaten the peanut butter sandwiches. It is not surprising that Bob ate a lot of peanut butter, which he believed gave him the energy to carry on with his studies and work.

Another establishment that Bob would visit was the Antelope Café where for twenty-five cents he could get a hamburger and a glass of milk. On one occasion, when he only had fifteen cents, Bob went into the Antelope Café that was located in the downtown area close by the Connor Hotel, and asked if he could get a hamburger and a half a glass of milk for fifteen cents—the owner obliged and Bob still remembers how good that hamburger tasted.

With the arrival of summer 1941, Bob sought employment to earn money to keep him at the university. He and two friends, Dean

Ryder and Bryant Bailey, got jobs working in the coal mine at Hanna. This would mean real money on a regular basis over the summer. Father Robert had arranged for the jobs through a request to the mine superintendent. It was an embarrassing situation for Father Robert, not wishing to be beholden to anyone, but the jobs did mean a lot to Bob and his two comrades.

The work involved outside labor, for which they had to wear hard-toed shoes and a hard hat, and they had to attend safety classes. They worked seven hours each day. The mining company paid each of the young men on a portal-to-portal basis which meant that their work time (for five dollars per day) did not start until they entered the mine opening (the portal) and finished when they left the mine.

A similar payment scheme was used in mines in northeast England, where the miners were paid from the time they reached the coal face until they left the face, even though it might take up to an hour to reach the coal face. A local mine being three miles from the coast meant that the miners had to travel almost five miles to reach the coal face that was one or two miles from the coast under the North Sea to begin work and another hour or more to travel from the face to the mine surface. Eventually, the Mineworker's Union was able to negotiate that the miners would be paid from the time they clocked in and entered the cage to descend into the mine.

Bob and his friends started by working on the tipple and picking the slate out of the coal.

This was the same many years later in the mines in northeast England, when young boys fresh out of school at fifteen (the official school leaving age, and they weren't labeled or looked down upon as dropouts) would start working as belt boys. Their sole function, other than to instigate playful but dangerous pranks, was to remove slate from the coal as it was transported along the conveyer belts from the coal face to the mine cage shipping point, from where the coal would be taken to the surface. Many of the belt boys ended up with a part or the whole of a finger damaged, which required surgical removal.

Bob and his two friends were then assigned to pick and shovel work. One of their jobs was to pick up the overflow from the mine cars that had been loaded. They used long-handled spades and would throw the material over the wall of the gondola—an open railroad car with a tipping trough used in mines, also known as a *tippler* or *chaldron wagon* or *mine car.* So they were throwing the coal upward for nine or ten feet over the walls of the gondola.

At that time, a new mine was being built next to the present Hanna mine to enable greater access to the coal and higher production figures for the whole mine. New buildings were being erected, and it was all handwork with picks and shovels. One job was to excavate a basement by hauling the material out by wheelbarrows. Then, when it was time to build the foundation, Bob and his friends would haul the cement into the basement using wheelbarrows. Fortunately, the wheelbarrows were small.

Another job involved unloading lumber, sacks of mine powder, and sacks of dynamite from boxcars. Then they would load the dynamite into boxes and take them up to the dugout and unload the boxes there. One day Dean Ryder was ahead of him and he dropped a box of dynamite; Bob was lucky. Those were the days when dynamite was a tricky material to handle. Fortunately, the nitroglycerin had matured and did not explode. Had the nitroglycerin wept and formed small drops of liquid on the package, it would have been different. The episode did make Bob think about his good fortune for a while.

***

After working for the summer, Bob made preparations to return to the University of Wyoming for the fall semester. All was well, and he approached the new academic year with confidence. He was to continue his work toward an engineering degree when death again entered his life. It was Bob Cooper, his roommate at the house on Custer Street in Laramie and the aforementioned owner of the coupé, who had succumbed to the Grim Reaper. It was while he was still in Hanna that Bob heard that Bob Cooper had drowned in East Allen Lake, about twenty miles east of Hanna and to the south of Medicine Bow. Bob Cooper and an unnamed fraternity brother and another unnamed young man from Medicine Bow had gone out onto the lake—ostensibly to fish—and for reasons unknown, the boat had overturned and all three were drowned.

Bob can still recall the experience vividly. He was walking along a street in Hanna toward the school late in the afternoon when a friend, Bernard Lucas, told him about the accident. Bob and Bernard, after seeking permission, took Father Robert's pickup and drove to Medicine Bow, at which time the doctor from Hanna was working on Bob Cooper. He was spread-eagled on his stomach, and the doctor from Medicine Bow (whose name is lost in the decades since that day) was injecting a needle into his back, but there was no hope for Bob Cooper. He had been in the water too long and life had left him before Bob and Bernard arrived at the scene.

***

On his return to Laramie in the late summer of 1941 to resume his studies at the university, Bob looked for a place to live. Being a member of the St. Mark's Episcopal Church in Hanna, he was fortunate to find a place at the Sherwood Hall for Boys, the building directly east of St Matthew's Cathedral and currently named Hunter Hall. Bob was in awe when he entered the building as he took in the sparkling clean shine of the place. At that time they had a basketball court and a formally-run boys' school. In later years, Sherwood Hall became a school for girls and took the name Ivinson Hall.

Bob obtained a job as a monitor, which gave him a free room on the uppermost (third) floor of Sherwood Hall. He had a little money saved, having worked for the coal mine during the summer, but he still needed to work to eat. Fortunately, he was able to return to his job at the Connor Hotel, working for his meals, which was convenient, as he could walk the one-block distance from his room at Sherwood Hall to the hotel. Thus Bob returned to the daily grind of work and classes related to his engineering studies.

When Bob lived at Sherwood Hall, there was a young man who also lived there and whose modus operandi was to visit the shops on First Street and trade an heirloom, such as a watch, for some whiskey. Thereafter, he would return and threaten to turn in the whiskey traders if he didn't get his watch back.

Bob kept a constant eye on him. It was never clear where the tradable heirlooms came from or who had been the original owner. But the young man's life of crime did not cease. He was finally expelled from the home because of his habit of harassing young women, and he was never heard of again. In more general terms, the behavior of the boys at the school varied from the occasional minor incident to being very well behaved.

The position of monitor at Hunter Hall and the job at the Connor Hotel was a fortunate situation for Bob. All seemed to be well with Bob's world, but the world in Europe was in turmoil.

War was spreading across Europe, but America's days of peace were running out when Bob returned to the UW campus the late summer of 1941 to register for his classes at the University of Wyoming. But dealing with the war, being isolated from it by several thousand miles, was not Bob's highest priority. His university education and his job to support his quest for a degree were his top priorities.

Throughout this time, America struggled to maintain neutrality, but the peace was fragile, and even the isolationists who advocated non-involvement in the European war eventually conceded that it was only a matter of time until Americans would be fighting and dying overseas. At the time of Bob's registration for the 1941–42 academic year, the attack on Pearl Harbor by the imperial forces of Japan was not even on the horizon. To most Americans, Pearl Harbor was an unknown place—a lagoon harbor on the Island of Oahu, situated to the west of Honolulu. But within weeks, the name Pearl Harbor was to be a rallying point—akin to the Alamo—in the quest for the United States to seek retribution for the unannounced Sunday-morning attack on some of the ships of the Pacific Fleet that lay at anchor there.

CHAPTER 4: PRELUDE TO WAR

The diplomatic rhetoric that occurred in the weeks before the attack on Pearl Harbor made many people, including Bob and many of his friends, aware that the clouds of battle were now on the horizon. The focus was on Europe, and the possibility of the entry of Japan into the war was not given much attention.

France had fallen to the armies of the Third Reich, and the Royal Air Force had managed to stymie the Luftwaffe in September of 1940, but London and other English cities were being bombed on a nightly basis. In addition, using the code name Operation Barbarossa, Germany had invaded Russia on June 22, 1941, and German armies were sweeping farther and farther into the Russian heartland.

America's peace was fragile, to say the least. To the realists, it seemed inevitable that the United States would soon be in the fight against the Axis powers. To the pacifists, America should or would not enter the conflict. Being a realist, Bob enrolled in the University of Wyoming Civilian Pilot Training Program. When war came, he wanted to be ready to fight for his country—in the air.

At first, the program was not looked upon with any favor by the US military. However, the possibility of war in Europe revitalized the program, leading to an expansion of its curriculum to a larger segment of the US colleges and universities. In May of 1939, the first nine schools were selected. Nine more were added in August 1940, eleven more in March 1941, and fifteen more by October 1941, before the US entered World War II. By the program's peak, 1,132 educational institutions and 1,460 flight schools were participating in the Civilian Pilot Training Program (CPTP).

The program taught young men to fly for military purposes, and there was no charge. Bob immediately took advantage of it and started to learn to fly at Brees Field (currently Laramie Airport) flying a Luscombe—a high-wing light aircraft that could cruise at ten to twenty miles per hour faster than many other aircraft on the same power.

Prior to 1940, the United States Army had approximately 4,500 pilots, including just over 2,000 who were active-duty officers, just over 2,100 reserve officers, and a little over 300 who were national guard officers. As war seemed more likely, the number of needed pilots had grown rapidly from 982 in 1939, to approximately 8,000 in 1940, to over 27,000 in 1941. Even with these record numbers, more pilots were still needed. At the time, the United States Army could not sufficiently handle the training of the large number of flying cadets required. The US Army Air Forces relied on additional pilots from the CPTP and a large network of civilian flight schools under contract to the US Air Corps. They also conducted training in their own schools.

At that time, young men of many nations perceived themselves and their role in war as knights of the air. Partaking up-close-and-personal in the horrors of hand-to-hand combat with a rifle and bayonet was not to their liking. In fact, most young men conscripted for war service wanted to fly, but few achieved their aspirations. If they were accepted for flying duties, their emotions were stimulated at their status. A fighter pilot would be shooting at another fighter plane. The young men of the Lindbergh generation exulted in the notion of flying fast in nimble single-engine, single-seat aircraft that granted a pilot a power over his own destiny. Yet many of the young would-be-knights-of-the-air found themselves instead assigned to bomber crews that were committed to the aerial bombardment of enemy targets and not the cut-and-thrust of a fighter pilot.

Whatever the outcome for the young enlisted man, the watchwords were training, more training, and—if anything else was needed—even more training. Even if the bomber pilot was denied the thrill of throwing a high-performance fighter across the sky, it still took skill and courage to get beyond the seemingly monotonous task of flying for eight or ten hours, either in daylight formation amid flak and fighters or through lonely darkness.

Because of the high level of training provided by the CPTP, program-trained pilots did well while receiving additional training at US Air Corps flight schools. Between 1939 and 1945, the CPTP would train more than 435,000 pilots, logging over twelve million flight hours! Following the attack on Pearl Harbor, the CPTP became known as the War Training Service (WTS). From 1942 until the summer of 1944, WTS trainees attended college courses and took private flight training, signing agreements to enter into military service after their graduation.

Graduates of the CPTP and WTS programs entered into the US Army Air Corps Enlisted Reserve. Most graduates continued their flight training and commissioned as combat pilots. Others became service pilots, liaison pilots, ferry pilots, glider pilots, instructors, or commercial pilots in the Air Transport Command. When the defeat of the Axis powers seemed imminent, and as it became clear that fewer pilots would be required in the future, the US military services ended their agreement with the CPTP and WTS in early 1944. The program was concluded in 1946 after having provided a much-needed service to the US Air Corps, both before and during World War II. The CPTP and WTS provided the US Air Corps with civilian pilots who could easily transition to military pilot training, thus speeding up the process of getting qualified military pilots into aircraft of all kinds and off to the front.

Thus, the decision to train civilian pilots also produced an unexpected but welcome side effect on the general aviation industry. The United States faced just as large a shortage of training aircraft as it did civilian pilots. The Federal Civil Aeronautics Authority (now the Federal Aviation Administration) regulations required a flight school that was participating in the CPTP to own one aircraft for every ten students enrolled in the program. Furthermore, the requirements specified for these aircraft narrowed down the field to only several models in production at that time, with most flight schools preferring the tandem seat configuration of the Piper Cub. As a result, several light aircraft manufacturers quickly entered the market with aircraft compatible with the Civilian Pilot Training Program.

With the flying lessons, his work, and university classes, Bob was settling into the routine of living in Laramie once more when the unthinkable (yet by some observers it was expected) happened.

And then, the realists who had anticipated America's entry into the war proved to be correct.

On December 7, 1941, Japan, which already had been at war with China since 1937, attacked the United States at Pearl Harbor as part of a plan to establish dominance over East Asia and Southeast Asia. Japan also attacked European possessions bordering on the Pacific Ocean, quickly conquering a significant part of the region.

At the time of the attack on Pearl Harbor, Bob was having breakfast in the kitchen of the Connor Hotel. He recalls looking around the table and wondering out loud about the location of this far-away place that did not mean much to him. He didn't even know where it was. Meanwhile, throughout the country, newspapers were preparing headlines to announce that the country was at war with Japan. The *Honolulu Advertiser* was one of the first newspapers to recognize that the country was at war—the headlines of the first extra edition of the *Advertiser* published on afternoon of Sunday, December 7, screamed "WAR!" in three-inch black letters. After the Japanese attack on Pearl Harbor, the United States could not ignore Japan's intent to take over the Pacific. The US Congress officially declared war against Japan on December 8, 1941.

With twenty-twenty hindsight, perhaps the attack on Pearl Harbor was foreseeable. Japan had been an ally of the United States and Britain in World War I. The Japanese military arm had captured a German base in Tsingtao, China, and after the war, they had prospered through expanding trade, becoming a recognized political and economic force in eastern Asia. But their triumph had been followed by the great earthquake of 1923, which destroyed approximately 50 percent of Tokyo. This was followed by economic disasters in the form of an overabundance of rice, which drove prices down, and tariffs imposed on Japanese manufactured exports by Western nations. Exacerbating this was the ever-increasing population, which threw a heavy burden on the economic policies of the country. By 1937 Japan, an island nation with fixed boundaries, held more than eighty million people in its limited space. The country needed to escape from the beleaguered state that was hampering progress while its resources were being depleted at a rate that dictated the need for expansion.

As part of the plan for expansion, which included gaining more natural resources, a market for their manufactured goods, and cheap labor, Japan invaded China. After a three-month battle, the Japanese took Shanghai in November 1937. With the capital Nanking then threatened, Chiang Kai-shek, leader of the Republic of China, hastily relocated to Wuhan. Nanking was taken in December 1937.

The United States government—surprised and shocked by the rapidity and violence of the Japanese attack—refused to export items to Japan that could be used in waging war, such as scrap metal. In the summer of 1941, all Japanese assets in the United States were nationalized (seized) by the US government. The enraged Japanese government signed a pact with Germany and Italy in September 1941. Japan, now aligned with the Axis powers against the United States, planned attacks—on Pearl Harbor, Guadalcanal, Midway, and the Philippines.

On hearing of the attack on Pearl Harbor, Bob's initial reaction was to volunteer for military service—which he did. And because of his love for flying, Bob set his sights on becoming a marine fighter pilot. The recruiting officer had told him that he should join the navy, then transition to the marine corps. Dutifully, Bob took all of the written tests and then reported for a physical exam in the old Half Acre Gymnasium at UW. The examination involved stripping naked and walking down a line of doctors who probed, measured, and tested each young man along the way. The last doctor in the line indicated to Bob that he should stand to one side. The doctor had spotted a large scar on Bob's abdomen.

Recall that in 1931 Bob developed a serious case of appendicitis, and his life was saved thanks to the ministrations of Dr. McDermott, the Union Pacific Railroad doctor. Part of the "payment," in addition to the cow and turkeys paid to Dr. McDermott for this near-miracle, was the large and plainly noticeable scar that remained on Bob's abdomen. The inner membranes of his lower abdomen had not been sewn correctly. And now the chickens—in this case the scar—came home to roost!

The scar had remained—a scar of that magnitude does not go away—and was, of course noticeable to the military medic who examined the area around the old incision and made the diagnosis, then gave Bob the bad news.

"I'm sorry," the doctor stated, "but you would never be able to stand dive-bombing. I rode in a dive-bomber recently. It exerted a tremendous amount of pressure which would tear your insides out because of the lack of structure of your abdomen. wall. I cannot pass you."

Not to be deterred, Bob left the gym to start the process all over again. This time he set his sights on the US Army Air Corps, which had been created by the US Army in 1907. It was renamed from the Air Service on July 2, 1926. The Air Service was part of the United States Army and the predecessor of the United States Army Air Forces (USAAF), established in 1941. On September 18, 1947, the United States Army Air Corps (USAAC) was folded into the United States Air Force, which became a separate military service on September 18, 1947, with the implementation of the National Security Act of 1947. This act created the National Military Establishment, which was later renamed the United States Department of Defense, which was composed of three branches: (1) the army, (2) the navy, and (3) the newly created air force. Prior to 1947, the responsibility for military aviation was divided between the army (for land-based operations) and the navy, for sea-based operations from an aircraft carrier and amphibious aircraft.

Learning by experience and now familiar to the routine of the medical examination, Bob managed to keep his arm over the scar when he walked by the doctors. As a result, he completed all of the tests and passed the physical with (no pun intended) *flying* colors. In June 1942, Bob took the Oath of Allegiance at Fort Warren, the army facility in Cheyenne, and was officially sworn in and enlisted as an *aviation cadet* in the United States Army Air Corps, after which he was sent home and told to await the call to active duty.

In spite of the warning by the military doctor, Bob flew twenty nine dive-bombing missions during his career without suffering any ill effects from the lifesaving appendectomy operation and the resulting scar.

***

In spite of protestations to the contrary and the expectation of eventually being drawn into the European theater of war, as America mobilized for global conflict, it became obvious that the United States did not have the existing military infrastructure to handle the number of men and women answering the call to arms. New facilities such as airfields had to be constructed almost overnight. New and expanded training programs for pilots had to be implemented. America now prepared for war.

Having completed the semester and wondering what to do with his time until the call to active duty came, Bob looked for a job. As it happened, Bob Lawson, one of Bob's roommates, was working for the Union Pacific Railroad (UPRR), and he alerted Bob to a job opportunity. Accordingly, Bob went to Cheyenne, applied for the position, and by July 1942 was working on a UPRR survey crew. Bob Lawson was a file clerk, and Bob Milliken was the chain man on the survey crew.

As the *chain man*, it was Bob's duty to assist in any way that was necessary, specifically:

1. to hold level the rod or distance meter reflector at designated points to assist in determining elevation and laying out stakes for mapmaking, construction, land and other surveys;

2. to call out readings or write the station number and reading in notebook;

3. to mark the points of measurement with elevation, station, or some other identifying mark;

4. to measure the distance between survey points using surveyors' tapes or electronic distance-measuring equipment, marking measuring points with keel (marking crayon), paint, sticks, scratches, tacks, stakes, or monuments;

5. to place stakes at designated points and drive them into the ground, sometimes at a specific elevation, using sledgehammers;

6. to cut and clear brush and trees from a line of survey using brush hook, knife, ax, or other cutting tools;

7. to obtain data pertaining to angles, elevations, control points, and contours used for construction, mapmaking, or other purposes;

8. to compile notes, sketches, and records of data obtained and work performed;

9. to direct the work of any subordinate members of the survey crew, of which there were none, as Bob was low man in the pecking order;

10. to perform other duties relating to survey work as directed by the crew chief.

A specific and important responsibility was to double-check the elevations and distances through several large snow tunnels in the Rock River and Medicine Bow area to ensure that trains and the cargos they were carrying didn't hang up going through. Bob was going to be busy as it soon became obvious to him that he was the survey crew.

The Cheyenne office was little more than a small room situated on the third floor of the Cheyenne UPRR depot, where quarters were shared with a district engineer who was prone to cigar-chewing but—to Bob's recollection—never smoked cigars. He merely chewed cigars in a manner that indicated he was trying for reasons unknown to get revenge on the cigars. He spat out the juice onto the wooden floor which, over a period of time, gave a unique coloring to the wooden floor and created a distinct aroma in the room.

In a way, Bob was accustomed to surveying, having helped Father Robert survey parts of the Ranch, but with much cruder equipment than was provided to the crew by the railroad. The equipment that he and Father Robert used consisted of a two-by-four crossbar with two two-by-four legs attached. One leg was shorter than the other. This gave Father Robert the grade for water flow. It was simple, economical, and effective.

While he worked in Cheyenne, Bob lived with Aunt Agnes (Father Robert's sister) and Uncle Harry Challendar. The house was in the 1100 block of East Twenty-First Street. Later, he lived with another aunt and uncle a couple of blocks away. From both houses, it was only a short walk to the depot, and when he was not working in the depot, he was out in the field.

The district he worked in spanned from Laramie to Ogden, Utah. Depending upon where they were surveying, Bob would start out by train or get a ride in a company (UPRR) station wagon to the place of his work. On occasion, as the work demanded, the crew would stay overnight in a Laramie, Rock River, Medicine Bow, Rawlins, Evanston, Rock Springs, or Ogden hotel, all of which were paid for by the railroad and were located near the UPRR main line. As the need arose, the crew members were often called upon to camp in the open. Through these activities, Bob gained firsthand knowledge of the Wyoming countryside outside of Hanna and Cheyenne and learned to appreciate the beauties of his home state.

The job was not without its disadvantages. Not paying attention to the heavy flow of rail traffic was a risk. It was also a shock to lose focus and then hear and see a steam locomotive coming head-on at the crew. The men always scrambled out of the way in time, but sometimes the survey chain didn't make it, and the crew chief was not amused by the number of times that the survey chain had to be spliced back into one single length of chain.

The ballast for the rail beds was available from various centers. In particular, there were large quarries west of Cheyenne, owned by the Union Pacific Railroad, where the ballast was excavated, loaded onto gondolas (open railroad cars with a tipping trough) and transported to wherever it was needed. By design, the rail lines ran in a downward grade to the ballast pit, which allowed the loaded cars to be released to roll down and link up with others in the train. This was always of interest to Bob!

To survey across the lines while loading was going on in order to complete the measurement, Bob had to lie on his stomach with his left side against an uphill wheel of a rail car with the end of the one hundred-foot tape beneath the rail car. His ears were always alert for the words: "Get out now!"

Upon hearing these magical words, he would he roll out from under the rail car just as a descending gondola hit the car and drove it over the spot where he had been lying just seconds before.

As Bob observed on several occasions, "Timing was everything, and the dice continued to roll my way."

And then there was the head of the engineers and the survey crew, Carl Marshall, who was renowned for his quick hot temper. Fortunately, it didn't take Carl very long to recover from his temper tantrums, and the crew members were not at all perturbed by Carl's lapses into verbal fury.

On one occasion, Carl lost his temper with Bob, who did not help matters when, having learned to stand up for himself, he mouthed off back at him. There were some tense moments, but Carl didn't fire Bob. He merely humphed or growled beneath his breath several times, glared at Bob, and then let the occasion pass.

Thus Bob was still working for the Union Pacific Railroad when the cold weather that was typical of the Wyoming High Plains arrived in November. He didn't have a hat, and the cold, brisk Wyoming wind whistled through his ears. He finally bought a pair of earmuffs that allowed him to work outdoors as long as possible.

Bob's UPRR experience was cut short when he was ordered to report in Denver on January 1, 1943. He was finally going on active duty. He left his work at the UPRR and went back to Hanna to prepare himself to leave Hanna for his military service.

His parents, especially his mother, were apprehensive, but Bob was anxious to go. On one occasion, they were listening to Bob Hope on the radio, and Bob Milliken happened to make the comment that before long he would be in one of Bob Hope's military audiences. The pained expression on his mother's face said it all. Her little boy—sons and daughters, no matter how old they are, remain little boys and little girls to their mothers—was going off to war.

***

Bob traveled by rail to Denver, alighted at the Union Station, and went straight to the Oxford Hotel—built at the height of the silver bonanza in 1891 and which survived the silver panic of 1893—that was and still is only short walking distance, almost just across the road from the railroad station. Early the next morning, he met other young men who were also reporting for active duty, and they walked as a group from the hotel back to the station and boarded a crowded train. It took no time for a joyous mood to prevail and the about-to-be military members started singing "California Here We Come." Because of the crowding, Bob had to share an upper berth with another recruit—it was what might be called *very close quarters*, but he survived. Traveling to California was a new experience for Bob—in his life he had never been further than Rock Springs or Cheyenne, and his world suddenly expanded.

As the train sped westward, Bob marveled at the changing scenery and was surprised to see palm trees as the train drew near the Union Station in Los Angeles. Once he disembarked, Bob left most of the other recruits, because he had to continue his journey to the Santa Ana preflight training base that lay southeast of Los Angeles. As soon as he arrived, he was confined to the base, quarantined, and introduced to the pleasures and rigors of army life.

***

With the expansion of the Air Corps, it became increasingly evident to the government and the existing army powers that be that there was an urgent need for closer cooperation between the two nearly independent elements: (1) the Air Corps, which was responsible for materiel and training functions, and (2) the Air Force Combat Command, which had formerly been the GHQ Air Force (General Headquarters Air Force) and which was responsible for operational functions and activities. As a result, the Army Air Forces (AAF) was created on June 20, 1941, to provide a unity of command over the Air Corps and Air Force Combat Command. Major General Henry Harley Arnold, also known more popularly as "Hap" Arnold, was designated Chief of Staff for Air and Chief of the Army Air Forces.

By December 1941, the AAF had grown to 354,000 men (of whom 9,000 were pilots) as compared to 26,000 men (of whom 2,000 were pilots) in September 1939. However, it had only 2,846 airplanes, of which only 1,157 were considered suitable for combat. The situation of April 1917 was being repeated—American flyers were soon to be called upon to combat enemy flyers who had superior weapons, in quantity, quality, or both.

On January 1, 1942, the United States Army Air Corps activated the Santa Ana Army Air Base and established the West Coast Air Corps Training Center there – flying training (basic, primary, and advanced) was conducted at airfields in the Western United States. On July 31, 1943, the camp was designated as the Western Flying Training Command.

A preflight Air Force Pilot School was also activated that taught aviation cadets the mechanics and physics of flight and required the cadets to pass courses in mathematics and the hard sciences. Then the cadets were taught to apply their knowledge practically by teaching them aeronautics, deflection shooting, and thinking in three dimensions. On January 8, 1943, the War Department constituted and re-designated the school as the 81st Flying Training Wing (preflight).

With the decline in the numbers of required pilot trainees as the war progressed, the Army Air Forces decided in October 1944 not to send more aircrew trainees to Santa Ana but to send them all to the AAF Preflight School at the San Antonio Aviation Cadet Center. The preflight school at Santa Ana remained open until January 1945, providing preflight training for Chinese students. It was deactivated on November 1, 1945, being consolidated into Central Flying Training Command at Randolph Field, Texas, and the facility was placed in inactive status.

During the early months of 1942, General Arnold saw that there was an acute shortage of pilots due to heavy losses of combat pilots. So he approved a plan, submitted by Jacqueline Cochran, a female pilot and an active member of the *Wings for Britain* organization that ferried American-built aircraft to Britain, and also the first woman to pilot a bomber (a Lockheed Hudson V) across the Atlantic. General Arnold used her as an advisor in training young women pilots to fly military aircraft within the United States, freeing the male pilots for combat duty. On September 14, 1942, the Women's Flying Training Detachment was established at the Houston Municipal Airport, with Jacqueline Cochran as its director. Three months later, because of a lack of military training facilities and housing in Houston, General Arnold approved moving the training program to Avenger Field in Sweetwater, Texas.

In May 1943, General Arnold authorized Jacqueline Cochran to oversee the development of a suitable uniform for the women pilots. The only caveat that he added was that the uniform *must* be blue. In concurrence with the new Santiago blue WASP uniforms, on August 20, 1943, General Arnold issued orders that the official acronym, without exception, for all Army Air Forces women pilots would be WASP (Women Airforce Service Pilots).

***

For Bob and his colleagues, arrival at the base meant immediate commencement of the indoctrination process. Each recruit was provided with the necessary basics: a training uniform, mess kit, and other items necessary for life in the boot camp. As training progressed and the young men completed the various stages of training, other items would be provided as required. One item that was evident all of the time was discipline, which was strict and never seemed to wane. Some of the older and more seasoned soldiers marveled at the naïveté of the new recruits and talked about the military system by sharing facts about army life that seemed to bear little relationship to reality.

The first days of the training program were filled with physical exercises and training, the nature of a range of medical treatments, and the effects of the medication. This was followed by preflight training, where Bob benefited from his membership in the Civilian Flight Training Program in Laramie.

Much of the training involved running, and the recruits got to walk only when they were hiking. Such walks took them to the Santa Ana beach, where they fired weapons such as the old water-cooled machine gun, the Thompson submachine gun, and rifles. The walk was a twenty-mile round trip. At the same time, the recruits were also trained in hand-to-hand combat, knife techniques, and bayonet fighting.

And there were also the Sunday parades, which involved standing at attention for an hour or more until the commandant and other dignitaries were all in place, after which the recruits would march in formation for review. Standing at attention was not an easy task, and there were occasions when one or more of the recruits would pass out on the parade ground. Bob managed to survive the Sunday morning activities without passing out by using a simple technique. He would push his hat high on his head and bend his knees slightly to keep the blood flowing.

After what seemed an age—in reality a week or two—the recruits, feeling that they were almost seasoned veterans, were allowed to take short periods of off-base leave. During training, Bob became friends with a fellow recruit by the name of Dick Miller. In keeping with the military tradition of alphabetizing everything, Miller and Milliken were next in line to each other. This friendship and the alphabetical relationship of their names meant that they were often able to take leave together, during which times they walked considerable distances.

The cadet training lasted approximately sixty days, and Bob accomplished his goal: He was one of a group selected for pilot training. His path would be from preflight training to primary to basic to advanced training and then to the silver wing badge, signifying that he was a flyer. The recruits not selected for pilot training were assigned to other duties: navigator or bombardier. Some were even declared to be unfit for duty and were discharged from military service.

The next step for Bob was to report for duty at the base at King City, California.

***

The war was already raging in Europe, which, although it was half a world away, did not seem real to many Americans. Unsurprisingly, the more distant a given country from the consequences of Axis aggression was, the less real the war seemed. But tensions were building in the Pacific, and the United States War Department began contracting with civilian flight schools to train pilots for the US Army. With the attack on Pearl Harbor, entry of the United States into the war became a reality and additional airports and flight schools were required in order to fill the need of the War Department for pilots.

In 1940, Palo Alto Airport Inc. won a contract and located a school at King City, which was an agricultural community, approximately 125 miles south of San Francisco, in the San Antonio Valley. King City had a population of 1,800 persons in 1940. The airfield was built on a 249-acre tract owned by the Spreckels Sugar Company and leased to the city, which in turn subleased the property to the school. Construction took place during the winter of 1940–41, the wettest in twenty-five years. The school welcomed the first cadets in March 1941. By May 1941, five buildings had been constructed to serve as barracks and a hospital, administration buildings, a mess hall, and two hangars were also completed. In the autumn of 1941, an additional hangar was added. The training center accommodated 280 cadets with a staff of 555 civilians and thirty-five army personnel. The Ryan PT-22, an open-cockpit monoplane, and the Boeing Stearman, a biplane, were the training aircraft of choice.

Cadets were expected to fly solo after no more than ten hours of dual instruction. If a recruit *washed out*, he went to the walking army (infantry). If he succeeded, he went on to two more levels of flight training before they were introduced to actual combat overseas. Bob succeeded.

As the Allies gained the upper hand in the war effort and enough student pilots were in the pipeline, the training contracts were canceled. King City was closed in August 1944, during which time approximately five thousand pilots graduated from primary training.

***

Bob recalls that he made a mistake when he enlisted. He had mentioned to the medical team that he had hay fever. When he arrived at the Santa Ana base, he discovered that was a foolish thing to have done. He had to report to the base infirmary, where a doctor started giving him a series of shots to test his allergies. Then the doctor came up with a liquid to be injected as a cure-all—a panacea for all diseases such as hay fever. This information went into Bob's permanent record, and he had to take the liquid—and his allergies— with him to the next duty station.

When Bob reported for duty at King City, he duly took the medicine and reported his allergies to the infirmary, as was the custom with anyone suffering from any kind of ailment. The doctor on duty told him that the medicine was powerful enough to induce death if he overdosed.

"Take no more than one half cc," the doctor said emphatically.

A sergeant then gave Bob a small bottle of medicine that was not marked with any form of direction or name but was supposedly a refill for his current medicine. The sergeant *thought* that the correct dose was either one half cc or five cc's. When Bob got back to his room, not trusting the latter advice that he had been given but realizing that the medicine could be injurious to his health, he deposited the bottle in the trash. He never reported back to the infirmary, and fortunately, his hay fever allergy never again bothered him.

***

It was at King City Primary Flight Training School (Mesa del Rey Field) that that Bob was introduced to the Ryan PT-22 (primary trainer), a two-man aircraft for instructor and student. Flight training came naturally to Bob, thanks in large part to an excellent instructor; and the trainer of choice (or necessity) was the Ryan PT-22.

The Ryan PT-22 was the military training aircraft used by the United States Army Air Corps and its successor, the United States Army Air Force, for primary pilot training. It was the first monoplane that the army had used for primary pilot training, as all previous pilot training aircraft were biplanes.

Since he already had a private pilot's license through the Civilian Pilot Training Program, Bob was several steps ahead of the majority of the cadets. One of the instructors was a pilot from Laramie. The instructor had one accident (to his credit or discredit!), as did most of the instructors trying to teach air discipline and air protocols to the students. Fortunately, most of the accidents were not serious.

Primary trainers presented the first of three stages of military flight training: primary, basic, and advanced. Prior to 1939, the air corps relied entirely on biplanes as primary trainers, but in 1940 it ordered a small number of Ryan civilian trainers and designated them as the PT-16. They were so successful that the air corps then ordered large numbers of improved versions, among them the PT-22. By the time production was completed in 1942, the air corps accepted 1,023 PT-22 aircraft. In 1942 the US Army Air Forces took delivery of twenty-five additional trainers, which had originally been ordered for the Netherlands.

The PT-22 fuel system consisted of a single tank mounted in front of the cockpit, and fuel was gravity-fed to the carburetor through a fuel strainer. A fuel selector valve, located on the left side of each cockpit, had three positions: (1) main, (2) reserve, and (3) off. The *reserve section* fed fuel from the reserve portion at the bottom of the aircraft's only fuel tank. The fuel gauge consisted of a sight gauge above the tank, visible to both pilots out the front of the aircraft. Oil pressure and temperature gauges were provided in each cockpit. The wing flaps were mechanically operated from a lever located on the left side of each cockpit, and adjustable elevator trim was provided by an elevator trim tab controllable from a hand-wheel mounted on the left side of each cockpit. Hydraulic brakes were provided for each wheel, controllable via the rudder pedals in each cockpit.

Often there would be six or more PT-22 aircraft in the flight pattern when the trainees were shooting touch-and-go landings—circling the plane over the field, going through the landing procedures, touching the wheels to the strip, then applying power to get airborne again to rejoin in pattern and repeat the process. All trainees sat in the front of the cockpit with the instructor behind.

Communication was by means of an open tube, with a mouthpiece for the instructor and ear phones for the student. There was no radio system in the plane. The trainees were the listeners and the instructors were the talkers. They were taught to immediately take their hands off the controls whenever the instructor said he was taking over. In one instance, Bob was lining up on final approach when he heard the instructor say: "I'll land it." Bob released his hold on the controls and the plane landed, bounced a bit, and rocked and rolled back and forth from wheel to wheel before the instructor grabbed the controls.

"What happened?" the instructor said in a demanding, almost incriminating voice.

"You said you would land it," Bob answered calmly, "so I let go."

"No," the instructor was adamant. "I said '*Now* land it!'"

Bob learned two lessons that day: (1) listen closely to the instructor and (2) the PT-22 could still make a relatively safe landing, even if the pilot was not in full control.

From King City the cadets were transported to Merced, California, in the San Joaquin valley, where they were introduced to the Vultee

BT-13 Valiant—the basic trainer flown by most American pilots during World War II. It was the second phase of the three-phase training program for pilots. After primary training, the student pilot moved to the more complex Vultee for basic flight training.

The BT-13 had a more powerful engine than the PT-22 and was faster and heavier than the primary trainer. The BT-13 required the student pilot to use two-way radio communications with the ground and to operate landing flaps and a two-position Hamilton Standard variable-pitch propeller. The aircraft had a fixed, as opposed to a retractable, landing gear and had considerably more horsepower. It was much bigger than the PT-22, about as big as the AT-6 (the advanced trainer) that cadets would fly in advanced training. The pilots nicknamed the BT-13 the Vultee Vibrator.

***

As a base, Merced also was a big step up, as it was a ceremonial base. That meant that bugles woke up the cadets, flag-raising and flag-lowering were all-hands-on-deck affairs, and parades and inspections were frequent. On the other hand, it was considered a *plus* that the barracks were just across the street from a swimming pool, which quickly became the focal point of the cadets' off-duty hours.

On duty, the cadets were taught to fly in tight formations as well as to take off, fly in patterns, and land without ever seeing the ground. Bob found that the best way to make such maneuvers was to move into position with the instructor's plane as he took off and then to stay in close formation with the instructor. Bob managed to focus on the instructor's aircraft and stay with him. After several attempts, the instructor could not shake Bob, and he could even land with Bob's aircraft at his wingtip, so he readily admitted that Bob was doing well as a format flyer.

Becoming a fighter pilot had always been Bob's dream, but when he talked it over with Dick Miller, he found that it gave him second thoughts. Bob wondered out loud to Miller if it would not be better to fly a multi-engine aircraft—a bomber or a transport—knowing this could lead to a lucrative civilian flying career after the war.

Miller was not sympathetic to Bob's out-loud thoughts and retorted: "You have always wanted to be a fighter pilot. This is your chance. Let's get into fighters and shoot things up."

So they both opted for fighter planes. Specifically, they chose the P-38, a double fuselage aircraft graded as a *pursuit* aircraft. However, to get into the cockpit of a P-38, Bob had to go to Williams Field in Arizona and learn to handle the AT-6 in advanced training. Williams Field—located in Mesa, approximately thirty miles southeast of Phoenix—was active as a training base for both the United States Army Air Force and the United States Air Force from 1941 until its closure in 1993.

The AT-6, a single-engine closed cockpit machine, was a capable airplane with a retractable gear. The cadets used it for gunnery training and dive-bombing work. At Williams Field, Bob was also introduced to the AT-9, a twin engine aircraft that Bob thought looked large and more cumbersome than the whale of an aircraft he had already been in. The aircraft had two big engines and four seats and was used to teach the cadets twin-engine flying, a skill that Bob would find valuable when he finally got into the cockpit of a P-38.

Miller and Bob took turns as pilot and copilot during takeoff and landing maneuvers and worked their way through various aerial manipulations. The AT-9 had some benefits, but speed wasn't one of them. The aircraft had a stall speed that was only a modicum lower than the flying speed. On final approach, the pilot had to use full flaps to keep the plane in the air long enough to get it on the ground.

On one occasion, Bob was piloting an AT-9 at low altitude when the door adjacent to where Miller was sitting sprang open. This event seemed to unbalance the aircraft, and even though it was at full power, the AT-9 immediately started to lose altitude. Since they were already at low altitude, there was not much space between the aircraft and the ground, and disaster was imminent. Instinctively, they developed a plan—Miller watched the controls so that Bob could reach across and pull the door closed. Finally at an altitude of less than one hundred feet Miller regained control and took the AT-9 back up to a safer altitude.

While at Williams Field, Bob also had sessions with the P-322, an early version of the P-38 in which the engines rotated in the same direction compared to the P-38 where the engines rotated in opposite directions. The P-322 was not a desirable aircraft. Some had been sent to Britain under the lend-lease agreement but were returned, having been found to be highly unsatisfactory, with an inferior performance in combat. The ones that Bob and his colleagues flew had been altered so that the propellers were counter-rotating. The propellers on both engines of most conventional twin-engine aircraft spin clockwise (as viewed from the pilot seat), while counter-rotating propellers generally spin clockwise on the left engine and counterclockwise on the right. That made a big difference, but the P-322 still didn't exhibit anything near good performance—it was too old and had too many maintenance and operational problems.

As an example, Bob had less than five hours flying time in the P-322 trainer when an extremely serious engine problem developed.

He had just turned on the downwind leg of his landing approach and was reducing speed in a 700-foot holding pattern. The starboard engine exploded, and Bob, looking at the engine, could see shards of metal sticking out of the engine covering—a sure sign, he thought, that the engine was not going to get better and needed serious repair or replacement if he could land the stricken aircraft. He immediately feathered the incapacitated engine and adjusted the controls for the P-322 to fly with the right wing high to avoid going into a spin. But even with full power and the control adjustment, the aircraft was losing altitude at an unhealthy rate. Bob knew that his best course of action was to continue turning until he was lined up with the runway, then get the plane on the ground.

While turning, he tried to drop the landing gear, but there were more problems. The hydraulics refused to work properly, and the wheels were not locked down. Immediately, he went to the back-up system (sometime called the system of last resort), which involved using the hand pump to get the wheels down and locked. Pumping the hand pump with one hand and flying the seemingly doomed aircraft with the other hand required skill, and Bob was still trying to line up with the runway.

He quickly concluded he was not going to make a successful landing and decided to call the field control tower to advise them that his only option was to forgo landing on the main runway and seek an optional landing area. At an altitude of approximately seventy-five feet, Bob managed to get the landing gear down and locked in place, and the flaps followed. Bob touched down with an ambulance, a fire wagon, and a rescue crew keeping pace all the way down the runway until the P-38 came to a halt. Fearing more trouble, Bob evacuated the cockpit in Olympic record time. This was his first experience at landing a P-38 with one engine completely incapacitated, and although the experience gained might be valuable, it was not an experience he wished to repeat.

The Lockheed P-38 Lightning was developed to an Army Air Corps requirement. It had a distinctive twin fuselage with a central nacelle (a cover housing, which is separate from the fuselage) containing the cockpit and armament. And fortunately, in designing the P-38, the Lockheed Company reversed the counter-rotation such that the tips of the propeller arcs move outward, away from each other.

Clustering all the armament in the nose was unlike most other US aircraft, which used wing-mounted guns with trajectories set up to crisscross at one or more points in a *convergence zone*. Guns mounted in the nose did not suffer from having their useful ranges limited by pattern convergence, meaning good pilots could shoot much farther. A Lightning could reliably hit targets at any range up to a thousand yards, whereas other fighters had to pick a single convergence range between 100 and 250 yards.

As part of the training program, the cadets, who were now adjudged to be able to fly, were allowed only one instructor-accompanied flight before taking control of the P-38 in a solo flight. To get that one flight, Bob had to make a sacrifice in which he was hunched over in the empty radio compartment behind the flight instructor. Part of the sacrifice for Bob was also being at the mercy of the instructor, who took the P-38 into a slow roll, during which Bob ended up lying on his back clutching his chest pack parachute with nothing but the thin cockpit canopy between him and several thousand feet of clear air.

And then there was parachute training, which was, to say the least, limited. Several practice jumps from a high platform were the only training Bob received. In addition, the flyers were ordered to pack their own parachutes. The men found this to be preferable to be sure that packaging of their individual parachutes had been done correctly and the somewhat delicate life-saving equipment would perform reliably if called upon to do so.

The focus of parachute training was on the proper exit by the pilot from the aircraft into the open air. There were no ejector seats in those days! After the exit the pilots were told to fold their arms across the chest with the right hand on the rip cord. The folded arms prevented fingers or an arm getting caught on the plane, resulting in serious injury. The hand on the rip cord reminded the pilot that he had to pull this to open the parachute. The rip cord was to be pulled when the pilot was clear of the stricken aircraft. Most pilots counted to three or four or five after exiting the plane while others shouted (to themselves) or mouthed the word *Geronimo* which gave them the time to clear the aircraft after the hurried exit.

In some fighter units of the Allies, the pilots were advised that a clean exit from the aircraft could be achieved by maneuvering the fighter into an upside-down position, removing the cockpit cover, and then allowing gravity to take over, ensuring a clean fall from the aircraft. However, the twin booms of the P-38 were not conducive to a clean exit. Some pilots were reported to have the parachute snagged on one of the rear stabilizers (tails) or the cross-boom between the tails, to the serious or fatal misfortune of the pilot.

Bob and his fellow airmen were advised to get out of the aircraft the best way possible, but the term *best way* was never defined. One pilot was reported to have slid down a wing to make his exit. Nevertheless, they were advised to ensure that the parachute and the man did not become entangled with the rear stabilizer of the aircraft. Then they were taught the correct technique for landing following a jump to prevent breaking a limb (usually a leg or ankle) on landing.

All pilots understood that an incapacitated parachutist was at the mercy of enemy soldiers and extremely irate German (in this case) civilians armed with pitchforks and other forms of edged or pointed weapons. As the war in Europe progressed and more missions were flown over Germany, there were many stories of Allied airmen being killed by civilians or by the Gestapo or by the SS after escaping from a disabled aircraft. Bob was determined that this would not be his fate.

The parachutes Bob and his fellow airmen used were of a round design and could be steered to a small degree by pulling on the risers (four straps connecting the paratrooper's harness to the connectors) and suspension lines that attach to the parachute canopy itself. This could be used to a limited extent to prevent the parachutists from landing in a treed area, which could lead to serious injury or death. However, mobility of the parachutes was often deliberately limited to prevent scattering of the troops when a large number of men parachuted together.

In spite of the disadvantages of parachuting, Bob liked the comforting thought of it being an escape route if a serious emergency arose. He also liked the parachute for another reason.

Being five feet seven inches tall at most, and weighing in at 135 pounds—Bob was smaller than many of the men who fitted into the cockpit of the fighter aircraft, especially the P-38. When questioned about his visibility over the rim of the cockpit, and the lack of a sore backside that plagued many P-38 pilots because of the infamously poor seat in the P-38, Bob's response was quite simple and sincere:

"When I'm in the cockpit sitting on my parachute *and* two cushions, my visibility is unimpaired!"

One can only assume that the parachute *and* the two cushions were sufficient to protect his backside from any ill effects from the notoriously uncomfortable seat in the P-38!

***

The cadets were also introduced to Link Trainers at Williams Field. The term *Link Trainer* (also known as the *Blue box* and *Pilot Trainer*) commonly referred to a series of flight simulators that were used as a key pilot instrument-training aid by the Army Air Corps. The trainers were crude by modern standards, but in 1943 it was cutting edge technology.

The trainer had all of the same instruments that would be found in the cockpit of a fighter aircraft. To add realism, the trainer was mounted in an enclosed cabin mounted on gears and pulleys. By the use of the gears and pulleys, the trainer was used to simulate flying without leaving the ground. With the cabin door of the trainer in the closed position, the cadet could see only the instruments. There were no outside reference points. This way the cadets learned to rely upon the instruments.

The enclosed cabin often confused cadets, and simulated crashes occurred often. The good news was that the cadets were always able to survive the simulated crash. But it was through the continuous use of the trainer that the cadets were able to gain confidence and show increasing signs of instrument-flying proficiency. But there was no substitute for actual experience, providing the pilot survived.

And so Bob and his colleague Dick Miller gained real experience on a cross-country flight to the Grand Canyon. Shortly after takeoff, Bob noticed the gas gauges were just above empty. They had made a cardinal error by failing to check—even double check—the fuel levels in the tanks before taking off. Realizing that there was either a shortage of fuel, as indicated by the gauges, or a problem with the gauges, they decided quickly to land at nearby Luke Field, Arizona, approximately thirty-five miles northwest of Phoenix. Luke Field was named after Medal of Honor winner Lt. Frank Luke Jr., who was born in Phoenix in 1897. He scored eighteen aerial victories during World War I in air battles over France before being killed at age twenty-one, on September 29, 1918.

The aircraft was amply fueled, despite the misinformation offered by the gauges. But it was too late in the day to complete the cross-country flight. The trip was canceled and they never did get to take the trip to the Grand Canyon courtesy of the military. And lesson learned—Bob never again failed to second-guess gauges without double-checking fuel levels before taking off.

And then it happened.

On November 3, 1943, Bob was commissioned as a second lieutenant in the United States Army Air Corps and was awarded coveted silver wings. Because none of their friends or relatives were able to attend the graduation ceremonies, Bob and Dick Miller pinned their wings on each other. Bob was now a fighter pilot, and he was fully qualified to fly the machine that would play a major role in his future—the Lockheed P-38 Lightning.

Bob's Graduation Day Picture

It was at this time that Bob was issued his Class A uniform and coveralls for flying. This was the only time he was issued clothing. Officers wore their rank insignia pinned onto the shoulder epaulets, while non-officers wore rank insignia and service stripes on both sleeves. A dress shirt and a four-in-hand necktie for formal and semi-formal functions was the order of the day.

The four-in-hand necktie is named after the *four-in-hand knot*, which is a method of tying the necktie. Also known as a *simple knot* or *schoolboy knot*, the four-in-hand is believed to be the most popular method of tying ties due to its simplicity and style.

Bob kept his uniform in excellent condition, not knowing how long it would have to last. Fortunately, there was always laundry service to keep his coveralls clean, either base laundry service or more often available through local women on an as-needed request wherever the base was located. Most men preferred the laundry services of the local women.

His practice paid off. The uniform and the coveralls lasted until his demobilization with an honorary discharge in June 1945, shortly after he took his last flight in a P-38, also in June 1945, when he flew from Langensalza, a city in Thuringia, Germany, and over part of Switzerland, landing back at Langensalza where he got out of a P-38 cockpit for the last time

Chapter 5: The P-38 Lightning

The P-38 Lightning—named the *Fork-Tail Devil* (*Der Gabelschwanz Teufel*) by the Germans—was a uniquely designed aircraft with the cockpit nestled on the wing between two counter-rotating engines. The engines were mounted on twin fuselages (twin booms) and tails connected by a tail boom (or horizontal stabilizer). The counter-rotating engines offset much of the torque and gave the P-38 turning and maneuvering advantages that exceeded those of other fighter aircraft. An additional benefit was that the P-38 could out-turn a single-engine plane, which would stall or snap-roll as the single-engine machine entered a sharp roll of 360 degrees (full circle) about the longitudinal axis, making control difficult in most cases.

The P-38 also was outstanding when it came to firepower. It had four 50-caliber machine guns and a 20-millimeter cannon, all mounted in the nose.

Starting in 1941, belly tank technology was added to the P-38 Lightning. The tanks (typically up to 200 gallons in capacity) were under-wing tanks fitted to the aircraft between the cockpit and the port side fuselage (left side boom) and starboard fuselage (right side boom).

The advantage of the belly tanks was that they increased the range of the P-38, but the primary disadvantage was that the belly tanks imposed a drag on the aircraft carrying them. A rule of thumb was that only about half the capacity of a streamlined drop tank actually goes toward increasing the aircraft's overall range. The rest goes to overcome the added drag and weight of the tank itself.

If the belly tanks were designed as drop tanks (to be discarded after they were empty), the fuel in the drop tanks was consumed first, and only when all the fuel in the drop tanks had been used would the fuel selector be turned to the airplane's internal tanks.

If the mission was of a short duration and did not require belly tanks, the place where the belly tanks might have been could be taken by two five-hundred-pound conventional drop bombs or drop tanks containing the highly flammable napalm. The name was originally used for the gelling agent that was mixed with a highly flammable petroleum-based liquid, but colloquially the name is used as the generic name of several flammable liquids used in warfare, often forms of jellied gasoline.

***

Although it was a fighter plane, the P-38 could—and often did—double as a bomber, although able to carry only half the bomb tonnage as a B-17 bomber (called the Flying Fortress). Some P-38 aircraft were fitted with bombardier type noses and were used to lead formations of bomb-laden P-38 aircraft to their targets. With supercharged engines, the P-38 could handle anything from high-altitude precision bombing to down-in-the-weeds dive-bombing. The largest bombs that Bob ever carried were two 2,000-pound bombs—one attached on the underside of each wing—in the place where the belly tanks would have been had it been a long mission. That barely allowed him to rise above the trees at the end of the runway on takeoff.

The nickname *Droop Snoot* was given to the P-38 Lightning, which had bombardier-type noses. These planes were fitted with the Norden bombsight that guided the bomb-laden P-38s to their targets.

***

Bob continued his training at various bases after Williams Field—such as Fort Ord (California) for work on the firing ranges and to check out much of the overseas equipment, including barracks bags, sleeping bags, and gas masks; and Glendale (California) Air Base, where he felt he was well on the way to becoming a *real* flyer and having real combat experiences.

At the Ontario (California) Air Base, Bob gained more time in a P-38, practicing maneuvers and formation flying. Bob's preference was always to fly solo when he could, and to do everything he wanted to, including a four-point roll—a quick series of quarter rolls.

However, the P-38 was often difficult to hold in level flight because of the heavy nose, but Bob found he could perform spin maneuvers. In the second spin, the P-38 started to lose altitude at the rate of approximately 5,000 feet per minute. Bob was deprived of time and altitude when he attempted to perform such aerobatics. By logical reasoning and a hidden voice in his head, he decided against this type of maneuver!

Officially, the P-38 pilots were prohibited from testing their aeronautical skills. But on occasion marine pilots flying F4U

Corsair fighters out of nearby El Toro Marine air base offered golden opportunities for honing the flying abilities of the P-38 pilots.

The Vought F4U Corsair, with its characteristic W-shaped wings, was developed early in 1938 at the request of the United States Navy. The idea was to design the smallest body aircraft that would be compatible with the most powerful engine available—the Corsair was the first US single-engine fighter to exceed four hundred miles per hour. When the Corsair appeared over the Pacific Ocean in 1943, it was the most powerful naval aviation aircraft. In the course of approximately 64,000 missions in the Pacific Theater, Corsairs downed 2,140 enemy planes while only 189 Corsairs were lost—a ratio unmatched in the history of aerial warfare.

Thus, when flying against such a machine as the Corsair, the skills of the P-38 pilots were sharpened by performing illegal aerobatic maneuvers against the equally-capable marine pilots who were flying aircraft that were at least equal to the capabilities of the P-38 machines.

And then tragedy struck. Miller and Bob (the alphabetical shoulder-to-shoulder pseudo-Siamese twins in the roll call line) were split up at the Salinas (California) Air Base because of the alphabetical order of their names. To assign pilots to various bases and duties, the officers using the method that has been in operation since time immemorial went through the names of the flyers alphabetically and chose alternate names for duty assignments. When it came to Miller and Milliken, Miller went to air reconnaissance at Moses Lake (Washington) and Milliken stayed with the fighter aircraft.

This move was ironic insofar as Dick Miller, the man who persuaded Bob to stay in fighter training, was not assigned to fly fighter aircraft. Air reconnaissance was no easy task. Typically, reconnaissance was carried out using an unarmed aircraft to lighten the weight and increase speed and maneuverability. But tragedy arose when Dick Miller was killed flying out of the Moses Lake base in a single-engine takeoff a short time after he was transferred there.

***

Milton Merkle, whom Bob first met at Williams Field, ended up in his group. Merkle was from Baltimore, was married, and had been a race driver. He was an Irishman with deep-seated feelings about Jews, Mexicans, African American, and just about anyone else that wasn't Irish. As a result, his background and concepts were very different from Bob's life as it had been in Hanna. In spite of this, Bob knew instinctively that he would stick to his wing in combat.

They flew together and whenever they could, they practiced formation flying, mock combat, dodging into clouds, and popping out unexpectedly in high-altitude high-speed games of hide-and-seek. Both men knew that there was always the chance that their flying habits could lead to danger, such as an unplanned (and fatal) meeting inside one of the clouds, but that just added more zest to the game. And they felt it was good training for real combat flying, when it made no difference to the enemy if fighting took place in a cloud. All flyers were trained to be hunter-killers no matter what the flying conditions and the abilities of the enemy.

Merkle was a good pilot, but so was Bob. Merkle thought that he was the better of the two, but Bob knew that Merkle was wrong. They spent many hours competing, but the point of who was the better man was never proved conclusively one way or the other. Instead, a mutual respect developed between them that was to last as long as they were together. But not all the pilots were like that.

There was a pilot we'll give the pseudonym *Bill Smith* to avoid embarrassment to his memory or to his family. Smith started the war as an infantryman at Pearl Harbor, where he claimed to have shot down one of the attacking Japanese aircraft using his rifle—a deed that was, in fact, noted in his military record. That evidence of fearless bravado gave Smith an opportunity to transfer from the ground to the air. He jumped at the opportunity and graduated from the flight training school, but he became and remained the proverbial *loose cannon*, subject to distrust and careful watching.

On one occasion, Bob was flying in a tight formation with Smith as wingman when Smith entered a climb as he was banking to the right.

Briefly, the *wingman* is a pilot who supports another in a potentially dangerous flying environment. The term *wingman* originally referred to the aircraft flying beside and slightly behind the lead plane in an aerial formation. The traditional military definition of a wingman refers to the position of that flyer in the flight pattern used by fighter aircraft. According to military protocol, there is *always* a lead aircraft and another aircraft that flies off the right wing of, and behind, the lead aircraft. This second pilot is called the wingman because he (in the modern Air Force, often *she*) primarily protects the lead flyer by watching his or her back.

As wingman, Bob prepared to slide to the right under him, assuming that Smith would maintain his flight pattern, and then as Smith recovered, Bob would slide his P-38 back under Smith's left wing. However, as unpredictable as loose cannons are, Smith lived up to expectations (or unexpectations), and instead of recovering, as Bob thought he would, Smith took the P-38 into a forward motion so that his aircraft came (literally and shockingly) within a few feet (Bob estimated approximately two feet) and on a near-collision course with Bob. Bob's view was limited. His windshield was filled with the extremely close-up view of Smith's aircraft and nothing else. If a collision had been a consequence of Smith's action, the story of this book was have been over. Fortunately, a collision was averted by Bob's flying skills and his quick instincts to get out of danger.

In fact, that was the first of several times when Smith's poor judgment and marginal flying skills almost spelled disaster for anyone within close range of Smith and his flying machine!

In another practice dive-bombing flight, they were on a run to dive-bomb a railroad bridge, flying in a direction from north to south. Bob had dropped his bombs and was taking his P-38 away from the target site when lo and behold, there was his colleague Smith coming at him, head on, and for reasons perhaps not even known to Smith, flying south to north and against traffic. The moment Smith released his bombs, Bob took his aircraft underneath Smith's P-38 and above the falling bombs.

Bob recalls that if he had spotted Smith one second later, their aircraft would have collided and been a fireball in the air. As usual, Smith was seemingly without any focus whatever, oblivious to it all, and never realized that he had been very close to meeting his maker.

***

Jumping ahead for information and a description of the antics of this very dangerous fellow.

Smith was just as oblivious in combat. Bob was flying on his right wing when Smith shot at and hit a German Messerschmitt 109 (Me-109), which immediately burst into flames. In military parlance, it was a hit insofar as the aircraft was destroyed, going to the ground in flames.

Smith's excitement got the better of him, and he lit up the radio with sound as he yelled: "I got one! I got one!"

Bob called for Smith to break right but he didn't hear Bob. Or else he heard Bob's words but wasn't in a state of mind to know what Bob had said. Smith was too busy yelling to see the German coming in at him from the right side. Taking his own initiative, Bob broke off from his formation position, turned into the German's attack, fired, hit the Me-109, and scored his first victory.

Smith's lack of discipline came up again when the squadron planes were returning from a prearranged bomber escort mission that was not to be. The squadron had reached the designated rendezvous point over France, but thick clouds prevented the P-38 flyers from locating the bombers they were to escort to Germany. The squadron was given the go-ahead to abort the mission and return to base in England.

At the time, Bob was flying the number three position in the flight—the position immediately to the left and just behind the left of Smith's aircraft, and the number four man was on Bob's left wing. It was not surprising that from past experiences, Bob didn't trust Smith's instrument flying or his judgment. So Bob moved slightly out of formation to the left where he could keep a close eye on Smith and have the maneuvering room that he would require if Smith got up to his usual anticipated antics.

With one eye on Smith and the other on his speed, Bob saw that they were getting deeper into clouds and losing air speed. Before Bob could warn him, Smith dropped the left wing of his aircraft and disappeared in a downward motion into the cloudy and overcast sky.

Bob took over as flight leader, set a course back to the base, and slowly brought his P-38 through the cloud, managing to avoid all of the barrage balloons. These were large balloons tethered to a ground base with metal cables. They were quite capable of seriously damaging low-level attacking aircraft, usually by the cables shearing through a wing. And he brought all of his flight members safely on go the ground. Smith eventually showed up alone. Bob believed that Smith had blundered around until he found a friendly place to land, which just happened to be his home base! Fortunately, he didn't exhaust his fuel supply.

***

But back to the past and the continued training that the flyers had to endure for their safety.

The flyers arrived at the Ontario base on January 1, 1944. That same day Bob flew over the Rose Bowl football game, and later he flew solo over a valley just north of the base, where he was able to unwind by putting the P-38 through its paces. He felt that he was at ease with the aircraft as though he and the machine were *one*. He took the P-38 from complex rolls to in-air stalls. Fortunately, the engines always started again after the stalling maneuver. He was able to take the P-38 to maximum speed (approximately 415 miles per hour) and then could take the plane into seven complete vertical rolls before losing air speed and dropping off. He would smile to himself at his abilities.

On one occasion, two of Bob's colleagues took off with the idea of sharpening their formation flying skills. As they buzzed Bear Lake, the two men misjudged their altitude, flew too low, and crashed into the water. Both were killed. Sadly, soon afterward another young pilot crashed and was killed as he also attempted to hone his flying skills.

Such incidents made the pilots take notice that sharpening any skills is not for the faint-hearted or for any pilot who was not up to full proficiency. But at age nineteen or twenty, who among them was not invincible?

***

And then the word of assignments came to the men while they were still at the air base in Ontario, California. Bob was assigned to the 429th Fighter Squadron, which, with the 428th Fighter Squadron and the 430th Fighter Squadron, was part of the 474th Fighter Group. That was part of the IXth Tactical Air Command Fighter Wing, which was in turn part of the 9th Air Force.

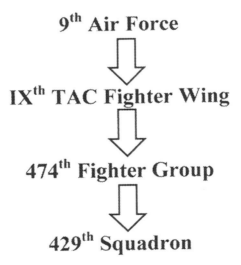

Lines of Reporting within the 9th Air Force

As the men made final preparations to go overseas, Merkle made a proposal. He had also been assigned to the 429th Fighter Squadron.

"Hey, Millie," Merkle offered, "I would sooner have you on my wing as anybody. Let's stick together when we go overseas. At least we will both know someone we can trust."

Bob agreed, and they joined up with three other pilots— Lieutenants Patterson, O'Neil, and Kirkland. It would be the five of them against anything the Germans could throw at them.

Having made the momentous decision to stick together, a celebration was in order. It took a full bottle of vodka to get Bob and his four colleagues from Salinas to Oakland, California, where they made their way to the Union Pacific Railroad congregating point. The bottle was empty by then, and the five young lieutenants were not feeling any pain but were slightly the worse for wear. As they were boarding the train, Bob noticed three *torpedoes* alongside the rails.

Torpedoes are small explosive charges that can be clamped over the rail so that when a train passes over them, the resulting noise alerts the engineer. The number of torpedoes in a sequence tells the engineer to slow down or stop. Knowing the purpose that the torpedoes served, Bob gathered up all of the torpedoes that he could find, placed them in front of the passenger car wheels, and waited for the train to start moving. When it did, all of the torpedoes exploded.

"Damn the torpedoes!" Bob shouted with unrestrained glee, as he repeated the order given by Rear Admiral David Farragut at the Battle of Mobile Bay on August 5, 1864. "Full speed ahead!"

Finally, the torpedo explosions notwithstanding, they were on their way. And like young men throughout history, they were determined that they would give their all for flag and country. They all did, and sadly, many did not return.

***

As with all trains on service to the military, each car was filled to the point of overflowing, and it was a struggle to find a place to stand, let alone to sit anywhere. One of the choice places to be was the smoking car, where the air was thick enough to cut with a knife—perhaps reminiscent of some of the nineteenth-century pea soup thick fogs of London. But with sufficient persistence and patience, a spot on the floor could usually be found.

As the train clumpety-clumped its musical way eastward, there was time to eat, drink, smoke, and sleep. It was a feeling of almost being home when the train crossed the border into Wyoming, arriving in Hanna at 2:00 a.m. to be replenished with water and coal—the life-saving needs for any steam-driven train. Bob had managed to find a place at a window when the train carefully maneuvered around the gentle curve that was just prior to the Hanna Railroad Station. The headlight of the engine flashed on his home, bringing back boyhood memories of those nights when a train light would shine briefly through his bedroom window. In his mind he pictured his parents sleeping, not knowing that the train whistle they might have heard in their subconscious was whistling their son's farewell.

At the station, only one person was in sight, probably the telegrapher going about his lonely duties while the town slept. Bob knew that he could not even say hello to the telegrapher. He reminded himself that doing so was not an option—he couldn't disclose any troop movements, not even his own. So he sat in silence, gazing at the town and all he was leaving, and wondering in the darkness when—the dangers of wartime flying notwithstanding—he would return.

***

Almost three days after the water and coal stop at Hanna, Wyoming, other stops had been made for the same reason, but they were of much less interest to Bob. The train arrived at Grand Central Station in New York. The flyers were transported to Fort Hamilton, New York, where they played the old but still in vogue army game of *hurry up and wait*. The men were ready to board the *Queen Mary*, but the ship was not ready for them. This gave them three or four days to see the city and, in their minds, paint the town red, which would involve attendance at various social activities in different parts of town—basically partying all night long, which had nothing to do with a pot of paint and paintbrushes.

Thus, night clubs attracted Bob and his companions like the proverbial moth to a flame. He saw some well-known comedians of the time, including a performer who played "Me and My Shadow" with an African American who doubled as the performer's shadow.

Like Bob, most of the flyers were from small towns and had never seen a big city, especially the biggest city of all—New York. Much energy was spent visiting places of interest, especially the Empire State Building. The men were young, and the jingle of coins in their respective pockets made them feel alive. However, all things can come to an end. One of the flyers even managed to get mugged and somehow managed to end up naked in a dark alley.

Suddenly, the order arrived on February 22, 1944 that it was time to board the *Queen Mary*. Bob does not remember much about boarding, except that 15,000 men (soldiers and airmen)—slightly below the record of 16,082 American troops that she carried on one crossing—boarded continuously, and the ship was loaded and ready to go within twenty-four hours of the commencement of boarding. Bob's memories of leaving New York Harbor are still vivid.

He stood at the rail and watched the Statue of Liberty fade in the distance. The ship was crowded, but he felt alone. The reality of war was at the forefront of his mind. On the other side of the Atlantic, men his age flying planes with Nazi markings were waiting to test their skills against his skills and the skills of his colleagues. He could not even imagine how this would turn out. He knew that his flying abilities would be put to the severest of tests. Perhaps the illegal and forbidden aerobatics he'd practiced would be useful. Perhaps not.

***

In spite of being built as a luxury liner, the *Queen Mary* was outfitted for war as a troop carrier and did not have luxury accommodations. When war broke out, the ship was taken out of passenger service, stripped to the bare essentials, and reborn as a high-speed troop transport. Because of her speed, the *Queen Mary* (also known as the Grey Ghost) sailed unescorted—her powerful engines allowed her to outrun any German U-Boat (*Unterseeboot*— undersea boat, submarine). Her sister ship the, *Queen Elizabeth*, was also used as a troop ship and was likewise able outrun a U-boat. Each ship could make the crossing from New York in five days. But outrunning a U-boat was one thing; being ambushed by a U-boat lying in wait in the mid-Atlantic was completely different and could be fatal.

The Battle of the Atlantic was still ongoing and the period known to the U-boat commanders as the *Happy Time* (June 1940 to February 1941), when U-boat groups (*wolf packs*) roamed the Atlantic and sank Allied shipping almost at will, was over. But the danger from the U-boats never ceased. Any Allied ship crossing the Atlantic was subject to fatal attack by torpedoes from the U-boats.

But in reality—known through rumor to some of the crew but amazingly unknown to the military passengers—there was another dark side to the voyage. Adolph Hitler had offered the German equivalent of $250,000 and the Iron Cross to any U-boat Captain that could sink the *Queen Mary*—the largest troop ship used during World War II and a major carrier of men and armaments. To add further to the dark side, on October 2, 1942, the *Queen Mary* had collided with the light cruiser HMS Curacoa. At the time, the *Queen Mary* was carrying 10,000 troops of the US 29th Infantry Division to join the Allied forces in Europe.

The *Queen Mary* was steaming an evasive zigzag course—eight minutes to starboard, eight minutes to port, then resumption of her base course for four minutes before starting the cycle again, which the aged *HMS Curacoa* could not match due to deterioration of her engines. She was hard pressed to keep pace with *Queen Mary*. The captain of the Curacoa opted to forego the zigzag course so as to be able to maintain a position from which to provide effective anti-aircraft watch and U-boat watch.

At about two fifteen in the afternoon, the *Queen Mary* started the starboard turn for the first leg of her zigzag, cutting across the path of the *Curacoa* with insufficient clearance, striking her amidships at a speed of twenty-eight knots (about thirty-one to thirty-two miles per hour) and cutting the *Curacoa* in two, which sank in six minutes, approximately one hundred yards from the *Queen Mary*. Due to the risk of U-boat attacks, the *Queen Mary* did not assist in rescue operations and instead steamed onward with a damaged bow. Hours later, the convoy's lead escort returned to rescue ninety-nine survivors from the crew of the *Curacoa*, which had totaled 338 men.

The loss was not reported until after the war ended. Under the Protection of Military Remains Act (1986), the wreck site where the

Curacoa went down is designated a *protected place*. Even though the loss was not reported officially until the end of the war, a ship the stature and size of the *Queen Mary* entering port with a damaged bow would not go unnoticed. Rumors would abound, and the active Official Secrets Act (legislation in the UK and Commonwealth countries that provided for the protection of state secrets and official information) seems to have been an effective barrier to rumors and talk. Keeping such talk and rumor from fifteen thousand military passengers was no mean feat!

As a gesture of good faith in the ship and to acknowledge the safety of traveling in her, Winston Churchill traveled on the *Queen Mary* three times during World War II and considered it his headquarters at sea. In fact, he even signed the D-Day Declaration onboard.

It was into this cauldron of war that Bob and his colleagues were introduced as they boarded the *Queen Mary*. The war was no longer 3,500 miles away; it was here and now, on board the *Queen Mary* in the Atlantic Ocean.

***

Sleeping accommodation for the fifteen thousand men on board consisted of *hot bed* assignments. Lots were supposedly drawn for the order of sleeping, but in reality the sleeping time was assigned by orders from the officers. In a hot-bed assignment, each man would sleep in a bunk for eight hours, then surrender his place to the second man who, after eight hours, would surrender his place to a third man. Then the cycle would repeat itself for another twenty-four hour period. The non-sleeping time of sixteen hours per day was free time—as far as a man could be free in the limited space of the deck and narrow passageways of the ship.

The bunks were stacked four or five high, and there was just enough room to walk between the rows. When it was Bob's turn to climb up and slide into a bunk, he gave thought to the position in which he wished to sleep. Turning over in such cramped quarters was a major problem and almost impossible to do if a larger-than-average fellow in the bunk above caused the bed to sag. Because of the sleeping arrangements, the odor of bodies was strong in the poorly ventilated sleeping area and filled Bob's nose. The only respite that Bob had was to pull the blanket over his head and concentrate on the less objectionable aroma of the wool.

In reality, the men spent eight hours in bed, eight hours on deck, and eight hours standing in line for meals—the meal lines were so long that when a man had finally worked his way up to the buffet-style food line and received his food, he would eat the food, return his mess gear for washing, and immediately proceed to the rear of the mess line and wait for the next meal to be served. Bob found that the meals were not exceptional but were acceptable, and food seemed to be plentiful. It was not the policy of the US military powers-that-be to starve soldiers, sailors, or airmen!

The men learned to eat what the British citizenry and soldiers, sailors, and airmen were eating: powdered eggs, powdered milk, dehydrated fruit, dehydrated potatoes, Brussels sprouts, turnips, and cabbage along with (the less than gourmet) Spam. There was also the occasional treat to supplement the spam—in the form of horse meat. Being from a farm, this didn't bother Bob, but the rumor was rampant on board ship that by the time they reached the designated British port, and as if to attest to this rumor, several of the farm boys would imitate a horse whinny, especially the whinny of a horse being obliged to pull a fully loaded wagon for the first time.

Fresh water does not seem to have been a problem aboard the ship, and water for bathing (bathtubs rather than showers) seemed to be plentiful. Bob does not recall there being any form of water rationing aboard ship.

And then there was Bob's duty assignment! As a brand-new second lieutenant, Bob was put in charge of a large group of enlisted men, and one of his duties was to ensure that the bathtub assigned to these men was clean at all times. When not in use, the tub had to be sparkling clean. If not, Bob could expect a serious talk from the captain in charge, whose duty was to oversee bathtub cleanliness and to determine if any tub did not measure up to the required standards of cleanliness. The standard was defined by the captain in charge and may have depended upon his mood at the time of the inspection.

The general sleeping and non-sleeping activities of the men were interrupted on one occasion during the night when the *Queen Mary* stopped dead in the water. The word was quietly passed from officers to men of the need for absolute *silence.*

Bob can smile now at the thought of trying to maintain silence among fifteen thousand men. Under the circumstances at close quarters aboard ship, the typical noise might decrease a little if an order came down the line for silence but it would not get to the base level of *quiet.* But the men knew that this was different, and a thick heavy silence stretched from bow to stern.

"A German U-boat is on the prowl," was the word passed among the men.

"It hasn't picked us up yet," the story continued, "and the ship is under an engine stop order so that the U-boat crew can't hear us."

"Sound travels well over water," came the ultimate words, "especially at night, so everyone has to be quiet. No talking!"

The *Queen Mary* became the *Grey Ghost*—floating in silent trepidation. But, as luck or fate would have it, the U-boat commander and crew—if there was a submarine—did not pick up the presence of the *Queen Mary* and her complement of passengers. When the *all clear* was given, the engines were restarted and the *Queen Mary* continued majestically on her way.

Submarines definitely were in the vicinity. On one occasion Bob saw an explosion and fire north on the horizon. An Allied ship—probably a tanker sailing as part of a convoy—and some or all of her crew was heading for the bottom of the very deep and cold Atlantic Ocean.

When not monitoring the enlisted men's bathtub, another of Bob's duties was to stand guard on the stern of the ship. Sailors bragged that the *Queen Mary* was so stable that you could put a glass of water on the rail and not spill a drop. They lied. The *Queen Mary* had a pronounced motion, accenting the rise and fall of its bow and stern.

There was nothing to guard against back at his post in a deserted passageway in the stern, but Bob did succumb to seasickness. Approximately 15,000 other men had the same affliction. The good news was that the chow lines got shorter. The bad news was that new lines formed for a spot at the ship's rail. It was a miserable two or three days before they finally made a landfall in Scotland in early March 1944.

Many naval officers breathed a sigh of relief, because ships that had outrun the German U-boats had been torpedoed close to shore by German E-boats. The E-boat was a fast-attack craft (German: *Schnellboot*, or *S-Boot*, meaning *fast boat*). It was part of the *Kriegsmarine* during World War II and was able to cruise at forty or fifty knots. Its wooden hull meant it could cross magnetic minefields unharmed. It is commonly believed that the British used the term *E* for *Enemy*, hence the use of the name *E-boat* instead of *S-boat*.

There had not been any briefing on the customs of the British— with the exception of learning to eat food similar to what British civilians and military personnel ate—so the men were landing in an area where living and social habits were unknown to them. A priest on board had offered some advice, but the men decided that as a priest he had a limited view of how to behave, so his advice was taken lightly or not at all. However, the men had been warned by high-ranking officers about the penalties for misbehavior and advised that they were going into a friendly country. The citizens were not the enemy, so the Americans had better behave themselves *or else* …

As usual in the armed forces, the sentence was never completed, and the *or else* was never defined. Thoughts about the punishment could be worse than the punishment itself.

Americans arrived by the tens of thousands—young men in olive drab continued to pour into Britain. In the first three months of 1944 the number of troops and flyers had doubled, to 1.5 million. In fact, of the eighty-nine divisions that comprised the United States Army, twenty divisions now could be found in the United Kingdom, with thirty-seven more either en route or earmarked for the European theater of war. They arrived through Liverpool, Swansea, Cardiff, Belfast, Avonmouth, Newport, and Glasgow, but most came into Glasgow and adjacent Greenock, more than 100,000 in April alone, 15,000 at a time on the two *Queens—Elizabeth* and *Mary*—each of which could accommodate and transport an entire division of men and their equipment.

Since the *Queen Mary* was too large to maneuver into a dockside position in the Port of Glasgow, the men disembarked using the typical navy netting-style rope ladder—not the most comfortable way to disembark from a ship of any size, but effective nevertheless. For safety reasons, each man was secured by a rope tied to the deck rail. Falling into the water next to the large ship was not an option at this or any stage of the trip. At the bottom of the rope ladder, the men transferred to a smaller craft that took them to the shore. Everything was neat, clean, and orderly and was a marked contrast to the junkyards and billboards that visitors could (and still can) see when approaching many American communities.

Once the water transport arrived at dockside and the men disembarked, each man had his name checked from a clipboard. And each soldier wore appropriate head gear and a field jacket and carried a large celluloid button that was color-coded according to the section of the ship to which the man had been assigned for the trans-Atlantic voyage. Each man also carried four blankets to save cargo space. On the occasion of Bob's arrival, a brass band and Highland pipers greeted them on the dock. Scottish children raised their arms in a V for Victory sign. Spirits were high.

Bob and his colleagues were in the Port of Glasgow for only a short time—three days of quarantine to check for any disease that was not welcome in the British Isles. Once cleared of any infectious diseases, the men were moved quickly to a rail terminal, where they boarded a train in orderly fashion using a typical army-style two-by-two arrangement to be taken to 1,200 military camps and 133 military airfields across Britain. Bob and his fellow airmen were told that they would be traveling to an airfield in southern England. The men had heard of the bombing of the area by German aircraft, and to a man, they agreed—the fireworks were about to begin.

As the train pulled out of the station, they were able to observe the obvious and colorful posters that proved to be ever-present at every station through which the train passed. Under unprecedented pressure, the British public had been called upon to show great stoicism and were forced to accept stringent measures to survive, such as rationing and blackouts. To ensure that the people at home did indeed survive, the British government mounted a determined propaganda campaign to maintain the spirit and well-being of the people and to impress upon them austere but vital policies. The slogans that characterized these propaganda campaigns, such as "Your Talk May Kill Your Comrades," "Take Your Gas Mask Everywhere," "Be Like Dad—Keep Mum" (*Mum* is still means mother in Britain, and it also means silent), and "Careless Talk Costs Lives." There were also posters encouraging women to enlist or work in factories: Serve in the WAAF with the Men Who Fly; Women's Royal Naval Service: Join the WRENS; and Women of Britain, Come into the Factories. The posters also demonstrated that the propaganda was aggressive or artistically conservative to engage a wide audience, but that subtle humor and design was just as persuasive and popular. As the train passed through the various stations, the posters passed a message to the men: They were now in a war zone.

Bob read the message on the posters and knew he had truly become a wartime pilot. He would now find out if all of the hours of flight training (dutifully recorded in his "Pilot's Flight Log Book," which is still in his possession as part of the Milliken family archives) were to be of any help.

He hoped so!

***

As the train from Glasgow wended its way southward, through the green field and soil-rich pastureland as well as large towns such as Carlisle, Manchester, Birmingham, and Southampton before finally turning west to Warmwell, the men—as if to remove the thoughts of war and death—had one thought for the immediate future: to see more of the English countryside!

Bob realized he was in the war when, on March 12, 1944 (four months and nine days after his graduation from pilot training on November 3, 1943), he saw the base—Warmwell—that was to be his home for an indeterminate time. The area was peaceful, as is often the case in the English countryside, where well-tended gardens were the order of the day and the war seemed to be in another time and another place. There were many such bases located throughout the length and breadth of the eastern and southern counties of England. War planes of various types—bombers and fighters—were taking off around the clock. Enemy-occupied France and the rest of Europe, later dubbed Fortress Europe, was approximately twenty-one miles across the English Channel at the nearest points. Heavily fortified Germany was just beyond the western coastal countries. Those would be their battlefields where Bob would join the war in the early weeks after his arrival in England.

Warmwell, located some three miles inland from the south coast that overlooked the English Channel and four to five miles east-southeast of the town of Dorchester in the county of Dorset, reflected that serenity and gentle terrain so typical of southwest England. The rolling hills surrounding the base were heavily grass-covered, as were the entire landing and dispersal areas.

In spite of British Prime Minister Neville Chamberlain's attempt to bring "peace in our time" by attempting to negotiate with Germany, Warmwell (like many other preparations) had been built in 1937. It was originally called RAF Woodsford. The airfield was renamed RAF Warmwell on July 1, 1938, to avoid confusion with Woodford, near the city of Manchester. It was a grass field amongst the low rolling hills and stands of woods typical of southwest England. RAF Warmwell was also approximately eight miles from Nazi-held France.

RAF Warmwell had been allocated for use by the Royal Air Force (RAF) to American fighter units in August 1942 but was not taken up at that time, and RAF units continued in residence. United States Army Air Force (USAAF) Spitfire and Republic P-47 Thunderbolt squadrons occasionally made use of the airfield as a forward or transit base. While under USAAF control, Warmwell was known as Station USAAF Moreton, although a squadron of RAF Typhoon fighter aircraft remained stationed at Warmwell. For security reasons the base became known as USAAF Station AAF-454, then by its station ID, XW, rather than its location.

As did many fighter-command airfields in England, the Warmwell air base used a grass field—nothing fancy—just well-trimmed grass for the fighter aircraft to take off and land without incident. The runway ran parallel to the coast so local buildings would not be in danger of being damaged by aircraft in trouble during takeoff or landing. There were sufficient aircraft-related incidents over occupied Europe without having incidents at the home base!

***

In spite of the apparent serenity of the idyllic rural life at the time of the arrival of Bob and his colleagues, there was copious evidence that the war was not too far away, even close by. Barbed wire and anti-aircraft guns ringed the base, the guns manned 24–7, and several burned-out buildings gave Bob and his colleagues their first face-to-face observation of the realities of war, with more to follow as the months passed.

The base also showed quite clearly the results of once having been heavily bombed, and the naked chimneys and unused building foundations served as sobering reminders that the enemy was little more than a stone's throw over the English Channel, which acted as a throat to the North Sea (known as the *German Ocean* until about the time of World War I). The RAF Typhoon squadron was on constant alert, as was an air-sea rescue unit, both of which were in frequent contact with the Germans and their victims.

Bob and his colleagues quickly settled into their new quarters and enjoyed the opportunity to get cleaned up, get a change of clothing after the long journey from New York, and with little else to do that first day, set about getting to know each other and taking stock of their situation. The men were allowed to write home to let their families know that they were well, without giving away anything about their location. Anything else and the censor would cut out or black out the offending lines of information.

But it was not the war that caused the most discomfort for the men. Most of the squadron members were from the warm and dry areas of the United States—none more so than Bob, from the dry, dusty, windswept High Plains of Wyoming. And here they were, thrown into a base in southern England, which is spectacularly green and lush. But this occurred at a price. The air was humid and the whole area was wet from frequent rainstorms, low clouds, fog, and a climate colder than most of the men were used to. More often than not, the sun seemed afraid to make an appearance! And Bob and his fellow airmen also had to acclimatize themselves to the vastly different British currency that was based on the duodecimal system, which uses a base of twelve, rather than the decimal system, which uses a base of ten. Adding to this confusion were the changes in diet and water, so it was not surprising that many of the officers and enlisted men of the squadron succumbed to any number of colds and sore throats as well as other internal problems, which (fortunately) soon passed.

The pilots flying the fighters and the bombers were young and confident in their skills but apprehensive about each mission. As is often the case in war, many never returned. Some died in the air. Others were killed in disabled and burning aircraft that crashed into European cities and countryside. Others were captured, subjected to Gestapo torture and questioning, then were either murdered or languished for years in prisoner-of-war stockades. Some parachuted from stricken aircraft and, managing by luck or good judgment to evade capture on the ground, eventually found their way back to England to fly and fight again.

***

Since the end of World War II, RAF Warmwell has been mostly consumed by a gravel extraction operation, although two Bellman Hangars are still in use for fertilizer storage. The control tower has been converted into a dwelling. Many would pass it by without knowing of its former history. Another airfield building has been in use for many years as the village hall. RAF Warmwell was formerly known as Woodford. The name was changed during the war because there were several other military airfields with similar-sounding names. A memorial to RAF Warmwell is situated on the edge of the Crossways residential estate, which was originally part of the airfield. Finally, as a tribute to the men who fought and died from Warmwell, a number of the roads around the housing estate have been named after the aircraft and pilots that were stationed at the airfield.

***

The young American flyers who arrived at Warmwell were first examined for any form of disease (unspecified but subject to the imagination) and were kept on base for at least three days, after which they quickly made new friends, much to the displeasure of some of their British comrades in arms.

Generally, the British welcomed the young Americans, but whenever they went into a pub (a public house where beer is sold and consumed), some attendee of the evening festivities might be heard to mutter knowingly: "There are only three things wrong with the Yanks: they're overpaid, oversexed, and over here."

The source of this saying is unknown, but it was used frequently in reference to the American military during the war and has managed to survive with gusto since World War II. The American military was paid at a much better rate than their European allies and they were also *over here*—in England. The other category of the expression has not been fully proven. And the Americans had money to spend on whatever took their fancy. The typical American staff sergeant was paid approximately $96 per month at the then current rate of exchange, which matched the monthly pay of a British captain and was almost double the pay of an equivalent English sergeant. The ruse used by the US military establishment of paying the men twice per month did not hide the large differential in the pay scales!

Shortly after their arrival, the flyers learned about intricacies of mail censorship. Mail censorship is the inspection or examination of mail and can include opening, reading, and total or selective obliteration of letters and their contents, as well as of postcards, parcels, and other postal packets.

Mail being sent to the United States and other countries of the Allies was read before being allowed to make its way to its recipients—including wives, parents, and girlfriends. As an officer (second lieutenant), Bob read and censored the mail written by the enlisted men. But he was sufficiently low in the military pecking order that as a junior officer his mail was read and censored by senior officers.

The new arrivals who had not heard the golden rule would hear of it. It was the *bottle-to-throttle* rule and the sleep rule.

In their wisdom, and knowing that soldiers and airmen of all ranks are likely to consume alcoholic beverages on occasion, the upper brass had decided (even ordered) that there would be no drinking within twelve hours of a mission. Since most missions were decided on an *as-needed* basis and not announced until shortly before the commencement of the mission, this meant virtually no drinking on base. Any man found guilty of ignoring this rule would be subject to a severe reprimand or even worse. The word *worse* was never fully defined but left open to the imagination and could include a reduction in rank or imprisonment or both, which in turn could lead to a dishonorable discharge at the end of the war.

The *sleep rule* was much simpler and very much to the point. *Sleep when you can. If there is a mission you will be needed immediately and you must be awake and alert!* There were no obvious penalties for appearing sleepy at the start of a mission. The pilots knew that being drowsy slowed the reflexes and could lead to death at the hands of a German pilot.

But the sleep rule was not an all-day every-day situation, and in true military style, there always seemed to be duties or exercises to perform during the non-flying hours.

As if denial of alcohol on base was not bad enough, the men had to simulate what it would be like to go *into the drink* (a phrase commonly used for ditching an aircraft into the sea). Many disabled aircraft were forced to crash land (*ditch*) into a body of water, particularly the English Channel or North Sea. Parachuting from a stricken aircraft and landing in the sea was also covered by this expression.

To simulate exiting an airplane after ditching at sea, the men were loaded into a Link trainer-like contraption and dumped into a swimming pool. This included a fully-clothed flyer being dropped into the pool, after which he had to clamber aboard a *life raft* (rubber dingy).

The first challenge was to get out of the simulator, which was not easy, especially when the simulator was turned upside down in the pool. Once free from the simulator, there was no cause to rejoice, as the second challenge loomed ahead. Getting into the raft while struggling with wet clothes and heavy equipment was also difficult, but the alternative of floundering in the water with the possibility of drowning was the less acceptable of the two options. Bob passed the tests, but he was always uneasy flying over the channel, and he was in no hurry to test his water-survival skills in a real-life scenario.

Bob's next move, for a short time, was to the city of Hull, in the county of Yorkshire, situated on the North Sea coast near to the town of Grimsby—a seaport on the Humber Estuary in the County of Lincolnshire—where he resumed training and practice missions. According to legend, Grimsby was first founded in the ninth century by a man named Grim, supposedly a Danish fisherman. But Grim was an alternate name for Odin, the leader of the Viking gods, so it's more likely that the town was named by Viking raiders who plied their trade on the east coast of England at that time and decided to settle there.

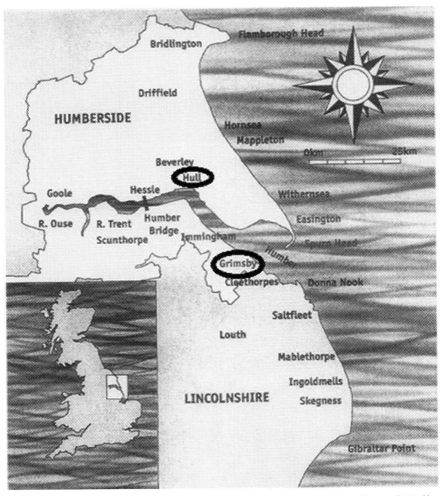

The East Coast of England Showing the Location of Grimsby and Hull

***

On one occasion, a truck with a driver was supplied to shuttle Bob and several of his colleagues to spend some leave time in nearby Grimsby. Armed with their .45-caliber pistols (live ammunition was issued all of the time, not just when it was needed—England was still in a state of readiness for a possible invasion) and in a state of euphoria where they were feeling no pain, they were returning from the alcohol-consuming outing when the air raid warning sounded. There was a bomb shelter near the barracks, but it was simple and primitively built and most unlikely to survive a nearby hit let alone a direct hit.

Instead of going into the shelter and taking their slim chances should a bomb land nearby, they got caught up in the excitement of being under fire for the first time, of seeing German planes spotlighted in the sky by the cone of searchlights, and of hearing and seeing anti-aircraft fire lighting up the night. When bombs began dropping in the area, Bob and his colleagues decided to add to the defense of the realm by firing their pistols at the German invaders. They were not credited with any *kills*, and no one on the ground was injured. Moreover, thanks to the prior training that they had received with the Colt 45 M1911-A1—which was the standard issue sidearm of Army Air Corps officer—no one on the ground was injured, but during the adrenaline-pumping incidents of combat, mistakes were made, and flyers accidently shot at each other as well as at civilians.

Originally manufactured for use in World War I, the gun (designed by John Moses Browning) featured the large, hard-hitting .45-caliber round and seven-shot magazine. This semi-automatic pistol operated via the recoil to force the top slide backward to eject the spent casing and chamber the next round. Browning also designed the Browning Automatic Rifle (BAR) as well as the .30- and .50-caliber machine guns used in the field, on vehicles and tanks, as well as on fighter and bomber aircraft. In addition to the Colt 45, Bob and his colleagues also received training with the water-cooled machine gun and the Springfield rifle.

Some days later, Bob left Hull and went to London by rail, then on to Warmwell. On April 23, 1944, as if to reaffirm what they had been told in Ontario, California, he was officially assigned to the 429th Fighter Squadron, nicknamed The Retail Gang because the word *retail* was given to the squadron as a code name to be used in radio transmissions.

The members of the 428th, 429th, and 430th Fighter Squadrons, which made up the 474th Fighter Group, were billeted separately, so other than fighting together, there would be little chance to get to know the members of the other squadrons. When the pilots of the three squadrons flew at group strength, there were thirty-six aircraft—typically eighteen from each squadron—flying as a team. Although each squadron had twenty or more aircraft and twenty to twenty-five pilots, making a total of sixty to seventy-five pilots in the group, there were always pilots who needed a break or aircraft that needed attention before being sent out on more missions.

***

At the end of the war, group casualties amounted to eighty-seven pilots killed in action. This number did not include pilots who had been wounded in action or pilots who were captured and became prisoners of war.

***

Finally, Bob had found his home within the air command structure, and he felt that he was getting somewhere rather than remaining (unofficially or officially) unassigned. He was joined in the squadron by his friend Lenton F. Kirkland (aka Kirk, later shot down during the Battle of the Bulge); Milton C. Merkle, who would be killed a few days later; William J. Patterson, who was later shot down but returned to fly again; and John W. O'Neil, who managed to survive and who was known to admit that he had been subject to less sensational experiences.

Kirk and Bob bonded immediately, sharing stories of home and embarking upon new adventures together. Their country-boy early lives and experiences gave them common views and outlooks and formed the basis for many an interesting conversation. And thereby hangs a tale.

Shortly after they had arrived at Warmwell, a small English aircraft was assigned to Major Glass, the squadron leader. It was a two-seater, a *tail-dragger*—aviation jargon for an aircraft with a conventional undercarriage, although some military personal prefer to use the term in reference to an aircraft with a tail-skid instead of a tail-wheel. In addition, this aircraft had controls unlike any Bob had ever encountered. Kirk and Bob were assigned to fly a three-leg cross-country journey in the plane, taking turns at piloting the aircraft. They made the major decision by the centuries-old tried-and-true method of decision-making—Bob tossed a coin, he won, and took over the aircraft for the first leg of the journey.

They were supposed to land at two bases, then return to Warmwell. Bob made the first landing and made a reasonably by-the-book comfortable landing, or at least as comfortable as the landing could be in such an aircraft. Kirk, who had lost the coin toss, dutifully took over for the second leg of the trip. The destination was a bomber base. On the approach to the landing, the plane was too high, and the aircraft had to be put down more quickly than desirable. Being heavier than air, the plane dropped like a stone, hit the ground hard, and blew a tire, leaving Bob and Kirk stranded at the base with a damaged airplane and no good excuse or reason for how the aircraft got into such a condition.

The base crew towed the plane back to the flight line, and the search for a new tire commenced, but without any luck. Bob and Kirk had to spend the night at the bomber base. With still no sign of the possibility of a replacement tire being available the next day, they decided they should return to Warmwell and report for duty, whatever the consequences may be. They were lucky enough to be able to hitch a ride to Warmwell on a Douglas C-47 Skytrain (USAAC designation) or Douglas Dakota (RAF designation), a military transport aircraft developed from the Douglas DC-3 airliner that was used extensively by the Allies during World War II. It bore the unofficial nickname *Gooney Bird* (a common name for the albatross).

The Douglas DC-3 Sleeper Transport first flew on December 17, 1935. The military version was designated by the United States Army Air Force as the C-47 Skytrain, but it was more widely known by its unofficial name. The C-47 was the mainstay of Allied troop carrier and transport operations during World War II. The DC-3 also became the mainstay of several commercial airlines well into the 1950s and, in some cases, the 1960s.

On arrival at Warmwell, Bob and Kirk were met by Major Glass. Not wishing to waste any time and knowing that the ire of the major would fall onto their shoulders, they quickly related their tale of woe. Major Glass had lost his little toy and did not know when or even if the aircraft was going to be returned to him in any form of working order. After relating their story, Kirkland and Bob stood stiffly at attention in front of his desk. They knew that the major was about to "blow his top" (USAAC terminology) or "hit the roof" (RAF terminology).

"You left your parachutes in that plane," he thundered, with a pregnant pause to allow his anger to sink into their brains. "Now you're going back to that base to get them, and you had better not come back without them!"

Again, the decision was made by the tried-and-true method of decision-making. Bob tossed a coin and he lost, which meant that he was to return to the bomber base to retrieve their parachutes. Fortunately, he located a Jeep and a driver —who welcomed a day off-base—and plotted a course back to the bomber base. The driver and Bob left Warmwell in the open Jeep, circled the north part of London, found their way to the bomber base, (most importantly) had a meal break, collected the parachutes, and made it back to Warmwell in good time. Bob didn't want the major to suspect that the journey had been a welcome outing. Whether or not the major's aircraft was ever returned to Warmwell and the major is lost in the fog of history.

***

Passes for leave (permission to go off base—typically a weekend pass for three days) were issued when the occasion allowed it and the number of missions a flyer had logged dictated that he needed a break. For example, after the fiftieth mission, a flyer might get a ten-day recreation and relaxation pass. Many of the fifty-mission pilots were in a condition known as *flak-happy*, which could impair judgment and lead to endangerment of the life of the pilot.

The passes and the rail service, which still managed to run efficiently despite the continued bombing by German aircraft, gave the flyers the chance to visit London. Bob and Kirk went on leave to London (only once) and to Bournemouth (on several occasions). Bournemouth, a resort town close to the base, had a pavilion where they held tea dances with young ladies present—every soldier and airman's dream.

Later on, as Bob's involvement in the war became a reality, passes would be issued to airmen only after an undefined number of missions, the number being subject to change and dependent upon the ongoing battle actions.

With very few exceptions, the British people—civilians and military alike, in spite of the comments about the Yanks being "over here"—were glad to have the *colonials* on their side. Everyone always had a good word for the Americans, even the railroad gatekeeper posted at a crossing near to the fighter base. Whenever a train loaded with supplies or troops was approaching, the gatekeeper would emerge from his clean, white-painted shack, lower the bar across the tracks, and stand proudly, guarding the crossing until the train was gone and the roadway was safe once more. No one was going to cross the railroad line with a train coming on his watch!

***

Bob was assigned to fly his first combat mission from Warmwell on April 30, 1944. The war would last for another year plus eight days. He and three of his colleagues—Patterson, Smith, and Parker—were designated to fly in a group fighter sweep-over around the area of Rouen, Le Mans, and Tours. Shortly after takeoff, Bob discovered a problem with his P-38 and elected to abort his mission. He had been taught in training to be safe rather than sorry, so he opted for safety, but the aborted mission was still entered into his record, and he felt it left a black mark against his name for the remainder of the war.

On May 2, Bob flew his second mission, on which he would take part in a flight over Belgium in what was called a *fighter sweep*—an offensive mission by fighter aircraft to seek out and destroy enemy aircraft or targets of opportunity in an allotted area of operations. His third mission was scheduled for May 5, but that one was scrubbed (cancelled) at the last minute, and the only flying he did that day was at the Officers' Club dance, where a new game was invented. The game involved each airman chopping off with scissors as many neckties of his colleagues as possible before someone got his necktie. According to Bob's memories, it was a festive affair, but he does not recall who was declared the winner or even if a winner was declared.

On May 7 at 8:00 a.m., the squadron was assigned to escort B-26 Marauder bombers headed for targets in occupied France. Bob was flying wingman for one of his colleagues, Lieutenant Paul Munger.

The wingman position was always off the right wing and slightly behind the flight leader's aircraft and was called the *number two man*. They were flying at assigned altitudes, weaving back and forth to keep pace with the slower B-26 bombers that they were escorting. It was a beautiful day, a blue-sky day with the occasional fleecy cloud hanging as if waiting for something, and the bombers were just skimming the top layer of the clouds.

As they were flying in a protective cover over the bombers, Bob looked down and saw tracer bullets hitting the tail of one of the B-26 aircraft. The realization hit him that the tail gunner had been killed in the fusillade. The tracer bullets continued to hit the B-26, which peeled off to the left, smoke streaming from an engine. The plane was stricken beyond help and spiraling to the ground. Bob saw two parachutes open as two crew members—from a crew of seven—bailed out of the falling aircraft. This was his first sighting of a causality of the air war. He learned later that the two parachutists were captured and spent the remainder of the war in a prisoner of war camp. As the bomber continued to fall, Bob—ever watchful—looked around and caught a glimpse of a German fighter aircraft disappearing into the clouds.

"Bandits hitting the bombers!" he radioed to his colleagues.

Other pilots sighted more fighters and sounded similar warnings. The group leader, Colonel Wasem, ordered Bob's P-38 flight to fly above the bombers and give them give them *top cover*, which meant they were to fly above the bombers to protect them from German fighters coming in from higher altitude and fly down at enemy fighters coming in from lower altitudes. Then he took the other P-38 flights down to attack. They went into a *Lufbery circle*, a World War I tactic that was named after Gervais Lufbery.

***

Gervais Raoul Lufbery (March 14, 1885—May 19, 1918), born of an American father and a French mother, was a fighter pilot and flying ace in World War I. He served in the French Air Service, and later the United States Army Air Service in World War I. He is sometimes listed as a French ace and sometimes as an American ace. Sixteen of his seventeen combat victories came while flying in French units. Lufbery was killed on May 19, 1918, during an attempt to intercept a German reconnaissance aircraft when the German gunner's fire hit the Nieuport 28 biplane (a French fighter aircraft) that Lufbery was piloting.

The Lufbery circle was a purely defensive tactic that could be mounted only by flights of aircraft working together. It involved forming a horizontal circle in the air when attacked. Theoretically, each plane would protect the plane in front. It was thought that an attacking fighter would be unable to attack any member of the formation without coming under fire himself. However, the tactic was intended for slower, less capable aircraft when attacked by enemy fighters. Lufbery circles were most often used by bombers, although in some instances it was also used by obsolescent fighter aircraft against more advanced fighter types as a way of avoiding attack. Bomber formations using Lufbery often had the benefit of dorsal gunners that further defended against attack.

The tactic did not work at all well in World War II. Good visibility didn't help in this case—the German fighter planes swept in and quickly shot down three P-38 fighter aircraft.

***

Milton Merkle, whom Bob had first met during training at Williams Field, was his first colleague to be killed in action. He was flying as wingman for Colonel Wasem, monitoring the bomber frequency and relaying messages from the bombers to the colonel. Merkle didn't have any chance to react to what was happening around him. His P-38 was shot down in flames by German fighters.

Merkle and Bob were bunkmates. When they first checked into the barracks, they flipped a coin to determine who went to the top bunk and who got the bottom bunk. Merkle lost and was stuck with the top bunk. Now the bunk above held only memories of a friendship that ended so early. Bob had the unenviable task of examining Merkle's footlocker and collecting any items that could be sent to his (Merkle's) wife. But there were also other casualties that day.

The two other pilots who did not return that day had also lived in the same barracks room as Bob. One of them was killed, but the other man parachuted over the Alps, successfully evaded capture, and got back to Allied lines. He survived the war and continued to a full career in the military, making the transition to the Air Force when the Army Air Corps evolved and morphed into the United States Air Force in 1947.

Bob believes that his flight was attacked by one of the best squadrons in the Luftwaffe (German Air Force), which the Allied flyers had given the name the *Abbeville Boys*. (Their official name was Jagdgeschwader 26 or JG 26, also called Fighter Wing 26, and the *Schlageter Wing*.) They were equipped with the most modern Messerschmitt or Focke-Wulf fighter aircraft and flew out of the airfield at Abbeville, located near the Somme River in northern France.

The unit got the name as part of its involvement in the reoccupation of the Rhineland on March 7, 1936, in violation of the Treaty of Versailles and the Locarno Pact. The locals adopted the unit, and suggested that it be renamed after a local nationalist hero, Albert Leo Schlageter. Leo had been shot by the French in 1923 for attempting to destroy railroad tracks taking coal from the Rhineland back to France as part of the war reparations imposed on Germany in the Treaty of Versailles. The political policies of France did not allow any coal to be sold in Germany even if they wanted to pay for it. Germany was short of coal during this time. As a result, many German people had no coal to warm their homes. This local German was protesting this fact. That's why a Gothic *S* on a white shield was put onto the left cowl of all unit aircraft.

At one time, Adolph Galland (a World War II German fighter ace) flew with the Abbeville Boys. He was a Luftwaffe general and flying ace who served throughout World War II in Europe. He flew 705 combat missions, and on four occasions he survived being shot down. He was credited with 104 aerial victories, all of them against the Western Allies. His trademark was a Mickey Mouse cartoon painted on the side of his FW-190. He commanded the German fighter forces and was demoted after disagreeing with Adolph Hitler. Most persons who disagreed with Hitler had an appointment with a firing squad shortly thereafter, but Galland still survived the war.

During the May 7 battle, one of Bob's squadron colleagues scored hits on a German fighter. However, since no one saw that plane go down or could confirm the destruction of the enemy aircraft, the P-38 pilot was credited with only a probable kill. The P-38 pilot was later killed, on September 12, 1944.

The young pilots came out of the May 7 fight with the realization that they had learned how to fly. But now came the real lesson—they were learning how to fight. In fact, with relatively few hours in the cockpit of the P-38, Bob was still learning how to master the aircraft.

The size of the P-38 did not give true account of its maneuverability, and the twin engines required considerable attention. But Bob knew that he would make the best of the situation. He was doing what he always wanted to do. He was a fighter pilot, and before going into combat, he would always say one prayer that sustained him throughout the war: "I do not want to die, but if I must die, I want to die like a man."

Flying in combat was—in modern parlance—a *rush* that was like none other. He was engaging in combat enemy aircraft that were flown by men who may have been at least equal to his abilities. He executed high-speed maneuvers through the air, firing short bursts at the enemy, and constantly stretching and almost swiveling his neck to make sure no one was behind him with intent to do him harm.

On the downside, he had to learn to live with the loss of colleagues. Perhaps death that had entered his life during his pre-teen and teen years allowed him to accept the death of friends. Of the five young pilots who shipped overseas together (including Bob), two were killed in action (Merkle and Kirkland), and one (Patterson) was badly burned when he was shot down in a dogfight. Like all other pilots,

Bob learned to accept the losses of war. He still remembers that he never got used to the losses of his comrades, but he learned to handle the emotion that went with each loss. It was not easy.

Ultimately Bob had several contacts with German planes and engaged in four dogfights. Many of his colleagues never saw an enemy plane or fired their weapons in combat. Bob learned that the German pilots were much like the Americans, and most of the Germans were not dedicated Nazis. First and foremost, the non-Nazis were Luftwaffe pilots, and they were well-trained. Many Luftwaffe pilots had also received real-life training in the Spanish Civil War (1936–39), flew in Poland and France (1939–40), and honed their skills during the Battle of Britain (1940). Unlike many American pilots who were assigned a specific tour of duty, whether as number of missions flown or time spent on active duty, Luftwaffe pilots (like their RAF counterparts) flew until they were killed, captured, or so crippled they couldn't get into the cockpit. There was another cause of the death of pilots. Those with marginal skills, whatever the insignia on their uniforms, would not and did not survive.

By the time the United States entered the war, the Germans pilots were some of the best that Germany and the Luftwaffe could offer. They were battle-tested and had numerous combat kills recorded on the sides of their planes. As the young American pilots sharpened their flying skills, the superior numbers of the Americans and their newly developed fighter aircraft allowed them to outmaneuver and outshoot the enemy. German fighter aces were shot down, and their less skilled replacements suffered the same fate. But in May 1944, the war still had a long way to go before it would be over. Allied pilots were being killed or wounded and need to be replaced.

American replacements pilots were sent to the various units as they were needed. These were young men who had never seen the dangers of an air battle, and they replaced the more experienced squadron pilots who had failed to return from missions. The new recruits would soon learn that training flying and combat flying were two different things. They would get their baptism of fire in good time.

After surviving several combat missions, Bob and his fellow pilots felt much older than their new comrades in arms. They had become battle-scarred veterans.

***

At that time, a flyer in the United States Army Air Corps received $240.20 per month. Of this total, base pay and longevity pay was $150.00 per month. Flight pay was $75.00 per month, and there was a subsistence allowance of $21.70 per month for a grand total of $246.70, from which $6.50 was subtracted for insurance. This was the contribution to the program that gave each of the airmen life insurance coverage in the amount of $10,000. In addition, Bob had life insurance through the Miner's Union. Through Father Robert's continued payments for membership in the union and Bob's paid-up membership for his summer work at the mine, there was an additional $10,000 life insurance policy.

Pay varied in other branches of the United States military. A private in the infantry might receive $50.00 per month base pay plus a $50.00 bonus each month for hazardous duty and an additional $10.00 per month for being in a combat zone. Married men might have received additional pay on top of this amount.

Anyone in the military could be fined for misbehavior, such as failure to perform. The amounts varied, but a common punishment could be reduction in rank, which, of course, carried with it a reduction in pay.

But one item was particularly disturbing to Bob and his comrades, and it was not related to pay. They heard that the United Mine Workers Union had called for a strike (a cessation of work by the members of the Union). The pilots felt that whatever the grievances voiced by the members of the union were, the United States was at war, and it was not the time for a strike by any workers while young American men and women were fighting and dying in the European and Pacific theaters of war.

Chapter 6: Start of Missions

Identifying both friendly and enemy aircraft in the heat of battle is a necessary part of pilot training. It's equally important for the pilots to recognize friendly aircraft—being shot down by an enemy is disastrous enough, but being shot down by a friendly aircraft is to be deplored. To some observers, being shot down by friendly fire is a part of war and therefore acceptable collateral damage. The pilot on the receiving end of the friendly fire would have a different opinion! The pilots honed their aircraft identification skills in a small building at the Warmwell base.

Bob paid particular attention to this exercise because being able to recognize of enemy aircraft could mean the difference between life and death. To this end, he studied the aircraft silhouettes and information about each type of aircraft that covered the main walls of the building. He quickly learned to identify planes from the top, side, and head-on views, and in split seconds could distinguish which were friendly and which were enemy aircraft and not so friendly.

Bob became an expert at this form of recognition, and he remains convinced that it saved his life many times over.

The room was set up so the flyers could see how the gun sights would look during various angles of attack. While his colleagues were sitting outside trying to catch whatever sun filtered through the cloudy English skies, Bob spent hours studying silhouettes, memorizing identification data, practicing the gun sight configurations, and calculating how much to lead the target during various angles of attack. The hours he spent in study and observation paid off in combat. He always knew what he was shooting at, he always fired very short bursts, he was confident his bullets would go where he intended, and he rarely missed.

Bob also spent considerable time in another Warmwell building, the Officers' Club, which was not much in any sense or interpretation of the name—an open room with a billiard table and some castoff chairs. The snack menu was limited—tea, toast, and marmalade. But it was a place where the pilots could get away from the war for a while and build enduring friendships. Bob still has a taste for Scottish-style marmalade, especially the kind with the strong taste containing thickly cut pieces of orange peel.

Often pilots of the Royal Air Force (RAF) joined the Americans at the Officers' Club. They were avid singers, and the Americans were quick to join in and did not hesitate to sing ditties about the king and queen—some pretty off-color. But if any of the Americans made adverse comments about the royal family, more than singing would break out.

As the days passed and other pilots started to pay more attention to the identification of enemy aircraft, not forgetting it was just as important to identify friendly aircraft. The more their recognition skills improved and study hours increased, the more confident the young flyers felt in their individual abilities—at least in their ability to recognize enemy aircraft. All of this time, as he studied the silhouettes of the German aircraft, Bob could remember Father Robert's words when they were hunting pheasant and other game birds:

"Shoot when you are certain and shoot accurately, with the correct lead of the bird. The shot must arrive at the place where the bird will be. When the bird goes down, you must have made sure he cannot get up and escape."

***

On May 11, 1944, Bob and his squadron comrades once again flew fighter cover for a B-26 Marauder bombing raid to the Beaumont area of northern France. As with most missions, they encountered flak—the German anti-aircraft fire: *Fliegerabvehrkanone*—airplane defense cannons, or *Flugabwehrkanone*, flight defense cannons— on the outward journey and on the return journey. Fortunately, the squadron did not lose any aircraft or pilots.

Two days later, on May 13, the squadron flew a long mission lasting six hours and fifteen minutes. Bob was flying on his squadron leader's wing, and each P-38 carried belly tanks so there would be enough fuel to go the distance. When a German fighter aircraft was sighted in the distance, the squadron leader gave the order to drop their belly tanks and *bust'er*—go to full throttle.

When Bob dropped his belly tank and hit full throttle, the P-38 came to an abrupt, almost worrisome slowdown. He had failed to change the fuel feed from the belly tank to the wing tanks. By instinct, he quickly made the switch, restarted the engines, and tried to catch up with his squadron colleagues, especially the squadron leader, who no longer had a wingman and was pursuing an enemy aircraft. Once back at base, the squadron leader asked Bob what happened, and he admitted his mistake—somewhat red-faced—but other than a serious look from the squadron leader, the incident was not pursued any further. He knew that Bob would learn from his mistake and would not repeated it.

Bob flew several other missions in May, escorting bombers or conducting sweeps, with flight times lasting anywhere from minutes to several hours. He also recorded his first dive-bombing and strafing assignments and would fly many more of those in the months ahead. As an afterthought, he noticed that the scar resulting from his childhood appendectomy had not given him any trouble during the dive-bombing. In spite of the seemingly dire prediction from the military medic at the time of Bob's examination, there was no feeling of discomfort or any sign of damage to the scar from his appendectomy. Bob smiled to himself.

"So much for medics," he thought, but then he realized, "the toughest predictions to make are those about the future!"

Throughout May, the top Allied command was involved in intense planning cycles and increasing the necessary preparations for the allied invasion of Normandy. Parks and all open lands in southeast England were filled with guns, planes, tanks, trucks, and other heavy equipment. The narrow two-way roads were clogged with traffic, and to make matters worse, the roads were changed to one-way only as the equipment was moved from the parking areas to ports and harbors for dockside loading. Anyone wishing to get from the coast to an inland area would have been hard pressed to do so. Mail of any sort to and from the men was forbidden, military protocol was strictly observed, and all troops were confined to their respective bases. The men were so busy saluting the high influx of officers that there was no time for off-base activities such as sight-seeing. The realization that something big was in the air was the source of one rumor after another.

As the men were wont to say: "There were lots of guys beating their gums and imagining lots of nothings!"

On May 29, the squadron was sent out on a six-hour mission to Berlin—generally known as the *Big B*—to act as an escort to B-17 bombers. The flak got heavy as they neared the target area, and the squadron was ordered to break formation and to get out of the way as the bombers plunged ahead through the flak to make their drops. German fighter aircraft were spotted at the edges of the bomber formation like wolves watching a herd of deer or elk as if waiting to pounce for the kill, but the FW-190 fighters beat a hasty retreat when the P-38s flew at them with the purpose of engagement.

Minutes later, as the B-17 formation started into a turn, Bob, sensing something not quite right, looked up and saw that he was directly underneath a B-17 with the bomb bay doors open. Instantly he knew that the bombs were only moments away from being dropped. Having no wish to be physically included in the drop, he quickly found other air space, realizing that being under a B-17 when the bombs start falling is not conducive to continuation of his good health.

To Bob and his comrades, the change in tactics made the promise of an imminent invasion of Europe become even more evident. The squadron assignments changed from being escorts to bomber groups to bombing bridges, railroad marshaling yards, and enemy lines of communication and supply. On June 2, 1944, every available plane in the 474th Fighter Group was sent on a dive-bombing mission in France. The target was a bridge that provided a transport route over the river for enemy vehicles taking men and supplies to the front line. The bridge was destroyed.

The squadron received word at 4:40 p.m. (1640 hours in military jargon) on June 5, when the flyers were called to a briefing at the Officers' Club. Military police standing guard at the doors made sure no unauthorized personnel got in. Military police never smiled, but something about their demeanor made Bob and his comrades curious but wary of the consequences of the meeting.

When all of the officers were assembled, the briefing commenced, as always, on a solemn note. The flyers were curious and concerned. And then the news was announced that they were to be a part of the most significant and the most thoroughly planned mission of the war. D-Day and the invasion of Fortress Europe was about to begin. The term *Fortress Europe* or *Festung Europa* was being used by Nazi propaganda to refer to the plans of Adolf Hitler and the Wehrmacht to fortify the whole of occupied Europe to prevent invasion from the British Isles. Not to be deterred by the enemy propaganda machine— directed by Herr Josef Goebbels, the man who almost single-handedly developed the field of propaganda into an art form—a massive flotilla of ships and boats of all descriptions had set out from numerous points on the south coast of England and were forming up into a gigantic convoy just south of the Isle of Wight.

At the same time that the ships were leaving coastal England to convey troops to the Normandy beaches, Bob and his colleagues were sitting quietly and listening intently to the plan, as the timing and proposed route of the invasion fleet was diagramed and explained and the overall intentions and expectations of the invasion were presented. Bob and his colleagues in the 429th Squadron were assigned to patrol and cover the area of the English Channel (*la Manche*—the Sleeve— is the name that the French call the English Channel) where the fleet would cross, that is, the area between the Isle of Wight and the Seine Bay, to the east of the Cotentin Peninsula, on the coast of France.

An estimate of enemy resistance was given by Intelligence. Radio call signs and code identification to planes, ships, and ground forces were announced by Communications. A message was read from General Dwight D. Eisenhower, Supreme Commander of the Allied Forces—a message that launched the greatest invasion that history had ever known.

After the message was read, Group Chaplain Leon Milner stood and offered a prayer. It was simple, but the nineteen words that he spoke were felt in the hearts and minds of the assembled squadron—flyers and ground crew alike:

Give us strength, courage, guidance, and understanding in the days to come, and protect us and our fellow men.

***

The evening of June 5, Bob was one of the P-38 pilots assigned to give the sailors and soldiers cover and protection from enemy aircraft, which the planners were certain would make their presence known. Bob's flight patrolled the right flank of the invasion. The reason for the selection of the squadron was simple and hopefully effective. The distinctive silhouettes of the twin-boom P-38 aircraft meant that there would be less likelihood of a nervous, trigger-happy ship's gunner mistaking the P-38s for German aircraft. In addition, the aircraft had white invasion stripes painted on the undersides of the wings for further identification, but even with those precautions, a few aircraft were lost to friendly fire.

They patrolled from 7:30 to 11:00 p.m. (1930 to 2300 hours) and flew at 1,500 feet over the fleet, and all the while they maintained strict radio silence. There was one call of enemy fighters over the beach, so they made a low-level sweep in that direction, but there was no sign of any enemy aircraft. All was quiet below. The Germans still had no inkling of the presence of the invasion fleet that lay just over the horizon. The invasion still remained a secret.

When Bob and his colleagues landed back at the Warmwell air base and were getting out of their aircraft, the main invasion air armada started passing overhead. For forty-five minutes there were red (port wing) and green (starboard wing) navigation lights and all manner of Allied aircraft—bombers, fighters, transports, and gliders—stretching from horizon to horizon as far as the eye could see. The transports and gliders were carrying paratroopers and special forces soldiers, who were the spearhead of the invasion force. The men were to be dropped behind enemy lines before that main invasion force landed on the Normandy beaches to seize and hold strategic points until relieved by troops arriving from their beach landing. All through the night the steady drone of airplane engines could be heard. The base was alive with noise.

Even though they were tired, Bob and many of his comrades were too excited to sleep. An air support unit stationed on the field was equipped with several heavy cranes. These were moved up near the landing strip for use in clearing the runway of aircraft damaged in landing.

Moments later, a C-47 came in on rough engines and landed without incident. The engines did not flame or explode, so all seemed to be in order.

The Douglas C-47 Skytrain or Dakota was a military transport aircraft that was developed from the Douglas DC-3 airliner. It was used extensively by the Allies during World War II as a troop and cargo transport and remained in front line operations through the 1950s. It is a safe assumption that several of these sturdy aircraft are still in operation in some parts of the world, kept in service by parts from their disabled cousins as they rotted in some aircraft graveyard, along with bailing wire, and (that old staple) duct tape.

However, the copilot and flight engineer stepped out of the plane as the ambulance drew up alongside. They reported that the C-47 pilot was inside, dead. He was probably one of the first casualties of the invasion to be flown back to England. The aircraft had transported paratroopers to a drop zone east of the planned invasion beach, and, timing being everything, all of the men had made the jump but one. The flight engineer informed the pilot of this and the pilot decided to circle the area once more to allow the remaining paratrooper to make the jump and join his unit. While circling the drop zone, the C-47 was struck by small-arms fire—possibly rifle fire—from the enemy troops on the ground. One of the bullets entered the cockpit, killing the pilot instantly. The paratrooper had made his jump and the copilot brought the plane back to the base.

***

On Tuesday, June 6, 1944, Bob's twenty-second birthday, but known as D-Day to thousands of other military personnel who were about to invade Europe by way of Normandy, he was on alert. The mission was to provide coverage to the invasion fleet. As he sat in the cockpit of the P-38 at the end of the grass strip that was otherwise known as the runway at the Warmwell base, the engines of his P-38 already warmed up and ready for instant takeoff, he decided to write a letter to his parents. After the briefing that the flyers had the night before and the all-night drone of aircraft passing over the base on the way to France, he knew by instinct that this day was to be a historic day. This was a day that he and millions of other people would always remember, so he decided to put his thoughts into writing and to share his feelings with the two people who were closest to him—Father Robert and Mother Anna.

He fingered his Hanna High School graduation ring. It was a more recent birthday gift from his father and mother. When he was a senior in high school about to graduate and leave for the idyllic academic climate of the University of Wyoming, he couldn't afford to buy a class ring. His parents had shared his disappointment and made up for that disappointment by purchasing the ring for him after the fact. Bob still has the ring and treasures it as much as he did the day he first saw it.

Finally, the letter completed, Bob was ready to return to the war. His P-38 was one of approximately 11,000 Allied aircraft that swept over the invasion area while Allied troops made the landings. Although the war in Europe was to go on for another eleven months, the D-Day landings—named Operation Overlord—marked the beginning of the end of World War II in Europe. The landings involved almost 7,000 vessels, including landing craft and equipment barges. In terms of personnel, there were 200,000 seamen who were the crews of the 59 convoys that carried 130,000 soldiers, 2,000 tanks, and 12,000 other vehicles to the beaches of the Cotentin Peninsula. But the end of this war was still an unknown event in the future, and there was more flying and fighting on Bob's calendar.

As Bob and his colleagues swept over Omaha Beach, they had no idea of the carnage taking place on the ground. Defense was fierce from a series of German machine gun entrenchments where the dreaded MG-42 cut a swath through the landing forces. The men who went down did not know what hit them as they fell dead onto the wet sands of Omaha Beach. They had not known what to expect.

Nor did Bob and his fellow pilots know what to expect from the Luftwaffe. The pilots were supposed to fly up to five daily sorties each to disrupt any invasion, but German aircraft losses in the past five months exceeded thirteen thousand aircraft, more than half from accidents and other noncombat causes. The Luftwaffe group responsible for western France had just 319 serviceable planes facing nearly 13,000 Allied aircraft. On D-Day they would fly one sortie for every thirty-seven flown by their adversaries. After the war it was known that American planes were gray, British planes black, and Luftwaffe planes invisible.

Bob was one of the gray devils that flew over and gave cover to the invading American forces on June 6, and enemy aircraft did not challenge the squadron. The Luftwaffe remained unseen. This was a momentary relief to the squadron, but many of the pilots took it as a sign that life would not be so easy once the Luftwaffe regrouped and brought aerial combat to the Americans.

On June 7, 1944, as Allied forces attempted to get themselves organized and move inland from the beaches, Bob was on a critical mission in France to bomb the railroad line on the Cherbourg Peninsula, which ran from Flers, through Domfront and Mayenne, to Laval. Considerable rail activity had been observed on this line, which usually indicated troop movements and supplies for the front line enemy soldiers. The orders were to destroy the transport routes, harass enemy convoys, and delay supplies and reinforcements reaching the enemy.

The mission was a success. Major Glass, the wing commander, made two direct hits on the railroad tracks. Another flight claimed two, possibly three, direct hits on the tracks farther north. The bombs from the P-38 flown by Colonel Wasem, the group captain, dropped onto a railroad embankment, causing the earth to collapse onto the track, which effectively prohibited passage of any train traffic until a cleaning crew could clear the track. Another P-38 pilot scored four direct hits on the tracks and station at a junction east of Mayenne. On their return, the squadron pilots could see the fires seemingly burning out of control in the cities of Caen and Flers.

On his second mission of that day, Bob was assigned to dive-bomb a railroad bridge at Flers, a high-priority target spanning a deep channel that had a good flow of water in the river.

He returned to base safely but had no hard evidence as to whether or not his bombs hit the target. But he did line up his approach correctly, and when he pulled up to a higher altitude after making the drop, he was confident that he had scored hits.

***

Bob's confidence in his bombing abilities was confirmed five decades later when he visited Flers with his son, Greg. A group of French citizens who had witnessed the dive-bombing attack from a vantage point on the ground had seen the bombs miss the bridge but hit the railroad tracks thirty feet away from the bridge. The rail line had been destroyed, effectively delaying the Germans from moving reinforcements and equipment into the Normandy beach defensive areas. With the bridge gone, the Germans would have a difficult time crossing the river.

***

The next day, June 8, the squadron flyers left the Warmwell home base in weather that was poor to say the least to bomb and destroy a coastal artillery battery that had been shelling the invasion force on the Cherbourg Peninsula and also hitting ships of the invasion armada just off the coast. The men had been briefed beforehand that to destroy or even damage the coastal gun, they would have to place their bombs squarely into a small open area.

For this mission, each of the P-38 aircraft was loaded to the maximum with two 2,000-pound bombs. Taking off from the Warmwell base field, Bob's P-38 skimmed the tops of the trees and was caught in propeller wash—the current of air created by the action of a propeller from a P-38 ahead of him, causing his P-38 to dip below tree level. One wing tip tore through tree branches, but fortunately, he emerged intact from his encounter with the lush vegetation of the English countryside, quickly recovered his composure and control of his aircraft, and continued on the mission.

Once over the target, Bob lined up for his approach and released his bombs at 1,800 feet from a 35- to 45-degree dive angle. Thirty-one bombs from the squadron exploded in the target area, and the pilots saw large clouds of dust and smoke covering the target as they left the area. They could only assume that the German coastal battery had been destroyed.

And there was good news for the flyers on their return to base. But as always, with good news there is bad news.

The good news was that the squadron was given a commendation for their role in the attack. The commendation was made by Lieutenant General Lewis H. Bremerton, commanding general of the Ninth Tactical Air Command—formerly Major General Lewis H. Bremerton, who had been in operational command of the US 9th Force.

The bad news was that Smith, the squadron's own personal loose cannon, had been promoted to *first lieutenant*, in what is often called a *typical military decision*, although some of the pilots described it in other language that cannot be printed here. And the remainder of the flyers, those who knew what they were doing in the air, remained at the second lieutenant level. The disappearance of Smith caused the men to wonder about his fate.

And if one thing is certain in all military organization of all countries, it is the efficiency and speed of the rumor mill. There were stories coming out of Normandy that the Germans were murdering Allied prisoners.

The first murder may have been that of a wounded Canadian private, bayoneted by an SS trooper who shouted curses at his victim as he impaled him. Eight more prisoners were told to remove their helmets, then were shot. Their bodies were dragged into the road and crushed beneath tank tracks. A French villager collected the remains with a shovel. Six others were frog-marched through a kitchen and shot in the head. The chaplain attached to the Sherbrooke Fusiliers was stabbed through the heart. Other Canadian prisoners, after surrendering their pay books, were bludgeoned to death or dispatched by a bullet to the brain.

On Thursday, June 8, the killings continued. Summoned one by one from a stable used as a jail, each condemned man shook hands with his colleagues before being led into a well-flowered garden, where he was shot. Forty prisoners assembled in a field near the Caen-Bayeux road were ordered to sit facing east; SS troops brandishing Schmeisser machine pistols advanced in a skirmish line and opened fire, killing nearly three dozen. Several who bolted were soon recaptured and sent to prison camps.

Now known as the Murder Division, the 12th SS Panzer Division would be accused of killing 156 defenseless men, nearly all Canadian, in little more than a week, igniting a cycle of atrocity and reprisal that persisted all summer.

Once this was known, it removed any trailing remnants of remorse that the flyers felt. This was war, and everyone knew that *war is hell*. They would continue to do their duty, flying the P-38s to destroy German facilities and German soldiers.

The other news was that four new second lieutenants received postings to the squadron: Harold D. Bledsoe, Orville R. Cester, Dennis R. Chamberlain, and Glenn W. Goodrich. Unfortunately, as is the case in war, death was ever-present among the flyers, snatching from life the young men eager to fight the enemy. Three of the newcomers did not survive for long: Goodrich was killed on July 18, Chamberlain was killed on August 3, and Bledsoe was killed on August 10, 1944.

***

At the start of the June 8 mission, Bob had a minor argument with the trees at the end of the Warmwell takeoff area. These trees, because of their height, were recognized as a danger to every aircraft that took off from the airfield. The squadron commander had sent several requests to the RAF for tree removal, but—perhaps to the surprise of no one—all responses were in the form of lame excuses (in the opinions of the squadron pilots) for the trees to remain. Had this continued, Bob knew that sooner or later the trees would disappear— by hands known or unknown—before they caused a major accident with serious injury or loss of life.

Then, as if by an afterthought and just as the squadron was to about to move to France, local English workers hired by the RAF appeared at the base and started cutting down the troublesome foliage. And although it was of little worry to Bob and his comrades because the trees had been cleared but, to add insult to injury, the RAF billed the US Army Air Corps for the cost of tree removal!

***

With the intensity of the war now building, Bob and his colleagues, along with other squadrons, were given low-level bombing and strafing missions almost daily to cover and assist the Allied invasion forces and to stall German reinforcements and troop deployments. But the Germans were staunchly defending every acre of Fortress Europe to the last drop of their blood (and the blood of anyone else that happened to get in the way). The enemy response to the incursions by Allied flyers was increasing in ferocity. Anti-aircraft fire from ground positions was plentiful and continuous. As a result, most of the losses recorded by the squadron came from ground fire.

When diving onto a target and receiving ground fire, Bob could see tracers coming up at him. At first they appeared to be moving slowly, but then would seemingly speed up and—at least he continued to hope—they would pass by his P-38. The speed of battle and the tracer shells was so great that there was not even the time to whisper a silent prayer. It was possible only to give thanks for survival after the return to the air base with very little damage to his P-38 from the ground fire.

The squadron attacked extremely important tactical targets, which were heavily protected by rings of 20-millimeter and 40-millimeter guns. Targets such as railroad marshaling yards and German airfields also had the renowned 88-millimeter cannon—a German anti-aircraft and antitank artillery gun that was widely used throughout the war, and was one of the most recognized German weapons of the war. Unfortunately, the only way to get at the targets was to come in low at treetop level, an elevation less than one hundred feet. Each time, the squadron knew the guns were waiting but could do nothing to avoid the fire. Group losses were heavy.

***

At this time, June 12 1944, even Field Marshal Rommel, commander of the German forces on the western front, admitted to his wife in a letter that "the battle is not going at all well for us." Not knowing this at the time, the Allied forces were keeping up the pressure to move further inland from the beaches and push back German defenders. As part of the push, orders came down to the squadron from the military brass that missions were the order of every day. As a result, Bob and his colleagues flew more search-and-destroy missions on June 10, 11, 12, and 14 and returned to base without incident. By this time, the presence of German fighter aircraft over the Normandy coastline had diminished, but there was always the intense and terrifying anti-aircraft fire, when the flyers had time to think of it.

As Bob was taking off for another patrol over the invasion area on June 15, the unfamiliar but dangerous smell of smoke attacked his nose. He took the plane into a circle of the base field and called the members of his flight to determine if they could see anything amiss with his P-38. The reports were all negative—there were no obvious signs of smoke or fire. With the smell of smoke still in his nostrils but hoping that all was well and being unable to detect anything wrong inside the cockpit, Bob turned on the mission heading and started to increase his altitude at a steady rate of climb. The old adage "where there is smoke there is fire" was about to become a reality.

At twelve hundred feet, the port-side engine caught fire. Bob took the aircraft out of formation—he was last in line—and went into a dive in an attempt to extinguish the fire but, as fate would have it, that maneuver didn't work, and he only succeeded in fanning the flames. To make matters worse, he could feel the temperature increasing in the cockpit, and the cockpit was starting to fill with smoke—always bad signs—as the fire made itself very obvious! Flames were licking back the length of the fuselage, and he had to switch the oxygen supply to *full* in order to breathe. This made the flow in the lines rich in oxygen, but also served as fuel for the fire. Glancing from side to side, he realized that his altitude was too low to allow him to bail out, even if he had time, which he did not. His only option was to get the aircraft on the ground. And that had to be accomplished very quickly, immediately if possible.

But there was another problem. Bob had to feather (shut down) the port-side engine. With that engine out of commission, if he turned the plane to the left, into the now-dead engine, he would likely lose control, go into an out-of-control spin, and crash. If the aircraft didn't spin and crash, flames from the left engine would blow into the cockpit. The options were not good. Even if he followed the training protocols to prohibit uneven flight to retain control of the aircraft, Bob's survival would require all of his skills plus a lot of luck.

The aircraft was now obviously in trouble, with the flames dangerously close to the cockpit. As if by instinct, Bob lowered the starboard wing and put the seriously ailing P-38 into a maneuver known as a *sideslip*.

In normal flight, as the aircraft proceeds forward there is no sideslip. In the sideslip condition, the longitudinal axis of the aircraft remains parallel to the original flight path, but the airplane no longer flies straight along its original track. The horizontal component of lift forces the airplane to move sideways, almost crab-like, toward the low wing. In other words, Bob had put the P-38 into a sideways motion in a forward direction. Whatever words describe a sideslip motion—crab-like or otherwise—it's a dangerous maneuver, and the pilot runs the high risk of losing control of the aircraft. Either way, Bob's options were limited. Danger existed no matter which course of action he chose. He continued to sideslip the P-38.

He repeated the sideslip maneuver twice to force the flames to be directed away from the aircraft, and on the third time he managed to get to where the aircraft was sideslipping toward the runway. Fortunately, he still had enough control of the P-38 to bring it to level flight and land, smoke and fire streaming behind him. Without further thought and in the interest of personal safety, he was out of the aircraft almost before it came to a halt, and stood at the edge of the runway taking deep breaths while the fire crew extinguished the flames and saved what was left of the P-38.

As Bob allowed his mind to go over the event, he made a mental note to apologize to his colleague Herman Lane, since he was flying Herman's plane that day. Herman took Bob's profuse apology in his stride, almost as if it had never happened.

"Planes are easily replaced," Herman acknowledged, "but pilots are in short supply."

These were indeed wise words. Sadly, Herman himself would die in aerial combat a few weeks later.

***

In spite of the fire incident, there was no rest or time for recuperation. The next day, June 16, Bob was assigned another P-38 and took part in a bombing and strafing mission on a marshaling yard and railroad bridge at Vire, a town located in the Basse-Normandie region and within striking distance of the Utah and Omaha beaches. The squadron destroyed a locomotive, some buses used for troop transportation, several trucks, and assorted railroad cars. At this time, any action that delayed the German military from shipping supplies to the army attempting to stonewall the Normandy invasion was a positive action.

It was at this time that the German Seventh Army, which had been pushed back from the Normandy beaches, was seeking a more stable defense base from which the Allied advance could be halted. They chose the area around Falaise to set up their defensive wall. Falaise is a city on the river Ante, a tributary of the river Dives, approximately nineteen miles southeast of Caen. This was a mistake. The area came to be known as the *Falaise Pocket* and served to be the death knell of the Seventh Army. It was also the time that Adolf Hitler gave the command to commence the V-1 rocket (*Vergeltungswaffe*, vengeance weapon) attacks on London. Time was becoming of the essence, as it was widely believed by the German military that such weapons could win the war for Germany if London was destroyed, or if not, lead to truce negotiations.

Three days later, on June 19, Bob was in a flight led by Captain Merle Larson. Bob's nemesis, Lieutenant Smith, was the assistant flight leader.

Recall that earlier I discussed this pilot to whom I gave the pseudonym Bill Smith to avoid embarrassing his family. Smith started the war as a soldier at Pearl Harbor, where he claimed to have shot down a Japanese aircraft using his rifle. (It was noted in his record.) That feat gave him an opportunity to transfer from the ground to the air, and he made it through flight training, but he remained the loose cannon that he was, even in the sky.

They had completed part of the bombing mission when Captain Larson's plane was hit. The plane was close to Bob's P-38. Bob watched as Larson pulled up, his left engine flaming, then leveled out, got out of the cockpit, slid off the right wing, and pulled his parachute cord. Fortunately, the parachute opened and Bob watched Larson as he descended. Bob circled in a protective action to ensure his comrade landed safely. He saw Larson land on the edge of a wooded area and run for cover among the trees.

Smith took over the squadron and ordered the men to follow him and to strafe anyone—civilians or German military—who made moves to approach the area where Larson had landed. Civilians who were friendly to the Allied cause would remain under cover lest they be captured, tortured, and shot by the German military—usually the SS or Gestapo, who had the task of *interviewing* captured aircrew. On the other hand, military personnel and civilians who were sympathetic to the Nazi cause were known to do serious bodily harm to flyers who had parachuted into occupied countries from stricken aircraft, especially bomber crew.

Larson was captured by the SS. True to form, he was beaten many times, starting when he was first captured and throughout the time he was in enemy custody. Instead of being sent to a prisoner of war camp, Larson was imprisoned in a concentration camp—an extermination camp—where most of the people held in such a camp were shot or gassed and the bodies cremated. The name of the camp is lost behind the curtain of history, but it was a mental and physical strain on anyone so interned. Somehow Captain Larson managed to survive to be released at the end of the war.

Bob and many of his squadron colleagues were convinced that Larson's treatment was wholly or in part due to the order from Smith to strafe the civilians as well as the military personnel. The SS and

Gestapo needed no excuses to practice their brutality, but Smith had given them excellent cause for the harsh and brutal treatment of Captain Larson.

***

On June 22, 1944, as American forces besieged Cherbourg in Lower Normandy, the squadron flew two missions. Bob flew on the second mission as the wingman of the squadron leader. The targets to be bombed were the railroad marshaling yards located in an area between St. Quentin and Compiègne in northern France.

The town of St. Quentin is named after Saint Quentin, who is said to have been martyred there in the third century. The Glade of the Armistice is located in the Compiègne Forest, the site of the signing of two armistices: the 1918 Armistice between the Allied Forces and Germany that brought an end to hostilities in the World War I, and the 1940 surrender of France to Germany. Adolf Hitler had specifically chosen the location, and had the original signing carriage moved from Paris to Compiègne, as an irony for the defeated French.

As had been the case on other missions, the flak was heavy but in spite of this the mission was a success. As they left the target area, Bob could see flames over the marshaling yards at a height of approximately five hundred feet. The attack destroyed thirty to forty freight cars full of supplies and also destroyed railroad tracks and a bridge. The group did considerably more damage to German transportation efforts on June 23, when the pilots strafed a fifty-car train carrying a full load of heavy field guns and anti-aircraft guns to the Front Line.

The following day, June 24, the wing commander led the group on an armed reconnaissance mission to Nantes, a port city in western

France located at the southern end of Normandy, on the banks of the Loire River, at the confluence of two Loire tributaries (the Erdre and the Sèvre Nantaise), and approximately thirty-five miles from the Atlantic Ocean.

One of the squadron pilots (Bob was not close enough to see his aircraft identification numbers) dropped a thousand-pound bomb on the middle of a train near Cholet, which lies just to the east of Nantes, and the bomb destroyed three railroad cars and several yards of railroad track. Two other pilots strafed the locomotive while another pair of flyers dropped their bombs, and although they missed the target, the bombs did severe damage to a heavy (possibly a two-ton) fuel truck. None of the rest of the group hit anything worthy of note, but their efforts were assured to cause the Germans considerable discomfort.

On a slightly more humorous note, Second Lieutenant Thomas L. Coleman, a ground (non-flying) officer, was assigned to the squadron on June 24. He and Bob quickly became good friends. Coleman captured everyone's attention even before he finished unpacking all of his belongings in his new barracks. He was cleaning his .50-caliber carbine, pulled the trigger, and discovered it was loaded. The bullet went through the walls of several rooms, but did not draw blood at any point along the way. Coleman had arrived!

On June 26, Bob was on patrol giving air cover to the naval task force approximately fifteen miles northeast of Cape Levy, which lay to the northeast of Cherbourg on the English Channel coast. Looking down he could see the battleships Arkansas and Texas accompanied by an assortment of heavy cruisers, light cruisers, and destroyers as well as countless other craft ranging from mine sweepers to transports and fuel tankers.

While patrolling over the ships, Lieutenant Munger had trouble with his left engine and returned to the field. He came in to land with his flaps down. (The flaps reduce the an aircraft's speed on landing, also shortening the landing distance.) The tower told Munger that the wheels of his P-38 were not locked into position. He was ordered to circle instead. By this time it was too late. The airspeed of the P-38 was down to 90 miles per hour, enough lower than the stall speed of approximately 99 miles per hour that he belly-landed the aircraft, giving himself quite a bumpy ride. Fortunately, Munger was not injured.

***

Within a day or so of the June 26 mission, Lieutenant General Omar N. Bradley, commander of the First U.S. Army, sent the following letter of commendation to Major General Elwood "Pete" Quesada, commanding general of the IXth Tactical Air Command:

Will you please express to the officers and men of your command my appreciation of the fine work they have been doing and of the close cooperation they have given the ground troops. Their ability to disrupt the enemy's communications, supply and movement of troops has been a vital factor in our rapid progress in expanding our beachhead.

I realize that their work may not catch the headlines any more than does the work of some of our foot soldiers, but I am sure that I express the feelings of every ground force commander from squad leaders to myself as Army Commander when I extend my congratulations on their very fine work.

General Quesada forwarded the letter to his fighter group (the 474th Fighter Groups) and added his own commendation:

I hope that each lad who is doing so much to make our effort successful gets as much pleasure out of the expression of General Bradley's appreciation as I do.

The Fighter-Bomber boys are doing more to make this campaign a success than anyone ever anticipated. The versatility of our effort is a tremendous contribution. The manner in which each boy has performed his mission and manner in which he has exercised initiative is a source of great pride.

Now that we are operating from bases on the far shore, I hope all will do their utmost to continue the high standards of efficiency that have been exemplified in the past. Remember that our work is really just starting. In other words, it is all over but the fighting.

Bob admired General Pete Quesada. He was a fighter pilot and he understood his men. Whenever the flyers broke the rules to buzz the field or engage in some aerobatics after scoring an aerial victory, he would always look the other way and pretend not to notice their antics. He not-so-secretly enjoyed seeing his *boys* (*lads*) showing off. If others objected to the antics and aerobatics of the *Quesada boys*, the general would quietly remind them of the dangers they faced on a daily basis, and he always protected his pilots by explaining: "Fighter pilots are fighter pilots."

***

The missions continued. On June 29, the squadron made an armed reconnaissance strike in an area bounded by the cities of Dreux, Chartres, Alençon, and Argentan, where German activity was heavy and constant. While the flights were forming up and climbing out after hitting the targets, one of the P-38s was straggling behind the remainder of the aircraft. Soon after passing over L'Aigle, a town in the Lower Normandy region of France, the pilot took his plane into a turning climb and disappeared into the grey clouded sky. He could not be contacted by radio. Two German FW-190s were seen in the area and may have played a direct role in the disappearance of the P-38. There was also the possibility that the aircraft had been hit by the particularly vicious and ever-present flak.

In the reality and sadness of war, Bob seemed to know by instinct that his colleague would never return and whatever the cause of his demise, another good man had been lost.

The next afternoon, June 30, Bob was part of a twelve-plane raid on targets east of Alençon, France. The pilots spotted numerous horse-drawn wagons along the way—a sure sign that the Germans were running short of motorized transportation—and they scored bomb hits on a power station, railroad tracks, and trains. All flyers made it back to the base in time for a quick shower, dinner, and a dance sponsored by base personnel and local residents.

June 30 was also the day that Captain Larson was to have received his fourteenth Bronze Oak Leaf Cluster to the Air Medal. Recall that Larson's plane was hit during a mission on June 19. Bob had watched as Larson managed to get out of the cockpit and parachuted to a grove of trees. If Larson was captured, he would suffer many months of captivity before the decoration was presented to him.

Bob received his first Bronze Oak Leaf Cluster to the Air Medal. The Oak Leaf Cluster was awarded in lieu of subsequent medals. So Bob at this time had two Air Medals. By the end of the war, he earned sixteen Air Medals.

***

Under Army Air Corps regulations, one Air Medal was awarded for ten missions. Thus, Bob received seven medals for the sixty-eight combat missions that he flew. An Air Medal also was awarded for each enemy plane destroyed or damaged. Bob had five confirmed enemy aircraft destroyed and four aircraft damaged for another nine medals, bringing his total to sixteen. There are three silver clusters and one bronze cluster on his Air Medal ribbon—each silver cluster is for five awards and the bronze is for a single award.

***

By early July, the Allied forces had moved inland from the beaches. One million Allied soldiers had come ashore in Normandy and were moving into France, but in well-defended areas the ground advance was limited to six miles inland. The German defenders held on tenaciously, and the areas of tough resistance had to be softened up by continuous air strikes. Bob and the other members of the Fighter Group were a necessary part of the softening-up process. And then US Independence Day dawned!

All of the squadron celebrated on July 4, the day that the American colonies published the Declaration of Independence from Britain on the way to becoming the United States of America. And American airmen were willingly and bravely defending the original mother country of the colonies.

The day started with a bombing assignment to destroy a double-track railroad bridge at Cérences near the west coast of the Cherbourg peninsula. Heavy clouds and a low ceiling made it extremely difficult to locate the target, and variable crosswinds diverted some bombs from the target. Even so, the bridge was knocked out for all practical purposes when hits severed the railroad line at both ends of the bridge. Later in the day, Bob flew another mission, providing top cover for some other aircraft. Then a surprise loomed on the evening horizon!

Neither Bob nor any of his comrades expected the British to be in favor of a July 4 celebration. He knew that families all over the United States would be engaged in some form of cautious celebration, but the war would put a damper on many celebrations, as families mourned the loss of the soldiers, sailors, and airmen who had given their lives to the current cause of liberty from tyranny.

But Bob and his colleagues misjudged the attitude of the British pilots and ground crew members. They held no grudges for the actions of the ancestors of these modern-day Americans in a long-forgotten war. They were focused on the friendship that existed in this current war and on defeating an enemy that was ready to subjugate all of Europe and many other parts of the world.

The Americans didn't have any additional supplies to help mark the occasion, and they happened to mention this fact to some of the RAF pilots after dinner that evening, which had been designated by the Americans as being appropriate for indulging in several extra after-dinner beverages. The RAF flyers were saddened to hear the Americans' descriptions of former glorious Fourth of July celebrations in the United States with the displays of fireworks in parks and other associated events. In England, it being wartime, blackout of all lights was the order of the day. This meant no lights at all were to be visible under any circumstances. Even the windows and doors of civilian homes were covered by blackout curtains. They could not allow even a crack of light that could be seen by enemy aircraft crews, who would use the light as a potential target. In other words, the use of fireworks for any reason in any demonstration or celebration was strictly forbidden.

Without trying to be too obvious, the RAF boys probed the Americans further about the fireworks. The whole idea was vague to some of the RAF personnel and new to many others. They were interested in what went on at these shows—the fireworks displays and the manner in which the displays were accomplished.

Possibly not wishing to expose their plans but now armed with sufficient knowledge of the July 4 events, two British flyers excused themselves and went outside, striding off toward the control tower, seemingly on business. But this was business that defied the usual description. They waited there until the tower operator walked into the back of the tower to take a look at the view. Then they rushed in and helped themselves to anything that might be of use for their purpose: Very pistols (used for firing colored signal flares), other types of flare guns, and an ample supply of ammunition.

Suddenly, the conversation among the attendees in the Officers' Club was interrupted by a commotion on the outside lawn. All personnel rushed to the window, wondering if there had been an attack by enemy aircraft seeking to make a last statement that all was not over. But that was not the case.

Feelings ran deep. Perhaps a few tears were wiped from moistened cheeks when the Americans saw the two English flyers comically chasing each other back and forth across the lawn like the Keystone Cops, the Three Stooges, and the Marx Brothers combined, firing red and green signal flares at each other, presumably without attempting to hit and injure each other. As fast as one of the RAF boys could reload, he would turn and pursue his friendly opponent until the other could reload on the run. After a few minutes of this, one of the lads ducked through the door leading to the bar. As if to signal "I am the winner," the second RAF pilot fired a parting shot in the direction of the Officer's Club. His aim was not just bad, it was terrible, and a red ball of fire shot through the open window of the men's lavatory. Then the evening fun really started!

It seems that an RAF wing commander was alone in this sanitary haven of peace and quietness at the time, but the sounds that Bob and his colleagues heard were more like the sounds of a yelping pack of coyotes on the Wyoming prairie as they circled to attack their next still-living meal.

The rank of wing commander is a commissioned rank in the RAF and also in the air forces of many other Commonwealth countries. It ranks above squadron leader and immediately below group captain. Currently, it has a NATO ranking code of OF-4, and is equivalent to a Commander in the Royal Navy or the US Navy, or a Lieutenant Colonel in the British or the Royal Marines… But back to the flare.

The active flare didn't show any respect for rank and it seemed to gather momentum. Bouncing from wall to wall, it circled the room, while the wing commander, trousers in disarray, leapt from his sanitary privacy only slightly ahead of the flare. By this time others had assembled, and more flare guns were brought up from unknown sources to add more color and light to the event. Presumably the wing commander was not amused!

The operator in the control tower sensed the futility of trying to stop this brazen violation of behavior that was unbecoming of officers in the Royal Air Force, in which emergency signals were being put to a use other than that intended. He gave in to his own impulses. From his vantage point high in the tower, he shot volley after volley of fiery lights into the evening sky, with complete disregard for any existing blackout regulations.

Nevertheless, everyone had a great time, and it turned out to be a truly inspiring Fourth of July.

***

On July 6, two days after the infamous but enjoyable July 4 celebration, the squadron was assigned to provide cover for an armed reconnaissance mission between Châteaudun—located about 28 miles northwest of Orléans and about 51 miles south-southwest of Chartres, on the river Loir, a tributary of the Sarthe—and LeMans, located on the Sarthe River.

The squadron, along with the 428th Squadron and the 430th Squadron, bombed and strafed a railway yard in northwest France that was used to supply the German front lines with weapons, ammunition, and other necessities. Considerable damage was done to buildings and sidings. As the flyers made their way back to the coast, the weather was clear, with only a few clouds in the sky. Bob, flying on Smith's right wing, saw tracers in the distance, and two explosions before the aircraft involved came in view. One P-38 was engaged in a dogfight with four German fighters. All four were FW-190s.

And this is where the realities of aerial combat became real. The destruction of aircraft and death of the pilots was the hardest part to handle. In addition, aerial combat was not easy, as you might think from playing modern video games. It was as if the P-38, like all other aircraft, was on a moving platform—one that moved up and down and from side to side continuously. To make matters ever more difficult, the enemy aircraft moved in the same manner. Destruction of the enemy was not guaranteed, even with the guns mounted in the nose of the P-38 so that the pilot could bring his guns to bear on an enemy aircraft more accurately than if the guns were mounted in the wings of the aircraft.

The American pilots climbed to an altitude of 10,000 feet and attacked. One parachute was already in the air. Smith shot at an

FW-190 and hit the aircraft with a deflection shot at close range that must have scored a hit in a crucial spot. The German went down in flames. Another FW-190 was attacked from a five o'clock position. Bob called for Smith to break right, but Smith ignored protocol. He was too occupied with his success and was distracted by his call to the flight leader.

"I got one! I got one!" Smith yelled excitedly.

Bob could hear Smith's exclamation over the intercom, so Bob had to leave Smith and break right into a tight turn to take on the FW-190.

For the first time since arriving at Warmwell, Bob and his colleagues were equipped with G-suits (gravity suits), which helped to prevent blood from being pushed down a flyer's body during a tight turn, leaving the man in a momentary black-out and vulnerable. Bob's suit worked perfectly, and he never lost sight of the German. With combat flaps down and at full throttle, Bob kept turning inside of him and began pulling his sights up to him.

Combat flaps are the leading and trailing edges of the wing flaps, which can be lowered at high speed. These flaps reduce the angle of attack for a given lift coefficient and flatten the load distribution to postpone flow separation on the outer wing, resulting in significant delay in the occurrence of buffeting, increasing the inaccuracy of flying and shooting.

But before Bob could fire, he had to break off to engage a second FW-190 coming in. Quickly, he took the P-38 into a right turn with the German but actually went through a 360-degree horizontal turn, aligned his sights on the FW-190, and fired a short burst. The German pilot rolled left and went into a dive. Not to be outdone, Bob executed a roll-over dive to follow him—he was in a near-vertical dive with the FW-190 now several thousand feet below.

Glancing to his left, Bob saw another FW-190 firing at a pilot in a parachute. It didn't appear that the German had hit the parachutist, and as the attacker passed the chute, he turned into him, and he started a right turn toward Bob, who cut him off with a short burst. The German dived and Bob followed. When Bob caught up with the FW-190, he realized that they both were running out of maneuverable air space—the ground was a little too close and the sky was not close enough! They were at a very low altitude, and Bob realized that he was going to overshoot the enemy aircraft, so he took his P-38 into a climbing left turn of 360 degrees so that the P-38 would outturn the FW-190.

As he set up his turn, Bob couldn't see the enemy pilot, and after Bob had completed the 360-degree turn, feeling like his neck had turned completely around twice and would look like a corkscrew, he spotted the German aircraft off to the right, skimming some treetops three or four hundred yards away.

Turning again to get on the enemy's tail, Bob closed the distance between his P-38 and the FW-190. The German went lower. At one point he was so low that he had to increase altitude to fly over some power lines. Bob saw that coming and just cleared the power lines. As he closed with the German, their propellers skimmed the ground. The German pulled up to clear a haystack and Bob followed, firing an occasional burst whenever he could. Then the FW-190 went over a small grove of trees to the right and as he cleared the trees, he climbed sharply to the left to approximately five hundred feet and leveled out.

Bob continued to close on his enemy, firing short bursts but shooting so that his bullets led the enemy aircraft. He could hear the gentle whisper of a familiar voice in his ear.

"Steady, Bob. Steady." He could hear Father Robert's voice as if he was in the cockpit. "Lead the bird so that your shot arrives at the same place at the same time as the bird."

As Bob closed with the FW-190 to about seventy five yards, the German pilot jettisoned his canopy. Bob could see his black flight helmet, his tan flight suit, and the stark white of his parachute webbing as he climbed out of the cockpit and onto the left wing of the FW-190. In flying terms, because of the speed of the aircraft—on the order of 300 to 350 miles per hour—this was up close and very personal.

At that point, Bob made a decision. The FW-190 was finished, and he was not going to shoot at a man in his parachute, even though he was an enemy. The German pulled the cord to release the parachute, and the force of the lifesaving canopy as it opened jerked the pilot off the wing of the FW-190. He passed directly beneath the P-38. As he left the stricken plane, the German pilot hit the rudder. Bob learned later, that the man's right arm had been was broken as a result of the impact. The parachutist eventually landed. A group of civilians were heading toward the wood where the German had landed. It was a group of locals, who probably had serious thoughts of injury in mind for the pilot, but the German Field Police arrived and the locals melted into the wooded area.

In the meantime, the FW-190 was going down fast. Bob wanted to get the final moments of its flight on film, but he didn't have time to switch on the camera.

It was policy for each fighter plane to be equipped with a camera that required manual activation before it would record the actions. Cameras were useful for the debriefing session after the flight; the photographic record was able to confirm the pilots' observations of a successful (or unsuccessful) shooting engagement or bombing run.

The FW-190 half-rolled to the right, then went into the ground nose first, where it exploded in flames. The flaming wreckage skidded along the ground, and came to a rest parallel to a fence line.

Bob pulled up to rejoin his flight. As he did, the cannon of the P-38, overheated by the extended firing, let off three or four rounds as if the aircraft itself, also pleased with its performance, recognized and saluted Bob's first aerial victory. He had used 145 rounds of 20-mm cannon shells and 1,194 rounds of .50-caliber ammunition in the fight. Two of his colleagues, one his wingman, confirmed Bob's victory.

That day the fighter group scored victories of various kinds. While strafing one marshaling yard, the pilots had destroyed sixteen freight cars and an engine and damaged eight flat cars. At another yard they destroyed two engines and five flat cars and damaged *sixteen flat cars. The score at a third yard was thirteen flat cars damaged and one locomotive destroyed. In addition, considerable lengths of rail track were damaged in the process, some irreparably.

***

Long after the war, Bob purchased a book about the Luftwaffe from which he learned that the FW-190 pilot was one of Germany's leading fighter aces. He broke his arm while bailing out of the stricken FW-190 but recuperated and returned to the air, during which time he shot down several more American flyers.

Looking back, Bob often regretted his decision to spare the pilot's life and does not have any doubt that he could have shot him off the wing as he got out the cockpit. If he had killed the pilot as he hung under the parachute canopy, several American families would still have their sons, brothers, and husbands.

***

The P-38 pilot who had parachuted from his ailing aircraft and was being shot at by the FW-190 pilot, being from a different squadron, was unknown to Bob. While there were claims of such actions from both the Allied and German sides, Bob realized the tragedy of such an action when he saw one of his own colleagues being shot at in his parachute. But this had a happy ending.

***

Eighteen days later, Lieutenant James F. Frederick came looking for Bob, but Bob was on leave and not on base. Frederick was the P-38 pilot in the parachute, and he wanted to personally thank Bob for shooting down the FW-190 pilot who had been strafing him. Frederick witnessed much of Bob's dogfight as he was descending and he was close by when the German landed. Frederick told Bob's tentmates that he had attempted to shoot at the German, but he couldn't cock his .45-caliber pistol because his hands were too badly burned. After telling his story, Frederick had to leave the base, and to this day Bob has not had the privilege of personally meeting or communicating with him.

***

The mission pattern was repeated on July 11, when Bob flew as wingman for his squadron leader. The squadron lost one plane on takeoff; the port-side engine on the aircraft caught fire. The pilot, as per flight training regulations, jettisoned his bomb and belly tank, but couldn't keep the P-38 in the air. He guided the plane to a belly-landing in a wheat field at the end of the runway. The P-38 plowed up almost one hundred yards of dirt before coming to a halt against a stone wall. Fortunately, the pilot got out and scrambled to safety just before his plane exploded in a ball of fire.

This served as a reminder to all pilots that returning to home base did not necessarily mean that safety was guaranteed. Danger lurked over the shoulder of each pilot every day of their service.

The squadron continued on their mission. Bombs were dropped from 1,500 feet, destroying two locomotives and damaging three others. Six fuel cars also were damaged. One of their flights strafed thirty-five to forty fuel cars and caused considerable damage and destruction. Another flight destroyed tracks and a truck, then strafed and damaged a radio tower. The third flight strafed and destroyed vital fuel storage tanks. All in all, it was another successful mission.

When they returned from the mission, Lieutenant Lenton F. Kirkland Jr. received word that he was a father. His daughter was born July 6. Unfortunately, Kirkland (Bob's friend Kirk) had only five and a half months to live and would never have the joy of seeing his daughter.

Although Bob did not fly on July 14 (Bastille Day in France), he remembers the day well. The squadron lost another pilot during an attack on a bridge in France. Going in for his attack, the P-38 seemed to have been caught in the bomb blast of the plane in front of his and was last seen doing a complete roll and exploding when hitting a stone building. It was always sad when a colleague was killed. In this case, the pilot was on his second tour of duty. He had gone home, got married, then came back to fight again.

***

225

Decades later, when Bob returned to France, he visited the pilot's grave in the American cemetery situated near the Normandy beaches. As is always the case when men are lost in war, he is forever young in Bob's memory.

***

On July 18, the 474th Fighter Group (all three squadrons were involved) went into action against German fighters, shooting down ten enemy aircraft, of which six were recorded as *kills*, and damaging fourteen enemy aircraft. Smith's wingman, a recent replacement from another squadron, had trouble when his left engine caught on fire. The wingman seemed to have the P-38 under control and was trying to gain more altitude when last seen. During the post-mission debriefing, Smith, hard on the tail of an FW-190, didn't miss his wingman until the P-38 had disappeared from sight.

Another colleague, albeit from another squadron in the fighter group but still a fellow pilot, was shot down before takeoff on July 19. An aircraft from another squadron was parked away from the active take-off area, positioned for bore-sighting—a procedure in which the aircraft was positioned horizontally and all guns were sighted to converge at a specific location downrange. The guns being in the nose of the P-38 made this a somewhat simpler procedure than for other fighter aircraft, where the guns were positioned in the wind, but it was still necessary for the P-38 to do it.

The pilot of the P-38 was in his plane, waiting for the go-ahead to taxi and take off for an armed reconnaissance over France. Just then, the guns on the unmanned parked plane ran amok and fired several bursts. Bullets fanned out in several directions as it twisted and bucked from the recoil of its machine guns. Gasoline spurted from gaping holes in the wing tank of the P-38. The pilot was not injured, but had to stay home. Ironically he was shot down on the ground. There was one casualty, however—a ground crew officer who cut his knee on (of all things) a broken beer bottle while performing a commendable Olympic-style hop, skip, and jump as he dived for cover.

It was back in the air for Bob on July 20. The squadron bombed St. Côme du Mont, the site of much activity and a strong defense by German forces on D-Day and still showing packets of resistance. But the results of the raid by the P-38s could not be observed due to bad weather.

July 20 was also the day of the failed attempt to assassinate Adolf Hitler. With the Norman battlefield still deadlocked, Hitler was able to attend to reprisals and to shoring up his regime. The failed assassin, Colonel Claus von Stauffenberg, and at least two hundred others were be executed—shot by an impromptu firing squad, hanged, beheaded, poisoned, or garroted—sometimes on film for the amusement of SS guards, while thousands more were jailed.

***

As a side-note, there had been discussion in England within the Allied High Command of sending an assassination squad to kill Adolf Hitler. After much discussion the plans were abandoned. It was felt that Hitler was doing as much to hinder and constrict the German war effort as the Allied forces. The Allied High Command believed that replacing Hitler with competent generals would prolong the war and lead to a negotiated peace rather than unconditional surrender.

***

Before the month ended, Wehrmacht officers would be required to demonstrate fealty by giving the stiff-armed Nazi *Heil* rather than the traditional military salute. To some Allied observers, they saw this as the beginning of the end for Germany. To those men on the front battle lines it meant that the regime would be anxious to shore up their hold on Germany and the fighting would increase in ferocity. On hearing the news, Bob and his colleagues could only grit their teeth for the oncoming battle.

Smith went down a week later. A plane from another squadron collided with his aircraft, tearing off most of his outer wing panel. Smith attempted to get his plane under control, and then bailed out when it started spinning. Squadron members saw his chute open just before it disappeared into the clouds. When the squadron returned to base, Smith's whereabouts was unknown, and the pilots feared the worst.

But there was another side to Smith's disappearance—his poker losses.

Although Bob was not an avid player, he frequently took part in poker games—the off-duty pastime of many pilots. In such games, it was not unusual for the pot to go as high as six or seven hundred dollars. This was big money by any stretch of the wartime imagination (or even modern-day imagination) and much more than a pilot's monthly pay, which was typically on the order of two hundred dollars. Smith decided he was a poker player, too—the size of the pot being an inducement. But he generally (in fact, almost always) lost money. When such losses occurred and after some pleading from Smith, Bob would loan Smith the money to tide him over until the next payday. Bob was always concerned that someday Smith would be shot down and not return, leaving him out of pocket. The opposite side of the coin was that if Bob was shot down, he would not need the money!

The bad news was that Smith's aircraft *was* shot down, and he owed Bob five hundred dollars when he bailed out from his stricken aircraft.

The good news was that Smith survived his parachute descent back to Mother Earth and retuned to friendly territory. From here he was able to get rides back to the base, and he had not forgotten what he owed Bob; he readily paid Bob what he owed him.

Without a word other than thanks, Bob willingly took the money.

CHAPTER 7: DAISY IN THE SKY

The previous chapter described the manner in which Bob came to the rescue of an American pilot, Lieutenant James F. Frederick, who had bailed out of his doomed aircraft. As Lieutenant Frederick was parachuting to earth, he was attacked by a German pilot. He was in serious danger with a high likelihood of being shot and killed in his parachute. Bob's actions saved the life of Lieutenant Frederick and discouraged the German pilot from any further shooting at the American as he and his parachute floated gracefully but unprotected to the ground.

It is only within the last decade that Bob's identity has become known to the family of Lieutenant Frederick. This chapter is included in its unaltered form and with the kind permission of Scott Frederick, the son of the pilot whose life Bob had saved.

Scott diligently searched the records for several years until he came across Bob's identity. Thankful correspondence from Scott to Bob ensued.

This chapter is part of the correspondence and is reproduced here with Scott's permission. It serves as a tribute to Lieutenant Frederick and his colleagues who had to leave their stricken aircraft, some of whom survived. Sadly, there were also many who did not.

This information was also kindly provided by Scott Frederick, son of Second Lieutenant James S. Frederick, a P-38 pilot in the 428th Fighter Squadron, 474th Fighter Group. And this is his translation of the part of the original version of Mademoiselle Schneider's notebook written at the time the events described therein occurred (July 6, 1944 to August 1, 1944). As an aside, Bob's squadron was the 429th Fighter Squadron of the 474th Fighter Group.

This chapter, along with the next one, also brings to the reader the realism of war and presents information that shows the life-threatening dangers that French Resistance fighters had to endure. This is not the stiff-upper-lip-and-grim-smile danger that Hollywood movies are made of. This is the flirting-with-capture-torture-and-death danger that the members of the French Resistance faced on a daily basis.

To these citizens of France who fought the war in the only way that they knew how—using guerilla tactics to provide resistance to the enemy—we owe our sincerest and heartfelt gratitude.

The story is as follows.

***

2nd Lieutenant James S. Frederick, Jr. or *Jimmie* as he was called was a P-38 pilot in the 428th Fighter Squadron, 474th Fighter Group.

The 474th had arrived and was stationed at Warmwell, Dorchester, England, on March 12, 1944. Warmwell was a British fighter base that had been turned over to the Army Air Corps as the United States built up its military in preparation for the invasion of Europe. The 428th Squadron went operational in April 1944 initially flying cover over convoys in the English Channel or escorting bombers to or from Europe. In preparation for D-Day (June 6, 1944), the missions were changed in late May from convoy cover and the 428th Squadron began attacking strategic targets such as railroads and bridges in France.

On June 5th the 428th Squadron flew cover over the invasion fleet as it made its way across the channel. Missions intensified as the Squadron continued to attack German transportation routes helping to stop the reinforcements that were heading for the beach heads.

July 6, 1944 found the 428th Squadron flying two missions as top cover for its sister squadrons, the 429th and 430th—the second mission started late in the afternoon and covered the area northwest of Le Mans. Now a 1st Lieutenant, Jimmie was in Blue Flight with his friend 2nd Lieutenant Robert J. Rubel flying as his wingman—the two men had formed a close friendship when they had met at the Santa Ana, California, Air Base during basic training. While Jimmie went on to be assigned to the 428th when it was formed, Robert was assigned elsewhere until he was assigned to the Warmwell Base in May.

The weather over the target area was clear with an unlimited ceiling and unlimited visibility (in the parlance of flyers, this was *ceiling and visibility unlimited, CAVU*) but there was still danger in the skies—at 4:15 p.m. four FW-190s burst onto the scene. Guns started blazing immediately and before the Americans could respond to the threat Lieutenant Rubel's P-38 burst into flames. Jimmie watched horrified as Rubel's aircraft nosed over and plummeted to the earth. He had but a moment to think of his friend as he took immediate evasive action as an FW-190 tried to get on his tail. Frantic radio calls brought the 429th Fighter Squadron up into the fight.

German Ace, Oberleutnant Wolfgang Ernst—the rank of Oberleutnant is approximately equivalent to rank of 1st Lieutenant—pulled in behind Jimmie and fired. Bullets tore in to Jimmie's left engine and ignited the inboard gas tanks. Flames swept in to the cockpit—burning his ankles, hands, lower arms, and face—as Jimmie struggled to undo his harness. He managed to roll the P-38 on its back, but hesitated a moment in order to get away from the combat zone before bailing out.

Lieutenant Robert Milliken of the 429th Squadron entered the fray and immediately engaged one of the FW-190s. Another of the FW-190s was shot down as Milliken was following his first plane. He turned inside the FW-190 and began to pull his sites through the enemy aircraft but had to break off as another FW-190 came in at 5 o'clock. Milliken turned to the right in a three hundred and sixty degree turn, pulled his sites through the enemy aircraft and fired a short burst. The FW-190 dove to the left and Milliken followed in a near vertical dive following. Looking to his left he saw the American pilot floating to earth under his parachute.

Unknown to anyone at that time, the dogfight was being observed by friendly forces. Just west of the French village of Montmerrei, Suzanne Schneider, a member of the French Secret Army was in a wagon with three other countrymen when the air battle broke out above their heads. They watched one of the P-38 aircraft that exploded before hitting the ground—the pilot, Lieutenant Rubel was killed. They ran into the nearby trees to avoid the bullets and shells hitting the earth around them watching as the other American pilot parachuted toward the ground.

Oberleutnant Ernst brought his plane back around with the intent of strafing Jimmie as he swung helpless beneath his chute. Fortunately, Ernst missed with his first burst of gunfire and as he passed Jimmie, he started to turn again. On the ground the French watched as the German plane started to turn. To their surprise, and pleasure, another P-38 hidden by the trees and coming in low at high speed climbed and shot at the FW-190.

Lieutenant Milliken gained altitude as he stayed on the tail of the FW-190 and fired another burst cutting him off and forcing the German to a dive. Milliken followed firing shorts bursts hitting the FW-190 and severely damaging the aircraft. At this point the plane was doomed—Ernst jettisoned his canopy and slid onto the port-side wing where the force of the wind blew him off and into the rudder of the FW-190, breaking his right arm. He managed to pull the ripcord and his chute opened and he was carried away from the doomed aircraft.

West of where Suzanne Schneider and her compatriots watched these events, three year-old Jean Claude Clouet watched as Jimmie slowly drifted toward a field to the north of their farmhouse. Bullets were still hitting the ground nearby as Jean Claude's mother rushed out of the cottage to take him inside—bullets from aircraft in a dogfight show no preference for pilots or citizens. As she reached Jean-Claude he called out, "Mama, look at that big daisy up there!" as Jimmie, suspended under the apparent *daisy*, disappeared behind some trees. He landed in a field near some blackberry bushes and once more upon firm earth Jimmie quickly shed his parachute, Mae West, helmet, gloves, and goggles shoving them as deep into the brambles as possible.

The *Mae West* was the colloquial name given to a personal flotation device (abbreviated as PFD and also referred to as, lifejacket, life preserver, life vest, life saver, cork jacket, buoyancy aid, flotation suit) which was designed to assist a wearer, either conscious or unconscious, to keep afloat if an aircraft was downed at sea.

Looking around, Jimmie saw Ernst coming down in a field to the north. Pulling his Colt Model 1911 service pistol—a semi-automatic weapon designed by John Browning and the standard-issue US military sidearm from 1911 to 1985—but he found he could not pull the slide to arm the gun as his hands were too badly burned. Instead Jimmie ran eastward, toward a heavily wooded area where he sought cover. He pushed through the trees and brambles for several minutes before stopping for a moment to assess his injuries. He was in great pain with second and third degree burns that circled his wrists— the heat had been so intense that the crystal face on his watch had melted. The burns on his ankles were the worst and the shoe laces on his boots were ashes. His face felt hot and swollen and had suffered some burns as the flames in the cockpit had licked hungrily toward his head.

Pushing on Jimmie spied a small cottage. Hiding in some bushes he waited, watched, and let his racing heart slow as he looked for any sign of life but the forest remained quiet. Slowly, quietly, painfully, he crawled through the underbrush keeping hidden as much as possible. Finally, close to the door he got up and gingerly tried the handle, but the door was locked. The adrenalin was still coursing through his body and, walking around the building, he found a window that he was able to open with some difficulty and he crawled inside. The cottage was small, consisting of a single room with a stove and table at one end and a bed at the other. A curtain served as a separator between the bed and the rest of the sparsely-decorated room. Still feeling the pain that seemed permanent, Jimmie crawled onto the bed, pulled the curtain covering across the bed, and started to consider his next moves. His main thought was to assure that he did not get caught by the enemy.

He did not have much time to think before he heard the sound of a key turning in the door lock. Fearing the worst but realizing that enemy soldiers, especially the SS and the Gestapo, did not bother with keys and locks—a well-placed jackboot or rifle butt would assure entry through any troublesome door. For safety reasons, most pilots—and Jimmie was such a pilot—never carried the gun with a round already in the chamber; accidental discharge of a primed weapon within a cockpit could have disastrous effects. His hands were still throbbing to remind him of the pain but, nevertheless, with some struggle and pain, Jimmie was able to operate the slide and ready his pistol with a bullet in the chamber before the door finally opened—his body, racked with pain, he moved the safety lock to the operate position and the pistol was now ready for action. The gun held eight rounds in the ammunition clip, just sufficient to put up a fight if the person entering the cottage was an enemy soldier. The door opened slowly and he heard the sound of soft footfalls—not the coarse stomp-stomp of jackboots. Jimmie's brow furrowed and questions raced through his brain, but he was still on his guard and the pistol in his hand was ready and threatening.

Unseen to Jimmie, who remained behind the curtain, Suzanne Schneider entered the cottage. A glance told her that a window was open—she knew that the window had been closed when she had left the cottage earlier and that she had locked the door but her senses told her that someone was inside. Thinking someone from the French Resistance, known as *the Maquis*, had entered and sought refuge in the cottage she spoke softly in French using words that were non-committal in case the intruder was a German:

"Fin d'alerte"

End of the alert (all clear).

The Maquis (aka *maquisards*) were rural guerilla bands of French Resistance fighters during the Occupation of France in World War II. Initially, they were composed of men who had escaped into the mountains to avoid conscription into *service du travail obligatoire* (STO, *obligatory work service*) of Vichy France to provide forced labor for Germany. To avert capture and deportation to Germany and remain free, they became increasingly organized in active resistance groups consisting of men and women.

More from the tone of the woman's voice rather than the French words, Jimmie allowed himself to relax a little but still held his pistol in readiness. The soft footstep told him that the woman was approaching the curtain. Jimmie gently pulled the curtain aside to see the woman face-to-face. Something told him that this woman was not an enemy—he quickly disarmed his pistol by moving the safety catch to the "on" position—the pain in his fingers prevented him from moving the hammer to the "rest" position. Having done this as the woman watched him, Jimmie then stretched out his hands in a gesture of friendship. With a look of surprise on her face, the woman's gaze quickly took in his flight suit, with and the signs of the burns, but his heart sank as she stepped back. She walked quickly to the door and as she locked the door and pulled the curtains over the window, Jimmie breathed a sigh of relief. At this moment names were not exchanged—capture of one by the enemy could lead to identification of the other through sessions of severe questioning—often known as *torture*.

Gently taking him by the arm, Suzanne led Jimmie to the table, helped him take off his flying suit, and she dressed his wounds—never had she seen such burns. Being prepared for such an event, food had been placed in strategic hidden locations within the cottage. Suzanne offered him food and gave him some cider highly alcoholic which sent heat coursing through Jimmie's veins. For almost one hour, they attempted to talk through signs and gestures and what little English she knew. Then she made Jimmie lie down on the bed to rest. She could see that his eyes were beginning to swell from the heat and smoke that he had endured before he left his ailing aircraft.

In the meantime, Robert Pettier, who owned the cottage and had been with Suzanne earlier that day, arrived knowing that Suzanne had gone to the cottage to check on its condition and should have reappeared by now. He was somewhat inebriated but welcomed Jimmie to France. Not needing Robert to hover around her and Jimmie, Suzanne sent him off to the nearby Maquis camp to secure the service of a bilingual Canadian infantry captain—who had parachuted into the area on an undefined mission. Pettier returned with the Canadian Captain, a Captain in the Maquis, and a local farmer. The Canadian and Jimmie immediately lapsed into an animated conversation for a few minutes when Robert, who had been standing at the door on watch, turned pale, and announced with a look of apprehension in his eyes:

"*Les Allemands sont à l'extérieur.*"

"The Germans are outside."

A German patrol was approaching in a truck along the road that passed close by the cottage. Closing the curtain in front of the bed where Jimmie lay, Suzanne sent Pettier and the Maquis captain farmer to tend to her cows while she stepped outside and started picking up firewood.

The German truck stopped short of the cottage and ten soldiers got out—fortunately they were not SS or Gestapo but their presence was enough for extreme caution—capture could mean that Suzanne and Robert would be the focus of an immediate firing squad and

Jimmie being sent to the Gestapo headquarters for interrogation. Neither was an acceptable or pleasant option.

A lieutenant (*leutnant*) and sergeant (*feldwebel*) approached while the other soldiers alighted from the truck and stood in line, ready for action. The lieutenant and sergeant, without any form of greeting or any expression of the formalities of the day, started to question Suzanne about the air battle that had taken place earlier. Feigning ignorance about the whereabouts of the downed pilot Suzanne answered their questions persuasively while at the same time leading the Germans away from the cottage as she collected more firewood. Finally, seemingly satisfied with Suzanne's answers and her demeanor, the Germans departed but added, as if to have the last word that they would be back.

Fearing a return visit very soon, Jimmie was moved to an alternate, but much smaller, accommodation in the form of a shack in the woods that evening. By the next day the burns had caused his face to swell and day his eyes had swollen shut. Several times each of the next two days Suzanne would visit Jimmie to bring food and milk and to change his dressings.

On Sunday, July 9, three days after he was shot down and injured the swelling around Jimmie's eyes had diminished enough for him to see and he was introduced to three other allies who were being hidden by the Maquis. They were 1st Lieutenant Richard Reid, an American P-47 Thunderbolt pilot with the 493rd Fighter Squadron (48th Fighter Group), Canadian Flight Lieutenant George Murray (a Spitfire pilot), and Private James MacPherson a Canadian soldier who had parachuted into the wrong Drop Zone on D-Day.

Word came through the Maquis *grapevine* that the Germans had brought in dogs to search for these men so the four allied soldiers left the shack under the guidance of two members of the Maquis. As always names were not exchanged and the men were led in single file—a Maquisard in front, the other in the rear—through fields and wooded areas which gave them as much cover as possible. A fine rain was falling that afternoon as they were taken to a home just south of Montmerrei—a small French village with less than five hundred inhabitants located in the Department of Orne in the region of Lower Normandy. The guides determined that they could not safely stay there and continued to move on foot toward the village of St. Hilaire-la Gerard some seven miles away—again through stands of treed areas, across fields, and roads.

Twice they were almost caught by the Germans. On one occasion, they had to dive behind a hedgerow alongside the road they were traveling on when a German patrol approached. A soldier with the markings of the rank of corporal on his uniform questioned one of the guides who had bravely stayed on the road to sidetrack the enemy. The next close call was when they dashed across a road only to have a German motorcycle patrol roar past a few seconds later. By this time, the burn injuries to Jimmie's right leg were causing him serious pain and he and his colleagues were finally taken to a large isolated barn near St. Hilaire-la Gerard.

On Monday July 10 1944, four days after D-Day and being shot down, it was Jimmie's birthday—he had reached the ripe old age of twenty three! On that same day, he was seriously disappointed to hear that 1st Lieutenant Richard Reid, the P-47 Thunderbolt pilot and the two Canadians—Flight Lieutenant George Murray and Private James MacPherson—had decided to leave the next day. Jimmie would have loved to be the fourth man in the party but his wounds prevented him from accepting the rigors of prolonged travel to the Allied lines. As a result of the journey from the Pettier cottage to St. Hilaire-la Gerard, the pain in his legs had increased and he was worried about infection.

The dirty, dusty barn—albeit a safe haven for the moment—did not offer much in the way of medical attention but certainly offered the possibility of capture by the Germans, which could have been much worse than any infection,. Jimmie was fed by the farmer during his stay in the barn, and his resolve strengthened, and the thought of capture, although still a possibility, started to fade from the front of his mind. Finally, on July 13 Jimmie was taken south to another farm house owned by the Tancray family, a farmer, his wife and eighteen year-old daughter Jeanne.

At the Tancray farm Jimmie was afforded a small room that adjoined the barn. One of the biggest drawbacks was that the farm lay right alongside a major east-west road that was frequently used by the Germans, who were constantly stopping at the farmhouse looking for food or cider. But in the care of the Tancray family Jimmie got what had been lacking since he was shot down—medical care, and excellent care at that. Every day the local medic, Dr. Lemeunie, who just happened to be a member of the Resistance, stopped at the farm to change Jimmie's dressings. It became a source of wonderment to Jimmie as to who might not be a member of the resistance!

As the days passed and his wounds started to heal, each day Jimmie's life was again permeated by thoughts that the enemy might discover him. The biggest threat came one day when a German Tiger II tank—a 75-ton behemoth with a six-man crew—stalled outside of the Tancray farm.

This was a German heavy tank—the *Panzerkampfwagen* Tiger *Ausführung B (Design B),* also known as *Königstiger*, King Tiger or Royal Tiger—that typically had a crew of five: commander, gunner, loader, radio operator, and driver. The presence of a sixth man was not unusual and was often seconded from another tank or unit when a tank needed immediate repair. Even though the seven-inch front armor of the Tiger II was never penetrated in battle, a tank (no matter what the model) was unable to sustain an attack from Allied aircraft. The crewmen—seeing a nearby barn—obviously decided that the vehicle would be better protected by being in the barn and under cover. There, they reasoned, they could work on the tank without interruption and without fear of attack by Allied aircraft. With much trouble and complaint from the spluttering engine that belched black smoke from the aromatic fuel, the crew were able to move the ailing vehicle into the safety of the barn.

The next four days were days of incredibly high stress for Jimmie—each day he was unable to leave the room for fear of being caught and he was afraid to sleep for fear of snoring, and giving away his presence. On the other side of the thin wall of his room was a workbench where the Germans frequently performed the necessary repair and maintenance. He could hear them talk, even breathe. Another problem was keeping Jimmie supplied with food and water. Jeanne Tancray would bring Jimmie his meals though she had to sneak them in so that the ever-watchful tank crew would not see any extra dishes lying about. To be caught would mean instant death for Jimmie and for each member of the family—tank crews were not known for taking prisoners—so it was with a (quiet) sigh of relief when the repairs were finally completed and the tank departed in the midst of a noise that only heavy tank engines can make and with thick black smoke emanating from the elevated tail pipe.

Once again Jimmie settled into a quiet but ever-watchful day-by-day existence. When possible, he was given frequent updates from the family and Maquis visitors of the approach of the Allied forces.

On July 25, 1944 the United States First Army launched Operation Cobra from St. Lô, the breakout offensive from the Normandy beachheads and hedgerow country. The attack was successful in tearing a gap in the German lines allowing the Allies to start their race for the borders of the Third Reich. By now Jimmie's burns had improved to the point that he could travel again. Unknown to him different factions in the Resistance were discussing (in reality they were arguing about) his fate.

One group of Maquisards wanted to put him on the road to Spain while the other group saw no sense in this as the Allies were not too far away—a matter of miles—and while Jimmie's injuries would allow some travel he was not fit enough for prolonged travel. Fortunately for Jimmie, the latter argument prevailed—his initial rescuer, Suzanne Schneider, had taken a strong interest in his welfare and visited him a number of times as he was moved from place to place. She was a moving force in keeping Jimmie from the perhaps fateful choice of having to travel to Spain through German-occupied areas. To get him further away from the arguments of the first faction—the send-him-to-Spain faction—Suzanne took Jimmie back to the cottage where she had first discovered him and there he met up again with a number of his new French friends.

On July 28 Jimmie was taken to the home of the Brû family—approximately two miles away from where he had been staying and a little over a half mile south of Montmerrei. It was a large family with ten children including five year-old André Brû who, as young as he was would play a role in maintaining Jimmie's freedom.

The following morning, July 29, a rumor of spread that the hated and despised *Gestapo* was in the area so Jimmie was moved to a nearby forest by what he called self-styled Resistance members. There he was reunited with his three former travel colleagues—Reid and the two Canadians, Murray and MacPherson. Their attempt to get to the American lines had ended in failure and now they were back in the Montmerrei area. At that time, the area abounded with German military units as they had assembled to attempt to stop the Allied advance—all to no avail but at the time the outcome was not known. Being behind enemy lines and being caught was not conducive to continued good health—like the tank crew, many German units were not amenable to taking prisoners and being shot after capture was not an acceptable alternate fate.

The four soldiers felt, unfairly, that these Resistance members were not up to the task of getting them back to friendly lines and so left and returned to the Brû family farm that same day. There was little they could do to help the family except peel potatoes and clean string beans, which they did willingly enough in order to help pay a little of their board and lodging.

Each night they slept in the barn but during the day they confined their activities to a little shed between the house and barn which had one door and a very small hole in the wall that served as a window. Fortunately, one of the other three men had a pack of cards so they played *Knock Rummy*, a matching card game that is based on the card game of *Rummy*, to pass the long hours. Later, Jimmie estimated they played 2,000 or more games during their stay.

In the game, the players draw for deal, and the player with the lowest card deals first. When two people play, each is dealt ten cards; when three or four play, seven cards; when five play, six cards. Each face card counts 10 points; each ace counts 1 point; other cards count their pip values. The players either draw or take the up-card, and then discard as in Rummy, but they do not meld cards on the table or lay off on each other's melds. Any player, before discarding, may knock (quietly under the circumstances surrounding the small shed), ending the hand. He then separates his melds from unmatched cards, and announces the count of the unmatched cards. Each opponent then separates his melds from unmatched cards and announces his count as well. The player with the lowest count wins the difference in counts from each opponent plus 25 points if he goes rummy. If any other player ties the knocker for low count, that player wins instead of the knocker. If the knocker does not have the lowest count, he pays a penalty of 10 points plus the difference in counts to the player with the lowest count, who wins the hand.

As anticipated, the Gestapo and SS paid the family informal but regular visits for food, cider, and other supplies (for which they did not pay or offer any form of barter). During each of these visits the men were constantly on the alert for fear that one of the children would allow the Germans to discover them. But not a one of them ever betrayed - by thought, word or deed—the men hidden in the little shed. The Germans had set up headquarters in a chateau located less than a quarter mile from the Brû farm and were inspecting the power lines running by the farm to determine if the lines could be adapted to provide electricity for the chateau.

On August 2, Jimmie and his colleagues again gathered in the shed to pass the time by playing cards. The weather was clear and warm and they left the door to the shed open to catch whatever breezes came their way. As they played and talked amongst themselves, five members of the Gestapo walked onto the farm, around the corner of the shed, and stood before the open door, looking up at the power lines, talking in an animated fashion all of the time. The harsh guttural sounds of the German dialects continued as another hand of cards was being dealt when a shadow fell across the doorway.

The cards froze in the hands of the four men and their card-playing faces were replaced by seriously frowned faces. Jimmie and his colleagues looked up and could do nothing but remain still, as if comatose, as they stared at the backs of the enemy discussing the power lines. Just as one of the Germans was turning to speak to one of his colleagues, five-year-old André Brû rounded the corner of the shed and unobtrusively closed the door to the shed. For some time the card players remained as still statues—threatening to turn blue as they held their collective breath—until the voices and footsteps of the Germans receded. It took them some time to recover from this experience and—lesson learned—they never left the door fully open again.

In spite of this isolation, the men were able to keep up with the current news—the Brû family also had a hidden radio, which was an offense punishable by summary execution if discovered by the Germans. Through this simple, but illegal piece of equipment, the news of the St. Lô break-through and the heart-warming details of the swift and steady advance of the Allies were gratefully received. Upon hearing that the Allied Armies were only fifty miles south of Montmerrei, the two Americans—Murray and Reid—left the farm on August 10th and headed in a southerly direction in an attempt to find US troops. The Canadian—MacPherson—stayed with Jimmie, who still continued to suffer pain and anguish from secondary infections around his ankles that prevented him from embarking on long journeys by foot.

Murray and Reid had identified a possible route that the Allies would take as they moved toward Paris but their progress was slowed when they reached the road south. Thousands of Germans soldiers were using the road to move north. This was not the smart goose-stepping army that had marched their way through France four or more years before. This was an army in retreat and disarray knowing that to slow their pace would lead to fierce fighting with many deaths. It was likely that these enemy soldiers were escapees from what became to be known as the Falaise Pocket, which was fought from early-to-late August 1944 and was the decisive engagement of the

Battle of Normandy that allowed the Allied forces to move further inland and away from the beach-heads of D-Day.

Finally, the flood of enemy soldiers dwindled to a trickle and then ceased. Murray and Read retained their composure and concealment in the treed areas and behind the large hedgerows (called *boucage* by the French) which had already gained infamy during the Normandy Invasion as being difficult obstacles to traverse and excellent hiding places for enemy tanks and machine gunners. These hedgerows were created as boundary markers between fields or as windbreaks from the coastal wind, and over time, they grew into substantial barriers. Most originally started as piles of stones dug from the fields or rudimentary stone walls but over time, soil and plants and even trees were added or grew over these walls, providing bulk and height. The hedgerows of the boucage present a difficult obstacle to bypass, being composed of rocks, soil, and small trees and bushes. The berms can reach heights of up to five feet with an additional 8 to 10 feet of bushes, shrubs or trees on top.

It was ironic that the hedgerows that had given cover to German defense forces were now giving cover to Allied soldiers who knew that being caught by retreating German forces would not be very pleasant—death would have been immediate. Time passed—minutes became hours—and then Murray and Reid heard the sound of marching feet as boots contacted the road in rhythmic unison. Fearing the worst and knowing that SS units always marched in time, they remained hidden. As the sound got nearer, they saw—to their surprise, amazement, and joy, that the soldiers advancing north along the road were Americans. Throwing caution to the wind, the two fugitives hailed the advancing troops who were very cautious on seeing two very strange men emerging from the cover of the hedgerow. Much to the joy of Murray and Reid, they were able to prove who they said they were and were accepted. Word spread like wildfire about the two fugitives from the Gestapo/SS and sundry other nasties who may have wished to take revenge on Allied soldiers.

Meanwhile, back at the farm, that evening MacPherson and Jimmie could hear the distant rumble of artillery coming up from the south. The following day, August 11, brought the sighting of an Army observation plane which heightened Jimmie's excitement that the Allies would soon arrive in the area. That afternoon they could hear American artillery shelling a village about five miles away.

Anxiously they waited throughout the day of August 12 for some sign of the Allies. Growing impatient, they decided to go out to try and contact American troops that evening, but the Brû family urged them to stay one more day, which considering the high potential for meeting distinctly unfriendly faces on the road, they reluctantly agreed to do and realizing that, like the tank crew and with the same the thoughts that had passed through the heads of Murray and Reid, the retreating Germans were very unlikely to accept prisoners.

The next day, August 13, brought another day of tension and barely-contained excitement. The sound of artillery that grew moved closer as the day moved into late afternoon. At 5:30 in the evening the sounds of heavy tracked vehicles could be heard passing by the farm. Peering out of the windows of the barn, MacPherson and Jimmie grew excited as elements of the Free French 2nd Armored Division commanded by General Leclerc—they did not see or meet the General—passed on the nearby road. Hastening outside—*at the double* in military parlance—MacPherson and Jimmie were able to stop a vehicle, by waving and shouting wildly with less than a modicum of caution, and they identified themselves as Allied soldiers. They were directed to go to the town of Mortrée where American forces could be found. Prior to the release of Mortrée by American

Forces, a German rearguard delayed the American progression hence the continued sounds of artillery fire. With help from members of the Resistance, the French took minor roads to bypass the obstacle and move toward Paris.

Later that evening the two men, feeling much more relaxed not to be fugitives behind enemy lines, walked the one and one-half miles to Mortrée where they found elements of the 5th Armored Division. In the town Jimmie received much-needed medical attention and both men were able to get his fill of food—an army marches on its stomach and the food was plentiful. Much to his delight, Jimmie got his first chance to use a toothbrush since he had been shot down six weeks earlier.

On August 14 Jimmie was *invited* (ordered) to a debriefing session and completed his *Escape and Evasion Report*. August 15 was a day of celebration when he was joyously reunited with his squadron at Air Base A-11 in France and later that day he was flown back to England—his personal effects had been left at RAF Warmwell and he returned there to retrieve them.

He anticipated being returned to his Squadron but while in England Jimmie learned that he would not be able to rejoin the 428th Squadron in combat operations as he had been hidden by the Resistance and could endanger them should he be shot down again, captured, and succumbed to torture. He was torn between returning to his Squadron but rather than place his French rescuers in jeopardy that would surely happen if he was shot down in combat and made prisoner there was only one choice and that was to return to the United States. After nine days of rest and further medical attention to his ankles Jimmie returned to his squadron in France to say good-bye. While he was there he went to visit the tents of the 429th Fighter Squadron to look up Bob Milliken to thank him for saving his life.

Jimmie located Bob's tent and entered only to find that Bob was on leave for a few days and unfortunately they never met.

Jimmie returned to England and in mid-September he flew to La Guardia Field in New York—which was named after New York mayor Fiorello La Guardia (in office from 1934 to 1945). It was not then known as it is today as La Guardia Airport, which is one of the three airports serving the New York area. The modern name was officially applied when the airport moved under the control of the Port of New York Authority by means of a lease with New York City on June 1, 1947.

His first evening in New York was spent walking down Broadway looking at American girls, eating ice cream, and not having to look over his shoulder for signs of enemy soldiers as well as grim-faced men in field-grey SS or black Gestapo uniforms. He had only one scoop of ice cream while he was on active duty in Europe but he certainly tried to make up for it by spending the seemingly outrageous sum of $1.50 on various ice cream concoctions during his first five hours of freedom in New York—at five cents per scoop this amounted to thirty delicious and thoroughly enjoyable ice cream cones.

From New York Jimmie went home to visit his parents in Alhambra, California. As luck would have it—*timing is everything*— Jimmie had sent them a cable shortly after being rescued informing them that he was well. Three hours after receiving the telegraph from Jimmie, his parents received word from the War Department that the search for their downed son had not provided any evidence that he was still alive and they (the War Department) did not hold much hope for his survival.

Shortly after arrival in California, Jimmie was reassigned to Portland Air Force Base in Oregon where he was a Flight Operations

Officer and eventually promoted to the rank of Captain before leaving the Air Corps in 1946.

For the six weeks Jimmie had been wounded behind enemy lines he had experienced severe pain, extremely stressful situations, as well as an uncertain future that could have ended with the blast from a muzzle of a German gun or imprisonment and torture until execution in a Gestapo jail. Through his own perseverance, his will to survive, and the assistance from some incredibly brave French patriots whose actions could have resulted in their own execution, Jimmie survived.

CHAPTER 8: JOURNAL OF MADEMOISELLE SUZANNE SCHNEIDER

The information presented below, like that which forms the previous chapter, was also kindly provided by Scott Frederick, son of Second Lieutenant James S. Frederick, a P-38 pilot in the 428th Fighter Squadron, 474th Fighter Group. It is Scott's translation of the original version of the notebook written at the time (July 6, 1944, to August 1, 1944) by Mademoiselle Suzanne Schneider. It presents the events described therein as they occurred. She took the time to nurse Lieutenant Frederick back to health. Her efforts and contribution must not be ignored.

The information obtained through the journal of Mademoiselle Schneider also presents further details of the events of Lieutenant James Frederick as well as important information that show the dangers that Resistance Fighters—the Maquis, rural guerrilla bands of French Resistance fighters, called *maquisards*—had to endure. The Maquis were composed of men and women who had escaped into the mountains to avoid capture and deportation to Germany. As the war progressed, they became increasingly organized into active resistance groups. Summary execution or perhaps days of extremely painful torture followed by execution faced any Maquisard who was captured, and they endured such dangers every day. To these brave men and women we owe our heartfelt gratitude.

Briefly, and to allay any confusion, although the name Schneider suggests a German (possibly even Bavarian) origin, families with similar names can be found throughout Europe, particularly in Alsace France. Mademoiselle Schneider was a French citizen, and it is possible that, in the lack of any further information, her family originated in the Alsace region (its capital is Strasbourg) in northeast France.

The name *Alsace* can be traced to the Old High German *Ali-saz* or *Elisaz*, meaning *foreign domain*. An alternative explanation is from a Germanic *Ell-sass*, meaning *seated on the Ill*, a river in Alsace. The region, as part of Lorraine, was part of the Holy Roman Empire, and then was gradually annexed by France in the eighteenth century, and became formally a province of France. Alsace is frequently mentioned with and as part of Lorraine and the former duchy of Lorraine, since it was a vital part of the duchy, and later because of German possession as the imperial province Alsace-Lorraine (1871–1918), was contested in the nineteenth and twentieth centuries. France and Germany exchanged control of parts of Lorraine, including Alsace, four times in seventy-five years. Many citizens of France either living in the area or whose families left the area for various reasons may appear to have German names.

***

In occupied Western Europe in 1940–41, the Nazis encountered many active or potential collaborators. The leaders of Vichy France were eager to pursue a partnership with Germany. Had this plan gained the support of many people in France, it could have led to French belligerence against its old enemy, Britain. But Hitler's economic exploitation of France, notably by imposing an artificially high exchange rate for the Reichsmark against the French franc, progressively alienated the French, even before the 1943 introduction of forced labor in France, the detested *Service de Travail Obligatoire* (STO, obligatory work service).

The Maquis (also known as *maquisards*) were rural guerilla bands of French Resistance fighters who were active (at the risk of life and limb) during the occupation of France in World War II. Initially, they were composed of men who had escaped into the mountains to avoid conscription into *Service du Travail Obligatoire* of Vichy France— which highlighted the division and confusion of French loyalties that had been apparent since the 1940 surrender—to provide forced labor for Germany. To avert capture and deportation to Germany and remain free, they became increasingly organized in active resistance groups consisting of both men and women.

In mainland France, the Resistance enjoyed support from only a small minority of people until the introduction of forced labor by the Germans in 1943, which persuaded many young men to join Maquis groups, in which they afterward fought for France. To challenge the occupiers was difficult and highly dangerous because much of the French aristocracy was believed to be in collaboration with the Germans, as well as with the Vichy regime that governed central and southern France until the Germans took them over in November 1942.

As a tribute to Mademoiselle Schneider and her compatriots, the translation of her journal-diary is reproduced here unchanged—except that italicized words have been inserted to clarify distances, measurements, and clarifications for the reader—in the form translated and provided by and with the permission of Scott Frederick. This is the best and most realistic way to present Mademoiselle Schneider's thoughts and deeds to the reader.

Calendar for year 1944

January
Mo	Tu	We	Th	Fr	Sa	Su
					1	2
3	4	5	6	7	8	9
10	11	12	13	14	15	16
17	18	19	20	21	22	23
24	25	26	27	28	29	30
31						

2: ◐ 10: ○ 18: ◑ 25: ●

February
Mo	Tu	We	Th	Fr	Sa	Su
	1	2	3	4	5	6
7	8	9	10	11	12	13
14	15	16	17	18	19	20
21	22	23	24	25	26	27
28	29					

1: ◐ 9: ○ 17: ◑ 24: ●

March
Mo	Tu	We	Th	Fr	Sa	Su
		1	2	3	4	5
6	7	8	9	10	11	12
13	14	15	16	17	18	19
20	21	22	23	24	25	26
27	28	29	30	31		

1: ◐ 10: ○ 17: ◑ 24: ● 1: ◐

April
Mo	Tu	We	Th	Fr	Sa	Su
					1	2
3	4	5	6	7	8	9
10	11	12	13	14	15	16
17	18	19	20	21	22	23
24	25	26	27	28	29	30

8: ○ 16: ◑ 22: ● 30: ◐

May
Mo	Tu	We	Th	Fr	Sa	Su
1	2	3	4	5	6	7
8	9	10	11	12	13	14
15	16	17	18	19	20	21
22	23	24	25	26	27	28
29	30	31				

8: ○ 15: ◑ 22: ● 30: ◐

June
Mo	Tu	We	Th	Fr	Sa	Su
			1	2	3	4
5	6	7	8	9	10	11
12	13	14	15	16	17	18
19	20	21	22	23	24	25
26	27	28	29	30		

6: ○ 13: ◑ 20: ● 28: ◐

July
Mo	Tu	We	Th	Fr	Sa	Su
					1	2
3	4	5	6	7	8	9
10	11	12	13	14	15	16
17	18	19	20	21	22	23
24	25	26	27	28	29	30
31						

6: ○ 12: ◑ 20: ● 28: ◐

August
Mo	Tu	We	Th	Fr	Sa	Su
1	2	3	4	5	6	
7	8	9	10	11	12	13
14	15	16	17	18	19	20
21	22	23	24	25	26	27
28	29	30	31			

4: ○ 11: ◑ 18: ● 27: ◐

September
Mo	Tu	We	Th	Fr	Sa	Su
				1	2	3
4	5	6	7	8	9	10
11	12	13	14	15	16	17
18	19	20	21	22	23	24
25	26	27	28	29	30	

2: ○ 9: ◑ 17: ● 25: ◐

October								November								December						
Mo	Tu	We	Th	Fr	Sa	Su		Mo	Tu	We	Th	Fr	Sa	Su		Mo	Tu	We	Th	Fr	Sa	Su
						1			1	2	3	4	5							1	2	3
2	3	4	5	6	7	8		6	7	8	9	10	11	12		4	5	6	7	8	9	10
9	10	11	12	13	14	16		13	14	15	16	17	18	19		11	12	13	14	15	16	17
16	17	18	19	20	21	22		20	21	22	23	24	25	26		18	19	20	21	22	23	24
23	24	25	26	27	28	29		27	28	29	30					25	26	27	28	29	30	31
30	31																					

2: ○ 9: ◐ 17: ● 24: ◑ 31: ○   7: ◐ 15: ● 23: ◑ 30: ○   7: ○ 15: ● 22: ◑ 29: ○

I have taken the liberty of making minor corrections to the journal dates. The diary as written—during the pressure of occupation soldiers forever on the lookout for partisans—was a day off in places. I have changed the day to match the date (as shown in the calendar reproduced above for any reader who wishes to place the timeline in perspective). If I am incorrect I apologize to the memories of the late Mademoiselle Schneider, her compatriots, and the late Lieutenant James Frederick.

Finally, the value of the French franc in 1944 was approximately one fiftieth of a US dollar (FF50 = 1 US$). US$100 in 1944 dollars is worth US$1,333.33 in 2014 or US$100 in 2014 would be worth $7.50 in 1944. The conversion of 1944 francs to US dollars has been made according to these formulas. Hopefully the numbers will give the reader some idea of the amount of money that was used to assist Allied soldiers and flyers escape from the clutches of the Gestapo (Secret Service). This money came from the pockets of French citizens.

***

Thursday, July 6, 1944, 10:00 in the evening

Just west of the French village of Montmerrei—a commune in the Orme Department of north-western France— Mademoiselle Suzanne Schneider, a member of the French Secret Army was in a wagon with three other countrymen when the air battle broke out above their heads. They watched as Lieutenant Rubel's plane exploded before hitting the ground. They ran into the nearby trees to avoid the bullets and shells hitting the earth around them watching as a pilot parachuted toward the ground.

I do not want to go to bed without noting down some of the impressions of the day. In spite of fatigue, I have no desire to sleep. I should like this to be tomorrow morning already, in order to know how the child passed the night who came down from the sky and is sleeping in the shelter 200 meters (*220 yards*) from here. I am tempted to go see him, but let us be reasonable, he could take me for a German and be disturbed. So, let us go back. This morning at 9:00 o'clock Mademoiselle Jeanne (Miss Jeanne Tancray, now Mrs. Maquere) came as usual to listen to the communiqué (*news*); that all is going well and in a month we will be delivered (*liberated*).

At 9:30 this morning I took her back to the road past a German auto mounted (*manned*) by four men, of which one is a lieutenant. It is going very slowly. The signalman is watching the sky. Immediately an English plane shot over the enemy car, and with a sudden turn it is hurled into (*over*) the hedge 200 meters (*220 yards*) from us. The balls (*rounds, bullets*) of the machine gun riddled the road, and the plane, seeing nothing, followed another trail (road). A quarter of an hour passed. The German signalman is coming to ask me for two horses. I indicate to him that the nearest are at the Locoy's (Lecoq's, farmers and neighbors of the Clouet's) and the Clouet's place. Is it not better to clear away their neighborhood as fast as possible?

Another quarter of an hour passed. The German returned to his post. He had found nothing. I take my bicycle and go to the blacksmith's house. Indeed the farms are deserted. Only the curious children are looking from behind the doors. I call the little Clouet girl (Ginette). She tells me that her parents (Louise and Eugene Clouet, farmers), frightened at the sight of the German, fled and she is going to meet them, telling them that their horses are going to be taken away. The Lecoy (Lecoq) family did the same. Not a man wished to be seen. Sad soldiers, truly. I do not wish to compromise them, and on the other hand I cannot enter their houses thus with the German, if they are running the black market. I am not a collaborator. I finally make Therese Lecoy (Lecoq), 12 years old, listen to reason. Her little brother, Pierrot, has her by the skirt. It is she herself, trembling, who indicates where the horses are.

The German saw the people flee, but he has what he is asking for. I explain to the Commandant (*name unknown*) that the people are in the fields, that I am forced to return Frankart (a local member of the BOA, Bureau des operations Aeriennes, similar to US OSS, United States Office of Strategic Services) and the boys of the Maquis (predominantly rural guerrilla bands of the French Resistance) are waiting for me and the little girl cannot return alone with her horses. He said to me that a man will go with her to put everything in place.

It is noon. Pettier (Robert, who owned the cottage, le Malheureux, where Frederick first hid, was not a member of the Resistance) returns from his rounds with communiqué (*news*) and announced to me that an animal (not specified, possibly a horse) which he is keeping got out (*of the enclosure*) and we will go together to look for it in the woods this afternoon.

At 3:00 o'clock we go out in the wagon; we look for an hour and have found nothing. Arriving at the top of Val Heureuse (a high spot on the road not far from the cottage), a plane battle suddenly broke out; a double fuselage (plane) came down in flames with a frightful crash. Two enemy planes fall in flames. A second double fuselage (plane) bursts into flames in its turn, but instead of falling heavily as the first, it continues its course at a height of about three kilometers (*a little more than one and three quarter miles or 10,000 feet*). After several seconds appeared the Allied parachutist who came down easily. But what a horror! A German plane goes toward him with the intention probably of bringing him down. Marcel (*Collet*), Roger (*Collet*), (the Collet's lived at le Valheurux), Pettier and I turn around among the oak trees to avoid the bullets coming over us. In my life I shall not forget this sentence of Marcel's.

"Look, everyone, it is marvelous."

In fact an unforgettable spectacle was presented to our eyes, horrified at first, them marveling. A third double fuselage plane (flown by Robert Milliken) with a sudden movement brought down the German plane which had not been able to reach the parachutist whom we saw still coming down easily. Anguish caught us again.

The German parachutist comes down in his turn and appears to be not more than ten meters (*approximately 33 feet*) above our ally. Provided they do not meet on solid ground, the German would kill the American. Such is their custom. The fight lasted twelve to fifteen minutes. Two Allies destroyed and five Germans (*destroyed*).

Thursday, July 6, midnight.

One hears the bullets hitting quite near. The first fallen plane is burning. Quickly all four (*of us*) go in that direction. It is 500 meters (*approximately 550 yards*) away. But at 200 meters (*220 yards*) we see a parachutist three-quarters burned, hanging in an oak tree. At the foot of the tree is (*we can see*) the hand of the flyer still holding the control of the aircraft. We went in the hope of disengaging him, and we found only pieces of skin. The plane burst in the air and the pilot was burned before he could move. Poor child, coming so far to deliver us, and finding (*meeting*) such a horrible death.

The flames were nearing the wood. It is impossible for the moment to attend to the remains of the unfortunate one, for the Germans arrived. We went to a house inhabited by the priest (L'Abbé Poulet). On the road Pettier found his animal. We left, each in his own direction. The collaborators are even more feared than the Germans. The Val du Malheureux—the poor cottage where (*James*) Frederick was—is waiting for me with the Maquis.

Arriving before the school house, I find a German cyclist carrying a burned German pilot. I think that, wounded as he is, he probably did not see ours. Oh, God, if I could find him, with what joy I would hide him and cherish him as my child. I decide mentally that after making a tour of the house, I will explore the woods. In a few minutes I returned. I had locked the door but, because of the heat, the windows were open.

"Return" I replied "the way is clear" thinking I was dealing with my friends, the Maquis.

The curtain which is in front of the bed moved and I see something I wished appear to my raptured eyes. No, I am going crazy, and nevertheless, those two hands stretched toward me. I took the hands.

It is true; the dear American child is there, burned badly, but so happy in spite of his suffering that he must endure. How I want to take him in my arms. He began to put on the pomade (salve). I help him take off his contraption (*flight suit and*), his revolver. I bandage him. My hands are trembling. Never have I seen such burns.

He eats some eggs, takes some tablets in a little cider, drinks some coffee with (*fresh farm*) cream, and combs his hair before the glass. He makes me understand that he is happy because neither his eyes nor his chest are touched. For an hour we talked (*through gestures*). He has already retained many French words and when I advise him to rest, he stretches out on the bed, where I hope with the permission of the master of the place (*Pettier*) he will pass the night. How happy I am, but how he must suffer. The perspiration runs down his face. His eye lids are beginning to swell. Ah, Pettier returns singing. He has been drinking as usual. I want him to be quiet. I do not want him to disturb the rest (*sleep*) of my child. He is surprised and happy. At the same time the sight of the burned pilot disgusts him.

There is in the Maquis a Canadian Captain. He speaks French. He came down in a mission and forgot (*was not able*) to set off again (*to leave to continue his mission*). He is a deserter (*separated from his unit*) but it is up to us to sustain him and not to judge him. Pettier is going to get him so I will know what my child wishes to drink and eat. At 8:00 o'clock he returned with the Captain, Frankart and Louis Bellavoine—a farmer living in St. Christophe, near Montmerrei. The Captain has been talking with the aviator for five minutes. Louis, who is near me at the entrance of the wagon, became pale.

"The Germans," he said to me, "are outside."

But we did not lose our composure. I sent Louis and Pettier to take care of the cows.

I pretend to gather wood. The Germans question me. I pretend to be surprised and go a few meters to meet them. They are at least ten meters (*approximately 33 feet*) from the aviator. The interpreter speaks French very well.

"Good day, madam. There are many planes which have fallen near you, aren't there? Are they Americans or Germans?"

"I don't know, sir. I am afraid of the shots (*bullets*) and I did not go near."

"And didn't you see the parachutists fall 150 meters (*approximately 165 yards*) from you?"

"Yes, sir, I met him opposite the school house of Montmerrei. I even noticed that he was very badly burned."

"Ah, yes, but perhaps it was ours whom you met."

"I do not know, sir, how the American aviators are dressed" and all the other questions they asked, (*such as*) how many kilometers they covered (*went*) along the road as the bird flies. Finally little by little, while replying, I led them along the road (*away from the farm*). They are going to come back tomorrow. They are ten, I am alone in answering them, but I won the first round. The German truck left and I returned joyously to the shelter. But all the men went outside. The Captain and Frankart went out by the window and left the parachutist. Where are their heads? (*What are they thinking?*) I answer the (*German's*) questions and they abandon me with the child. If the Germans had returned, we would both have been shot. For my part I would prefer that to the martyrdom of (*torture by*) the Gestapo, but this poor child who will be 22 years old the 10th of this month (*Jimmie Frederick turned 23 that year*). His birth date was July 10, 1921). Now he is not secure (*safe*) here.

We must take him to the shelter in the woods where no one will find him. People are very comfortable there. I spent the night there. I slept well. This day leaves a good impression on me. I was not afraid. Tomorrow I will organize the life of this child. I will call him by his name. Tonight I can only wish him good night.

Friday, July 7, 1944

I did not sleep well waiting impatiently for the day in order to see my parachutist. I noticed last evening that his right eye was hardly visible. I am going for milk, but let us (*I must*) hide this notebook. The Germans may come. It is 9:00 o'clock (*in the morning*). After having milked the cows I went to carry breakfast to this dear child. Goodness, what he must suffer. His two eyes are not visible. His eyelids swollen by the burns, and he finds the means to smile. What courage! He drinks and eats well. That gives me pleasure and very little trouble. He has on him some good salve (*ointment*). I have seven liters (*almost 15 US pints*) of milk for him to drink as much as he wishes. I think that is his favorite drink. So much the better. Milk is at the same time an antidote. I think he must need to go to the cabinet (*toilet*). I want him to understand that he does not need to be embarrassed, that although he is a grown man, I consider him as my child. But he does not see clearly and I cannot speak his language. I change his dressings and go to get Pettier who is coming to see him. He takes him (*Jimmie*) by the two hands, and going backwards, leads him to the little corner, which he did not wish to understand with (*explain to*) me and he understands immediately with a man. That shows great delicacy.

I hardly had time to see the Canadian Captain yesterday, and he seemed cold and bossy, and my little Lieutenant is so gentle. I want to know what he wants to eat. I am going to send for the Canadian and that will be settled. During this time I am going quickly to

Montmerrei to try to find some preserves for him. It has been three years since we have had any, but for him I would have the courage to beg.

At 11:00 o'clock I return from the town. I am happy. I am bringing back a little bowl of stewed rhubarb. Madame Leulier (Madame Alice Leulier and her husband Adrien owned the local bakery and grocery shop in Montmerrei), who furnishes all she makes for the Maquis, gave it to me. She is glad that he fell near me that she puts me on guard. The collaborators are looking in the hedges for the second fallen American. I assure her that no one can find him. My water is boiling for the second dressing. I go to see him, taking milk, bread, butter and the preserve. The Captain and Frankart came to see him in my absence. They do not have the courage to come to the house nor to stop and wait for my return, distracting him a little (*spending some time with him*). I find only a paper.

"Give him milk and change his dressings twice a day."

How angry I am. I did not need them to know that. I will change his dressings as often as necessary. What I wanted to know is what he would like to eat. He has just eaten and drunk without seeing clearly. I put butter and preserves on the bread in little bites. I put it in his mouth like a little bird. He drank the milk with pleasure. He made me understand by putting his hand at his throat that he is not hungry. Then he stretched out his two hands in spite of the suffering which his wrists make him endure, to make me understand that he is grateful - dear, dear, child. How I would like to surround him with more comforts, but his security comes before all else.

How the time has passed fast since yesterday. I did not stay long with the Maquis. I am sorry I told the Captain and Frankart of the descent of this child near me. They do not sympathize so I shall not ask them for anything. They dared to make fun of my sensibility toward this child. These two men from now on I judge to be undesirables, to say nothing more. A bright idea comes to me. Roger Collet, very well educated, knowing how to speak a little English, is worthy of knowing my dear child. I am going to look for him. It is 7:00 o'clock in the evening. My cows are milked. The milk is heating. I am going to take advantage of it by noting down the events of the afternoon.

Roger Collet arrived at 2:30 with the pomade (salve, *ointment*) and the dressings. He has just dressed the ankles. I myself dressed his head and wrists. He was so happy to talk with Roger. But it was a blow to him when he told him that (*his colleague*) Rubel was dead. Then I knew that he was his friend and that they lived about twelve kilometers (*approximately seven and a half miles*). James was from Alhambra and Robert (*Rubel*) from Los Angeles their friendship developed in England when Robert joined the 428th Fighter Squadron) from each other. I know that his name is James. Roger left at 4:00 o'clock promising him to return tomorrow. At 5:00 o'clock I brought him coffee and milk, bread and butter. He stretched out and rested until 8:00 o'clock.

I have just learned something that revolts me. This morning George Desiroix (Descroix, lived in Montmerrei) and Marcel Collet went to see the mayor to tell him that they had picked up the remains of the noble child (*Robert*) Rubel. They were very badly (*not well*) received (*by the mayor*).

"Put everything in a sack", he said to them, "and bury it where you wish, but not in the cemetery."

How shameful to hear a mayor talk thus—the mayor was named Aubert and, while not a collaborator, is a coward. He acts like the last of the collaborators. The two young people returned to the Val Huereuse. They met Pettier and he decided that Mr. Collet should make a box secretly from the Germans. Poor Rubel. Of his head there remains only the skin covered with beautiful brown hair, two hands one of which still held the control of the plane, some strips of flesh from his thighs, probably weighing in all hardly two kilograms (*almost four and a half pounds*). Madame Louet—should be "Madame Clouet", living in Montmerrei but no relation to Jean-Claude (*Clouet*)—took a lock of his hair. In case the parents could not come to get the body of their son, she would send what remained of their child.

I have just had supper. I let Pettier finish his meal alone so I can stay as long as necessary by my James (*Jimmie Frederick*), to change his dressings, make him eat and teach him some words of French, as he remembers everything. If he can stay a month here, with the help of Roger we will understand each other very well. At 9:30 I return. Poor child (Jimmie Frederick), his head is more swollen than this morning, but he has very little fever which reassures me a little. Good night, dear child, a French woman watches over you.

Saturday, July 8, 1944

Today I got up early in order to be as quickly as possible near him whom in my heart I call my child. His dear face is still more swollen than yesterday, but after washing his eyelids, his eyes are slightly visible. Roger came at 10:00 (*in the morning*). A scene (*an argument*) about Rubel has just taken place with his father. Since the mayor did not want to bother with this unfortunate one (*Robert Rubel*), the patriots dug the grave in the cemetery and ordered a coffin from the carpenter since the mayor refused to do it. Then he threatened them with prosecution for violation of the cemetery. How shameful and how vain are the threats. Rubel will be buried this afternoon. The religious service is ordered. Roger will be the only one not to attend. He promises me to come this afternoon to stay with James.

We have had dinner. (*A man, code name*) Josec—a member of the Resistance though not a good one—came with fresh supplies and told me that James' revolver had been offered by the Canadian Captain to Frankart. It is an easy thing, indeed, to give gifts when they belong to others. I was then right to think that those two are undesirable. Marcel Eriseff (a man of goodwill and a member of the Resistance, but a drunkard) came in his turn to see my James, like a curiosity. How these people displease me. Selfish and worthy of being the servant of Frankart, not working except for gain. Did he not say that thanks to the Captain he would be an aviator? Poor fellow, no education, son of an alcoholic, he limps and without glasses he cannot see anything at two meters (*six feet six inches*). Underneath his appearance of a good boy, (*but*) he is a liar and undisciplined. Just today Mr. Collet said he would make a search of the quarter. At any rate, let us distrust him.

5:00 o'clock in the evening. Roger and I spent two hours with James. Those two spoke English and French. Returning to the house, we found that Mme. (*Madame, Mrs.*) Collet sent him some cakes by her son. Pettier was furious. The priest, since he was a true collaborator, had the service an hour earlier so that the patriots were not there. The mayor went to see the Germans and told them that all this had been done without his authorization. The German officer replied that it was regrettable, because it would have been more correct if we had been told in order to give honors to this soldier. So thanks to this timorous Mayor, this noble aviator did not receive the honors which were due him. We decided to put a cross on the tomb of Rubel, with his name and the date of his death. We will put flowers on it, and if after the war the parents can come for the remains of their child, we will show them a monument worthy of him. The helmet and headpiece of Rubel are in the hands of the mayor. He does not deserve to have in his hands these relics. We should rather have Mr. Collet keep them in order to give them back himself to the family. But Mr. Collet will not stay here after the war and none of us can take charge. We are all the future prey of the Gestapo.

Sunday, July 9, 1944, 10:00 P.M.

Today marked the twenty-third birthday of Lieutenant James Frederick. He spent it recovering from his still-painful wounds.

Everything is very fine. My child (*Jimmie*) left, and in what a state, poor thing. This morning at 8:00 the Frankart crew came saying they were followed by the Germans. I gave them shelter, and the three parachutists (*the Canadian Captain and two other allied airmen*) who were with him asked me for permission to lie down near James. Frankart before the next day is to go further with them. They had dinner and prepared their beds for the night. The Germans have lost their trace (*trail, track*). At 3:00 in the afternoon the Eriseff boy came like a crazy man. The police dogs were on the heels of the Frankart crew, and as he (*they*) had found shelter near my pilot (*Jimmie*), it is necessary that he leave also. I try to intervene. If they take him away, it is death that awaits him who is getting along so well.

He (*Jimmie*) has no fever this morning, and sees clearly. Roger, who had brought him such good things, how happy we were to spoil him, and now a fine rain is falling. It is necessary to take off the bandage which he has on his eyes in order that he can walk. Marcel takes them to the Montagne's—Mr. and Mrs. Montagne were living in Montmerrei—(*hidden*) in a barge (*cart*) of firewood. I go by another road with the blankets and rejoin them. I profit by changing James' bandage, and I think that tomorrow perhaps I can see my child again. Mrs. Montagne (Mortagne) brings him milk. A child of 14 years passes. A piece of sheet iron falls on the shelter. Impossible for the men to stay here. Their refuge is discovered. What to do? I stay with them while the men look for a solution. They will be taken away tonight.

At St. Hilaire-la Gerard, at Mr. Martin's (house)—the Martin family lived in St. Hilaire la Gerard—and took (*Jimmie*) Frederick there to stay with the Tancray Family, (*with whom*) I am acquainted. I could go to see my child, but I am very troubled. His hands are burning (*painful*). He asks to lie down. His legs hurt him, and tonight there are twelve kilometers (*approximately seven and a half miles*) to go on foot across fields. I tell everyone good-by and James goes out of the shelter to embrace me. I hold back my tears but courage leaves me when I arrive at the house. Pettier and Frankart wept at the fate of the poor child.

Today, Roger comes to celebrate the 22(*nd*) (*23rd*) birthday of James. What a disappointment, to know he left without hope of returning, for I told no one where they went.

Noon: Charles, Regional Head of the secret army (*the French Resistance Movement sent help to downed Allied flyers*), came for three days. He must hide. He is tracked. He tells me why the Chateau of the Courviere and the Major German State are not healthy. His radio was tapped when he sent his messages. I told him the story of my aviator, and my torment. A man of heart and honor, he understands me and promised to have James returned here because he knew his officers and their way of acting with our allies. He is going to see Frankart so that he will bring back the revolver (*referring to James's handgun, a Colt 45 M1911-A1*).

Monday, July 10, 1944.

I did several errands for Charles. He recommended precautions toward the Maquis. Pettier takes the communiqué (*news*) to too many people. I reassure him and am going to show him where the English post (*hideaway*) is. It is 20 meters (*approximately 22 yards*) from the shelter, empty now of my dear child. Tomorrow morning I must take between four and six pounds to Joseph Montagne (Mortagne). Marcel Eriseff will take it to carry it to the Martins. Perhaps he will see the parachutist and I will have some news.

Tuesday, July 11, 1944, 3:00 in the morning

I should say Wednesday, since it is 3:00 a.m. Finally I note down the day Tuesday, which was well used. This morning I waited at Joseph's (Mortagne) for the return of Marcel Eriseff to have news, but he could not see anyone. I got ready to leave the courtyard. I saw three men pass. I recognized the three parachutists, among who was the Canadian Captain who also recognized me. He made me understand that they were going to be prisoners before the end of the day. I crossed the town of Montmerrei, talking to them in order to throw the Germans off the scent. I made them know that the big chief (*the Canadian captain*) is at my home now (*I am the head of my household*). They did not want to walk further. Their guides were walking 200 meters (*approximately 220 yards*) ahead, must return back. I called Marcel Eriseff who is going to look for Charles in order to lead him to the five men. I returned to the Val du Malheureux to prepare dinner. Charles returned at 1:00 o'clock and gave the order for the guides to go and tell their chief that if he had no other solution than to put these three men on the road, he would take charge of them himself. The three men are hidden in a hedge.

Charles, troubled, sends me there. He is afraid they will take these men away. I stay with them until 8:00. I must return to get supper. I make the Captain promise not to follow anyone. As soon as I arrived at the house, Charles with Louis Quandieu (a hardware dealer who was deeply connected to the Resistance) went to look for the men. They are going to eat here and then Marcel Eriseff will go to lead his Captain to Lemoine (a pork butcher in the Resistance) while I take the others to Louis. I do not keep any papers on me but I take my 6/35 (*a small six-shot 35 mm revolver*). In Montmerrei we almost crossed a German patrol. The two men lay in a ditch. The Germans did not see anything. They are with Louis, each in a bed. They need rest. The American pilot cannot walk further. I returned here at midnight. I have not had supper. Charles calls (*to see*) me. He is happy that everything went well.

Wednesday - July 12, 1944

Charles left after breakfast. He must give his word so that James will be returned to me. He had already told the young man sent by the head of St. Hilaire, and since James is at his house, he will not refuse to let me see him.

Thursday, July 13, 1944

I went to the tomb (*grave*) of (*Robert*) Rubel to take a bouquet. I gathered some flowers there which I intend to take to James (*Jimmie Frederick*). (*I felt*) Disappointment on arriving at the house (*where*

James had been taken). James had changed in the morning. Why? Because those two were very sympathetic.

"Go to Martin's," he says to me, "and try to take James away, because I am afraid they will play an ugly trick on him."

Arriving at Martin's, I exposed the purpose of my visit. Then this man became very angry.

"It is you," he said, "who prevented the three parachutists from following their road (*route, plan*)."

"Yes, sir, after the orders of our chief (*head of the local Maquis group*)."

"But do you know that you run the risk of having all of us shot with those people who know our names?"

"No, sir," I replied.

"These men are allies and more than that, they risked their lives to deliver us. It is the least we can do to protect them."

"A truth with sentiment", he said to me. "Not only will you not see (*Jimmie*) Frederick but in 15 days I will put him on the road to Spain."

Friday-July 14, 1944

I have made the acquaintance of (*code name*) Marsouin (*Porpoise*). That is his war name. His (*real*) name is Mazeline, (*and he is*) a school teacher, 29 years old. I tell him my troubles.

"It is not advisable," he said, "for Martin to put on the road this young man (*who is*) scarcely healed. Besides, there are orders. They must stay at their point of fall until the arrival of their own people. Go there tomorrow for me for I am afraid that Charles will be offended and will not do what is necessary. As for Frankart, I shall see him and require him to put back the revolver where the Captain had taken it."

Frankart said to me also that Martin had been receiving for a long time food and clothes from England. What did they do with them? One thing is for sure - we have nothing in the Maquis and I am going to ask you to buy some for us, all that you find. Frankart has 850,000 (*francs, worth approximately US$17,000 at that time or US$226,000 in 2014*). How did they get them (*so much money*)? (*Probably the*) Black market and parachuted merchandise—and we, the kindly patriots, are forced to beg for all these conscripts (*Allied military personnel*) that the Gestapo is looking for.

Saturday-July 15, 1944

My trip to St. Hilaire simply told me that James is getting along as well as possible and that is all. I am going to return there Monday. If I can know where he is, we will go and get him at night.

Sunday, July 16, 1944

Last night I awakened suddenly at 2:00 in the morning. It was Marsouin who came to say that for three days he had no bread. Then I went to Leulier—the baker—who gave me six loaves of bread of six pounds (*six loaves of bread totaling approximately six pounds in weight*), and (*he*) promised me more tomorrow. I found a calf at Joseph's, (*it was valued at*) 2800 (*francs, approximately US$56 in 1944 or US$746.50 in 2014*) and he did not want me to pay.

"When our purse is empty it will be time."

Amedée—whose real name was Arnold Crouin was a good friend of Jean-Claude's father and used to slaughter animals to feed the Resistance—brought it in his cart, the boys also who furnished cider for nothing to everyone, and to think that if the collaborators knew it, the Gestapo would make only a mouthful of (*noise about*) it.

Monday, July 17, 1944

It was impossible for me to go to St. Hilaire (*a small village located in the south of France*) today, but Mrs. Montagne saw Martin who told her that I could not see him, but that he could not send him on the road before eight days. His ankles were bad again. Marcel Eriseff, learning that, was remorseful for without the story of the police dogs, James would have been cured here quickly between us two.

"Roger" he said, "it is necessary that I do as much as possible to help Suzanne to get him out of there, for it is my fault alone that he is there."

Tuesday, July 18, 1944

I hired the horse from Bisson (lived at la fenderie Montmerrei (*the enchanted Montmerrei*). Frederick passed through his farm when he was led to St. Hilaire la Gerard) to go to Argentan, but I went simply to take food to the camp of the Maquis. One calf of 2000 (*francs, approximately US$40 and worth US$533 in 2014)*, five loaves of bread, beans, and brandy. They have no more money. It is necessary that they pretend to be collaborators.

Wednesday, July 19, 1944

For the third time I return to St. Hilaire without seeing James. It is Martin's son, George, who received me.

"You saved him," he said to me, "and I understand your desire to embrace him before he leaves. But today you will not see him. He is leaving in eight days alone on the road to Spain. Promise me not to let him see the dangers of the road, and the eve of his departure you will see him."

I promised but I swear that I will do all I can so that he will not take the road to Spain.

Thursday, July 20, 1944

Marcel Eriseff is remorseful of his thoughtless conduct. Not only James could die as a result of the fever contracted by one night of fatigue and rain, his wounds open to the air, but the road to Spain is ready for James, and Marcel understands very well that the poor child will not make it 20 kilometers (*approximately twelve and a half miles*) without being taken, so it is necessary at any cost to save him.

"You know," he said to me, "the three others did not complain."

"But", I replied, "It is not a question of that. Everything is ready for him here."

He promised to try to bring him tomorrow.

Friday, July 21, 1944

This evening Maquinguy (*Maquigny*), informed (*who has been told*) by Marcel Eriseff, came to tell me that the child was forever lost, that he was leaving the 28th for the road to Spain. Finally all is perhaps not lost, since I must go to say good-by to him the 27th. But tears flowed that I could not hide. My despair is great. Everyone respects my sorrow.

Saturday, July 22, 1944

I saw Marsouin (July 15, spelled as Masson) who said to Martin that if he did not give back this young man to us and as a result something happens to him, he alone will bear the responsibility of it. Sunday, Monday, Tuesday, nothing abnormal. The communiqué (*news*) is very good and the Germans on Caen experience many losses.

Wednesday, July 26, 1944

I left the wagon after breakfast without telling anyone where I was going. I was so afraid of losing a final meeting. Marcel Eriseff had gone before me to Martin's. Mrs. Martin was alone. Her son George was at Montmerrei in order to get acquainted with the shelter of the three parachutists. He had two passports and would have liked to persuade one of them to leave with James. He follows the order of his chief regretfully, for he is attached to James. At 5:00 he had not yet returned. I stayed alone to wait for him and at 6:00 he arrived.

"You came to say good-by to him," he said to me.

"No," I replied, "I came on behalf of the Lieutenant to tell you that the three parachutists are with me, that tomorrow he is going up to the Maquis where he will rejoin a (*return to the*) base. The Lieutenant wants Frederick to rejoin his comrades, if that is his wish. But if you put him on the road to Spain, you will be responsible."

"No nonsense," he replied. "I deliver him back to you and he led you half way."

He confided to me that James had as much good manners as the Captain had little, that he would have wept to put him on the road to Spain, but that he owed obedience to his chief, but the Lieutenant was over him. He was very happy with the outcome, and he even went to look for a piece of James' plane as a souvenir. They said good-by to each other as good friends.

In the course of the trip James spoke to me of his fiancée Betty, who is English and loves him very much. Arriving here at 10:00, what a scene, Josec warned me but nothing touched me since my child was there. Pettier is forced to milk the cow. Mrs. Collet has not her milk. I shall leave tomorrow morning saying to Roger that his friend is there. How happy they will both be. Pettier, lying down, argues while we two drink milk. Of what importance to me are the reasons of a man who is drunk? I saved that child twice. I was able to reconcile my duty and my affection for him. He will no longer sleep in the shelter but in a bed with Josec. I think he understands the reproaches with which I am assailed, for before going to bed he embraces me tenderly.

Thursday, July 27, 1944

I carried (*went for*) the milk early. Mr. Collet answered me. He came with Roger to listen to the communiqué (*news*) with James. They commented on it. Roger will return tonight as well.

Friday, July 28, 1944

Yesterday my dear James, evoking (*thinking of*) his family so far away. Poor child, how I understand his sorrow, and how cruel of me not to be able to say one word of consolation. He gave me his chain from his neck and a lock of his hair. They will never leave me, and if ever any misfortune comes to him, I shall send to his mother this holy souvenir of her child. Tomorrow he will get dressed fully, and Monday he will go up to the Maquis with his comrades. This troubles me and reassures me at the same time for the Gestapo is beginning to

277

have doubts. Then he has a bad leg again. Up (*at Maquis camp*) there is a doctor. The Captain and the Commandant, both teachers, are very kind. Every two days I go up to the camp. I can see James and take him the milk which he loves so much, the only thing they lack.

Saturday, July 29, 1944, early morning—just after Midnight

Marcel Eriseff came to say that the three parachutists (*the Canadian captain and the two other allied airmen*) would like to see James. This causes me an indefinable uneasiness. Why? At 9:00 I went to take James to Lemoine's house where the (*Canadian*) Captain is (*hiding*). From there others would come for them. It is again necessary for me to be separated from my child who embraces me before leaving. Two kilometers (*approximately one and one quarter miles*) to go on a black (*dark*) night. I am not afraid.

Sunday, July 30, 1944, 11:00 in the evening

I have finally found iodine for James' leg. I am going to take it to him at the Bru's (*house*). Their reunion seems to be a plot. The Captain was triumphant. James was anxious. Roger Collet came this evening and was disappointed. James had not yet returned. They all arrived at 9:30. The Captain ordered James to bring the linen which Roger gave him and the linen he gave him yesterday. Roger and his mother were to return tomorrow, to see James, and James did not want to sleep in his bed. The linen which he left yesterday was not washed. I intended to take it to him up there in two days. They told me they wanted to sleep all four together to talk, but that tomorrow morning when I leave their breakfast, James will return with me to talk with Roger and his mother.

Monday, July 31, 1944, 10:00 in the evening

Cursed be Marcel Eriseff who invented the story of the (*use of*) police dogs (*to find James*) which made (*forced*) James leave on July 10, bringing on him (*causing him* to develop) the fever. Cursed (*also*) be the Canadian Captain who did not like James because James, (*being*) a man of honor and duty, had nothing in common with him (*the captain*) (*nor with all*) who all who approached (*sided with*) him (*the captain*)—except Marcel Eriseff, deprived of intelligence— judged him (*the captain*) to be without (*did not have any*) scruples. Am I going to have the courage to write what is tormenting me so much, or am I simply going to drown this page with tears? What a pity that I cannot speak their language (*English*), for perhaps James would not have left. If he was cured, I would not be so troubled, but his leg still has a wound (*the size of which is*) as large as a hand. Captain Misfortune (*as Mademoiselle Schneider called the Canadian captain*), did he not reply at Bru's when they said (*asked*), after the war you four will all come back to see us?

"No," replied the Captain, "three only" (*the captain replied quickly to exclude himself from any return visit*).

He did not like James, and he had the presumption to tell me last evening that he wanted James to sleep with them. This morning I got up early and in two baskets I put all that was necessary for the breakfast for the three men. James was to return here for breakfast to be able to talk with Roger (*Collet*) and his mother. How fast I went to go to look for my child, but arriving at the shelter, nothing (*there was no one*).

Thus, those four men I saved had left in the night without leaving me a word, leaving me to (*in*) despair. How I got back to the house I do not know. Madame (*Mrs.*) Collet saw me, came to me, and mixed her tears with mine. Roger arrived then and did not find any explanation of our sorrow but the breakfast intact. He tried with Josec to reassure us saying that the Germans were too busy to occupy themselves with them and that they would pass the lines easily. Perhaps but his leg with the fever (*his high temperature*) of (*that accompanies*) gangrene (*infection*) is lying in wait for him. Did I do right in saving this child from the Germans? Yes, he would have been shot. They would have wanted to avenge (*revenge for*) their five planes (*that were*) destroyed.

On May 30, 1944, Martin Bormann, Hitler's secretary, sent a notice to local authorities that no citizen should be punished for assaulting or killing downed Allied airmen. In occupied countries the airmen and anyone assisting them would be held liable for aiding the enemy and summarily executed. Fighter pilots, who strafed at low level in the last phase of the war, incurred special hatred.

Yes, the great (*main*) culprit is Marcel Eriseff. Without him (*Eriseff*), he (*James*) would have stayed here and with Roger would have awaited the arrival of the Allies. Marcel Eriseff wants to be an aviator after the war. He is afraid of danger. He is fearful and gave proof of lack of discipline today.

The four aviators were to go up (*to the Maquis camp*) this evening with the Maquis Commandant. All the men wanted to prepare good beds for them. Marsouin (*the Porpoise*) had ordered breakfast for fifteen (*persons*). They were all then to go up to a depot of arms. I had trouble in finding enough to eat for so many. Fortunately Amedée (the butcher, who real name was Arnold Crouin) gave me a good roast of veal. There were no preserves (*condiments*). The group of which Marcel Eriseff was a part of (*member had*) all dispersed.

Frankart cashed 1000 francs (*approximately US$20 and worth approximately US$267 in 2014*) for Marcel and 1000 for Louis. I inform them, as for me, I cashed 2000 (*francs, approximately US$40 and worth approximately US$533 in 2014*) to go to pay the expenses of the three parachutists. I know what the Captain paid, but I am going to give what Marsouin (*the Porpoise*) has said. The Normans are very stingy. May this money do them a lot of good (*spoken sarcastically*). Marcel Eriseff approved of getting so much money, but he stayed to one side. He did not want to go up to the Maquis. Let us not insist, and let us mistrust him (*Eriseff*).

Marsouin (*the Porpoise*) arrived first and came happy to take these four men under his protection. He was very disappointed. He went alone to the (*Maquis*) camp. All this changed his program (*schedule*). His men will not come for breakfast, but everyone will go down this evening. They are going tonight to transport a depot of arms. I am going to prepare the accounts. He gave me yesterday 200 francs (*approximately US$4 and worth approximately US$53 in 2014*) to pay the expenses of the three parachutists although the Canadian Captain came down in a mission and had already (*been*) paid. But the Normands (Normans) are so stingy. This afternoon I went to Lemoine's (*home*) to pay for the Captain (*not to come back*). They are very happy that he (*the Captain*) has left, for the Bru's are very imprudent (*lacking in good judgment*). They see only the interest (*personal financial reward*) that this operation brings them. They risk nothing. They bring (*are given*) bread, meat, and money which helps them in raising their family. I should like to possess their morals (*spoken sarcastically*). Unfortunately it is nothing. I wonder if I am not losing my reason, for when I went to the Bru's to take the money, I had a vision of James jumping through the window. This would be something to wish for, but it is impossible. He left on the road, limping, for his leg was very bad. If only the gangrene (*infection*) does not set in with that fever, but nothing will bring an end to my disturbance (*unhappiness*).

Tuesday, August 1, 1944.

I did not sleep all night. The men traveled all night with the arms (*and are all armed*). A small carriage broke down under the load, and it was necessary under threat of a revolver to requisition in the dead of night horses and carriage to cross the road and pasture land. The men carried it all in their arms across the woods. This morning not a trace remained of anything. All the men were present. Only under his appearance of a good boy (*under the presence of being a good man*), Marcel Eriseff took to his bed (*supposedly he was sick*). It is not he who will help to save France. Madame Leulier (*one of my friends and another Resistance fighter*) had to put me on guard against him. Liars are dangerous. Did he not make enough fuss over James' revolver? More than ever let us (*continue to*) distrust him (*Eriseff*), for the people that (*whose personal*) interests dominate (*their actions*) are dangerous. Roger comes each day for the milk and to listen to the communiqué (*news*). When we are alone we talk of our James.

"Dry your tears" he tells me. "In four or five years we will see him again."

I dare not reply to him what I am thinking. I shall (*may*) be dead before then. I do (*not*) accuse the poor child (Jimmie Frederick). He was dominated by the Canadian Captain (*the senior officer of the group of Allied flyers and, in keeping with his rank, the person in command*), but I am sure that he will have regrets at (*if he knew he was*) causing me pain.

CHAPTER 9: ONCE MORE UNTO THE BREACH

In July Bob earned the second and third oak leaf clusters to his Air Medal. The awards reflect the number and intensity of the missions they were flying in support of the advancing ground forces. The fliers were in the air almost as much as they were on the ground.

Bob got credit for only one, but he flew two missions on July 30. Both were in the area of Chartres, where they encountered heavy flak while cutting rail lines, shooting up box cars, and raking a German convoy. The missions kept coming.

On August 1, he was on a dive-bombing sortie in the Laval area. The next day it was the same thing, this time in the Amiens area where they hit and destroyed three trains. Amiens is a city and commune in northern France, approximately seventy-five miles (120 kilometers) north of Paris. It is the capital of the Somme department in Picardy.

On August 4 the squadron hit an airfield east of Amiens, then strafed and bombed railway traffic. In all, they destroyed a locomotive, blew up twelve to fifteen railroad cars, damaged a building, and destroyed six trucks and an official-looking black sedan that got caught in the gun sights of one of the P-38 pilots.

Two new pilots joined the squadron on August 3: Ben Higgins and Robert Liberenz. Higgins was later killed, and Liberenz got off to a rocky start. Shortly after joining the squadron, Liberenz was flying on Bob's wing, but instead of protecting Bob's flank as a good wingman should, he broke formation and took off on his own to strafe a bus, after which Bob could not trust the man. He had left his designated place in the formation and exposed his colleagues to danger if an attack by German fighter pilots had occurred.

***

The last mission from Warmwell was flown on August 5, 1944. The following day the 429th Squadron moved to France and was based at A-11, an airfield located inland from Omaha Beach, a short distance south from the town of Isigny on the Cherbourg peninsula. Advance contingents from the squadron had already departed, and subsequently all non-flying personnel and equipment crossed the Channel in LCTs (landing craft tanks) to Omaha Beach.

The designation "A" and a number indicated an *advanced landing ground*, the term given to the temporary advance airfields constructed by the Allies during World War II in support of the invasion of Europe. The airfield was used by the 474th Fighter Group from August 6 to August 29, 1944.

To build the base, approximately 2,000 trees, including an entire apple orchard, were uprooted and destroyed to lay down the perforated steel mesh for a runway. Shelter halves were erected until tents could be obtained. The base could finally be called "home" on August 31,

1944. The squadron would no longer have to fly across the Channel to hit designated targets. The move extended the squadron's range and kept the men close to the front line ground troops.

Soon after the move to A-11, Bob was just leaving his tent to walk up to the flight line when an explosion rocked the area. Running to help, he spotted a man's shoe, which was about all that was left of one of the men caught in a bomb blast. It has been a US bomb—a ground crew was transporting the bomb, which may have contained unstable explosives or had a defective arming system. Whatever the reason, the bomb exploded, and two men of the squadron's ground crew were killed. They were the first A-11 casualties.

Bob's Zippo cigarette lighter was another (far less important) casualty. Since the base lacked facilities, movies were shown outdoors. They were projected on the cleanest sheet available while the audience sat on stumps, grass, or overturned buckets. A young French boy stood next to Bob one evening; he invited the boy to join the viewing, making a place for him close by.

"Nice kid," Bob thought after the movie ended and he left to go home. It was then that Bob discovered that the *nice kid* had picked his pocket and his Zippo lighter was missing.

***

Back at the war, American and British ground troops were pushing forward, and the Germans were on the run. They finally had been forced out of their foxholes and hedgerows. As they fell back, the bomb targets and strafing lines of the squadron moved forward. The more German installations and transportation the fliers could destroy, the faster the Allied troops could advance.

On August 12, the 429th Squadron flew two missions. Bob was on the second, a trip into the Louvier-Paris area.

The squadron descended on the airdrome at Evreaux, which was littered with He-111s (Heinkel 111s—German aircraft).

At least two hangars were destroyed. Two of the squadron pilots accounted for one each, and another hangar was damaged by a third squadron pilot. Elsewhere on the field, another squadron pilot made a direct bomb hit on one plane while Bob and another colleague damaged at least three more aircraft. As a result of this mission, the German airfield had received significant damage, and so claims by the P-38 pilots during the debriefing session were kept to a minimum. A later survey by the squadron leader showed that at least some of the planes were repairable, if not actually immediately available for operation.

After takeoff on August 13, the squadron was directed to a special target. More than a hundred German vehicles were reported to be in a wooded area. As the fliers approached the area, they could see large fires burning. They bombed the area from an elevation of 3,000 feet, adding to the flames and damage already done to the vehicle concentration. The squadron aircraft took some flak in the process, but there were was no major damage to the aircraft—all planes and pilots returned to base.

The Germans grouped very large guns to defend major targets, and the squadron encountered intense flak during most of the missions, even at high altitude. One thirty-six-plane mission took the men over the Keil Canal. The weather was clear and their group leader spotted gun emplacements on the east side of the canal. The airmen could hear a high-pitched tone in their earphones, signaling that enemy gunners on the ground were zeroing in on the squadron formation. As the sound peaked in intensity, Bob could see flashes, and he knew that anti-aircraft rounds were coming his way.

Immediately the fliers began *jinxing* on the leader's command—jinxing involves making sharp turns left and right and changing altitude to throw the gunners off target. Black flak clusters erupted all around the formation, and then they broke through into clear air. Quick radio checks confirmed that the formation was intact and there were no casualties. The mission was acknowledged to be routine; they encountered flak outward bound, attacked the target, and all aircraft and fliers returned safely to base.

It was different for the bomber crews who were unable to take radical evasive action when the anti-aircraft gun crews targeted them. They had to hold course and continue on while the flak tore holes in their formations; losses of bombers and their crews were severe.

At lower altitudes, the squadron regularly encountered 20-mm and 40-mm anti-aircraft fire, and the tracer rounds were visible as they arced up toward the aircraft. The tennis ball-size rounds appeared to start slowly then would rapidly gain speed and, with luck, would flash by the aircraft. On one mission Bob blundered over a field that lit up with tracers and he was enveloped by them. Tracers went above, below and on either side of the plane, but by some miracle, none of the tracers hit his P-38.

Revenge is sweet, and Bob had a dose of sweetness on a dive-bombing mission.

When he pulled up after releasing the bombs, a German gun about three hundred yards away opened up on the aircraft. He nosed over and directed his tracer shells into the gun emplacement. Rocking the plane, he hosed his tracer bullets left and right to cover the total emplacement, the gunners, and stored ammunition. The entire area disappeared in a ball of smoke and flames. He didn't have time to look back for a detailed damage assessment, but he knew instinctively that he would not have to make a second run over that target.

***

When not flying, the men were adjusting well to tents and living a relatively civilized life with crude showers and latrines, enjoying a steady diet of K and C rations.

K rations were a staple for the squadron, and the newer C rations were a welcome change. C rations were full course meals, everything from canned meat to crackers, chocolate, and coffee, with orange marmalade, cigarettes, chewing gum, and toilet paper thrown in for good measure.

The tents were among trees that survived after the runway was hacked out, but they had to share the trees with swarms of yellow jackets. These flying animals attacked in squadron formations whenever packets of food were opened. Bob was never stung, but several of his colleagues had allergic reactions to yellow jacket stings and ended up in the infirmary.

***

A night mission came to the squadron on August 14. The fliers were tracking a flight of German bombers—Junkers 88s (Ju-88s)—but never located them. As they crossed over the ground battle lines, everyone opened up on the squadron—Germans, Americans, British, and anyone else in the area. They could hear the planes, but they couldn't see enough to identify the fliers as friends or foes. The British even turned on powerful searchlights to point the way for their guns.

Some of the fliers had to dump their bombs and take evasive action. Knowing they were over friendly forces, they made sure the bombs they dumped were not armed and would not explode on impact. But if the unarmed bombs happened to land on some of the knuckleheads shooting at them, maybe they would knock some sense into the members of the ground forces! Fed up with the situation, the squadron headed for home where, to make matters worse, as the aircraft came in for landings, their own anti-aircraft guns opened up.

Bob was turning on his final approach to the runway when his instrument lights went out. There he was, coming in with full flaps and using a flashlight to check the air speed when a heavy stream of .50-caliber tracers went by the port wing of his aircraft. The airfield gunners were getting close to shooting down one of their own, but somehow the trigger-happy individuals missed everyone. They just lit up the night sky and further stressed already jangled nerves. The squadron landed in complete darkness, and the fliers trudged off to their waiting tents, muttering and grumbling about the science and safety of night fighting.

***

On the ground, the German Seventh Army was nearly surrounded in what came to be called the Falaise Pocket. The pocket was centered in the region around the town of Falaise which lay approximately twenty miles south of Caen.

In the summer of 1944, as the Allies advanced out of Normandy, the American forces swept forward farther and farther east. With Patton's forces moving so fast, General Bradley saw an opportunity to trap an estimated twenty-one German divisions—or to be more accurate, the *remains* of twenty-one divisions. If General Patton's Third Army swung north to Alençon and the Canadians could reach Falaise, only fourteen miles would separate them. General Montgomery accepted the plan, and one of General Patton's corps moved swiftly toward Alençon and pushed through the town to reach the outskirts of Argentan on the evening of August 12.

The Canadian troops reached Falaise on August 16, twenty hours after American and French troops launched the Anvil landings in southern France against slight opposition. As General Patton's army hurried eastward, Hitler authorized a strategic withdrawal from Normandy.

In the so-called Falaise pocket, the German Seventh Army—approximately 150,000 soldiers—suffered relentless Allied air and artillery bombardment. The *Blitzkrieg* had come full circle; the ones who had doled out such an attack in 1939 (against Poland), in 1940 (against France), and in 1941 (against Russia) were now on the receiving end of Allied vengeance.

They had only one way out, and the 429th Squadron flew over the area constantly to help close the back door. The Polish First Armored Division, fighting as part of the 21st Army Group and the First Canadian Army were in the thick of that fight. The Polish division raced ahead of British and Canadian forces to seize vital positions and seal off the pocket. They suffered some 2,000 casualties and lost more than a hundred tanks in the process. They also captured more than 5,000 German prisoners.

While the Allied troops were pounding the Germans from three sides of the Falaise Pocket, Allied planes were hammering them from the air. Some Germans managed to escape from the pocket, but on the evening of August 19, Polish and American troops met at Chambois, closing the Falaise gap. Allied fighters and fighter-bombers destroyed thousands of vehicles in the pocket. But for two more days, German fugitives trickled through. In the end, the Germans lost 10,000 killed at Falaise, and five times that number were taken prisoner. Rumors spread that the German armies in France were destroyed at Falaise, but this was not entirely true. They suffered some 240,000 casualties during the campaign, and forty divisions were wrecked, but an additional 240,000 men and 25,000 vehicles moved out of the pocket and crossed the Seine eastward between August 19 and August 31.

***

The most dangerous missions were *zero* missions—so-called because bad weather or other reasons prevented the fliers from finding or hitting the target.

Bob had a zero mission on August 16, when the squadron was assigned to escort B-26 bombers to a target southeast of Paris. They flew for two hours and forty-five minutes, and then were recalled because of bad weather. By the time the squadron got back to the British sector, the fog was so thick the pilots could barely see the engines on either side of the cockpit. The formation broke up, and it was every man for himself. Pilots landed wherever they could find a friendly field. Bob landed at a field designated B-Q, which was unknown to him then and remains so to this day. All he knows is that he got down in one piece. For him, that was mission accomplished.

Planners at Allied headquarters (SHAPE) learned through the French underground that a castle—Diors Chateauroux—was the local headquarters for the Gestapo, the German secret police. The most experienced pilots from three P-38 fighter squadrons were picked for a special mission to destroy the castle, Gestapo barracks, and administrative buildings within an airdrome, and the railroad station. The Gestapo officers and men were committing atrocities in the castle, including the torture of suspected underground members, Jews, and others. They executed two French resistance leaders just a few days before Bob and his colleagues were to drop their bombs.

The pilots were given a special briefing on August 17. It was a very hush-hush affair, and only veteran pilots from the three squadrons were in on it. Each squadron was assigned to hit specific targets. Bob and his wingman were assigned to hit the castle and barracks.

The P-38 aircraft were each armed with a 1,000-pound bomb with an eight-second delayed fuse for the castle and a 100-pound fragmentation bomb for the barracks. They would approach at low altitude, and they needed the eight-second delay to get clear of the blast. It would not be a fitting end to be blown out of the air by their own bombs.

The weather en route to the target area was terrible, and the planes were forced to fly on instruments most of the way. Some of the pilots turned back or were recalled, and Bob did not know if they would make it. Then suddenly they broke from the cloud to find themselves over the target area.

Bob went in first, and his wingman followed. They made their bombing runs from south to north. As Bob cleared the top of the castle, he released the 1,000-pound bomb, which pierced a wall just below the roof line. His wingman also scored a direct hit. One of the two bombs exploded immediately after the eight-second delay, but for some reason, as they found out later, the other bomb didn't explode until several hours later. The castle was literally blown away, and dust and debris covered the whole area. After the explosion of the first bomb, Bob and his wingman turned to strafe the area, while other pilots bombed and strafed the nearby German barracks. The railroad yards and depot were leveled. All pilots and planes returned safely.

***

Records indicate that Bob and several of his colleagues went on a five-day leave to London starting August 19. The French Second Armored Division and the US Fourth Infantry Division entered Paris on August 24, 1944, where they found French Resistance units largely in control, with scattered fighting still going on in the outskirts of the city. Liberating Paris signaled to the world that the Allied tide was sweeping relentlessly toward Berlin.

Smith rejoined the squadron on August 21. His story of evasion and escape is interesting.

After bailing out of his plane, his parachute snagged in a tree moments before landing. While he was disengaging himself, he wrenched his back. Luckily, some Frenchmen were the first to find him, and they, in turn, put him in the care of the Maquis, the organization of Free French who were fighting German occupation troops at every opportunity.

The pilots of Bob's squadron had become aware of the dangers that could befall a pilot parachuting from his doomed aircraft. If he was not shot by an enemy pilot as he descended, there was Nazi (and civilian) malevolence toward the Allied fliers responsible not only for the bombing of German cities but also toward any Allied flyer. In fact, on May 30, 1944, Martin Bormann, Hitler's secretary and trusted aide, sent a notice to local authorities that no citizen should be punished for assaulting or killing downed enemy airmen. In occupied countries the airman and anyone assisting him would be held liable for aiding the enemy and would be summarily executed. Fighter pilots, who strafed at low level in the last phase of the war, incurred special hatred.

As soon as Smith recovered from the wrenched back, he wanted to get back to his outfit and move away from the potential of being executed. To make matters worse, he was told by his rescuers that there was no means of returning him through the enemy lines. All he could do was wait, which was a difficult thing for Smith to do. Before long, he was going out with the raiding parties of the French Maquis. It seems that from time to time the Allies would supply the Maquis with guns and ammunition and other essential equipment. Even Jeeps were dropped by parachute from cargo planes—part by part.

The Maquis, as Smith observed, would get six or eight of their group together, pile into a fast automobile, and make occasional uninvited visits to the Germans who were garrisoned in small villages nearby. Smith accompanied them several times and was amazed at their timing and coordination.

The Maquis would determine from inside sources the precise time that the Germans would be changing their guard or gathering in a formation. Then, on a prearranged notice, the French villagers would be advised by the Maquis to get off the streets or find cover nearby. At the right moment, the Maquis would race through the village streets in their long black sedan and open fire on the Germans from both sides of the car. Smith said that the Chicago gangsters of the 1920s and 1930s were just a bunch of jokers compared to this outfit. He would sit down low in the back seat and toss out hand grenades on both sides of the road while the others manned the machine guns.

Smith's experience was not atypical. Many downed pilots picked up by the French became involved in behind-the-lines resistance activities before they were repatriated. Those that rejoined their squadrons had some great stories to tell. As a rule, pilots with too much knowledge of French resistance activities were not allowed to rejoin their squadrons. They were sent stateside to avoid the risk of them being shot down again, captured, and forced under torture to tell what they knew.

***

The aircraft piloted by the squadron leader, Major William Bowman, was hit by flak on August 23, and Bowman was forced to bail out over Bernienville. He made a delayed jump from 5000 feet, opening his chute just before touching down in an open field. Squadron pilots orbited his descent and saw him land safely. They returned to base confident that he would probably be back with them soon. That turned out to an incorrect assumption. Bowman was captured and spent the rest of the war in a German prisoner of war camp.

Major Bowman was one of the outstanding leaders of the 429th Squadron. He faithfully attended the postwar squadron reunions, a quiet man respected by all for his talents as a pilot and for his leadership example. He led from the front and was not a desk-bound commander. When he went down, the pilots felt that the soul of the squadron went with him. His son later became a navy admiral and was in charge of Pacific air operations. More than a half century after his dad was shot down, Admiral Bowman made it possible for several of Bob's squadron mates and himself to land on an aircraft carrier (the USS Constellation), spend a night on the ship, and experience a catapult takeoff.

***

There was some jubilation on August 24 when General LeClerc and his French soldiers entered Paris—the commencement of the liberation of the French capital. The Parisians though the liberators were American but soon learned that the liberators were French. Joyous shouts of the citizens became even louder and continuous.

Barricades were opened by the Parisians and church bells rang. But as always, there is somber news to offset good news.

August 25 was the day that General Dietrich von Choltitz, who later committed suicide, surrendered Paris to the Allied Forces. It was a day of jubilation for the Parisians and many Allied troops, but it was a Black Friday for the 474th Fighter Group.

A group mission was launched against three enemy airfields on the east side of the Seine, which were used by German fighter groups. Many of them were in the air and ready to fight when the US planes attacked. Bob was not flying that day, but those in the air experienced heavy losses. The squadron lost several pilots, while seventy-three kills were claimed. The actual number of confirmed kills is probably less than that, as there is not much time for detailed accounting during aerial combat. Several pilots might sometimes claim the same kill. Other planes thought to be on their last legs were only damaged and managed to limp their way back to home base. Some twenty sites where German planes went down have been documented, so it is confirmed that the group downed that many enemy aircraft.

Patterson was shot down during the fight. He was burned, but survived. At the time of research for this book, he was still living, and Bob has talked with him on frequent occasions.

Milton Merkle, whom Bob first met during training at Williams Field, was not as lucky. He was killed.

Another one of Bob's close friends was Lenton F. Kirkland (Kirk). He and Bob were both country boys with common views and outlooks and had bonded immediately at their first meeting. They shared stories of home and embarked upon new adventures together. Kirk shot down two German planes, moving him ahead of Bob on the squadron scorecard. Kirk now had three confirmed kills while Bob remained with one confirmed kill.

Bob was in the air on August 27 when a specially modified P-38, affectionately referred to as a Droop Snoot, flew with them. The Droop Snoot had the nose guns removed and a glass gondola installed to accommodate a bombardier.

Seventeen planes were to fly in formation and drop bombs on command from the Droop Snoot. The theory was that bombs from seventeen planes landing in a tight concentration would have a profound impact on the Germans. The theory was good, but was trumped by poor visibility. The Droop Snoot's bombardier couldn't get a good fix on the target, so the squadron had to dive and bomb the target without direction.

The squadron participated in a fighter sweep on August 31. All roads in the patrol area were congested with German traffic trying to escape from the Falaise Pocket. Bob saw everything from tanks and half-tracks to horse-drawn carriages and armored cars on the road, and he strafed everything that he could get in his gun sights.

The carnage was heavy and a mass killing—something that fighter pilots were called upon to do and something that Bob has pretty much blotted from his memory. He does remember bombing the head of the column and the rear to stop movement, then strafing and bombing everything in between. On this mission, one of the P-38 pilots took his aircraft from Bob's wing to strafe a bus, which went into the ditch, killing the occupants. Altogether the squadron destroyed fourteen motor transports, damaged fourteen more, and also severely damaged a Tiger tank.

While they were flying this mission, ground personnel packed up all of the squadron gear and equipment for a move to A-43. As the front lines pushed toward Germany, the 429th Squadron kept pace. American ground forces were a little more than eighty miles from the German border, and in some instances, the squadron bomb line was only two or three miles from the Belgian border. Time was running out for the Thousand Year Reich.

The day ended with the welcome return of Bill Patterson, another one of Bob's colleagues from training camp. Shot down during a mission, he had quite a story to tell.

***

Patterson had wisely decided to leave his stricken aircraft, and he had parachuted into a clearing in the woods near Compiegne but the Germans picked him up before he could make his way to some cover nearby. He was taken to a German field hospital but did not receive any attention because they were overcrowded and too busy caring for their own wounded to look after an American flier with back and arm injuries. The Germans didn't even take time to interrogate him. He was just left alone.

Just as Patterson and his captors arrived at the field hospital, he saw other captured pilots and soldiers in outdoor pens or cells. Those who were not wounded were loaded on trucks and shipped farther back behind the lines. The situation didn't look very good. Patterson didn't get much to eat and decided anything would be better than his present situation; and he still needed medical attention.

After a few days there, Patterson spotted a chance to escape. With two other prisoners, he managed to break out after dark one night, and they worked their way out through the enemy lines. He knew that his own lines were not very far away. The three Americans finally stumbled into British hands. As he recalled, they got medical attention at the Limey first aid station.

While they were walking back through the German lines to their own lines, the three Americans actually saw what everyone had suspected for some time—the Germans were using ambulances to transport ammunition to the front. In this way, the ammunition traveled with the immunity reserved for any vehicle bearing the Red Cross insignia. Once the ammunition was off-loaded, evacuating German soldiers climbed in and were moved to the rear.

After the British tended to Patterson's wounds, he was given time to rest, and then he hitchhiked back to the 429th.

***

Late in August, Bob was awarded his sixth bronze oak leaf cluster to the Air Medal—he now had seven Air Medals. At the same time, five new second lieutenants joined the ranks of the 429th: Richard V. Riggs, Donald K. Ross, William R. Ryan, William Safarik, and Richard Stein. On September 12 1944, Stein flew his first mission as Bob's wingman and scored his first kill.

***

Prior to leaving A-11—south of Isigny and near to the D-Day landings at Omaha Beach—for the new base, Bob had a day off, and he ended up in an area where Allied convoys from the port of Cherbourg were forming. He happened to catch one that was loading cans of gasoline. The group running the convoys was called the Red Ball Express—a cargo express service begun in late August. Each truck had a red ball about twelve inches in diameter painted on its sides.

Within a short time after the commencement of the Express, seven thousand trucks carried four thousand tons or more each day on one-way highways to First and Third Army dumps, typically a three-day round-trip. MPs posted 25,000 road signs in English and French, and Cub planes monitored the traffic flow. The trucks of the Red Ball Express were given the highest priority on all roads and highways. But other problems arose very quickly. The vehicles used 300,000 gallons of gasoline per day, and to expedite the delivery of supplies, drivers sometimes loaded six to ten tons of cargo on vehicles equipped to carry two tons. Not surprisingly, the Express became known as *truck-destroyer battalions*.

Red Ball Express trucks ran on two parallel routes. One route was one-way to the front lines, the other was one-way back. Regardless of vehicle type or the rank of officers riding in them, all had to give way when the Red Ball Express was rolling. Military police stationed at major crossroads enforced the rule. No exceptions. The trucks were hauling troops and vital supplies to General Patton's army, giving momentum to the rapid advance toward Germany.

Furthermore, and despite a twenty-five-mile-per-hour speed limit, seventy trucks on average were wrecked beyond repair every day. On one stretch marked Steep Hill and Dangerous Curve, eight gasoline semitrailers in a single convoy flipped over, followed by eight more the next day. In fact, of the 15,000 US Army vehicles rendered useless in Europe in the autumn of 1944, 9,000 were trucks littering French byways.

Bob joined a driver in the cab of his truck. They drove and drove, then drove some more, and the number of miles covered remained a mystery. There was only one stop—to refuel the truck and get something to eat. Bombed-out buildings and ravaged vehicles littered the landscape. A strange pungent odor permeated the air, and Bob knew it came from rotting bodies. They drove on and Bob mused that they were passing through enemy territory, but they met no challenges and were moving fast. Even so, they never did catch up with Patton. Instead they were directed to an off-loading area where the truck was emptied. Then it was back to Cherbourg. Bob has never forgotten the day he rode the Red Ball Express.

***

The new airfield, A-43, lived up to its name. It was all grass and the group headquarters was located in an old chateau near to Saint Marceau in France.

Known as an *advanced landing ground* (the term given to the temporary advance airfields constructed by the Allies during World War II in support of the invasion of Europe), A-43 was near to Saint Marceau in the Ardennes region of Belgium. It consisted of a single 5,000-foot prefabricated runway. In addition, tents were used for billeting and also for support facilities. An access road was built to the existing road infrastructure: a dump for supplies, ammunition, and gasoline drums, along with drinkable water and a minimal electrical grid for communications and station lighting. The 474th Fighter Group used this base from August 29 until September 6, 1944.

Tents at the east end of the strip housed engineering, tech supply, parachute, communications, operations, armament, ordnance, and other administrative units.

The pilot's mess area, orderly room, and squadron supply were farther down the main road. An outdoor privy was isolated and starkly visible at the south end of the camp. The privy was outfitted with the bare (no pun intended) necessities, but no screening or walls. As Bob was sitting there enjoying the view one day, several young ladies came floating down the river. They politely ignored him and looked away, or at least that is what they appeared to do.

301

The tents for the men were on the banks of the River Sarthe, just across from an old flax mill. Bob took a picture of the mill for his scrapbook. He took an identical picture decades later when he returned to France. Everything had stayed the same, except the mill is no longer operating, the tents are gone, and the boys that once lived in them are old men with many memories.

It was interesting to watch French people harvesting flax from their fields. They dumped bundles of flax in the mill pond to soak and soften and then processed it through the mill.

The pilots used the mill pond for swimming and for paddling around in a one-man life raft. In addition to the watching, swimming, and paddling, they also had fishing, courtesy of the military engineers. Their approach was simple and very direct—hand grenades were thrown into river, everyone waited a few seconds for the blasts to subside, and then they waded in and scooped up stunned fish in their helmets.

By now Allied armies had swept beyond Paris and were fanned out across France and Belgium. In the sector assigned to Bob's squadron, Brest was in the cross-hairs. Troops trying to take the city were taking heavy fire from large guns on an island.

The 429th Squadron flew missions against the guns. Al Mills went down on September 3, when his plane was hit by flak. His squadron mates watched from the air as Mills belly-landed his burning plane, skidded to a stop, and scrambled out of the cockpit. It was the start of a nine-month ordeal that would take Mills through several German concentration camps, including the notorious Buchenwald.

The pilots were flying short missions—two or three a day—across the Brest peninsula, mostly over friendly territory and without much enemy resistance except from flak.

The overall mission of the squadron was to support two infantry divisions in their push to capture the ports of Brest, Lorient, and St. Nazaire. The targets were German fortifications, U-boat pens, harbor installations, and just about any other enemy assets worthy of bombing. Often the P-38s flew in low-level bombing runs, dropping the 1,000-pound bombs directly into the enemy gun emplacements.

As the Germans fell back and the Allied front advanced, the 429th continued to move forward, and on September 6, they moved to a new advance field, A-72, at Perrone. This was formerly a Luftwaffe base, and much of the installation had been destroyed when the Germans pulled out of the area. As Bob was taxiing out for the first time, the P-38 in front set off a land mine. The explosion went off directly behind him and directly in front of Bob. Fortunately, neither plane nor pilot was damaged, but there was a lot of noise and dust.

September 12 was a day Bob will always remember. He was assigned a mission to hit a target near Aachen, a city anchoring the German Siegfried Line between Belgium and Germany. Lieutenant Paul Munger was leading the flight of eight aircraft. The mission was to suppress German flak batteries, and two of the P-38s were assigned to bomb the batteries from low level, and six of them were escorts.

After attacking the flak batteries at about 3:00 p.m., the flight split up and began attacking targets of opportunity. Bob went down alone and strafed a truck parked in the shade of some very tall trees; he also hit the outer area of some anti-aircraft emplacements. There was no return fire—the guns were large-caliber, too big to fire at the aircraft at such a low altitude.

After strafing the truck, emplacements, and several searchlights, he noticed a suspicious-looking installation. As Bob dived down for a closer look, he could see that it was covered by netting, and as he flew along just skimming the ground, he could see that the camouflage was hiding a long, low building with a veranda on one side. A woman dressed in white was running along the veranda from one end of the building to the other. Bob assumed the building was a hospital, and even though he did not see any distinctive red crosses, he elected not to strafe that particular target.

Bob broke off his strafing when he got a radio call from Munger to form up and get ready to go home. All planes were low on ammunition, some more than others, but Bob had not found many targets, so he still had a good supply. Munger gave the pilots a rendezvous point, and heading for forming up the flight, Bob got his flight of four pilots together and led the flight in a high-speed climb.

As they climbed to join Munger and his flight of four, Bob looked up and saw a flight of German FW-190s. They were directly above, crossing diagonally from left to right. From his position, it seemed as though all aircraft were suspended in mid-air and everything seemed to be in slow motion. The German aircraft outnumbered the P-38s by about three to one. As he watched, Bob wondered why they didn't come in for the attack.

The P-38s continued to climb and weave, going all out. Bob lost sight of the FW-190s. Then Munger's flight was attacked, and Bob's flight headed for the fight. One of his pilots called, "Break right!" Some of the FW-190s approached them from the right rear and above. As the P-38s whipped right, turning into them, Bob's number three and number four men split off, leaving him with a second lieutenant—Richard Stein—on his wing.

Completing the right turn, Bob went into a slight dive to gain more airspeed, and then he pulled into a slight right-hand turn and a shallow climb. Approximately 1,000 feet above his P-38, an FW-190 was on a course that was crossing Bob's flight path. Bob was still pulling up a little, gaining speed, and coming around to get behind the German. When the FW-190 pilot saw Bob's P-38, he made the first of several tactical errors. The German had the altitude advantage, but instead of trying to position himself to where he could get on Bob's tail, he made a slight banking turn and went into a dive toward Bob. When he did that, both pilots were committed to actions against each other.

Bob pulled up to meet him—there was no other option—to turn left or right would have exposed the P-38 to a deflection shot, and if Bob pulled up sharply, the German would have a clear shot at the underbelly of the P-38. But if Bob kept up the turn he was in, the German could have made a weaving turn and come in on Bob's tail. He could have depressed the stick, but things were happening fast, and Bob didn't like that option either. So the P-38 and the FW-190 came at each other almost head-on, both firing, and Bob was awestruck by the firepower coming out of wings of the German aircraft. It looked like cannon fire.

Everything seemed to happen in a millisecond. During that time, Bob executed a very slight left roll to pull his fire into the FW-190. The German's tracers were whipping over the P-38 canopy and the bullets from the P-38 was passing under the right wing root of the FW-190.

The German had the momentary advantage, but he blinked first by failing to press his attack. If he had pressed his attack, he could have dropped his tracers to hit the canopy of the P-38. But the German hesitated and Bob pulled back on his stick, and fire from his four .50-caliber machine guns and 20-mm cannon tore into the German's right wing root and fuselage. The FW-190 exploded.

The German fighter was less than one hundred yards away, and Bob's air speed was about 250 miles an hour. There was no way to avoid the explosion. Bob closed his eyes and forged ahead, fully expecting to end up with the German's engine in his lap, but he made it through the smoke and flames without any significant fragments hitting him or the P-38.

Bob estimated that only four seconds had passed between the time that they sighted each other to the time he was flying through the German's debris. What remained of the FW-190 flipped over and dove straight into the ground. Stein confirmed the victory and reported that he had not observed a parachute coming from the stricken aircraft.

Turning again to the right—with Stein still on his wing—Bob saw another FW-190 below. The German had a P-38 in his sights. Moving to the rescue, Bob made a 20-degree dive on him, closed to about 250 yards at an air speed of 250 to 300 miles per hour, and made a twenty-degree deflection shot. Bob gave him a three-second burst and could see tracers from his P-38 hitting both wing roots and the cockpit. But since neither Stein nor Bob saw the plane go down or the pilot bail out, they could only claim that the FW-190 had been damaged.

Things continued happening fast. Looking up to the right, Bob spotted two FW-190s coming for them. He fired a short burst at the leader and Stein took on the number two man. As Bob turned to the left, he saw Stein's target flip over on its back, smoking very badly. The FW-190 exploded when it hit the ground. Stein racked up his first victory on one of his very first missions.

With Stein still on his left wing, Bob made a sharp right turn as he heard Stein's voice over the radio:

"Break right!" Stein warned.

The FW-190 that had been coming at him head-on was returning for another go. Now he was almost directly behind the P-38, firing, and he was very close, about 150 yards away. Bob could not turn into the German without giving him an easy deflection shot, so he went to an evasive maneuver that he had practiced to some degree but never put to use. Bob had kept the maneuver in reserve for times like this.

One of the favorite maneuvers of FW-190 pilots was the split-S, and used against a P-38, it gave the Germans a slight edge. To execute the split-S maneuver, the pilot must half-roll the aircraft into an inverted position and then into a descending half-loop, which results in level flight in the exact opposite direction but at a lower altitude. The Germans would probably expect the P-38 to gain speed as it rolled into a dive, and then maybe go into compressibility as the controls froze and fly into the ground or be easy prey for picking off.

But Bob had other ideas. He didn't follow the script. Instead of setting up a turn, he hit full right rudder, chopped his right throttle, came back on the stick, and applied right elevator. The move was performed so violently that the P-38 was thrown all over the sky, but it all happened so quickly and so suddenly that the P-38 may have disappeared from the guns of the FW-190.

Even Stein lost sight of Bob's P-38, and after the mission he questioned Bob quickly.

"What happened?" Stein queried. "You just vanished!"

Recovering from the violent maneuver, Bob found he had lost the German and gained a new wingman—Second Lieutenant Larry Baillargeon. Together they headed back to the main battle as an FW-190 that had been attacking P-38 planes pulled up from below Bob, who immediately gave the German a three-second burst as he passed in front—twenty degrees of deflection at about three hundred yards. The tracers arched into him and the left wing of the FW-190 exploded—Baillargeon confirmed the FW-190 plane was destroyed.

Bob then dropped into a right diving turn to gain air speed, and then pulled up as Baillargeon engaged and destroyed another

FW-190. Bob's attention was focused on an FW-190 flying straight and level from his left to right, putting them on a converging course. The German had about a hundred feet of altitude on the P-38, putting Bob at a slight disadvantage. If Bob pulled up, his angle of attack would have been less than desirable and he didn't have enough altitude to get on his tail. Trying such a move would probably have set up a head-on confrontation. He made an immediate sharp turn to the left, setting up a course away from the FW-190 at about forty-five degrees so that he could keep his cockpit area in sight. Then Bob gave the P-38 the full throttle.

Initially he flew straight and level, testing to see if the German was willing to attack—he was not.

Bob went into a dive to the left to gain air speed while watching the FW-190 over his right shoulder. The German continued to fly straight and level, a major mistake in a dogfight, as it takes only seconds for someone to come in and blow you away. A pilot had to constantly turn and clear the skies to make sure an enemy was not coming in the aircraft tail.

Bob dived to hit the blind spot of the FW-190, and he could tell that the German didn't plan to engage, so Bob continued to dive in a shallow right turn. He turned the P-38 more to the right until their courses were almost parallel. Bob held the P-38 in a dive while looking up at the FW-190 and gaining all the air speed that he could. When Bob had the P-38 at a level where he was actually ahead of the FW-190, he saw that the German wasn't weaving or taking any evasive action.

Bob pulled the P-38 into an Immelmann turn (a half loop executed in combination with a half roll) so that as the P-38 rolled out, he was slightly ahead of the German and facing rearward. From there Bob moved the P-38 toward the underbelly of the FW-190.

Once in position, Bob fired a two-to-three-second burst starting at one hundred yards and closing to fifty yards or less, from about forty-five to thirty degrees of deflection. He observed five or six 20-mm hits in both wing roots and in the belly of the FW-190. As he rolled to the left and dived to gain air speed, Bob knew he had hit the FW-190 hard, but he lost sight of the German aircraft and could only claim that another aircraft was damaged. Bob is still convinced that with all the hits he got into his underbelly and cockpit area of the FW-190, it would have been almost impossible for the German to survive.

As Bob was circling left, Stein and Baillargeon joined up with him again. They heard a radio call for help. One of their pilots had several FW-190s on his tail. There were a number of smoke columns from planes that had gone down—all German.

There were two columns of smoke close together, and Bob called to the pilot in trouble, "Where are you? I can't see you, but where are you relative to the double column of smoke? If you can, fly toward the columns of smoke so we can locate you."

Bob scanned the skies, but he couldn't see a P-38. But he did see three single-engine planes—Germans—flying in a loose formation. With Baillargeon on his left and Stein on the right, he dove down.

Bob had learned well from his previous mistakes. In his first dogfight, he dove on an FW-190 strafing an American pilot in his chute, but the German went into a split-S to evade him. Bob continued in the dive and came up behind the German so fast that he almost overshot the enemy aircraft. He had to take the P-38 into a sharp, climbing 360-degree turn or he would have overshot the FW-190, leaving him open to attack from the rear.

This time Bob was a little more cautious. He was flying at about three hundred miles an hour when he started leveling out of the dive. He hit the trailing plane with a fifty-degree deflection shot at a range of about two hundred yards. The FW-190 twisted and turned, then leveled out. Bob scored another direct hit on it with a short burst at 150 yards. The enemy aircraft started trailing white smoke and as Bob fired his last burst, he saw a line of solid tracers from the .50-caliber guns signaling that he was about out of ammunition.

Closing on the FW-190 and firing his last bursts, Bob saw the FW-190 on the left turning into what he thought would be a head-on attack. Instead he went to the left, and Bob realized that he was after Baillargeon, who engaged the German head-on, shot and damaged the FW-190, but did not get credit for a kill. The third plane in the formation evaded Stein.

Bob continued closing on the FW-190 that he had shot and that was trailing white smoke and flying level. Bob kept his sights on the German's tail and pulled the trigger. Nothing happened!

"I've got one down here on the deck, but I'm out of ammo!" he radioed. "Can anyone get down here and finish him?"

No answer. There had been only eight P-38s at the start of the action against twenty or more Germans. Bob didn't know it at the time, but two P-38s had been shot down, leaving only six. They all had their hands full. So it was just Bob with empty guns against a badly damaged FW-190.

Bob closed on the German until he was flying off the left wing of the enemy aircraft. The FW-190 pilot and Bob stared at each other across the gulf, each wondering what the other was going to do next. While the enemy ducked his head to check his instruments, Bob was running through his options. He wondered if he could flip up the German's wing and throw him out of control. Or he could decrease his speed and sever the tail of the FW-190 with one of the P-38 propellers. Another option was to ram the nose of the P-38 into the FW-190 tail surfaces. Or could Bob open his right window and give the German a few rounds of the Colt 45.

Then he quickly but carefully weighed the probable consequences. He might destroy the German aircraft, but if he crippled the P-38, he would be a liability to the rest of the squadron. They had enough on their plates without having to nurse Bob home in a crippled P-38. And even though the German's plane was smoking heavily, he might still have some fight left in it. The odds of bringing down the damaged plane with an unarmed P-38 were not good. So Bob pulled up and let him go. When last seen, the German was still in the air, smoke billowing from the stricken plane. In all probability, he did not make it back to base.

As suddenly as it started, the massive dogfight was over. The sky was clear of swirling planes, P-38s and FW-190s alike. Back at base the pilots tallied the score. The squadron had lost two pilots—Hazzard and Lane—and although heavily outnumbered, the P-38s had shot down four FW-190s and damaged six. Bob was credited with destroying two FW-190s and damaging three.

Both Lane and Hazzard ran low on ammo and were last seen heading home on the deck. One of them probably called Bob for help. If whoever it was had been able to vector Bob to his position, he might have been able to save him. Herman Lane, whose plane he damaged a few weeks earlier, was the high score man in the group. He was credited with four kills—one short of being an ace—as well as one probable, and three damaged enemy aircraft.

For his actions on September 12, Bob was awarded the Silver Star, the third highest combat medal to be awarded by the United States.

September 17 was another big day. The Allies launched Operation Market Garden to outflank the Siegfried at Eindhoven, Holland. It was a massive airborne operation, the second of the war. Thirty-five thousand airborne troops were to be dropped to take advance positions and hold them until Allied ground forces could link up with them.

The mission of the 429th Squadron was to spearhead the attack by attacking flak positions where US paratroopers were to land, then to fight off any enemy air attacks against the operation.

From Bob's vantage point, the paratroop drop site looked to be about five miles long, running north and south, and maybe a mile wide. The P-38s arrived and just had time to make a couple of turns when they saw some red panels marking where friendly troops had already landed. Another small airborne group was coming in. They were Americans, both paratroopers and glider-borne infantry. There were nineteen to twenty-five aircraft in the formation. When they turned upwind for landings, German anti-aircraft opened up. The fliers of the 429th Squadron did knock out some German gun positions, but that was not enough. Bad weather and limited visibility hampered their efforts, and many of the Allied planes and the troops they were carrying were lost to German anti-aircraft fire.

On the return, the squadron had all landed safely and the aircraft were taxiing to the flight line when Lieutenant Richard Stein attempted to touch down. The tower saw that his landing gear was not working and gave him a wave-off with a red flare. There was no radio contact with him, so Stein did not know what was wrong. All he knew was he could not land at the field and he headed off in the direction of Paris. He was not seen again.

Five days later the news came in from a controller at a field near Paris that a P-38 with only two of its three wheels down had attempted to land there on September 17. Unable to make radio contact, the tower had fired red warning flares, after which the plane

312

circled the field several times, and then flew northward. Stein tried to land at another field near Paris, and for a third time was warned off. He then apparently attempted to make it back to the airfield but time ran out. His plane crashed a few miles north of Beaumont and Stein was killed.

When Stein was attempting to land at the home field, Bob was out of his P-38 and did not see what was going on. If he had been in his plane or if someone had been more alert, they might have been able to fly up and help Stein by inspecting the exterior of the aircraft. He probably didn't know what was wrong, only that he could not land at the 429th base and that he had to find someplace to put his plane down before it ran out of fuel. Stein was on only his second or third mission—he had flown his first mission with Bob and got his first victory.

***

Orders came down from headquarters on September 18 promoting Bob to *first lieutenant*. He had been a second lieutenant for ten months. The brass on his second lieutenant's bars was worn to the point where he could almost pass them as the silver bars of a first lieutenant, but he decided against such an action. Bob bought shiny new first lieutenant bars and kept the worn ones as war souvenirs. The extra pay that came with the promotion meant a lot, but the rank itself did not make that much difference. In a fighter group, a pilot is not measured by the rank on his uniform. What counts is performance—how a pilot stays close to his wingman and the way he measures up in a dogfight.

***

313

Blaze bombs were strapped onto the P-38s for the first time on September 22. Each bomb started as a standard 163-gallon belly tank, the kind normally used to carry extra fuel for extended range missions. However, on this occasion the belly tank was filled with napalm, a jelly-like mixture that erupts in a wall of fire and sticks to everything it touches. A grenade inside the tank made sure the napalm exploded when the dropped tank hit its target.

The targets were in the middle of the Siegfried Line near Aachen, a primary transportation point for the Germans. American troops had been trying to capture a massive German pillbox in the line and were taking heavy return fire from it.

The P-38s attacked in trail formation. Each of the pilots had been briefed to drop the napalm about fifty yards short of the target so that the flames would splash over the pillbox. Any Germans not killed by the fire would be suffocated when their oxygen was instantly burned away.

Bob led his flight into the target, made a good drop, then turned right and banked away. As they were leaving the target area, the flight received a call from the ground. One of the tanks on Bob's P-38 had hung up momentarily, and when it was finally released it had landed in an area occupied by some of the American troops. They suffered some casualties. It was another case of friendly fire. Unfortunately in the harshness of war, mistakes and accidents happen.

***

As September ended, Bob continued to fly missions in support of Allied ground troops pounding the Siegfried Line around the clock. German troops were falling back, but they were not quitting. The squadron faced stiff resistance every time they flew, either from enemy planes or anti-aircraft guns. Bob does not recall the precise details of all of the missions but he knows that he flew at least six or seven missions, including fighter sweeps and two or more Droop Snoot bomb sorties.

A radio switch had been used to salvo the formation's bombs simultaneously, but it was not totally successful. The bomb patterns were scattered and the results inconclusive.

The squadron flew back to England on October 6. All available aircraft were sent on detached service for five days with the Eighth Air Force. The assignment was to escort heavy bombers hitting targets across France and Germany. Any German fighters taking on the bombers would have to fight their way through the 18 aircraft of the 429th Squadron first.

The escort missions lasted nearly five hours, a long time to be cramped in a cockpit, the pilot swiveling his neck, and watching for distant dots in the sky that might materialize into incoming enemy planes. Details of the escort flights have long since escaped Bob's memory, but he does recall that it was a welcome change of pace to again operate from an English airfield and experience how the bomber crews lived.

***

For many years after the war, Bob and his colleagues thought the August 17 mission on Diors Chateauroux was an unqualified success. The castle was totally destroyed and with it, so it was believed, the local Gestapo unit. However, as history sorted itself out, the pilots found that the original assessment was overly optimistic. Military intelligence got most of it right. The Gestapo had not been using the castle, but the Luftwaffe and many high-ranking Nazi officers, including Field Marshal Erwin Rommel, had been in residence. Just before the raid, the Germans were either alerted by collaborators or just got nervous and moved out. When the squadron bombed the castle, the high-ranking Nazis were gone.

The castle raid captivated Bob for decades after the war. It was a prime topic of discussion and speculation at his squadron reunions and was one of the few places that he could actually pinpoint where he had been. Many of the sites that the squadron dive-bombed or strafed were difficult to identify or were targets of opportunity that the pilots hit on the way back to base. It was different with Diors Chateauroux. Bob knew he had been there and wanted to go back.

It took fifty-seven years, but he made it back on November 2, 2001, when he visited the castle site with his wife, Zella. Their tour guide was Phil Canonne, a French professor of history and geography. Bob had been corresponding with him for some time. When he learned Bob and Zella were to visit France, Phil volunteered to accompany them and serve as the translator and guide. Phil's fiancée, Anne Manuelle Chaigne, also a professor, made the group a foursome.

Bob had five goals in mind. First, he wanted to visit the site of his July 6 victory. He did. When he went to the town of Montmerrei and saw a memorial to a friend killed on that mission, he talked to a witness of the dogfight who saw a German pilot parachute from his stricken aircraft. When Bob asked what happened to the German, the witness merely shrugged and said, "We do not talk about that."

Bob and Zella also visited the D-Day invasion beaches, toured Allied cemeteries where so many of his friends and colleagues were buried, saw a memorial honoring his fighter squadron, and, above all, they went to the castle site.

A reception committee was waiting when the groups arrived at the castle grounds. They were all there—the local mayor, the former head of the French Resistance movement, French underground members, and two elderly women. The women lived across the road from the castle and were eyewitnesses to the attack on the castle.

Casting his mind back to that day, Bob remembered seeing four or five people run out a side door when he rolled in to make his bombing run. One woman was dressed in white and he thought at the time that she might be a cook or servant of some kind. "Oh, yes," one of the elderly women nodded in agreement, "that was a cook. She was my cousin."

To Bob's relief, the local residents confirmed that no lives were lost when the castle was destroyed, and they held no ill feelings because of the bombing. On the contrary, they thanked him many times over. They said that even though the Gestapo was gone when the castle was hit by bombs, the raid did a great deal to hasten the departure of Germans still lingering in the area. The Germans knew the Americans would be coming for them, and they cleared out.

As word of Bob's return visit spread, other people with strong memories of World War II came forward. One man still had a life vest from one of the 429th fliers who had lost his life over France. Another had a helmet from a pilot he hid from the Germans after the American flyer was shot down. With French help, the pilot made it back to Allied lines.

The local residents went all out for Bob and the group. They took them to visit the grave of Bob's friend Richard Stein, where they had erected a memorial that has been tended almost daily for more than fifty years. They also took Bob to the memorial for the 429th Squadron, and he was able to locate where he had pitched his tent in the mud of the summer of 1944. The villagers have never forgotten what America did for them.

After Bob and Zella returned to the United States, he received a follow-up packet from Phil Canonne. In it was the casing of a .50-caliber machine gun shell. The cartridge was found on the ground the day after two P-38 fighters strafed and bombed the castle. Those planes were flown by Bob and his wingman. A woman who watched the attacks from her vantage point on the ground picked up two cartridges and kept them for nearly sixty years. She wanted to give one of them to Bob on the supposition that he had fired it at her enemy. The chances are high that she is correct.

Chapter 10: Belgium

While Bob was in England, the ground fighting in Europe increased to a high intensity as German defenders were pushed back from the Normandy beaches and the Allied forces made gains in France. Town after town fell to the advancing Allies, some towns at great cost, but at greater cost to the enemy defenders, as the Allied forces moved eastward toward the Rhine and Germany. In keeping with these advances, the squadron also moved to a large field in the Florenne-Juzaine region of Belgium designated as A-78 and used by the 474th Fighter Group from October 1, 1944, until March 22, 1945. This would be Bob's base of operations until other orders were received.

Rolling fields and dense woods could be seen in every direction. Unknown to Bob, the Ardennes was to become a hotbed of enemy activity on December 16, 1944, when a German counteroffensive was launched in an attempt to push Antwerp on the coast to cut the

Allied forces in half and secure enough territory to warrant a claim for peace.

The squadron shared the field with the 370th Fighter Group, flying P-47 Thunderbolts, and the 422nd Night Fighter Squadron, the P-61 Black Widow night fighters. Even though the movement to A-78 predated the Ardennes counteroffensive, it was still a dangerous time. Bob was forced to make an unintentional hot landing at the field when he returned from England on October 12.

***

Hot landing is the term given to landing an aircraft that may be suffering from dangerous weather conditions or mechanical problems that suggest damage to the aircraft from other sources, such as enemy fire.

***

October 12, 1944, was a day that was known in fighter pilot parlance as a *dead calm day*. The windsock at the airfield was hanging limp, and with no headwind to slow down the P-38, Bob would have to make a full-flaps landing. As he flared out the flaps to slow the aircraft to a reasonable landing speed to touch down on the runway, the P-38 plane just floated and floated. And then, as if the aircraft had a mind of its own, it floated some more. When Bob finally did touch down, he was far down the runway and, not wishing to stand on the brakes and probably damage the nose wheel, he judged that he still had room to stop before running out of runway. However, it was not to be.

John O'Neil, another pilot, didn't enter into Bob's calculations. He landed ahead of Bob, pulled off to the right, and then turned to cross the runway to get back to the flight line. For some reason, O'Neil didn't see Bob coming in. The propellers were still turning when Bob's P-38 caught up with O'Neil's aircraft. Fortunately, neither Bob nor O'Neil was hurt, but O'Neil's plane succumbed to the incident and was very badly damaged.

As is the case with all such incidents, it being a dead calm day and there being no apparent reason for the incident, an investigation was necessary. The finding of the investigation was that Bob had not raised an extension on the flap lever to move from combat flaps to full flaps. This oversight extended the descent of the P-38, causing the plane to float—like the proverbial feather in the wind—when it should have landed. Bob was not reprimanded, but like all good flyers, he did learn from the experience.

***

The next day, October 13, the squadron took off for a fighter sweep into Germany. Bob was leading the squadron's second flight when they came upon a formation of twenty-five German fighter aircraft just west of the Rhine. Within the time it takes to collect one's thoughts, American and German aircraft were engaged in dogfights all over the sky. And there was no time for admiring the scenery, the painted emblems on the other aircraft, or any type of panoramic view for any of the pilots, each man was focused on the enemy plane currently being engaged.

Bob saw a P-38 under attack by a German FW-190, and the German was winning. The P-38 pilot, Bob Ingerson, later told Bob Milliken that all he could see in his rearview mirror was the spinner on the German's propeller and bucket loads (he used different words) of hot tracer shells coming his way.

Ingerson pulled back on his stick and started climbing. The German stuck with him as both aircraft headed straight up. Losing speed at the peak of his climb, Ingerson looped over and dived, then started his climb again, but the German pilot matched his moves. Bob knew the climb and dive tactic wasn't going to work, and Ingerson was seconds from being shot down.

At the time, Bob didn't know that Ingerson was flying the P-38 and he radioed, "P-38 with the 190 on your tail. Don't climb! Turn with him! Turn with him!"

Ingerson must have heard the call because when he reached the top of his climb, Ingerson started a left-hand turn. He had lost most of his air speed and the German wasn't more than twenty yards behind him. Bob expected the German to open fire and shoot the P-38 down any second, so he went into a left-hand bank and put his sights ahead of and slightly higher than Ingerson's plane.

Again, Father Robert's words came to Bob: "Lead the bird so that your shot arrives at the same place at the same time as bird."

From his position, Bob had to shoot so far ahead of him that he could not see all of Ingerson's plane and the FW-190 was not in his sights. It was a desperate situation, so Bob just took what he judged was a good, long lead and fired a sustained burst.

"You got him!" Ingerson called as the FW-190 rolled over and went into a dive straight into the ground.

There was no sign of smoke or debris trailing the plane on its way down so Bob could only surmise that his bullets went straight into the cockpit, killing the pilot who slumped over the controls. Bob watched as the FW-190 crashed into a courtyard near a German farm—the aircraft hit the ground nose first, approximately thirty feet from the farmer's front door—and the tail of the aircraft stuck straight up from the wreckage, as if to mark the site and to inform Bob that he had his fourth confirmed victory.

Realizing that there was more business at hand, Bob scanned the sky and spotted another FW-190, whereon he immediately rejoined the aerial battle. He was able to get onto the German's tail, hit him several times, and in Bob's estimation, caused considerable damage to the enemy aircraft. The FW-190 dived into some clouds to lose his pursuer, but Bob circled. The German was not seen any more. The FW-190 was not seen to crash, and destruction of the aircraft could not be confirmed. As the air force rules clearly stated: no confirmed destruction of an aircraft by the attacking pilot or by a colleague, no kill.

When Bob looked around for other enemy aircraft, there were none. The sky that had seemingly been completely filled with swirling, battling planes minutes before was now totally empty. Then, as the squadron pilots collected their thoughts, the radio calls started coming in, and Bob and his colleague took their places once more in formation and looked like a squadron again. William Chickering, the leader of the other flight, had also scored a victory. Bob joined Chickering in formation as his right wingman.

Bob's last memory of getting into the dogfight was that he had been chewing gum. When he emerged from the encounter, his mouth was so dry from adrenaline, oxygen, and heavy breathing that the gum was stuck to the roof of his mouth like putty on a dry board. He moistened it as much as he could lest it dislodge in its dry state and lodge in his throat which he knew would be extremely uncomfortable, possibly fatal. Extricating oneself from the actions caused by choking while landing was not described in the pilot's Flight Instruction Manual.

Typically, when the squadron pilots approached the field at a low altitude, they would peel up into a left bank at the end of the runway, then go into a vertical bank, put the wheel levels down, drop flaps, and come in for a clean landing. Following that procedure, the whole squadron could get down in very short order.

However, for the first time, Bob was flying a plane with a hydraulic boost on the ailerons. When Chickering went into the peel-up, he did a roll. Bob's first instinct was to follow, but the hydraulic boost and Chickering's unannounced roll threw him off. He came out of his roll about a hundred feet high, and he had to go around again to make a clean landing.

As he taxied to the flight line, Bob saw a single-engine aircraft running up for takeoff. A Jeep was waiting for Chickering and Bob. Colonel Wasem wanted to see them immediately. The two pilots were not even given the time to take off their helmets or other gear. Immediately meant right now!

The colonel looked stern as he started to speak. As they stood stiffly at attention in front of his desk, the Colonel gave them a tongue lashing for breaking a standing rule against victory rolls. He concluded his sermon with a simple admonishing statement:

"And you, Milliken. Damn it, you couldn't even do a good one!"

Bob and Chickering were not the only pilots on the carpet that day. A general had been in the single-engine plane waiting for takeoff as the squadron was landing. He had witnessed the acrobatics and was not impressed! The general, via radio, gave Colonel Wasem a severe tongue lashing for their performance. Maintaining the military tradition that excrement rolls downstream, the colonel passed the general's regards along to Bob and Chickering.

***

At midnight on October 14, Bob took off on what was to become one of his most interesting missions. The target was the city of Cologne, which throughout the war was bombed in 262 separate air raids by the Allies, and thirty-one times by the Royal Air Force. Consequently, the city had become a lively and well-defended hot spot in the German homeland, and it was from this mission that Bob almost did not return.

Bob had flown night missions before, none of them particularly productive or something he wanted to repeat. Nevertheless, when volunteers for the Cologne mission were sought by Colonel Wasem (the squadron's commanding officer), Bob stepped forward. He wanted to get at least one night mission success under his belt. Another one of Bob's colleagues, John Johnston, also volunteered, making it a two-man show. Because of the dangers of night flying, the aircraft would not be in formation. Instead, the two fliers were to take off separately and proceed to the target independently.

Sitting in the ready room wearing red goggles to adjust his eyes to night vision, Bob heard Colonel Wasem call headquarters, and he was trying to tell them that the mission should be scrubbed, that it was too risky. Colonel Wasem made quite sure that Bob overheard what he was saying. It was Bob's first inkling of what might be coming his way as the night aged.

Wasem made an impassioned argument, but headquarters was not convinced and the mission was on. From Wasem's action, Bob knew that if he decided to abort the mission for any reason, nothing would be said about it. But Bob was not going to take that route. He had volunteered, the mission was a go, and he was in it for the full ride—and, he hoped, the return.

During the mission briefing, Bob was told to fly to Cologne under radio control, then dive-bomb German troops attempting to escape from the city. He would be escorted by a night fighter, a P-61 Black Widow.

The Northrop P-61 Black Widow, named for the American black widow spider, was, like the P-38, a twin-engine twin-boom aircraft that was the first operational United States military aircraft designed specifically for night interception of aircraft, and was the first aircraft specifically designed to use radar. The first test flight of the P-61 was made on May 26, 1942, with the first production aircraft rolling off the assembly line in October 1943. On the night of August 14, 1945, a P-61B of the 548th Night Fight Squadron named Lady in the Dark was unofficially credited with the last Allied air victory in the Pacific theater before VJ Day (Victory over Japan Day, August 15, 1945). The last P-61 aircraft was retired from government service in 1954. Bob never piloted a P-61 Black Widow.

On that day, October 14, 1944, fighter control had Bob flying at a higher altitude that usual—10,000 feet instead of 5,000 feet. There were some scattered clouds up there, and it was dark despite a partial moon. It was even darker down below. Everything was blacked out. Maintaining strict radio silence, the P-61 escort and the P-38 proceeded on course for Cologne.

Suddenly radio silence was broken by the flight controller. "You are being stalked by a bandit!" A German night fighter was looking to put Bob in his sights. As soon as the fighter escort heard the warning from base, he engaged the enemy bandit and Bob continued on without a wingman.

The flight controller, code named Sweepstakes, advised Bob that he was being stalked by another bandit. He looked down and around into the darkness, trying to spot the bandit, and he started to circle, hoping he could catch the German's silhouette against the partial moon or catch a glimpse of his engine's exhaust. Bob went through a lot of maneuvers before Sweepstakes radioed that the bandit had broken off. Maybe the German thought that he knew where he was and decided to back off to find an easier target. The hunter might have become the hunted.

Bob continued flying through the darkness, and when Sweepstakes told him that Cologne was very close, he could still see nothing. Blackness blanketed the ground, and he could not even see the city, let alone pick out targets for dive-bombing.

Reluctantly, Bob decided to abort the mission. Concluding that he was well over enemy territory, he went into a dive to drop his bombs on whatever was below when all of a sudden searchlights slightly ahead began sweeping the sky—the Cologne air defenses were seeking British bombers.

Bob was close enough to see bombers—Lancasters—caught in the cones of the German lights. As the anti-aircraft guns opened up, a volley exploded just off the left wing of the P-38 and lit up the cockpit as bright as day. He took the P-38 into a roll and then went into a deep dive. He released the bombs, pulled out of his dive at treetop level, and headed for home. The British Lancasters were giving Cologne more than the city could handle.

On the way home, Bob decided to give his sleeping colleagues a thrill. The base radio transmitter was always tuned to the IFF (Identification Friend or Foe) transponders on the aircraft. The signals they got from incoming planes told ground crews whether friendly aircraft or Germans were incoming. Another clue the ground crews used was sound.

German night fighters always had an engine out of sync. When crews heard that distinctive throb, they knew Germans were in the vicinity.

Approaching home base, Bob turned off his IFF transponder and throttled back just a little on one engine. Then he dived and buzzed the chateau in which the pilots were housed. The P-38 was doing well over three hundred miles an hour when the plane cleared the roof by about fifty feet. Bob admitted it was not the smartest thing he had ever done, but (as he was told later), the maneuver certainly sure got all of the pilots out of their beds. They thought a bandit was in their midst. The bad news was that Bob heard more about his stunt after he landed. The good news was that he had been to Cologne and back, he had evaded stalking Germans, dumped his bombs on enemy territory, and was home again in one piece.

Kirk scored another victory on October 21, giving him three kills. That same day the news came over the radio that the Germans defending the key city of Aachen had surrendered. A big hole had been punched through the Siegfried Line.

On October 28, General Eisenhower reiterated his plan for winning the war, which meant that there would be no end to the continuous missions for the 474th Fighter Group. After flying daily missions, Bob flew a two-aircraft night-bombing mission on October 29. He dropped flares to illuminate a railroad junction two miles east of Düren, a town in North Rhine-Westphalia and located between Aachen and Cologne on the river Ruhr.

When Bob's flares lit up the target, a pilot from the 428th Squadron swept in to bomb the junction. Unfortunately, the radio controller directed Bob to drop his flares from 10,000 feet, and the flares were close to being spent and extinguished by the time the pilot from the 428th was in position. He did complain about the poor lighting, and the results of the raid were inconclusive. Unfortunately, this was another night mission with unknown accomplishments.

One of Bob's colleagues, Lieutenant Munger, got far different results while test hopping a plane over the airfield on November 1, a typical cloudy Wednesday in western Europe. He encountered another P-38 flown by a pilot from the 370th Squadron. Naturally, a friendly dogfight broke out between them. During the fracas, an electrical short caused Munger's cannon to fire and the volley of 20-mm shells took out an engine on the other plane. The 370th pilot made a quick one-engine landing, with a chagrined Munger close behind.

Bob was given the unenviable task (in other words, he was ordered) of taking Munger's plane on a test flight to determine what had malfunctioned. He performed a series of maneuvers, but was not able to duplicate his experience. Then during a steep climb, Bob popped the stick forward and the guns fired. There was a defective contact in the cannon firing mechanism—and the discovery got Munger out of what could have been a lot of trouble.

Another squadron colleague and a good friend of Bob, Lieutenant Bill Safarik, was hit on November 5. He was flying a mission in support of the 28th Infantry Division when German flak badly damaged his plane. While limping back on one engine, Bill was unable to maintain altitude and attempted to belly-land near Liege. As he made his approach, his plane suddenly dropped into high tension wires and crashed. Bill's neck and leg were broken, and he was taken to a German hospital where he received what he thought was very good care. However, his war injuries plagued him for the rest of his life. Shortly before his death, doctors discovered some bone fragments that should have been removed at the time of his injury.

On November 7, Bob flew a leaflet drop mission—a form of psychological warfare in which leaflets (flyers) were scattered in the air to fall to the ground in an attempt to alter the behavior of German combatants and civilians. Four days later, on November 11—ironically, the anniversary of Armistice Day, which ended World War I hostilities in 1918—the squadron escorted a B-26 bomber group on a 90-minute radar bombing. Again, flak was a problem, as it was on all bomber raids, but Bob returned unscathed to the base. Shortly after his return, Bob was given a choice. He could stay with the squadron, work toward a promotion, and assist in operations, or he could go on leave to America.

At the time, it looked as though the war was on its last legs. The Germans were falling back, the Allies were advancing on all fronts, and the war in Europe was drawing to a close. New men were constantly being shipped to Europe from the United States, putting the 429th Squadron in the position of having more pilots than aircraft. It was too late for Thanksgiving, but Bob could make it home for Christmas, and so he opted for leave, reasoning that he could then go on to the war still raging in the Pacific.

But a trip home was not in the cards for Bob. While he was awaiting orders, Bob was assigned his own plane and another major event—known familiarly now as the Battle of the Bulge (the Ardennes Counter Offensive, *die Ardennenoffensive*)—would interfere with his plans for leave.

The Location of Bastogne and the Ardennes Forest in Belgium

Previously he shared a plane with Lieutenant Kirkland, Lieutenant Herman Lane, or whichever pilot was not flying that day. Now he had his own, a P-38 that he inherited from Ralph Morand, who had left the squadron for reassignment.

Lieutenant Lane was the same Herman Lane who had loaned Bob his plane that had been damaged on a prior occasion. At the time, Lane had remarked philosophically: "Planes are easily replaced, but pilots are in short supply."

331

Sadly, both Lane and Kirkland were about to be killed in action and would not see the end of the war.

Bob dubbed the plane Swat in honor of his father. The name and a cowboy on a bucking horse were painted on the nose of his aircraft—the cowboy and bucking horse were brown on a yellow background, brown and yellow being the colors of his alma mater, the University of Wyoming. Four swastikas (painted in reverse) signified his aerial victories, and a series of bombs—one for each mission he had flown—were also painted on Swat's nosecone.

***

Bob was surprised in 2006 when Corgi Toys—producers of a range of die-cast toy scale-model vehicles produced by Mettoy Playcraft Ltd. in the United Kingdom—featured his P-38 as one of its new releases. Corgi has a global market for its models of cars, trucks, farm tractors and accessories, locomotives, planes, and military equipment. Collectors value Corgi models for their authenticity and attention to detail. Bob's plane, *Swat*, was selected for Corgi's nose art series. The scale model release was accompanied by a short biography describing his war experience.

Corgi did not contact him prior to the release, nor has he been able to establish contact with anyone in the company to determine how or why his P-38 was selected. Bob first learned of the release when an old wartime friend called saying he had seen the scale model in a Walmart store. Bob's young friend, fourteen-year-old Tanner Shelton Cornay of Longmont, Colorado, presented him one of the scale models. He also got Bob involved with the Corgi website and catalog so that he could order models for his family members. Many of Bob's friends and acquaintances also ordered models and have asked him to autograph them. The Laramie newspaper interviewed Bob for a major story on the model release, and the story was later picked up in full by the Casper newspaper and given statewide exposure.

Richard Kimmel, now living in the Washington, DC, area, also contacted Bob. He had been a member of the 429th Squadron ground crew, and he painted the nose art on the P-38. Bob was able to get him a picture of a Wyoming license plate so that he could accurately reproduce the cowboy on a bucking bronco. It was great catching up on each other's lives and sharing memories of those who fought with them so many years ago. Little did Bob imagine when he was playing with model planes as a boy that several decades later collectors would be buying models of his plane and seeking him out for his autograph.

***

Late in November Bob stood at attention in front of the squadron formation while the Distinguished Flying Cross (DFC) was pinned on his uniform.

The Citation for the Distinguished Flying Cross.

First Lieutenant Robert C. Milliken, 0758036, during the period 23 April 1944 to 22 November 1944, has participated in 66 missions totaling 193 combat hours and 137 sortie points. Milliken, flying as element and flight leader, participated in the pre-invasion air offensive on Europe, the invasion of France, and in close support of our ground forces throughout their progress to and beyond the Siegfried Line.

In hazardous long-range escort missions involving every problem of navigation, on low-level dive bombing and strafing attacks, and in personal victories over the enemy in the air, Lt. Milliken has displayed outstanding aerial proficiency and a keen desire to seek out and destroy the enemy.

One example of his skill and outstanding flying ability was demonstrated on 13 October 1944 when the 474th Fighter Group was dispatched on a fighter sweep over Cologne, Germany. At 20 miles northwest of Cologne, two of the squadrons were attacked by a numerically superior force of enemy aircraft. Lt. Milliken, leading Yellow Flight of the 429th Fighter Squadron, and in his intense desire to destroy as many of the enemy as he possibly could, immediately ordered his flight to attack.

Diving to the attack, he obtained numerous strikes on a FW-190. The enemy aircraft in an attempt to escape split S'd to 1,200 feet and Lt. Milliken, displaying cool determination and courage, followed him down. It was only when the enemy aircraft became protected by clouds that Lt. Milliken was forced to give up the fight. Immediately following this encounter, Lt. Milliken observed a friendly aircraft being pursued by an enemy aircraft, and though dangerously low on ammunition, turned to its aid. In the action that followed, Lt. Milliken, displaying superior flying skill, sent the enemy aircraft down in flames where it crashed into a group of farm houses.

After all enemy opposition had been cleared, Lt. Milliken reformed his flight and led it safely to its base through closing weather.

In all his flying, Lt. Milliken has carried the fight to the enemy and in personal victories over the enemy in the air, has displayed a superior aerial proficiency which clearly exemplifies his marked aggressiveness. His courage and determination to seek out and destroy the enemy without regard to his own personal safety reflect great credit upon himself and the Army Air Forces of the United States.

The Citation of the Distinguished Flying Cross

Subsequent to the award of the DFC award, he received the following letter from the Governor of Wyoming, the Honorable Lester C. Hunt:

I note in the press that you have been awarded the Air Medal with Oak Leaf Clusters and the Distinguished Flying Cross.

As Governor of the State of Wyoming, I write to congratulate you upon receiving these awards and to wish you continued success through the balance of the war.

We will be looking forward to your return to Wyoming after the war is over.

Fork-Tail Devil

***

In addition to getting his own plane, other events caught up with Bob before he could visit the US as part of his leave package. The Allied Air Forces were supposed have air supremacy, but the skies were decidedly unfriendly. In addition, the Germans, thought to be in full retreat, rocked the Allies back on their heels on December 16, 1944. Hidden tank and infantry divisions, including the First SS Panzer regiment under the command of Lieutenant Colonel Joachim Peiper, launched massive attacks through the Ardennes Forest. The enemy counteroffensive was directed at reaching Antwerp and splitting the Allied forces in the north from those operating in the south. The Germans sent 2,500 tanks and self-propelled siege guns against the Allies. They were supported by twenty-seven divisions, including nine armored divisions.

While crack German panzer (tank) divisions were wedging into the central section of the First Army front, hundreds of German paratroopers landed behind the Allied lines, cutting communications, attacking command posts, and using English-speaking Germans to spread chaos and confusion. The Allies were caught totally off guard. Troops retreated up and down the lines. Many were cut off and forced to surrender. Others were surrounded, left to fight alone until air support and ground relief could somehow be organized. As the Germans pushed ahead and the Allies fell back, the front line on military maps depicted a deep intrusion—or bulge—into what had been Allied territory prior to December 16. The Battle of the Bulge had begun, and the Allies were losing the fight.

***

335

Bob and his colleagues had heard about captured American soldiers being massacred by the Germans. One example of such an atrocity was the massacre that was committed on December 17, 1944, by members of Kampfgruppe Peiper (part of the First SS Panzer Division), a German combat unit. The US soldiers were taken to Malmedy woods and shot. Other massacres were committed by the same unit on the same day and following days. The names Malmedy and Baugnez are stark reminders of the atrocities committed by the Kampfgruppe Peiper.

As word of the massacre spread, there was retaliation by US Army units against German prisoners of war during and after that battle. Initially, very few Waffen-SS soldiers were taken prisoner. An example of the aftermath of the massacre is the written order in which it was stated "No SS troops or paratroopers will be taken prisoner but will be shot on sight." A possible example of a related large massacre against Germans is the Chenogne massacre in late December 1944 in which Waffen-SS prisoners were shot in such a systematic manner that US Army Headquarters had to issue orders that Waffen-SS soldiers were to be taken alive so Army Intelligence would be able to extract information from the otherwise sullen and morose SS soldiers.

More than ever, after hearing news of the Malmedy massacre, Bob and his squadron colleagues were anxious to get back in the fight. By this time German forces had made a ten-mile wedge into the American lines. The weather was miserable—snowy, foggy, and cold—but clear enough for the squadron to fly missions on December 18. All the pilots scheduled were combat veterans with at least fifty missions under their respective belts. With Lieutenant Munger leading, the assignment was to bomb targets on the German side of the bulge and to take on any Luftwaffe planes in the sector.

En route, ten or twelve German Me-109s were spotted at 12,000 feet. They were in a dogfight with some P-47s. Munger's radio went out, so Kirkland took over as leader and immediately ordered the bombs to be jettisoned, after which the P-38s climbed to give the outnumbered P-47s a hand. Bob was leading a flight of four with Lieutenant Bob Murdock on his wing.

As they swept in to attack, Murdock called in three Me-109s coming in from one o'clock. Bob made a turn away to give the Germans the impression that they were trying to get away. As soon as the P-38s hit their blind spot, they came back down underneath the 109s. They were climbing in a high-speed flight toward scattered clouds. Visibility was not the best. The cloud cover extended down to within a thousand feet of the ground and as high as Bob could see.

The Germans that Bob was tracking were flying a reverse V formation. Murdock and Bob got into the blind spot of the German pilots, and as they came into range, he and Murdock maneuvered into a position about 150 yards behind them. Visibility continued to decrease, but the Me-109s were still in sight.

"I'll take the one in the middle," Bob radioed to Murdock. "You take the one on the left. When I count to three, fire."

Bob closed to within thirty yards and remained in the German's blind spot, counted to three, and fired in concert with Murdock's firing. They were so close that he almost overshot the German. Bob gave him a two-second burst with almost no deflection. The tracers whipped across the cockpit area and Bob saw .50-caliber and cannon strikes in the upper cockpit and the propeller of the Me-109. As if in slow motion, the aircraft slowed visibly and then rolled over into a spin. When Bob rolled sharply to follow him, the instruments of the P-38 started spinning. He had his artificial horizon and was in a dive deep in the overcast sky. Moments later, Bob could see light above, so he pulled back on the stick, popped out of the cloud cover and found to his amazement that he was flying between layers of clouds.

To one side, Bob saw a B-17 placidly flying on the same level. He placed himself on the left wing of the bomber and used it as a reference point to reset his instruments. Then he rejoined the squadron for the flight home. Murdock had also rolled to follow the Me-109 after it was hit and he confirmed that the German plane had crashed.

It was Bob's last mission and his fifth kill. He had achieved the status of Fighter Ace.

Meanwhile, Kirkland was keeping pace. He had destroyed two Me-109s—his fourth and fifth victories. Kirkland and Bob had simultaneously become *flying aces* (five confirmed kills were required to earn the designation) but the excitement for Bob was not yet over.

***

General Quesada called Colonel Wasem after dinner on Friday December 22 to advise the squadron that company was heading their way. A German armored column was expected to attack the base within an hour. Allied aircraft reported the German column was across the river Meuse, within fifteen miles of Bob's air base. The enemy tanks needed the fuel supplies, and they were about to make a determined effort to capture the fuel supplies.

As ground crews scrambled to defend the A-78 airfield, pilots were prepared to fly the planes out. With rumors, orders, and counter-orders swirling about, the squadron decided that safety and valor were one and the same and started packing to leave. The men destroyed items that could not be packed and transported. Bob put his Class A uniform and other gear in a barracks bag, then stowed it in the radio compartment behind the seat of his P-38. Everything else went into trucks, along with any families that had been housing the American pilots.

Bob was assigned to take off first. It was dark, with visibility less than fifty yards, and he would have to make an instrument takeoff—something he had not done since his student pilot days.

This should be interesting, he thought, as he didn't know where he was going.

The orders were to save the planes, to fly them somewhere safe. England was safe, but Bob didn't care to cross the Channel, so he decided to locate the river Seine and head for Paris. Why not? Paris was reputed to be a lovely city and had not been destroyed by the retreating Germans. But as Mr. Shakespeare had once observed, "To be or not to be," and for Bob and his squadron colleagues, it was not to be.

Just before takeoff, all activity was called off. The pending attack was a false alarm. The German column was not coming, or was not base-side of the river, or was not in the vicinity, or all of the above. It had been turned back approximately twenty miles away with heavy losses—losses that the German Army could ill afford.

Feeling relieved, Bob retrieved his barracks bag from the radio compartment and went off to bed while the Prumont family was getting resettled in their home and ground crews started unpacking trucks.

***

In the sadness of war, Lieutenant Lenton F. Kirkland Jr. was killed on Christmas Eve 1944 while he was leading a flight, escorting a flight of 250 B-26 bombers. On the return leg of the mission, Kirkland's plane was hit by flack and went down smoking. Other pilots saw him bail out. His chute opened and Kirkland landed as his P-38 crashed nearby. One pilot reported seeing Kirkland run into the woods. The 429th never saw or heard from him again. His body was recovered after the war and buried in Belgium.

***

When Allied ground troops pushed the Germans back, searchers from the 429th Squadron combed the area thoroughly, hoping to learn what happened to Kirkland and two other pilots who had gone down in the vicinity. They learned little. However, local inhabitants stated they saw a P-38 crash on December 27. Unless the locals got their dates wrong, it was not Kirkland—he went down on Sunday December 24. The pilot that the locals saw bail out was captured and marched away with guns pointed against his back.

Years after the war, when Bob was attending a Hanna High School reunion, he talked with a former infantryman who witnessed a P-38 crash on Christmas Eve in the sector where Kirkland went down. He made his way to the wreckage. There he found signs that the pilot may have been mortally wounded. The description provided by the former infantryman and the watch and other belongings remaining in the seriously damaged aircraft fitted the description of Kirkland.

It is extremely likely that the arm in the aircraft that the infantryman found was in Kirkland's and that Kirkland had died from shock or loss of blood after running into the woods.

The daughter that Kirkland never saw lost her father before her first Christmas. Seventy Christmases have come and gone, and Kirkland has yet to make it home. He lies at rest, as young as he was on the day that he died, with hundreds of comrades in a military cemetery in Belgium.

Chapter 11: The V-1

The planned trip home didn't materialize. While he was awaiting orders, Bob was assigned his own plane, and another major event—now known familiarly as the Battle of the Bulge (the Ardennes Counter Offensive, *die Ardennenoffensive*)—interfered with his plans for leave. The battle lasted from December 16, 1944, until January 25, 1945, putting cold water on any plans for leave any of the servicemen held.

During this time, Allied troops managed to delay and then fight back the German counteroffensive. The key crossroads city of Bastogne was surrounded, but the defenders kept fighting. It was at Bastogne that the commanding general of the US forces, General Anthony Clement McAuliffe, responded to the surrender ultimatum presented to him by the commander of the German XLVII Panzer Corps, General Heinrich Freiherr von Luttwitz, with a single word:

"Nuts."

This was reputedly explained to Luttwitz by the German interpreters as:

"Go to hell."

The British, agreeing with this comment but having a somewhat different take on the situation, interpreted the word as meaning:

"Up yours, mate!"

Then Allied reinforcements made it to the front, through the efforts of many, not the least of which was General George S. Patton and his Third Army Corps. The Allied lines stiffened and resisted further encroachment by German forces. And most important, the weather cleared. As a result, Allied aircraft, including Bob's squadron, were able to fly again and took control of the skies. Coordinated attacks with ground forces served to reduce the initial gains made by the German counteroffensive.

The siege of Bastogne was lifted, and all of the territory taken in this last-gasp effort by the Germans was recaptured. As the year ended and the month of January 1945 got under way, the Allies were shifting their efforts from the Battle of the Bulge to the Battle for Berlin. This gave a new sense to the Allied forces. The goal and the end of the war seemed to be in sight, but there was no doubt in anyone's mind that the German forces would fight ferociously to define their homeland. In reality it would be another five long months before hostilities in Europe would be officially at an end.

Thus, as with many Allied soldiers and flyers, the war was not over for Bob and for many of his colleagues. For many of the men, it was merely a shift in focus. Bob's combat flying ended early in January, when he was assigned to detached duty, temporarily working at or with another unit. In this case Bob was assigned to the 321ˢᵗ Fighter Control Squadron. His first assignment was to Verviers, a textile city and municipality of 41,000 people located in the Belgian province of Liège, which was the central headquarters for Fighter Control.

After Belgium had been liberated on September 9, 1944, the 327th Fighter Control Squadron was one of the first American units to set up headquarters in Verviers. The 327th were billeted in l'Athénée Royale, a downtown secondary school, but worked in nearby Stembert, a hamlet of white farmhouses and rolling hills in Eastern Belgium with a population of 5,770 that lay just west of the German border. With its higher ground, Stembert allowed better functioning of the radio equipment.

The first item that Bob noticed when he arrived at the headquarters building was a large situation board. It dominated the room, and the fliers sat above it on balconies, looking down at the board. Each pilot was equipped with a microphone and earphones so that he (there were no female pilots) could maneuver fighters in the air to keep ahead of events unfolding on the situation board. Each flight control had a number of airborne planes assigned to them, which they could vector to targets. The experience the men gained as combat fliers was invaluable to the planners in assessing targets and opportunities for those now carrying the fight to the enemy, which was still very much in everyone's mind.

When Bob reported for duty on the first night, he was tired and he did not know which cubicle was his, so he put his kit bag and other gear next to a large glass window covered by drapes, found a cot, and settled in to sleep.

During the night, without realizing it, Bob was introduced to the latest German weapon. He had heard a dozen or more explosions during the night, and when he arose the next morning, there was broken glass under the drapes. Pulling back the drapes, he discovered the large windows had been shattered. Someone told him that the culprits had been V-1 bombs that had landed only a short distance away.

The V-1 was a secret weapon, highly praised by Hitler and German forces. It was a rocket-propelled flying bomb, known more correctly as the *V-1 rocket* and more familiarly to Londoners as the *buzz bomb*. Once the motor stopped and the buzzing sound ceased and the missile started to dive, it was time to seek cover.

The V-1 Rocket, Also Known as the Flying Bomb or the Buzz Bomb

***

The V-1 (*Vergeltungswaffe*, retaliation weapon, vengeance weapon) was an unmanned, unguided, flying bomb. Since it was the first such weapon, it was designated the V-1. Although primitive by modern standards, it was the first weapon of the type that is referred to in modern parlance as a *cruise missile*. It was designed by the Fiesler Company and designated the FZG-76.

The V-1 was a liquid-fuelled, pulse-jet drone aircraft that could carry a 2,000-pound warhead. There was no navigation system, so the weapon was merely pointed in the direction of the target—typically a city in southern England. Simple gyrocompasses kept it level, and its range was reputedly controlled by a predetermined time. When the time expired, the wire holding the elevators was severed and they turned down with the result that the V-1 dived to the earth. Some observers claim that the V-1 did not have any timing device and the distance it flew was controlled by rocket power and the angle of repose at takeoff. Whatever the means of guidance, the explosion caused by the bomb could devastate English cities (from its inception) and western European cities, such as Liège or Antwerp (after the D-Day invasion), killing almost 23,000 civilians during the time the weapon was in use.

The V-2 rocket was very different from the V-1. The rocket was forty-six feet long, weighed almost thirteen tons, and carried a one-ton warhead. Reaching 3,600 miles per hour and an apogee of sixty miles, it could not be tracked or caught by Allied fighter aircraft, and it had an impact velocity comparable to fifty big train engines slamming into a neighborhood.

The V-2 was the handiwork of a young Prussian Junker named Werner von Braun, who belonged to the Nazi Party and the SS, and who since 1937 had been working on a liquid-fuel rocket at Peenemunde, formerly a fishing village on the Baltic Sea coast of Germany.

The first V-1 flew in 1942 at Peenemunde on the southern Baltic coast. A series of fixed launching sites were constructed in France, Holland, Denmark, and Germany to allow the Germans to shower V-1 rockets onto any part of southern England. However, German planning did not take into account a strong bomber and fighter-bomber offensive against the V-1 launch sites. This forced the Germans into creating mobile launch sites and launching some of the weapons from Heinkel (He-111) bombers.

The first offensive launch was on June 12, 1943. Once the Germans got into a routine, 150 to 200 V-1 rockets were launched each day. The British quickly became expert at spotting and shooting them down. Through the agency of fighter aircraft of the Royal Air Force and anti-aircraft guns, less than 25 percent of the launched V-1 rockets hit the target.

The English established defensive zones. First were the fighters (Mosquitoes, Spitfires and Typhoons), which patrolled the English Channel and the southern part of the North Sea. Then a thick zone of heavy anti-aircraft guns equipped with the first radar proximity fuses. And then a zone of light anti-aircraft guns and rocket projectors and finally barrage balloons. Once the Allies captured the launching sites, the target of choice switched to Antwerp, the main Allied port, which received a pounding by 11,988 V-1 rockets and most of the 1,766 V-2 missiles launched. Fortunately, the Allies overran the launch sites that could have deluged the Normandy beachhead with these high-explosive bombs, interfering greatly with the supply and logistics of an army in Europe.

***

Bob's first day, after the cleanup of the shattered glass in his assigned quarters to make sure that none of the shards found their way into his bed, was to study and take in the workings of the situation board, which was set up to display all of the information relayed from headquarters and gave a point-by-point description of troop and aircraft movement. Observers on the Allied front lines and behind the enemy lines relayed pertinent updates, and Bob became heavily involved in the business of running and fighting a war.

The Liège Fighter Control Center was in the downtown business district and across the street from a line of shops. However, Germany was close by—just across the Rhine River. Radar observers would pick up V-1 rockets when the Germans fired them in the direction of the center then would track them and extend the track to the highly probable impact cities—Liège or Antwerp.

When it was generally established where the V-1 rockets were heading, the men in the Flight Control Center would step out on a balcony and watch them come in. Each V-1 carried enough explosive to completely destroy (using Bob's own comparisons) a Laramie city block or virtually all of Hanna, the town of his birth and his youth.

Watching from the balcony on one occasion, Bob heard the engine of an active buzz bomb almost directly overhead and then the silence. He scanned the sky and saw the V-1 crash into a large brick warehouse building only a block and a half to the right of the Control Center. The warehouse erupted and then collapsed in a smoking pile of rubble. If the weapon had made a shorter flight, that resulting explosion would have wiped out the Fighter Control Center, and Bob and many of his comrades would have been V-1 statistics.

Bob developed a survival strategy for staying out of the V-1 impact zones when he was caught out in the open. When the warning sirens sounded and he could hear the buzz bombs coming in, he would get to a street corner. If the V-1 hit on his side of the street, he could dodge debris by ducking around a corner. If he saw that the V-1 was going to land really close, he could dash across the intersection in the wild (perhaps delusional) hope that he could reach shelter before buildings started collapsing from the explosion. The strategy seemed to have worked, as he was never injured during any V-1 attack.

However, on one occasion, it was close! He was in a movie theater when the sirens sounded. The audience was evacuated to an air raid shelter and then returned to their seats after the all clear. A second attack warning and evacuation followed, then a third attack, making it a long night. But Bob stayed with it to the end of the film. Its name is no longer part of his memory, but it must have been to warrant his presence through three buzz bomb attacks. He was in a state of mind where he decided that it would take more than a few buzz bombs to keep him from watching the movie until the end. He said he got his money's worth by seeing the whole movie!

But it was not always that lucky for the staff of the center. On at least one occasion, the buzz bombs made their presence felt.

The Officers' Mess was situated in an upper class hotel. There was a pleasant reading room on the second floor, just a short distance from the dining area. One evening, Bob was relaxing in the sitting room, listening to the chaplain playing a grand piano in the corner. He was sitting with his back to a window box surrounded by drapes and blackout curtains when he heard a V-1 coming in. The engine cut out, and he knew that it was going to be close. He also knew what shattered glass driven by a bomb explosion could do to the human body.

As if by instinct, he dived across the floor to take cover under the grand piano while the chaplain, still playing the piano, just sat on the piano bench and waited. Unfortunately, the bomb landed in the motor pool adjacent to the hotel, instantly killing the sergeant in charge and doing severe damage to several vehicles that were parked nearby. Fortunately, however, the blast was directed away from the hotel, so any further loss of life or injury to personnel did not occur and damage to the building was minimal.

Bob was in Liège for less than a month. During that time, 301 V-1 rockets landed in the city and nearby areas. The Germans were hoping to hit transportation or storage areas, but the buzz bombs, having no reliable guidance systems, seldom hit strategic targets.

On one occasion, a V-1 did land in the heart of Liège, in a large circular plaza surrounded by a bank and other beautiful buildings that may have included an opera house or municipal center. Knowing that assistance would be needed, Bob ran to the impact area and arrived just as first aid people and ambulances were also arriving. The bodies of many civilians who were unable to get into the shelters in time were scattered across the plaza in the ungainly but unmistakable attitudes of death. There was nothing he could do as the professionals tended the wounded, covered the dead, and consoled grief-stricken survivors.

Bob watched, and then turned to walk back to the hotel. An army truck was parked facing uphill on a slight grade with the tailgate open, and blood from the dead stacked inside was dripping slowly onto the street. He stepped over the growing dark-red stream and continued on his way. Liège inhabitants continued to live and die under the buzz bomb assault until the Allied troops fought their way across the Rhine. When the enemy was forced to move the launch sites deeper into the interior of Germany, Liège was finally out of range.

At the end of February 1945, Bob was assigned to a post as an observer for the Bonn Fighter Control Center. Having flown into Germany several times in his P-38, he finally entered Germany by ground. He was assigned quarters in an apartment building on top of a hill, just four or five hundred yards from the downtown area of Bonn, where he worked out of city hall. Being an observant fellow, he had noted a power plant with a tall chimney was close by where he worked.

During some off-duty time, he went back to the squadron, checked out a P-38, and flew over Bonn. He was upstaged by a P-47 pilot who buzzed the city at a low altitude, then pulled up, and rolled over the power plant chimney. Being a fighter pilot and a breed apart from other pilots, and having the confidence that anything the P-47 pilot could do he could do better, Bob buzzed the headquarters building at such a low altitude that a woman who saw him coming dived into the dirt. Then to further demonstrate his flying abilities, Bob took the P-38 into a perfect slow roll over the towering chimney. But not all stories have happy endings. He learned later that the P-47 pilot was court-martialed for his antics, but there were no reports of Bob trying to outdo him, and he escaped without even a reprimand for his acrobatic maneuvers.

Four days later, Bob was less confident about getting away from trouble. In those days, there was no such thing as just going for a walk to get some fresh air. Caution was needed as sporadic exchanges of fire persisted for many weeks. Chalked on building walls were slogans such as *Berlin bleibt Deutsch* (Berlin remains German) for those persons who refused to accept that Germany had been defeated.

Thus it happened that as he was walking to the Bonn headquarters, a German woman approached him, said something in German that he didn't understand, and stuck out her hand to give him an object. Thinking that it might be a thank-you gift, Bob took it before he saw what it was—a hand grenade. Fortunately, the safety pin was still in place, but he was not comfortable standing in the middle of a German city holding a grenade, which he assumed was live. Grenades had been known to be temperamental weapons, with the tendency to explode at any time, especially if they had been booby trapped.

He became extremely suspicious when the woman who handed the grenade to him made a rapid withdrawal in the opposite direction—she ran away!

It took Bob two seconds or less to realize he had to dispose of the grenade quickly. Leaving the safety pin in place, he threw the grenade as far as he could into the park woods, and then waited for the explosion. The safety pin worked—the anticipated explosion didn't happen. And he still hopes that no one ever dug up that grenade and pulled the pin.

Whether the woman who handed him the grenade had found it and wanted a soldier to dispose of it, or she was still fighting the war (there were many Germans with this turn of mind) and wanted to do her bit for the Fatherland by injuring or killing an American soldier, Bob would never know. For Bob, discretion (throwing the grenade away) was the better part of valor.

***

A day or so later, out of curiosity and deciding that they wished to see the enemy close up, Bob and Tom Coleman, a ground officer who had not made flight status, signed out a Jeep and drove to the fighting front where they parked approximately one quarter of a mile from the Rhine River. Not wishing to become an enemy target—they could observe the movements of steel-helmeted heads just across the river—they used a gravel pit for concealment.

Staying under cover—being a casualty of war at this stage of the proceedings and not wishing to be a statistic in an officer's log book was not palatable to either Bob or Tom—they worked their way carefully and cautiously to a house where they ascended a somewhat dilapidated and less-than-stable staircase to join five American riflemen who were observing movements of the enemy soldiers. The German trenches were clearly visible through an oval-shaped observation port. One of the riflemen loaned Bob his sniper rifle equipped with a high-power scope through which he could see the tops of German helmets moving up and down the trench line. Bob had a strong impulse to put a bullet through one of those helmets, but realizing that for every action there is a reaction, probably in the form of incoming mortar shells, he resisted, and gave the rifle back to its owner.

No one really wanted to stir up a fight at that stage of the war. It was obvious to the Allies that the Germans were finished, but since no one had told them they were finished, there had yet to be a formal surrender. And there were many Waffen-SS units. Meanwhile, both sides settled into a stalemate.

The Waffen-SS (armed SS) was created as the armed wing of the Nazi Party *Schutzstaffel* (SS or Protective Squadron), and gradually developed into a multi-ethnic and multi-national military force of Nazi Germany with units fighting alongside German Army (*Wehrmacht*) units but under control of SS officers. Adolf Hitler preferred that the Waffen-SS remain the armed wing of the Party and to become an elite police force once the war was won. These men were die-hards who would fight to and beyond the bitter end. If the units across the Rhine had been SS units, the consequences of shooting at and possibly killing the wearer of one of the steel helmets could have been disastrous. Fortunately, the only front line shooting that occurred happened when divisions rotated and those new to the line set up aiming stakes and sighted in their weapons ready to use should action break out. It did not.

After a short stay in Bonn, Bob and his colleagues received orders to assemble a convoy with radio equipment. They were moving up to the front line as forward air controllers. His group was assigned a half-track vehicle, a weapons carrier, and three Jeeps towing trailers with the radio crew and all their equipment. Bob rode part of the way in the half-track. It wasn't built for comfort, and if it had any shock absorbers (which seemed unlikely from the discomfort in his rump), they needed considerable adjustment. The shaking vehicle was a teeth-and-bone rattler to the point that Bob insisted the men had to take turns riding in the weapon carrier, then the half-track. Each one had to share the fun—and the pain and discomfort!

***

Allied troops made headlines and history when they captured the Ludendorff Bridge at Remagen, the only surviving span across the Rhine River.

The bridge was badly damaged, and there were fears that it would collapse before it could be strengthened. The Germans were fighting desperately to stem the flow into the heartland of Germany. Luftwaffe pilots, at least those who remained and risked venturing forth in the Allied-controlled skies, tried to destroy Allied bridgeheads and turn back the Allied soldiers. Allied fighter aircraft met the Luftwaffe head-on, creating heavy losses for the Germans, thereby allowing the advancing Allies to surge across the Rhine.

On March 7, 1945, a small advance party of the 9th US Tank Division, under the command of German-born lieutenant Karl H. Timmermann, successfully captured the bridge after two unsuccessful demolition attempts by the Germans. During the following days, the German Army Central Command desperately tried to destroy the bridge with multiple bomb raids. Because of the capture of the bridge by American forces, Adolf Hitler ordered a special court-martial, which sentenced five of the German officers to death. Four of those officers were shot in the close-by town of Westerwald.

With each crossing, the damaged Ludendorff Bridge got weaker and threatened collapse. Bob's convoy crossed the Rhine on a hastily constructed pontoon bridge a short distance upstream. On March 17, 1945, ten days after the completion of the pontoon bridge, the severely damaged Ludendorff Bridge collapsed. Unfortunately, twenty-eight American soldiers died as they went into the river with the bridge.

The hastily erected pontoon bridges proved to be a godsend for Allied troops. These bridges floated on water. Barge-like or boat-like pontoons supported the bridge deck and the varying loads of men, machinery, and equipment.

***

The Allied forces were streaming across the Rhine on pontoon bridges and water-worthy craft. In late March 1945, thousands of German troops were caught in what came to be called the Ruhr Pocket. Many had fought in the Battle of the Bulge and had been fighting and dying constantly during the period since that battle ended. And now that the German soldiers were defending the homeland, in many sectors of the front, the fighting increased in ferocity.

The Ruhr Pocket was a battle of encirclement that took place in the Ruhr area. The American artillery joined aircraft in pounding the Ruhr Pocket. Bob was not involved directly, but when the artillery shells passed over the position where he was on duty, they sounded like freight trains rumbling in a steady stream. No one, he thought, could stand up to this type of bombardment. To Bob and others, the outcome was inevitable.

By early April the battle was over. For all intents and purposes, it marked the end of major organized resistance on Germany's Western Front. More than 300,000 Wehrmacht and Waffen-SS troops were taken prisoner.

Bob had returned to headquarters with the 18ᵗʰ Airborne Corps, which consisted of the 82ⁿᵈ, 101ˢᵗ, and 17ᵗʰ Airborne Divisions, with other units being attached to the corps at various times. Part of his duties was to maintain contact with various fighter groups and squadrons so that he could divert them to wherever their firepower was needed.

On one occasion, a flight of P-51s checked for direction. Seeing that an opportunity had arisen, Bob advised them that a squadron of US tanks had not been able to successfully remove or bypass an extremely active German Tiger tank that was blocking their way.

The Tiger tank was a heavy German tank that had been developed in 1942 as a response to the unexpectedly formidable Soviet tanks encountered in the initial months of the invasion of the Soviet Union. The Tiger design included heavy armor and the almost unbeatable 88-mm gun that gave it an advantage of armor protection and firepower over the American tanks. Sitting where it did, the Tiger was a major hurdle for the US tank commanders.

Bob surmised that some of the Sherman M4 tanks might be the older model, which had an engine that was powered by highly flammable gasoline rather than the less-flammable (but still dangerous) diesel fuel. It was not surprising that the Germans gave the gasoline-powered M4 the nickname Ronson! Either way, whether gasoline-powered or diesel-powered, the Sherman M4 was no match for a Tiger tank.

Dutifully, Bob gave the P-51 pilots the coordinates of the Tiger, and the P-47 forward observer and his troops marked the target with some red smoke. The P-51s destroyed the Tiger tank, and the American tanks were free to move on further into Germany.

Much to Bob's surprise, a colonel monitoring the sequence complimented Bob on his efforts, and he offered Bob an after-the-war job as an American Airline pilot, if he would relocate to Chicago. It was a tempting offer, but nothing ever came of it.

The Flight Control headquarters were in what had been a small mansion on a hilltop. To the north, Germans began streaming toward it across an open pasture. They were finished and had enough. Caught between two advancing armies—Allies to the west and Soviets to the east—the Germans were making the best of a bad situation by surrendering in droves to the Allies. Bob took a short walk down into a valley and took photographs of 30,000 or more German prisoners just held out in the open. They were guarded by military police backed by two Sherman tanks, but they were not considering an escape. Their fighting days were over. It was just as well. It would have taken minimal effort for thousands of Wehrmacht soldiers to overcome less than a hundred US military police.

The MPs were able to keep the prisoners in line using the age-old military police weapon—the baton. Whenever one of the Germans started acting up or did something he was not supposed to do, one of the MPs would rap him with a baton. The German soldiers were quick learners. One rap was all it took to convert most of them to good behavior. The prisoners didn't have much in the way of shelter, but they did have water and sanitary facilities, and they were getting three meals a day. Even if those meals were American surplus K rations, it was more than they had been used to recently from their own command.

A short distance away and out of sight of the surrendered Germans, Bob saw a mountain of weapons. Most were Karabiner 98 Kurz bolt-action rifles chambered for the 7.92 x 57 mm Mauser cartridge that had been adopted as the standard service rifle in 1935 by the Wehrmacht. It was one of the final developments in the long line of Mauser military rifles. Although supplemented by semiautomatic and fully automatic rifles during World War II, the Karabiner 98 Kurz rifle had remained the primary German service rifle until the end of World War II in 1945.

Other items in the mountain included Mauser rifles, machine guns, mortars, odds and ends of uniforms, and other debris of war marking the German defeat. There was also a varied assortment of handguns, including the well-known Luger pistol, which were prime mementos for American soldiers to take home at the end of the war. Afterward, he often wished that he had picked up one of the Mauser rifles. It would have made a great hunting rifle to take back home to Wyoming. But he had no place to keep it safe and was not about to risk being branded a looter.

Looting and pillaging had been a common occurrence when the German forces entered conquered countries at the beginning of the war. Many of the soldiers were told to live off the land. Others just wanted loot, not to mention certain activities that conquering armies are wont to do.

Attempts were made to mitigate looting when the Allied forces entered Germany, but with little success. Many men, who had never stolen anything in their lives, as some of the stress of battle was removed from their daily living, suddenly turned to stealing anything that could be carried. Bob didn't wish to be a part of such activities, and he always found something else to occupy his mind when looting parties were out and about.

He did manage to acquire a motorcycle that he was able to use for transport within the city and in the country, although he did have to exercise caution. There were Germans (he didn't know if they were renegade soldiers or civilians) who were prone to take shots at US service men. This came to an end a few days after acquiring the motorcycle. His commanding officer requested (ordered) that the machine be surrendered to the military transport personnel.

On one occasion, as he walked along the cobblestone street of a village and explored a deserted second-story photo studio, Bob looked out of the window to see a weapons carrier bouncing up the street. In the bed of the weapons carrier were some shovels, various instruments, tools, and the body of an American soldier. The man's remains were curled up in a fetal position, just rattling around like a block of ice amidst all the tools and instruments. The experience of so much death over the past years had made many of the men callous in the way that they handled bodies, even bodies of fallen comrades.

***

Bob's next move was to Weimar, Germany, where he stayed for three nights and was billeted in the third floor of what had once been student housing. To Bob's surprise he found that he was within walking distance of the notorious Buchenwald concentration camp, which about a month before his visit had been liberated by Soviet soldiers from the murderous ministrations of the camp guards.

The Buchenwald camp was located just a short distance east of Weimar. Bob couldn't agree that villagers could deny knowledge of the existence of the camp. He finds it difficult to believe that most German civilians could credibly deny knowledge of the concentration camps or the slave-labor system. They are like people who to this day insist that the Holocaust didn't happen and that the whole thing is a historical fabrication.

Bob had heard that the camp still had prisoners on-site and decided to investigate to find out what really had happened there.

As he walked toward the Buchenwald camp—one of approximately 350 camps and ghettos that were established by Germany and the countries allied with Germany—the eye-watering sting of smoke and the smell of burning flesh was still in the air. Trying to get the smell out of his nostrils, Bob heard a sound and realized that someone had taken a shot at him. He heard the bullet as it zipped past even before he heard the sound of the gunshot. It was close—too close—and another reminder (especially after the hand grenade incident) that for some German diehards the war was not yet over. Bob couldn't see the shooter, but he could only conclude that it was someone connected with the concentration camp or was one of the so-called innocent civilians living in Weimar.

After seeing the camp, with bodies not yet recovered from shallow depressions in the ground (they certainly couldn't be called graves) for a decent burial, Bob found it difficult to comprehend why anyone would deny what happened there. He went through the crematorium, then through the gas chambers, where he saw the tattooed skin on the walls. He saw lampshades made out of human skin. He talked with some of the survivors, saw the barracks where they were forced to live, and witnessed the primitive conditions under which they worked until their date with the crematorium came due.

As the Allies advanced toward Buchenwald, the Germans stepped up the slaughter. So many helpless men, women, and children were murdered that the camp's crematorium couldn't handle the carnage. A big open ditch was dug into which many of the bodies were dumped. Other bodies were burned or buried whenever possible.

Before death, the victims were stripped of everything—clothing, jewelry, glasses, hair, and even gold teeth. The ever-efficient Germans took everything of value, and then cast aside the most valuable thing of all—human dignity. Unbelievable numbers of people died at Buchenwald. When the camp was liberated, forty thousand prisoners were still alive—barely. And to make matters worse, the prisoners were surrounded by ten thousand unburied corpses and the ashes of hundreds of thousands.

During his visit to the camp, a prisoner was sitting outside a barracks—he was too weak to stand—caught Bob's attention and motioned him to come over. Looking carefully at the prisoner, Bob believed that he was a very old man—the hair that the man had remaining on his head was almost white—until he showed Bob a photograph and pointed to himself. The photograph was of a thirty-five-year-old man. It was the prisoner as he had been only two years or so before Bob's arrival at the camp.

Buchenwald prisoners were crammed into crude barracks where they slept side-by-side on board planks stacked floor to ceiling with barely enough room between layers for the prisoners to turn over. When prisoners died, they stayed wedged among the living until morning roll call. Then the bodies were dragged away and the living got on with the desperate task of staying alive another day. The only possessions a prisoner had were a rag for a blanket and a bowl from which to eat, which sometime doubled as a night pot. If they lost either their blanket or their bowl, death was a certainty.

Bob viewed a special concrete room underneath the crematorium ovens at Buchenwald where prisoners were tortured, strangled with piano wire, or hung alive on meat hooks, then stripped of everything down to body hair and gold teeth and sent along an elevated assembly line to die. He also learned that the crematorium ovens were built to accommodate one body at a time, but the SS, in the interests of efficiency, would load two bodies into each oven for final destruction.

General Eisenhower visited the camp shortly before Bob arrived. Appalled by what he saw and disgusted by the constant "we did not know" denials of the German civilians, he ordered the inhabitants of Weimar to be marched past the stacks of dead bodies lying in the ditch. Now there could be no denials. Weimar residents knew what had been going on under their noses, and through their silence and complicity they must bear the stigma of history.

Bob did not know it at the time, but one of his close friends, squadron colleague who was shot down, were sent to Buchenwald instead of a prisoner of war camp.

Stories that the camp survivors told Bob were reinforced by the experiences of this squadron pilot. The pilot confirmed that the Germans killed inmates as a matter of course, excusing it sometimes by rationalizing that they were only following orders or that they had to make room for legitimate prisoners of war.

***

Like Bob, Lieutenant Joseph F. Moser had grown up on a small farm, only Joe's farm was in Ferndale, Washington, and like Bob, he had dreamed of becoming a pilot since he was in school. His dream came true when he qualified to fly the P-38 Lightning. Joe was sent to Europe and was assigned to the same squadron as Bob. Joe survived forty-three missions, earning honors for outstanding skill in dive-bombing missions.

On August 13, 1944, on his forty-fourth combat mission, Joe's dream was shattered when he was shot down. He survived the incident, but his dream had ended and turned into a nightmare. Joe was one of the Allied flyers known as *terrorfliegers* (terror flyers) who was captured by the Germans and scheduled for execution by the SS.

In the summer of 1944, 168 airmen from the US, England, Canada, and other Allied countries who had been captured by the SS and Gestapo were shipped in crowded cattle cars to the infamous *Koncentration Lager Buchenwald* in Germany. This was an extermination camp, *not* a prisoner of war camp. Falsely accused of being "terrorists and saboteurs," the airmen faced a terrifying fight for survival and a race against time to escape their execution.

Joe was rescued just four days before he was scheduled for execution, only to spend over six more months in several POW camps. He ended up in Stalag XIII D in Nuremberg, where he and 15,000 other prisoners of war were liberated by American forces on April 29, 1945.

Joe made it back to Ferndale and lived to contact Bob. They have remained close friends ever since.

***

To the south, on April 28, 1945, Benito Mussolini was captured and shot by partisans while attempting to escape from northern Italy. On the afternoon of April 30, as Russian troops stormed the Reichstag building a mere four hundred yards from the Führerbunker (Hitler's bunker), the leader of the Third Reich killed himself and his wife. The remainder of the leaders of the Third Reich disappeared, although some arranged to have a meeting with death—by their own hands—in Berlin in April 1945.

There was much jubilation among the Allies at the news of the death of Adolf Hitler. He committed suicide by gunshot on April 30, 1945, in his Führerbunker in Berlin. His wife Eva (née Braun) committed suicide with him by ingesting cyanide. That afternoon, in accordance with Hitler's prior instructions, their remains were carried up the stairs through the bunker's emergency exit, doused in gasoline (called *petrol* in England and *benzine* in Germany), and set alight in the Reichs Chancellery garden outside the bunker. Soviet archives record that their burned remains were recovered and interred in successive locations until 1970, when they were again exhumed, cremated, and the ashes scattered over a wide area.

Accounts differ as to the cause of death; one that he died by poison only and another that he died by a self-inflicted gunshot, while biting down on a cyanide capsule. Contemporary historians have rejected these accounts as being either Soviet propaganda or an attempted compromise in order to reconcile the different conclusions. There is also controversy regarding the authenticity of skull and jaw fragments that were recovered. In 2009, DNA tests performed on a skull fragment that Soviet officials had long believed to be the last remains of Hitler did not confirm the identity of the skull. The mystery remains.

Following Hitler's death, Grand Admiral Karl Dönitz assumed the role of Führer and over approximately a two-week period attempted to buy time for German forces to escape westward from the Russians by staging partial capitulation and seeking to negotiate with the British and Americans. As history shows, this was not an effective strategy. The Allies marched on. SS General Karl Wolff had already concluded a unilateral negotiation for the surrender of his army in Italy on April 29, 1945; German forces in northwest Germany, Holland, and Denmark surrendered to Montgomery at Lüneburg Heath on May 4; resistance on the American fronts ended two days later, while the Red Army closed up the Elbe; General Patton's army reached Pilsen and might have advanced to Prague, but the Russians insisted on taking the Czech capital themselves. They finally accomplished this on May 11. Meanwhile, a delegation from Admiral Dönitz reached General Eisenhower's headquarters at Reims on May 5, seeking an exclusive surrender to the Americans. The supreme commander required a simultaneous and unconditional surrender on all fronts, which Reichs General Alfred Jodl, senior military adviser to the late Adolf Hitler, signed on May 7. May 8 was celebrated by all the Western Allies as Victory in Europe Day (VE-Day). If confusion exists about the official end of World War II, it is because Josef Stalin, the Russian leader, insisted on a further ceremony in Berlin, at which the Russians were full parties. This took place on May 8 and May 9, Russia's own declared date of victory.

***

From Weimar Bob was flown into Leipzig to set up fighter control there. He was in Leipzig only a few days when he was ordered back to Weimar, then flown to Czechoslovakia, where the men were going to set up a fighter control center at the front lines. That did not happen. Instead, Leipzig was turned over to the Russians, and Bob went back to Weimar, where he was when the war in Europe was declared to be over on May 8, 1945.

Everyone was ready for the war to end, and there was even more jubilation that it was now over. No longer needed as a forward observer, Bob rejoined his squadron at Langensalza (now Bad Langensalza), which is east of Kassel, Germany.

At Kassel Bob inspected a lot of abandoned German planes, including the Me-262, the world's first operational jet fighter plane. One of his enlisted friends got him a P-38 pistol, a gun similar to (in fact a copy of) the much-coveted German Luger. Bob packed the pistol in a wooden box with many of his other keepsakes, including a bona fide Luger, and some German flags that he picked up along the way.

That box and the souvenirs have survived many moves in the decades since. Zella carefully repacked the box each time they moved—which was often—and he still has the collection intact.

Bob took his last flight in a P-38 in June 1945. He flew from Langensalza, a city in Thuringia, Germany, over part of Switzerland. As he flew over two lakes in Switzerland, someone fired a few rounds at the aircraft. He concluded that the Swiss were not as neutral as he had been led to believe! He continued flying over the Swiss Alps, taking pictures until the camera froze up, then landed back at Langensalza and got out of a P-38 cockpit for the last time.

***

During his years in combat, Bob had been awarded the Air Medal, the Silver Star, and the Distinguished Flying Cross.

He was awarded an Air Medal for every ten missions that he flew in combat. The Silver Star was awarded for shooting down two German aircraft and damaging three others in one combat session. The Distinguished Flying Cross was awarded for shooting down an FW-190 that was intent on killing one of his comrades while Bob ignored his own imminent danger.

CHAPTER 12: WHERE THE DEER AND THE ANTELOPE ROAM

The following month, July 1945, Bob made preparations to journey home. It was a pleasant time, as he received a memorable farewell from those who flew with him and fought beside him, starting him on a leisurely trip home. The trip also gave him time to think of the past two years.

As he prepared to return to the United States and home, he knew that everything had changed. He was a US Army Air Corps pilot who had fought for his country. He had seen death and destruction and he knew that he had changed. He had lived through a time that many people never experience—a time of danger—but he had done what was needed, and proved to himself and others that he could be depended upon. And now he was going home where he would put such thoughts behind him and face life as it should have been.

He flew from Kassel Airfield near Weimar to Paris on a C-47 transport. The Douglas C-47 Skytrain or Dakota was a military transport aircraft that was developed from the Douglas DC-3 airliner. A fighter escort was provided for part of the journey by some of his squadron colleagues. They had all surmised during the previous two months that for some Germans the war may not yet be over. Then he flew to Stone, a base in Staffordshire, a landlocked county in the West Midlands region of England, where he was quarantined for a medical check to ensure that he had no infectious diseases. Then he was transported by rail to Wales. However, Bob did find the time while in England to walk in the fog and in Wales to play a round of golf with one of his colleagues.

At the time, it was Bob's habit to look to the sea and imagine his home in the United States, far to the west. Bob didn't know that a crashed P-38 was just offshore below the water line. It might have been a deeper nostalgic moment had Bob known of this—it certainly is a nostalgic moment now, at the time of writing.

Bob boarded a B-24 Liberator bomber, the type of aircraft that his brother-in-law Bobby Bell had flown during the war for the final leg home. The war might have been over, but this was not exactly a pleasure trip for Bob! The B-24 was notorious among American aircrews for its tendency to catch fire. Moreover, its high fuselage-mounted wing also meant it was dangerous to ditch or belly land, since the fuselage tended to break apart. Nevertheless, the B-24 had provided excellent service in a variety of roles thanks to its large payload and long range capability. Bob refused to be pessimistic, and his mood was one of joyous optimism.

However, as the aircraft left Wales, Bob could hear radio calls from other troop-carrying B-24s that were having engine problems. Some forged ahead, some returned to Wales, and unfortunately some never reached land. The aircraft on which Bob was a passenger took the great circle route past Greenland, landed at Reykjavik in Iceland for an overnight stay, then flew to Labrador, and from there the aircraft took Bob to a remote airfield located on the northern border of the United States.

As was the common custom during the twentieth century and remains the custom in the twenty-first century when soldiers return from war or active duty abroad, when Bob got out of the aircraft he instinctively knelt down, bowed his head, and kissed the earth—and he was not alone in performing that action.

The rest of Bob's military career was relatively anticlimactic, but exciting as he could sense that he was going home for good.

He traveled by train to New York and then boarded the familiar Union Pacific rail line for Santa Ana, California, where he waited to receive his discharge papers. As usual, it was a hurry-up-and-wait situation, and the thought that his service could be extended to serve in the Pacific Theater was always on Bob's mind. He thought in the meantime that a trip home to Wyoming would be beneficial and enjoyable. It would ease his mind from constant thoughts of service in the Pacific and relieve the boredom of the constant waiting. So he applied for and received permission for a fifty-day leave. After a seemingly endless two-day journey from California, he finally arrived in Hanna. There were no seats on the train, so he willingly stood or sat on the floor all the way. Getting home to Wyoming was his priority.

It was a leave he will always remember. He had a relaxing time hunting with Father Robert and Father's two brothers, John and Will, catching up on all the family happenings, and planning for his rapidly approaching future.

It was during this time that one day when he returned home after a day of fishing with Uncle John, Bob received the news that an atomic bomb had been dropped on each of two cites in Japan—Hiroshima and Nagasaki—and that the government of Japan had no choice but to agree to an unconditional surrender.

On August 6, 1945, the bomb known as Little Boy was dropped on Hiroshima. The detonation of this bomb generated the power of 12,500 tons of conventional explosive (TNT), created injuries of a kind never before experienced by human populations, and killed more than 70,000 people. Three days later, on August 9, the second atomic bomb, code-named Fat Man, was dropped on Nagasaki. The destruction matched the explosive power of 22,000 tons of TNT and killed at least 30,000 people.

There are modern critics of the bombing of Hiroshima and Nagasaki. But in the course of the war, it had been necessary to advance the cause of Allied victory without further loss of the lives of Allied soldiers, sailors, and airmen. By August 1945, to Allied leaders the lives of their own people had come to seem very precious, and in such circumstances, it seems understandable that President Truman did not halt the actions that carried the bombs to Japan.

At 7:00 p.m. (Washington time) on August 14, 1945—August 15 in Japan—President Truman read the announcement of Japan's unconditional surrender to a dense throng of politicians and journalists at the White House. The president then ordered the cessation of all offensive operations against the enemy. In Tokyo Bay on September 1, Japanese and Allied representatives headed by General Douglas MacArthur signed the surrender document on the deck of the battleship *USS Missouri*. The Second World War was officially ended.

The signing of the surrender documents by representatives of the Empire of Japan was the final act that brought a cessation of hostilities and brought World War II to a close. Before then, there had been much activity on the part of the Japanese government. At the end of July 1945, the Japanese government, despite realizing that the Imperial Japanese Navy was incapable of conducting operations and that an Allied invasion of Japan was imminent, was publicly stating their intent to fight on to the bitter end to defend the Japanese homeland. However, Japan's leaders (the Supreme Council for the Direction of the War) were privately making entreaties to the neutral Soviet Union (in respect to the war in the Pacific) to mediate peace on terms favorable to the Japanese. Meanwhile, the Soviets were preparing to attack the Japanese in fulfillment of their promises to the United States and the United Kingdom made at the Tehran and Yalta Conferences.

World War II was over. Bob's discharge papers were now a mere formality. He was home at last!

***

Sadly, Uncle John, who loved to dance, was killed April 1, 1946. He and his wife, Mary, were at a dance at the Garden Spot Pavilion in Elk Mountain, Wyoming. When a fight broke out between two of the local young men, a deputy sheriff who shouldn't have been handling a gun tried to break up the fight. When he hit one of the fighters over the head with a revolver, the gun went off, and the bullet hit Uncle John in the throat. He died almost instantly, leaving a widow and three daughters.

***

Back at Santa Ana after the leave, Bob was still trying to get some flight time. He managed to get a few hours in an AT-6 and was surprised when the former loose cannon we've given the pseudonym

Smith showed up as his flying partner. Against all odds, Smith survived the war and his bad habits.

***

Smith did compile a commendable record during the war and continued in the military as a career pilot. Years later Bob heard from someone in his squadron that he met Smith in the Orient when Smith was a major. After that Bob heard that Smith was in charge of radar warning platforms off the northeast coast and that he failed to get his crew off before a bad storm. Allegedly some men were lost and Smith was court-martialed. Bob has not heard from or about him since.

***

During his final days in the military and just before he received his discharge papers, Bob bought a 1940 Mercury convertible at a good price. He had plans, and he later sold the car to buy an engagement ring and ended up with an old Ford Model A given to him by his father. In the meantime, the officers were giving all of the men pep talks about reenlisting and making a career of military flying, but Bob was not interested. Without giving the ink time to dry on his discharge notice, he was on his way once again to his beloved Hanna.

He drove home in the newly-purchased convertible, accompanied by a pilot friend. They stopped briefly in Las Vegas, but Bob doesn't remember much about the city other than there was a carnival at one end of the town and a hotel at the other, a far cry from the Strip and neon glitz of the twenty-first century city. They spent one night in the hotel and the next in the desert. A problem with the car was the reason for the enforced desert camp, but they were able to continue the journey the next day when Bob discovered and repaired, a loose connection that had prevented the ignition mechanism from working correctly.

As they got closer and closer to Hanna, the car got lower and lower on gas. By late that night they had reached the Walcott service station, only twenty or thirty miles from Hanna, but the service station was closed. Bob was able to get the husband and wife owners of the service station out of bed to fill up the gas tank. He only had a $100 bill, and in those pre-credit card days, they were hesitant to take it. It would take all of their available cash to make change. But he was able to convince them that he was an honest local lad returning from active duty. They believed him, and he got enough gas to make it home.

Once he was home, Bob took off his uniform for the last time, donned civilian attire, and within days joined hundreds of other returning veterans enrolling for the 1945 fall semester at the University of Wyoming in Laramie. He had done his bit for the country that he loved and was ready to get on with the remainder of his life.

The war had made him rethink his future, and as a result he had changed his degree goals. He wasn't sure of his future, but he did know that he had no wish to continue his 1940 plans for a career in engineering. After a series of tests and interviews, his academic counselors pointed him in the direction of law school. They advised him that the fees for law school were high, and that he really could not afford to major in business administration.

***

Bob's life took another turn when he met John Roum, a former Navy pilot and a member of Sigma Alpha Epsilon fraternity. Because of John, Bob pledged that fraternity in April 1946. John and Bob also decided to go into business together—the airplane business. He decided to embark on an aeronautical future and left the University of Wyoming.

One of the members of the local Airport Board told Bob and John that they could not operate their business from the Laramie Regional Airport, also known as Brees Field, so he and John built their own airport, Laramie Airpark, located approximately one mile south of the city.

Their flying inventory consisted of two airplanes: an Aeronca Champion, which Bob had acquired, and a Luscombe that they owned jointly.

The Aeronca Champion (manufactured by the Aeronautical Corporation of America) was a convenient high-wing light aircraft for their business. It had been designed for flight training and personal use and entered production in the United States in 1945.

The Luscombe was a product of the Luscombe Aircraft Company, a United States aircraft manufacturer from 1933 to 1950. Luscombe had been founded in 1933 in Kansas City, Missouri. Like the Aeronca, the Luscombe was a high-wing, two-place monoplane that was ideal for flight training.

Since Bob had his flight instructor rating and John did not, the plan was for Bob to give lessons and for John to sell planes. The flight instruction activities brought in some money, but the sales activities did not. They were unable to sell a single plane. Seeing no prospects in the flying business, Bob sold his share of the company to John and went back to the University of Wyoming to get his engineering degree. And then Bob's life changed—forever.

***

A petite blonde with a lovely smile two years out of high school caught Bob's eye in January, 1946. He went stag (alone, unaccompanied by a young woman) to a dance at the Gray's Gable building (also known as the Quadra Dangle), a popular dance hall on what was then the northeastern outskirts of Laramie. The blonde, he learned later, was there with her brother.

Ignoring her brother, Bob (using tactics that he had fine-tuned when chasing enemy aircraft in his P-38) zeroed in on the young woman, introduced himself, and asked her to dance. Later he somehow persuaded her to let him drive her home. He was determined, even after this short time, that he was not going to allow Zella Bell to slip away and out of his life. Finding that they were compatible from the start, instead of taking Zella straight home, Bob took her to the Summit Tavern east of Laramie, together with two of his SAE brothers. That's Sigma Alpha Epsilon, *not* the Society for Automotive Engineers. By now Bob was a member of the Sigma Alpha Epsilon fraternity. Zella had not yet reached the so-called *responsible age* (adult age) of twenty-one, so was too young to consume alcoholic beverages, but she could dance with the best of them, and dance they did.

Setting twenty-one as the legal drinking age seems like a contradiction, since young men and young women are considered sufficiently mature at age eighteen to stand up and fight for their country, often dying in the process! Bob had witnessed many young people eighteen, nineteen, and twenty years old going off to war— willingly and without a word of complaint—but they were not legally allowed to have a glass of beer in a public bar!

Born January 5, 1926, at the home of her maternal grandparents in North Platte, Nebraska, Zella was the youngest of three children. Her father, Robert Lewis Bell, was born and reared in Missouri. He had two brothers and a sister. Like his father, he worked first in the coal mines, and then he went to work for the Union Pacific Railroad in his twenties. He started as a switchman and eventually worked his way up to conductor.

Zella's mother, Ruby Hopkins Bell, also was born in North Platte, the eldest of seven children. She had two brothers and four sisters. She was fourteen years younger than her husband, making her an understanding bridge between her three children and their somewhat distant father.

Zella's only sister, Lola, died in California in 2006. Her brother, Robert Lee Bell, lived in Salt Lake City, Utah, until his death in 2010.

The Bell family moved to Idaho when Zella was four. For the next seven years, they lived in a farming area before moving to Laramie, where Zella was enrolled in the fifth grade. Seven grades later, she graduated from Laramie High School. Zella attended the University of Wyoming from 1944–46 before family financial pressures forced her to drop out and go to work for a Laramie medical group. She was working for the medical group when Bob suddenly appeared on the scene and became a major part of her life.

Like Bob, Zella enjoyed dancing, going to movies, and having a good time in general. Other young men took their special girls for rides in whatever prewar jalopies they had acquired or could borrow. Bob courted his special girl in the Aeronca, the small single-engine type of aircraft that he bought as the first step in what he hoped would blossom into a commercial flying service. That didn't work out, but his airborne romance did. Bob sold his interest in the airport to his partner.

In the summer of 1946, Zella's mother asked Bob about his future plans. Specifically, she focused on if and when he planned to marry Zella. Without pausing for a moment, Bob's responded very casually:

"Next Saturday seems like a good day!"

True to his response, Bob and Zella were married that very Saturday, August 25, 1946.

Bob and Zella's Wedding Day—August 25, 1945

***

Michelle, their first child, made the family a threesome when she was born on October 30, 1947. Two more small Milliken family members came into their lives—Sherry was born on November 19, 1949, and Pam appeared into the world on July 22, 1951. The fourth child, Greg, was born on December 19, 1955.

Life's journeys have taken Zella and Bob down many roads, and they have crossed many rivers. The challenges and opportunities to be explored that they have faced together have been many. Those are behind them now, as are the days of their youth. Yet one constant endures—family friends—and here in Laramie they have been well and truly home.

CHAPTER 13: ZELLA'S STORY

Zella Faye Bell and Robert Carl Milliken were married in Laramie Wyoming on August 25, 1946. Since that time, Zella has been a major part of, and an equal partner in Bob's life. It is only fitting that Zella receive more than a brief mention but a very honorable mention in this book. Her role in the family is true to the role of frontier women: organized and in control of the house and children. She did not hesitate to drive from Wyoming to Florida with her four children at the time when Bob was registered for an advanced degree at the University of Florida even when the journey took her through Selma, Alabama, at the time when civil rights issues where rising to the forefront of American life.

Zella's willingness to play such a role comes from her ancestry that consists of many persons who were willing to stand up for their beliefs, no what the outcome might be. Because of this, the story of Zella's ancestry needs to be documented as an integral part of this book.

This is Zella's story.

***

The name *Bell* is predominantly of northern English and Scottish origin. Further investigation takes the name back to Middle English— *belle* or *bell* in various applications—most probably a metonymic occupational name for a bell ringer or bell maker, or a topographic name for someone living *at the bell*, which indicates either residence by an actual bell (such as in a town bell tower, which is centrally placed to summon meetings or sound the alarm) or *at the sign of the bell*, meaning a house or inn sign. (But surnames derived from a house or from the sign of an inn are rare in Scotland and England.)

The name *Zella* had several possible origins. A common origin is that Zella is a diminutive form of the German name *Marcella*. In the present case, Zella's mother took the name from the biblical Selah (Zelah), which was used as a female name in biblical times (and also in the in the late nineteenth and early twentieth centuries) and taken from the name of a city in the area settled by the tribe of Benjamin.

With that introduction, Zella Faye Bell (who, on August 25, 1946, would become Zella Faye Milliken) was born on January 5, 1926, in North Platte (Lincoln County), Nebraska. She was the daughter of Robert Lewis Bell (born March 4, 1889, in Deep Water, Missouri) and Ruby Gertrude Bell (née Hopkins, born June 24, 1903, in Round Valley Nebraska). Mother Ruby was one of seven children born to Grandmother Daisy and Grandfather Samuel—two boys and five girls.

Zella's Parents: (a) Robert Lewis Bell, (b) Ruby Gertrude Bell

Dr. T.J. Kerr (as shown on her birth certificate) was the attending physician at Zella's birth. She was born at the home of her mother and father, but there is also mention in her records that the birthing table was a kitchen table, which (although not the same table!) had also been of great assistance as an instrument during the birth of Bob Milliken.

North Platte is the county seat of Lincoln County, Nebraska. It is located in the southwestern part of the state, along Interstate 80, at the confluence of the North Platte and South Platte Rivers forming the Platte River. North Platte is a railroad town—specifically the Union Pacific Railroad. With the demise of railroad passenger traffic, North Platte is currently served only by freight trains, but during World War II the city was famous for the North Platte Canteen, where crowds of volunteers from North Platte and surrounding towns met the troop trains passing through North Platte, offering coffee, sandwiches, and hospitality.

Zella had two other siblings—Robert Lee Bell (born on August 31, 1922, in Platte Nebraska and died August 23, 2011, in Salt Lake City, Utah), and Lola Eileen Bell born on January 3, 1924. All three children were born in North Platte in the house of Grandmother Daisy Hopkins (wife of Grandfather Samuel Hopkins).

Father Robert Lewis Bell recognized the value of work at an early age. Grandfather George W. Bell was killed in a mine accident when Robert was thirteen years old. Being the oldest male in the family and therefore the man of the house, Robert announced to his mother—Rebecca Laura Gilstrap Bell—he would seek work and find a job in the mine. But he didn't stop there. He was determined to finish his education and was successful in his quest for a high school diploma.

Father Robert Bell saw duty in World War I. He was unmarried at the time of his enlistment. Although he lived in Beier, Macon County, Missouri, he was working on the Union Pacific line in Cheyenne when he went to the Fort Warren base (now the F.E. Warren Air Force Base). Being on the road, his activities were not really known in his town, and Robert, who was in uniform and in France one week after enlisting, merely announced that he was in the army by sending his mother a postcard from France bearing the words: "Hi Mom, I'm in the army." True to form, he was a man of very few words!

Robert had enlisted as an older man—he was 32 at the time—but the army still found use for him. Having railroad experience in civilian life, he was put to work on a military railroad that carried troops, supplies, and armaments to the front line. He was honorably discharged after the Treaty of Versailles was signed on June 28, 1919, putting an official end to the hostilities of World War I. The Armistice that commenced on the eleventh hour of the eleventh day of the eleventh month in 1918 was the day that the guns fell silent, but it didn't put an end to the war.

But Zella's story doesn't stop there and has an even longer history. Records indicate that her family had very old roots in the United States, going back as far as the mid-seventeenth century to the time of the Pilgrim Fathers (and Mothers) in Boston, Massachusetts. However, before starting this historical account, credit is due to Robert Bell (Zella's brother), who took the time and had the patience to trace the family lineage through various sources, especially through the Church of Jesus Christ of Latter-day Saints (LDS Church). It is only through his efforts that details of the family history became known and evolved into present form.

Robert Lee Bell, 1942

During his time in the Army Air Corps, which became part of the US Air Force, which in turn became a separate military service on September 18, 1947, Bobby served in various capacities, and always where the action was.

Sadly, Bobby died in 2010, being retired after a total of thirty-one years in the US Air Force and rising to the rank of Master Sergeant (E-7 rank). His grave is in the Greenhill Cemetery in Laramie Wyoming, the city in which Bobby was raised and educated.

The Headstone of Robert Lee Bell, Greenhill
Cemetery, Laramie Wyoming

The headstone is marked by engravings of the B-24 bomber of which Bobby was a crew member during World War II, and also the B-36, the B-52, and the C-17 cargo plane. Bobby worked on this aircraft after he reenlisted into the Air Force after World War II. As shown in the picture, behind Bobby's headstone is the headstone of his brother-in-law Charles J. Crawford who served in the US Navy during World War II.

***

The B-36 Peacemaker was a strategic bomber built by Convair and operated solely by the United States Air Force (USAF) from 1949 to 1959. It was the largest mass-produced piston engine aircraft ever made and had the longest wingspan of any combat aircraft ever built (230 feet), although there have been larger military transports. The B-36 was the first bomber capable of delivering any of the nuclear weapons in the US arsenal from inside its two bomb bays without aircraft modifications. With a range of 9,900 miles and a maximum payload of 73,000 pounds, the B-36 was the world's first manned bomber with an unrefueled intercontinental range. Until it was replaced by the jet-powered Boeing B-52 Stratofortress, which first became operational in 1955, the B-36 was the primary nuclear weapons delivery vehicle of the Strategic Air Command (SAC), and set the standard for range and payload for subsequent intercontinental bombers of the USAF.

The Boeing B-52 Stratofortress is a long-range, subsonic, jet-powered strategic bomber that has been operated by the USAF since 1955. The bomber carries up to 70,000 pounds of weapons and replaced the Convair B-36. Although a veteran of several wars, the B-52 has dropped only conventional munitions in combat.

The Boeing C-17 Globemaster is a large military transport aircraft that was developed for the United States Air Force (USAF) by McDonnell Douglas. The C-17 commonly performs strategic airlift missions, transporting troops and cargo throughout the world; additional roles include tactical airlift missions, medical evacuation missions, and airdrop missions.

This chapter is also dedicated to Bobby's memory. He is remembered for his bravery as a B-24 ball turret gunner. As the occasion demanded, he also served as the aircraft tail gunner—both positions were fraught with danger. And he is appreciated for his conscientious and thorough efforts at compiling the family history. His story is as interesting as any and is worth presenting here.

Men such as Bobby (and his brother-in-law Bob Milliken, whose life is the focal point of this book) never talk about or discuss their activities in war. Their stories have to be wormed out of them with care and diligence after they have returned home and restarted their lives. Such men as these are the true heroes.

***

Bobby was born in North Platte, Nebraska, on August 31, 1922, and later moved to a small town near the Tetons in Idaho. In 1936 his family moved to Laramie, Wyoming. He graduated from high school in 1942 and then worked on the railroad.

As early as Bobby could remember, he wanted to read. He would get a book, have one sister on each side of him, and pretend he was reading to them. All through life Bobby would read two or three books a day. He could glance at a page and see if any words were misspelled.

While in high school, Bobby delivered the morning paper in Laramie. The paper was the Laramie Daily Boomerang that stills serves the community today. One morning it was fifty degrees below zero. The wind was blowing, and at each house he would ask if he could step in and get warm. Not surprisingly, this was the last day Bobby delivered papers. So he started his own business selling cardboard boxes to grocery stores. He rode his bike to other stores, and they would give him their boxes. One business gave him a room in their store to store the boxes. A man in Laramie started collecting boxes and tried to take away Bobby's business, but Bobby had built up such goodwill with the various merchants that they saved the boxes for Bobby (this was in 1930, during the Depression), and he sold them for two cents to four cents each.

At the outbreak of the war in 1941, Bobby enlisted rather than being drafted into military service. He joined the Army Air Corps in 1944, where he was assigned to the 406th Bomb Squadron (the Carpetbaggers Squadron, or as the squadron was known in France, *Escadrille Carpetbaggers*) and served as a gunner on a B-24. Bobby flew thirty missions over German-occupied Europe.

The B-24 Liberator (designed by Consolidated Aircraft of San Diego, California) required a crew of eleven men: pilot, copilot, navigator, bombardier, radio operator, nose turret gunner, top turret gunner, two waist gunners, ball turret gunner, and tail gunner. The bomber was adopted by the United States Air Force in 1941. It was a four-engine heavy bomber with a more modern design than many World War II bomber aircraft and was hailed as a triumph of aeronautical engineering with a higher top speed, greater range, and a heavier bomb load than the better-known B-17 Flying Fortress (designed by the Boeing Aircraft company) with its crew of ten: pilot, copilot, navigator, bombardier and nose gunner, top turret gunner, radio operator, two waist gunners, ball turret gunner, and tail gunner.

Recall that the B-24 was notorious among American aircrews for its tendency to catch fire. Moreover, the aircraft lacked the strength imparted to the fuselage by a low-mounted wing, and the high fuselage-mounted wing of the B-24 meant it was dangerous to ditch or belly land, since the fuselage tended to break apart.

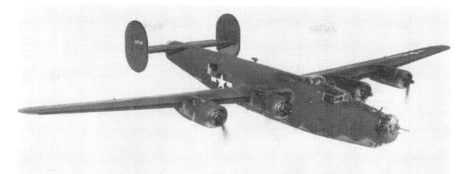

The B-24 Liberator

Bobby flew as a ball turret gunner—his slight stature of five feet seven inches and a weight less than 115 pounds made him an ideal fit for the ball turret, which hung from the underside of the aircraft.

The ball turret was a spherical-form altazimuth mount—a simple two-axis mount for supporting and rotating the turret about two mutually perpendicular axes, one vertical and the other horizontal. Rotation about the vertical axis varies the azimuth (compass bearing) of the pointing direction of the instrument, and rotation about the horizontal axis varies the altitude (angle of elevation) of the pointing direction. The turret was built to accommodate the gunner with nearly all the necessary equipment for defensive firepower (except for the ammunition storage) mounted either within or onto the spherical shell of the turret structure. What was less obvious was that the turret was vulnerable to attacks at various angles from below by enemy aircraft with orders to strike the soft underbelly of the bombers, and to flak from the land-based anti-aircraft guns.

As stated earlier, Bobby also served as the tail gunner as the occasion demanded. In the tail gunner position, the crewman defended the aircraft against fighter attacks from the rear, or *tail*, of the bomber.

He operated a mounted but flexible-movement machine gun with an unobstructed view from the rear of the aircraft. In this position, any tail gunner was a prime target for enemy fighters approaching the bomber from the rear. Both the ball turret gunner and tail gunner positions were fraught with danger, as the men in those positions were prime targets for enemy fighter pilots.

Bobby's missions were flown at night over France and Belgium. The purpose was to drop secret agents into the occupied countries. The crew couldn't see anything except the anti-aircraft fire coming at them from below. Bobby also never forgot the sight of burning towns with only the stark outline of the skeletons of damaged and destroyed buildings. In Germany he could smell the smoke even before they could see the towns burning. Because of their work, the squadron was often referred to as the Carpetbagger Squadron.

On his first mission, Bobby's sight window was broken by the first burst of anti-aircraft fire. In fact, a mission never went by that the B-24 did not receive some form of damaging enemy fire. And unless the enemy fire did heavy damage to the aircraft that caused difficulties in maintaining a planned flight path, it was not always easy to discern where the B-24 was hit the hardest.

For example, on December 11, 1944, on Bobby's seventeenth mission, the B-24 was involved in a terrifying crash as the aircraft retuned to home base at Woodbridge, Suffolk, England. The picturesque town of Woodbridge has a history dating back to pre-Roman times and is situated on the coast of the county of Suffolk. The history of the town was far from Bobby's mind as the aircraft approached the runway; the recorded time was 1938 hours (7:38 p.m.).

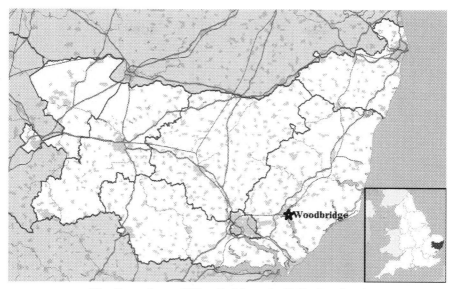

The Location of Woodbridge, Suffolk, England

The plane had taken several hits from the defending anti-aircraft guns. Flak and metal shards from the exploding shells had caused damage, but the flyers were uncertain of the extent or degree of the damage.

As usual, Bobby had been assigned to the ball turret for the mission, and as the returning aircraft approached the English Channel, one engine went out of commission. Then another engine was lost as they approached the English coast, and a third engine failed when they approached the runway. One operational engine of four is not conducive to maintaining aircraft stability, especially if the live fourth engine is coughing smoke and threatening to cease operation. With no options left, the pilot advised the crew over the intercom that a crash was imminent and they had to brace for impact—always an ominous command. Fortunately—timing is everything—Bobby had had just raised his ball turret back up into the body of the aircraft when the crash occurred. Unfortunately, he was not quite ready and had not been able to brace for impact, so he was thrown around inside the aircraft. Bobby was hit in the mouth by an unknown object as he heard the sound of trees being knocked down. Then he was instantly buried in dirt up to his knees as the soil filled the aircraft, which stabilized the motion of his body and most likely prevented further injury. The aircraft slithered and fishtailed to a halt in the open area next to the forest at the side of the runway.

Bobby was stunned, probably from the blow to the mouth. And he had an injury to his back. He didn't know it at the time, but the back injury would plague him for the rest of his life. One of his fellow crew members threw him from the plane, and he started to run with the other crew members. They turned around and looked at the plane. It was on fire, and the pilot and copilot were unable to escape from the burning plane. Bobby was in the hospital for three days, after which he returned to active duty.

Bobby returned to Wyoming, where he married Shirley Crawford in April 1946 at the LDS Church in Laramie. He then started at the University of Wyoming and completed his engineering degree. When the Korean conflict began, he reenlisted into the Air Force and also completed a degree in architectural engineering and drafting. During that time they lived in Texas, Nebraska, Puerto Rico, Washington, Colorado, Mississippi, Georgia, South Dakota, and California. Bobby served in Guam and Thailand during the Vietnam War. After retirement from the Air Force, Bobby worked on aircraft design for the McDonnell Douglas Corporation.

While in Thailand, Bobby was exposed to Agent Orange, which sent him to the hospital for six months. He was then sent to Puerto Rico for twenty-six months as part of the recovery process, after which time an allergy to sugar cane caused him to be sent to the US Mainland for final recovery. His legacy of serving his country continued with his two sons, Steven and Robert. Steven retired from the US Air Force as a Master Sergeant and Robert retired from the US Air Force with the rank of Major.

After his discharge from the Air Force, Bobby continued the work on the family history. It was shortly after the US withdrawal of troops from Vietnam that Bobby became engrossed in his quest for family history.

***

Using records from several parts of the USA, especially the genealogical files of the LDS Church, Bobby found that the ancestral lines of the Bell family can be traced back to England in the seventeenth century. Using these valuable records as a base, the family lines have now been traced further back through the Hopkins family (the family and ancestors of Zella's mother Ruby Gertrude Hopkins) and the birth of William Hopkins in 1620 (give or take a year or so), at the time when the *Mayflower* sailed from England to the New World.

The troubled times of the mid-seventeenth century arose because Charles I, the reigning king of England, believed that he was anointed by God and as a result had been given the divine right to rule. He cared little for the English landowners, less for the ordinary working people of England, and even less still for the governance of the country by the duly elected Members of Parliament, who were typically landowners. The chances of any members of the working class being elected to Parliament were extremely slim, if not impossible. Democracy was *not* alive and well (in fact it was dead) in England of the mid-seventeenth century!

Under these circumstances, life in England in the seventeenth century was tenuous, to say the least. At that time, the common people (the *silenced majority*—in modern times they would be called the *silent majority*) could not speak of or express an opinion as any man or woman engaging in free speech stood a high chance of being summarily killed or executed by roving regiments of Parliamentarian or Royalist troops. Therefore, anyone who had the wherewithal or the ability to leave the country took the chance and took passage on a ship to the American colonies (at that time, not yet known as the United States).

Thus started the English Civil War (1642–51), a series of political and then armed conflicts between Parliamentarians (Roundheads—so-named because of the short style of haircut and the shape of the helmets) and Royalists (Cavaliers). The First Civil War (1642–46) and the Second Civil War (1648–49) pitted the supporters of King Charles I against the supporters of the Long Parliament, while the Third Civil War (1649–51) saw fighting between supporters of King Charles II and supporters of the Rump Parliament. The Civil War ended with the Parliamentary victory at the Battle of Worcester on September 3, 1651.

The Long Parliament is the name of the English Parliament called by Charles I on November 3, 1640. It received its name from the fact that through an Act of Parliament, it could only be dissolved with the agreement of the members, and those members did not agree to its dissolution until after the English Civil War and at the end of interregnum in 1660. On the other hand, the Rump Parliament is the name given to the Long Parliament after the purge of December 1648 in which those Members of Parliament who sought a negotiated settlement with King Charles I were forcibly expelled by the New Model Army (Roundheads). The Members of the Rump Parliament regarded themselves as the lawful Parliament of the Commonwealth of England, but the derisive name first used widely in 1660 became its enduring nickname after the Restoration.

The Civil War led to the trial and execution of Charles I, the exile of his son, Charles II, and replacement of the English monarchy with first the Commonwealth of England (1649–53), and then with a Protectorate (1653–59) under the personal rule of Oliver Cromwell. The monopoly of the Church of England on Christian worship in England ended with the victors consolidating the established Protestant Ascendancy in Ireland. Constitutionally, the wars established the precedent that an English monarch cannot govern without the consent of Parliament, although this concept was legally established only with the so-called Glorious Revolution later in the seventeenth century.

Finally, another person of interest who lived in this timeframe and who has a place in Zella's lineage and is well deserving of a mention in this story is Theophilus Whaley (Theophilus Whalley). He was born in England in or about the year 1617 and reputedly died at an age exceeding one hundred years in 1720 in West Greenwich, Rhode Island. Theophilus moved to Virginia in the colonies for justifiable reasons. (See below.) He moved to Rhode Island from Rappahannock County, Virginia, where he sold his plantation in 1665 and married Elizabeth Mills in or before 1664. Elizabeth Whaley, a child of the Whaley-Mills union, was born in 1645 and died in 1715.

Theophilus was born of wealthy parents, university-educated in England, and waited upon hand and foot by servants until the age of eighteen, when he moved from England to Virginia (at an unknown date before 1638), where he served as a military officer. His rank is unknown, but considering his birth and background, it would have been high. He returned to England in 1642 at the start of the English Civil

War to serve in the Parliamentary Army under Oliver Cromwell—the Lord Protector of England who had displaced Charles I. And there is evidence to suggest that Oliver and Theophilus may have been related. If the identity of Theophilus has been deduced correctly—and there is no reason to doubt this—his regiment took part in the execution of Charles I in 1649. Moreover, it is highly likely that Theophilus was actually one of the Whalley brothers—Robert or Edward Whalley— but which one has never been clearly stated. Edward was one of the two *regicide* judges who fled England and were concealed for some time in Hadley, Massachusetts, among other places. If this is indeed the case, *Theophilus* was an assumed name, designed to cover his past after the ascension of Charles II (the son of the executed Charles I) to the throne in 1660 (the Restoration of the Monarchy).

About that time (in the year 1660), Theophilus (aka Robert but probably Edward) returned to Virginia with his son-in-law Major-General William Goffe, the other regicide judge, and bought land there. He married Elizabeth Mills (1645–1715) in Virginia, and two or three of their children were born there. Sometime between 1665 and 1680, Theophilus moved to Rhode Island, settling at the head of Pettaquamscutt Pond in Narragansett. He never spoke of his past while living in Rhode Island and quietly made his living there by fishing, weaving, and teaching. (He was fluent in Greek, Latin, and Hebrew.) He seems to have deliberately avoided public notice and public office, though he sometimes penned deeds and other legal documents for his less-well-educated neighbors.

Mysterious visits to the home of Theophilus and Elizabeth by distinguished men from Boston and elsewhere enriched the humble life they had chosen to lead. During Queen Anne's War (1702–13), as the North American theater of the War of the Spanish Succession was known in the British colonies, was the second in a series of

French and Indian Wars between France and England fought in North America for control of the continent. A warship dropped anchor in Narragansett Bay, and its captain, who claimed to be a kinsman of Theophilus and bearing the same surname, sent a boat crew to invite Theophilus aboard for dinner. Initially, perhaps overjoyed at hearing that a kinsman was in the area, Theophilus accepted the invitation. But given time to consider the situation, he changed his mind and refused the invitation. As he explained to a friend afterward, he feared a trap had been laid to take him back to England to suffer trial and retribution for his previous acts. This story confirms the suspicions of Theophilus's contemporaries that he was one of the regicide judges, a belief that persisted long after the announcement of his death.

Theophilus was on the tax rolls of Kingstown, Rhode Island, in 1687. In 1709 or 1710 he acquired 120 acres of land at nearby East Greenwich, which he gave to his only son, Samuel, the next year. He was buried with military honors near the home of his son-in-law Joseph Hopkins in West Greenwich. The children of Theophilus Whaley and Elizabeth Mills were Joan, Ann, Theodosia (Zella's ancestor), Elizabeth, Martha, Lydia, and Samuel. Only Martha's birth date (1680) is known, but all the children were born after the return of Theophilus to Virginia in 1660. Since Elizabeth Mills was only fifteen years old in 1660, it seems likely that the marriage came a little later, though before 1665.

Thus, Zella's ancestors who were born in England in the very early part of the seventeenth century set sail for the shores of America (the American colonies, which were not known as the United States until the name appeared in the Declaration of Independence) and the possibility of a new life in which they would be free to speak and express themselves without being persecuted for their thoughts and words.

***

Zella's mother was a descendent of the Hopkins lineage. Her ancestor William Hopkins first appears in the town records of Roxbury, Massachusetts, for January 19, 1656, which means that William had lived there for some time prior to the date of these records. (The actual date of his arrival in the town is not known.)

Willyum Hopekins was chosen to dige graves for the town, and he is to have for mens and wimmens graves, two shillings and for children under 10 years of age, he is to have twelve pence per child.

Twelve pence (pennies) was one English shilling. At best estimates, in 1656 two English shillings had an approximate worth of at least two hundred US dollars in the currency of 2014—a considerable sum at the time and even now.

Roxbury is a dissolved municipality, a neighborhood within Boston, Massachusetts. It was one of the first towns founded in the Massachusetts Bay Colony in 1630, and became a city in 1846 until annexed to Boston on January 5, 1868. The original boundaries of the Town of Roxbury can be found in *The History of Roxbury and Its Noted Personages* (Drake, 1978). Those boundaries include the Christian Science Center, the Prudential Center (built on the old Roxbury Railroad Yards), as well as everything south and east of the Muddy River, including Symphony Hall, Northeastern University, Boston Latin School, John D. O'Bryant School of Mathematics & Science, the YMCA, Harvard Medical School, and many hospitals and schools.

The next appearance of the name is in the baptismal records when, on March 6, 1660, three children of William Hopkins were baptized: William, Thomas, and Hannah. There seems to be no record of the death of William Hopkins, although a date has been recorded as November 5, 1688. Hannah died of smallpox on November 5, 1678. Both William and Hannah were members of the church presided over by the Reverend John Eliot.

Other records indicate that William was in Roxbury in 1656. It's possible that the three children baptized there in 1660 were the issue of a first marriage, and that he married Hannah Andrews, the daughter of Thomas Andrews of Dorchester, in 1660 or 1661 as a second wife, although there is no entry in the records to the effect that William was married prior to his marriage to Hannah Andrews.

Hannah Andrews demitted (resigned) from the Dorchester Church on February 22, 1660, and was called Hannah, the daughter of Thomas Andrews. This was only a month before the baptism of William's three children, and had she been his wife, the record of her resignation from the Dorchester Church would probably have so stated. Their fourth child, Mary, was baptized in 1662, which would give time for a marriage in 1660 or 1661.

Briefly, and with relevance to this historical account, Dorchester is a historic neighborhood of over six square miles in Boston, Massachusetts. The town was founded by Puritans who emigrated from Dorchester, England in 1630. This dissolved municipality, Boston's largest neighborhood by far, is often divided by city planners in order to create two planning areas roughly equivalent in size and population to other Boston neighborhoods. It is named after the town of Dorchester in the English county of Dorset – which coincidentally is close to the area that became known as the Warmwell Air Base. Puritans emigrated from there on the ship *Mary and John* a mere ten years after the time of the *Mayflower*. Dorchester, which now covers an area approximately equivalent to the city of Cambridge,

Massachusetts, was founded in 1630, few months before the city of Boston. It was still a primarily rural town and had a population of 12,000 when it was annexed to Boston in 1870.

The record in the Dorchester church (Dorchester Church Records, 1891, 22) says this:

22:2: 1660:

The day above said Hanah ye daughter of Thomas Andrews desired a letter of demittion to Joyn to ye Church of Rocksbery although she was not a stated member but by vertue of her parents covenant: and it was granted only bro. Breck (a Presbyterian) foster (an independent) & Mead would not act with ye Church.

Hanah (Hannah) was admitted to the Roxbury church a week later, February 29, 1660. A year and a week after her admittance came the baptism of the three children of William Hopkins. The New England Historical and Genealogical Register states:

Susanna dau. of Thomas Andrews married Hopkins in the record of Thomas Andrews will she is called Hanna Hopkins (Suffolk Probate Records, File 658). The will was dated 6 August 1667 and proved 4 days 6 months 1673. He bequeathed to his wife Ann who died 13 Jan. 1684 all of his estate during her natural life, and after her death, to his only son Thomas, he to pay to daughter Hanna Hopkins seaven pounds in current pay of New England an 20 s (shillings) a pecce to (for each of) her children as they shall come of age. But restricted to those born before the date of the will. William Hopkins put in a caution against the will, and witnesses to its execution testified that William Hopkins had told them that the differences had been composed.

Of the two children mentioned in the foregoing will, Thomas Andrews Jr. was baptized on June 23, 1639 (Dorchester Church Records, 1891, 151). As no record of Hannah's baptism is found in Dorchester, it is quite possible that she was born in England and brought to the colonies as an infant—a significant journey for anyone of any age in those days.

In 1664, a petition was submitted to the General Court from the inhabitants of Dorchester in which the names of Thomas Andrews Senior and Junior appear.

There is also reference to land belonging to William Hopkins and Abraham Newell that was sold to Isaac Newell, land called Totman's Rocks: "late land of William Hopkins and Samuel Ruggles, bounded w[est] by Dedhan highway and s[outh], on road to Gamblin's End, 24 Jan. 1671" (Suffolk Deeds, 7:309).

The name William Hopkins also occurs in other land transactions. For example, "William Curtis of Roxbury deeded to his son Isaac, land bounded on west by land lately of William Hopkins and the road leading to Gamblin's End." (Suffolk Deeds, 8:117) "The same land was sold and bounded the same." (Suffolk Deeds, 9:430) "The same land was sold and bounded the same described formerly of *William Hopkins*, June 20, 1698" (Suffolk Deeds, 19:99).

To continue this aspect of the genealogy, in a list of soldiers credited with military service under Captain Danile Hinchman appears this entry:

27 August 1675 William Hopkins (Soldiers in King Philips war, 1906, page 52 (Bodge) Again the name William Hopkins appears in the list of Hampton Men under Capt. Will Turner, 7 April 1676 (Ibid., 241). This is the list preceding the Falls Fight 19 May 1676.

These entries may refer to William Hopkins of Roxbury or to his son William Hopkins of Billerica.

The Town of Billerica is located twenty miles northwest of Boston and borders Lowell to the south. Incorporated in 1655, the town remained predominately agricultural until the mid-nineteenth century, when a major mill complex was built on the banks of the Concord River in North Billerica.

***

King Philip's War (1675–78), sometimes called the First Indian War, Metacom's War, Metacomet's War, or Metacom's Rebellion, was an armed conflict with Native American inhabitants of the area on one side and English colonists and their Native American allies on the other. The war is named after the main leader of the Native American side, Metacomet, known to the English as King Philip. Major Benjamin Church emerged as the Puritan hero of the war. It was his company of Puritan rangers and Native American allies that finally hunted down and killed King Philip on August 12, 1676. The war continued in northern New England, primarily in Maine at the New England and Acadia border, until a treaty was signed at Casco Bay in April 1678.

The war was the single greatest calamity to occur in seventeenth-century Puritan New England. In the space of little more than a year, twelve of the region's towns were destroyed and many more damaged; the colony's economy was all but ruined; and much of its population was killed, including one-tenth of all men available for military service. More than half of New England's towns were attacked by Native American warriors.

Nearly all the English colonies in America were settled without any significant English government support, as they were used chiefly as a safety valve to minimize religious and other conflicts in England. King Philip's War was the beginning of the development of a greater American identity, for the colonists' trials, without significant British government support, gave them a group identity separate and distinct from subjects of the Parliament of England and the Crown in England. It is this lack of support from the Mother Country but the insistence that the colonists pay taxes to the Crown that eventually led to the onset of the Revolution and the creation of the United States of America.

***

To continue the story of the Hopkins family, the known children of William Hopkins from church and baptismal records from the time:

1. Hannah Hopkins: Born January 3, 1657; baptized Roxbury, May 6, 1660, by Rev. John Eliot; married 1678 to Philip Goss; divorced him April 14, 1690; Philip remarried March 29, 1690, to Mary Prescott in Concord, Massachusetts; Hannah had her second marriage to John Murray on March 23, 1687.

   Record of the Commissioners of the City of Boston 6:93 show that Hannah was censured in the Church in 1678, but she confessed and was absolved (Roxbury Church records, 93).

   Other records indicate that Goss applied for a divorce on the grounds that she left him and married another man from Jamaica (the area known by that name that is in the modern Borough of Queens, New York).

2. William Hopkins: Baptized May 6, 1660, Roxbury, Massachusetts; he serves as soldier at Northampton under Captain Turner; killed by Indians in 1676.

3. Thomas Hopkins: Baptized May 6, 1660, Roxbury, Massachusetts; killed at Sudbury by Indians April 21, 1676, when he served under the command of Captain Samuel Wadsworth; Edward Cowell in a statement sworn of June 19, 1676, signed to the fact that he "went back and buried four men which were killed whereof Thomas Hanley and Hopkinses son both of Roxbury." (Ibid., 226)

   Note: Thomas Hopkins was reported to be in the garrison at Marlborough (a town adjoining Sudbury) on April 24, three days after the fight. There was also a Thomas Hopkins of Mashantatack, who died in 1698. He married Sarah, who died after 1699. He was a freeman in 1678 (meaning he owned land); on March 26, 1688, he sold to Edward Searle Jr. forty acres in Mashantatack. He removed later to the other side of the Pawtucket River, within the limits of Providence. His will, dated 10 Oct. 1698, Prove 13 Jan. 1699, names his wife executrix and gives to her his whole estate, house, lands, goods, and chattels (Genealogical Dictionary of Rhode Island 1887, 105).

4. Mary Hopkins: Baptized March 30, 1662.

5. Samuel Hopkins: Baptized November 15, 1663.

6. Margaret Hopkins: Born February 18, 1666.

7. Joseph Hopkins: Baptized March 8, 1667.

8. Elizabeth Hopkins: Baptized April 3, 1670.

9. Abigail Hopkins: Baptized April 30, 1672.

10. Ebenezer Hopkins: Baptized July 5, 1674.

11. Berthia Hopkins: Baptized December 5, 1675.

***

To move on a generation, Francis Hopkins (the son of Joseph Hopkins, born April 8, 1698), was born about 1720 in Virginia and died in 1778. He married Mary Joslin (Joshlin) in about 1740.

Apparently, the members of the County Court of Washington County were zealous Whigs and so aggressive in the enforcement of their views that it was difficult for a Tory to make his home anywhere within the bounds of this county without being prosecuted to the full extent of the law. A majority of these men recognized no distinction between an Indian who would scalp his wife and children and an Anglo who lent his influence to a government offering every inducement to the Indian to murder and plunder white settlers.

There were two major parties in England at this time, the Whigs and the Tories, and their thoughts and allegiances spilled over into the newly settled colonies.

The Whigs were first a political faction and then a political party in the English Parliament who contested power with the rival Tories from the 1680s until as late as the 1850s. The origin of the Whig Party lay in the belief in *constitutional monarchism* and in opposition to Tory belief in *absolute rule.*

The Whigs played a central role in the Glorious Revolution of 1688 and were the standing enemies of the later Stuart kings. James I, who followed Elizabeth to the throne of England, was the first Stuart king, but his son Charles I and grandsons Charles II and James II showed no fondness for the democratic process in word or deed! So James II was deposed by William II—William of Orange, the Protestant son-in-law and nephew of James II—and exiled to France.

Aided by his French hosts, James Francis Edward Stuart, the son of James II, took on the role of Pretender to the Throne (of England),

and his son (Charles Edward Stuart, aka Bonnie Prince Charlie) took on the role of the Young Pretender to the English Throne. They were keen to convert England back to a Roman Catholic monarchy.

Bonnie Prince Charlie remained a source of trouble until he was defeated at the battle of Culloden on April 16, 1746, after which he made a somewhat ignominious escape from the Scottish mainland as Betty Burke—supposedly an Irish spinning maid—in the care of Flora MacDonald and several boatmen of the local militia. Flora was the stepdaughter of the commander of the local militia.

The party landed at Kilbride, Isle of Skye, within easy access of Monkstadt, the seat of Sir Alexander MacDonald. The prince was hidden in rocks while Flora MacDonald found help for him in the neighborhood. It was arranged that he be taken to Portrer, Isle of Skye, and from there taken to Glam on the Isle of Raasay. Careless talk by the boatmen brought suspicion on Flora MacDonald, and she was arrested and taken to London for aiding the prince's escape. After a short imprisonment in the Tower of London, she was allowed to live outside of it, under the guard of a messenger (a jailer). When the Act of Indemnity was passed in 1747, a statute passed to protect and forgive people who had committed an illegal act, she was released.

Charles Edward Stuart evaded capture and left the country aboard the French frigate aptly named *L'Heureux* (meaning "happy" or "fortunate"), arriving back in France in September, where he spent the remainder of his life in exile. If he had been caught by the Duke of Cumberland (aka Billy the Butcher)—the son of King George II—after the battle Charles Edward would have certainly been executed in some indescribable and painful manner, as were many of his followers when captured by Billy and his redcoats.

During this time, the Whigs had been in full control of the government since 1715, and remained totally dominant until King

George III, who came to the throne in 1760, allowed the Tories back in. The Whig Supremacy (1715–60) was enabled by the succession of George I (the first Hanoverian to occupy the throne of England) in 1714 and the failed Jacobite Rebellions of 1715 and 1745, which were instigated by Tory rebels. The Whigs thoroughly purged the Tories from all major positions in government, the army, the Church of England, the legal profession, and local government.

As might be expected, the beliefs that carried over into the colonies led to aggressive persecution of the Tories by the Whigs. In fact, Colonel William Campbell was particularly aggressive in his prosecution of the Tories in the county, and by reason thereof, was the object of special hatred on their part. At this time there lived in the area that in later times became known as Washington County two men by the names of Francis and William Hopkins. Francis Hopkins was alleged to be a counterfeiter. At the May term of the sessions of the county court in the year 1779, he was tried on suspicion of having counterfeited, erased, and altered sundry treasury notes, the currency of this commonwealth, knowing the same to be bad.

In 1779 in Virginia, all bank notes issued between May 20, 1777, and April 1778 were removed from circulation since counterfeits had been issued, as Colonel Campbell said, by "our enemies at New York and are found to be spreading."

Francis was found guilty, fined fifty dollars (in the lawful currency of Virginia), sentenced to six months in prison, and ordered confined within the walls of the Fort at William Cocke's (now C.L. Clyce's), on Renfro's Creek, alias Spring Creek, until the county goal (jail) was completed. He was conveyed to Cocke's Fort but within a short time thereafter, made his escape and began a series of bold and daring depredations upon the Whig settlers of the county. He organized a band of Tories, whose major occupation was to steal the horses of the settlers and intimidate the citizens whenever possible.

With this background, Francis went so far as to post notices at and near the home of Colonel William Campbell, warning him that if he did not desist from his prosecution of the loyal adherents of George III, a terrible calamity would befall him, either in the loss of his property or his life.

Thus it happened on a fairly quiet and pleasant Sunday in the spring of the year 1780, Colonel Campbell, accompanied by his wife (who was a sister of Patrick Henry), and several of their neighbors attended a religious service at the Presbyterian house of worship known as Ebbing Spring Church in the upper end of this county. As they were returning to their homes, they happened to be conversing about the audacity of the Tory (believed to be Francis Hopkins), so bold and defiant in his declarations, and suspected of having posted these notices. Just as they arrived at the top of a hill, a short distance west of the residence of Colonel Hiram A. Greever, they observed a man on horseback on the opposite hill coming toward them.

Colonel Campbell was riding beside his wife, with an infant on the horse before him. One of them remarked that the individual meeting them was the Tory of whom they had been speaking, probably now on a horse-stealing expedition, as he was observed to be carrying a rope halter in his hand. Hearing this, Colonel Campbell, without stopping, handed the infant over to its mother and dashed out in front. Seeing the movement and recognizing the man he so feared and hated, the Tory wheeled his horse and started back at quite a rapid gait, pursued at full speed by Colonel Campbell and one of the gentlemen of the company, whose name was Thompson.

Never, it may be presumed, either before or since, has such a dashing and exciting race been witnessed upon that long level between the residences of Colonel Greever and Beattie's. Colonel Campbell dashed up alongside the fleeing Tory, who, seeing he would be caught, turned short to the right down the bank and plunged into the river. As he struck the water, Colonel Campbell, who had left his companion in the rear, leaped in beside him, grasped the Tory's holsters, and threw them into the stream, and then dragged him from his horse into the water.

At this moment Mr. Thompson rode up. Helping Colonel Campbell, they took their prisoner out on the bank and held what may be termed a drumhead court-martial. The Tory, bad as he was, had the virtue of being a brave, candid man. At once he acknowledged the truth of the charge preferred against him and boldly declared his defiance and determination to take horses wherever he could find them. But he was mistaken in his man, for in less than ten minutes he was dangling from the limb of a large sycamore that stood upon the bank of the river.

This is all that is actually written in the county records. There may be more. Elmyra McGuire Royse, a Hopkins genealogist, wrote 100 years later, that Draper (a historian) started checking and reported that Francis Hopkins was hanged by William Campbell and a Negro named Thomas about 1778 or 1779. It was said he was a Tory— amongst other things—but from a careful study, it can be concluded that the occurrence was occasioned by the fact that persons of Scottish and Irish ancestry were unhappy with the people who migrated down from Connecticut, New York, and New Jersey.

It appeared that Colonel Campbell chased Francis Hopkins and hanged him only because *he was told* that Hopkins was a troublemaker. Some witnesses of the time believe that William Hopkins in this account was the son of Francis Hopkins and that he was the William Hopkins who was discharged by proclamation issues in 1782 by the Term Court of Sullivan County, Tennessee. There is also the possibility that William was the brother of Francis Hopkins.

To continue the genealogy, Francis Hopkins married Mary Joslin (Joshlin) (born February 2 1771 in Exeter Rhode Island) and they had the following children:

1. Henry Hopkins: Born December 2, 1743; married an unidentified person.
2. Sarah Hopkins: Born December 26, 1744, in East Greenwich, Rhode Island.
3. Rachel Hopkins: Born May 21, 1747, in East Greenwich, Rhode Island.
4. William Hopkins: Born November 15, 1748.
5. Gardner Hopkins: Born July 16, 1750 in East Greenwich, Rhode Island; died June 4, 1832, in Morgan County, Kentucky. He married Mary Chambers on April 1, 1773, in Orange County, New York.
6. Mary Hopkins: Born April 9, 1753 in East Greenwich, Rhode Island.
7. Francis Hopkins: Born before 1759; died 1823 in Bath County, Kentucky.
8. Eldridge Hopkins: Born about 1759; died about 1799; married Elizabeth Waldon in Madison County, Kentucky, June 16, 1891.
9. Robert Hopkins: Born July 4, 1760; died March 26, 1824, in Nichols County Kentucky; married Elizabeth in New Jersey, 1776.
10. Hannah Hopkins: Born in March 13, 1766, in New York; died August 26, 1852, in Morgan County, Kentucky; marred Thomas Lewis on March 3, 1786, in Morgan County, Kentucky.

The following letter is addressed to William Hopkins of Roxbury from his daughter Hannah (married name: Hannah Gross-Murrey). This William Hopkins was the great-great-great-grandfather of Zella on her mother's side. The letter is reproduced in the same form as sent by Hannah to her father as the eighteenth century turned into the nineteenth century.

"Hono" [Honorable] father

There are to lett [sic] you understand that I am very will [well] in health. Hoping that these few lines will find you all in the same blessed bee God for it. I cannot but wonder of my not hearing from you in all this time I do think long to hear from you yt [that] I may understand of you and my childs wellfae [welfare] hoping yt in a small time ty [that] I shall see you for I wish it very long & tedious till such time as I am with yo & since I have been here in Jamaica I am married to a Joyner [carpenter] and have wh [with him] a sonne & about seaven months old. My child that I brought of New England who is now very will [well] & desires to remember his duty to yo & his kind live [love] in Gegerall soe having noe more at ye [the] present but with my and my husbands although unknown duty to yo & to my mother with love and service to my brothers and sisters & and all ye rest of my relacon [relations] in General and kind love to Mr. ffoster [Foster] & his wife & tell him yt I would be with him in time with Gods permission hopeing [hoping] yt he is careful of my son & yt that they agree will [well] together soe having noe more at ye present but craving yor … foe me I rep

Yor ever Dutifull Daughter

Hannah Murrey

If you send me alter please pray direct to ye care of Mrs. Hannah Hicks.

The reference to Samuel Foster (a non-family member) and his wife is to be expected since he owned the property adjoining the property of William Hopkins and was a close family friend. Also, it is interesting that the word *joyner* (a person who joins pieces of wood together) was used for *carpenter*. The word is still in use in Britain, although the spelling (*joiner*) in Britain is different from that written in the letter.

Adding to this history, in 1829, Andrew Bunton Sr. (Andrew Buntin Sr.), a grandson of William Hopkins as well as a relative of Martha Bunton, moved with his family west from Kentucky to Indiana, locating in what subsequently became Clinton County. Though at that time neither Clinton nor Boone counties had been organized, both counties were under the jurisdiction of Tippecanoe County. Clinton County officially came into existence on March 1, 1830, and was named in honor of DeWitt Clinton, the seventh governor of New York State and architect of the Erie Canal. The act forming the county was approved by the Indiana General Assembly on January 29, 1830. It created Clinton from the eastern parts of neighboring Tippecanoe County.

Andrew and his family were compelled to cut their way through the wilderness to Kirk's Cross Roads, there being no settlement south of Twelve Mile Prairie—now in Effingham County—west of the Little Wabash River (also known as the Little River, in Northeast Indiana). Two months after reaching their destination, Elizabeth (the wife of Andrew Sr.) died and was interred in the Bunton family cemetery. This was the first death in what became known as Jackson Township, one of fourteen current townships in Clinton County, Indiana, and named for President Andrew Jackson. The township was one of the original townships of Clinton County, created at the first meeting of the county commissioners on May 15, 1830, and remains the largest of the current fourteen. The first white settlers were Walter and Anthony Leek, who arrived in 1828, followed within the year by the Bunton family.

Shortly after settling in the township, Andrew Bunton Sr. gave Elihu Bunton (Andrew's son) $200 to purchase the quarter section upon which he resided. The total cost of the land at the time of purchase (May 4, 1832) was $400. Paying the $200 in cash, Elihu applied the proceeds of his farm to the payment of the outstanding $200. There is no notation that any interest was charged on the outstanding $200.

Martha Bunton (born: August 29, 1802, and the great-great-grandmother of Zella on her mother's side) was married to Eldridge Hopkins (born: February 13, 1800) and the son of William Hopkins (above) and brother of Hanah Hopkins Gross-Murrey.

***

Following the line further, but in a different part of the United States, the 1850 census of Macon County Missouri shows the following resident of the county: Peter Gilstrap, age 53, born in Kentucky. In his household were the following, presumably his wife and children: Amy, 36; Mary, 14; Tyre M., 12; Bright A., 10. Bright eventually became the father of Rebecca Laura Gilstrap, Zella's grandmother on her father's side of the family.

The listing of the children of Peter and Amy Gilstrap, which agrees so well with the census record for 1850, might have come from a personal record such as the type of record found in a family Bible. The name Gilstrap is most likely English—probably a name from a lost or unidentified place, possibly with a name such as Gil(l)sthorp(e), the first element being on Old English or Old Norse

411

personal name, the second being an Old Norse word for *hamlet*, or *settlement*, or possibly an Anglicized form of a Danish place-name from *Gelstrup* or *Gølstrup* in Jutland.

At her birth, Rebecca Gilstrap had older siblings: Lewis, 8; Daniel, 6; William T., 4; and James M., 2. Other records indicate that the Gilstrap family migrated from Wayne County, Kentucky, across the Mississippi River to the country along the southern border of Macon County, south of Callao. The records also show that the marriage of Bright A. Gilstrap and Permelia Ann Andrews took place on November 18, 1858.

The 1850 census of Macon County, Missouri, also shows Haley Andrews, age 53, born in Virginia. Others in the household included Jane, age 44, born in Virginia (evidently the wife of Haley); and Permelia Ann, age 8, born in Missouri. Digging even further into Zella's past, the estate records in the Probate Office, Courthouse, Macon, there are letters of administration for Peter Gilstrap that listed Bright A. Gilstrap as an heir, and for Haley Andrews that listed Permelia Gilstrap as an heir.

The oldest child of Alex (Bright Alexander) and Ann (Permelia Ann) could have been named for his father and her father—Peter Haley. Haley (or Hailey Andrews) was noted to live in Franklin County, Virginia, as recorded in the census of 1820 and in the census of 1830.

Zella's grandmother was born Rebecca Laura Gilstrap on May 17, 1867, before marrying George W. Bell (born October 4, 1862, in Independence, Missouri). An early record shows that Rebecca was born in Bevier, Macon County, Missouri, to Bright Alexander Gilstrap and Permelia Ann Andrews. Rebecca died on April 16, 1951, in Macon County, Missouri, and was buried in East Oakwood

Cemetery, Bevier. Rebecca was the wife of George W. Bell. They were married November 4, 1886, in Bevier, Macon County, Missouri.

***

Zella's story does not end here. Many adventures and other snippets of information can be derived from the family history. Perhaps one of the most interesting stories comes from more recent history. It relates to Zella's drive in the summer of 1964 to Florida to meet up with Bob after he had left Wyoming to further his education at the University of Florida.

The journey took Zella and the little Millikens (three daughters and one son) through Selma, Alabama. They had not intended to stop in Selma, but a burst tire that needed repair changed their plans. This was a time when civil rights and race relations in the United States were not on a firm footing, and even outsiders were looked upon with a high degree of suspicion.

Their forced stay in Selma began in the late afternoon on the outskirts of Selma. The suffering that usually goes with a flat tire became obvious. However, two high school students came to the rescue. When Zella asked them for directions to the nearest service station, they offered to change the tire, as the service station would "charge too much."

Zella was grateful for this courtesy, and since she and the children had already eaten, they went to the motel and stayed there overnight, without venturing out until morning, realizing that Selma was a hotbed of unrest. Zella was not willing to risk the drive to Florida without a spare tire, so the next morning she purchased a new one before they continued on their way.

***

In the 1960s, Selma became the focal point of unrest that eventually made it a key city in the history of the Civil Rights Movement. Opposition to equal rights was strong, but voter registration and desegregation efforts continued and expanded during 1963 and the first part of 1964. Defying intimidation, economic retaliation, arrests, firings, and beatings, an ever-increasing number of African Americans attempted to register to vote, but few were able to do so.

Medgar Evers, an African American civil rights activist who was involved in efforts to overturn segregation at the University of Mississippi, had been shot and killed the morning of June 12, 1963, by a member of the White Citizens Council—just hours after President John F. Kennedy gave a speech on national television in support of civil rights. Evers had become active in the civil rights movement after returning from overseas service in World War II and completing secondary education. He became a field secretary for the NAACP. As a veteran, he was buried with full military honors at Arlington National Cemetery. His murder and the resulting trials inspired civil rights protests as well as numerous works of art, music, and film.

In addition, John F. Kennedy, the thirty-fifth president of the United States, was shot and killed in Dallas on November 22, 1963. The alleged assassin Lee Harvey Oswald was later apprehended, but he was soon assassinated, too. The reasons for the president's assassination were never clear. Some people believed that it was because of the President's stand on civil rights.

In the summer of 1964, when Zella and the little Millikens were driving through, a sweeping injunction issued by local Judge James Hare barred any gathering of three or more people under sponsorship of the Student Nonviolent Coordinating Committee (SNCC), the Southern Christian Leadership Conference (SCLC), the Dallas County Voters League (DCVL), or with the involvement of forty-one named civil rights leaders. This injunction temporarily halted civil rights activity until Dr. Martin Luther King Jr. defied it by speaking at the Brown Chapel Church (and at the African Methodist Episcopal Church) on January 2, 1965.

The Milliken Children, May 1965 (from the left): Michelle, Pam, Sherry, and Greg

This church was a starting point for the Selma to Montgomery marches in 1965. As the meeting place and offices of the Southern Christian Leadership Conference during the Selma Movement, it played a major role in the events that led to the adoption of the Voting

Rights Act of 1965. The nation's reaction to Selma's Bloody Sunday march is widely credited with making the passage of the Voting Rights Act politically viable in the United States Congress.

Segregation in the schools still existed at the time of Zella's visit to Selma. It was not until 1968 that segregation in all forms of was declared unconstitutional by the Supreme Court. By 1970 support for formal legal segregation had dissolved. Formal racial discrimination was illegal in school systems, businesses, the American military, other civil services, and the government. Separate bathrooms, water fountains, and schools all disappeared, and the Civil Rights Movement had the public's support.

It was into this den of unrest that Zella and the little Millikens arrived in Selma. So with the potential for civil disturbances at any time, the tendency for the local hostiles to remonstrate with anyone they didn't see eye-to-eye with, and the heavy mistrust of outsiders, one night in a motel was sufficient for Zella. Once the car tire was repaired, she (with the Miniature Millikens) was relieved to be (according to the words of Willie Nelson) "on the road again."

CHAPTER 14: MEMORIES

It is almost seventy years since the end of World War II and Bob's eyes have dimmed, but his memories of the men that he trained with and flew with during the war are sharp and focused.

Like Bob, most of those men were just out of boyhood and still in their teens when bombs rained down on Pearl Harbor, changing forever the world that they knew. Overnight, high school dances and homecoming queens were pushed aside by recruiting posters, and nightly radio newscasts reported Axis advances while Allied defeats were many and Allied victories were few. Across America, men and women of Bob's generation stepped forward without hesitation to fight for and defend the United States and its Allies.

With proud justification, these men and women have been called *The Greatest Generation*—a term that arose to describe the generation of youths who grew up in the United States during the deprivations of the Great Depression, and then went on to fight in World War II, as well as those whose productivity on at the home front made a massive and decisive contribution to the war effort.

The actions and sacrifices made by the men and women of that generation must not be forgotten. Each person who served and wore the uniform of the United States has an individual story that *must* be told. Similarly, those who worked behind the enemy lines and those who worked on the home front all have stories to tell that must be heard. History must not be allowed to forget the contribution to freedom of these men and women.

The teenagers of today play war games on their computers. War was not a game for Bob and his comrades. There were no computers, and war was real. Their missions had deadly outcomes for both sides. In the context of this book, pilots on both sides were fighting for their respective countries and, most of all, for their lives. They had to get it right, not just the first time, but every time. They couldn't reboot or restart their computers. There were no second chances for Bob and his comrades. Success was necessary the first time and every time. Bombs from aircraft on both sides killed real people in English cities and in European cities and countries. Anti-aircraft fire and plane-to-plane cannon fire turned Allied and German aircraft into balls of flame that fell to the ground, often as unidentifiable pieces of twisted metal, and left grieving families of the aircrew in the wake of such events.

Enemy pilots fought back with skills honed during years of combat before America entered World War II. They were good. The American pilots had had to be better. Ultimately, superior equipment, skilled pilots, and massive home front production of the vehicles and weaponry of war tipped the scales. Still, luck—some called it fate or coincidence—intervened. Comrades were lost not only in aerial combat, but also in training accidents because of mechanical failures and because of weather-caused crashes.

Those young men—Bob's fallen comrades who will forever remain as young as they were on the day that they died—are offered lasting tribute through this book. The following list presents (in alphabetical order) with honor and remembrance the names of Bob's colleagues, the fallen warriors who made the ultimate sacrifice for their country. I apologize for any names that have inadvertently been omitted:

Harold D. Bledsoe
Ralph E. Byers
Dennis R. Chamberlain
Robert L. Coleman
Robert N. Cooke
Paul M. Daily
Glenn W. Goodrich
Jack P. Greve
Robert T. Hazzard
Paul J. Heuermann
Ben Higgins
Charles N. Holcomb
George Houston
Claude N. Kimball
Lenton F. Kirkland
Herman Q. Lane
Gene F. Loveless
Milton J. Merkle
Clarence C. Moore
John R. Northrop

Merle V. Ogden
Richard V. Riggs
Richard Stein
James G. Ware

Carefully tended roadside memorials in Europe mark where some fell and will remain there for generations. The remains of many other downed pilots have never been found, and their passing is marked only by now filled-in, charred craters on French and German battlefields or by rusted fragments of a P-38.

***

In recent years Bob has visited the graves of comrades buried in France and Normandy. They lie in hallowed cemeteries, surrounded by thousands upon thousands of other young Americans from ground units and naval units who are quietly remembered by family and friends every day. The skies above them are quiet and free of combat and are disturbed only by the vapor trails of the commercial aircraft that fly from city to city. To the survivors of the war—aging veterans on sentimental journeys—standing reverently at attention, those in the graves are as they were when they fell—comrades in arms, friends, and colleagues.

Another tribute that Bob pays to the men who flew with him comes from his own words, which mean much to the men and women of Bob's generation and should also be remembered:

I was fortunate that I got to fly. I got to fly the plane I wanted and I came home. It was something that I wanted to do because I love to fly and I was fighting for my country.

Robert Carl Milliken,
US Army Air Corps, P-38 Pilot (1942–46)
December 6, 2006, to the *Laramie Daily Boomerang*

Tributes are also due to all armed forces personnel and their support staff who fought during the war; and to people such as Mademoiselle Suzanne Schneider and her colleagues, who resisted the efforts of the occupying German forces and put themselves in danger by helping Allied pilots and soldiers, at the same time risking capture by the hated Gestapo. Had this happened, their fate involving torture and death was assured.

Their efforts must also be continuously remembered and not forgotten.

***

Finally, I offer my heartfelt thanks to Bob for his willingness to tell me this story. I also thank Scott Frederick for allowing me to publish his translated letters that document not only the trials and tribulations of his father, First Lieutenant James S. Frederick, a P-38 pilot in the 428th Fighter Squadron, 474th Fighter Group, but also the translation of the journal of Mademoiselle Suzanne Schneider, which provides valuable insights into the painful wounds suffered by Lieutenant Frederick and what it was like to live under the jackboot of Nazi Germany.

To them all thank you.

Note added: Zella Faye Bell Milliken died on October 25 2014. *Requiescat in pace.*

INFORMATION SOURCES

Ambrose, S.E. 1991. *Band of Brothers: E Company, 506th Regiment, 101st Airborne from Normandy to Hitler's Eagle's Nest.* Touchstone, Simon & Schuster, New York.

Anderson, B.J. 1985. *Army Air Forces Stations: A Guide to the Stations Where US Army Air Forces Personnel Served in the United Kingdom during World War II.* Research Division, USAF Historical Research Center, Maxwell Air Force Base, Alabama. January 31.
http://www.scribd.com/doc/1423777/US-Air-Force-usaaf-bases-in-united-kingdom

Atkinson, R. 2013. *The Guns at Last Light: The War in Western Europe, 1944–1945.* Henry Holt and Company LLC, New York.

Babcock, J.B. 2005. *Taught to Kill: An American Boy's War from the Ardennes to Berlin.* Potomac Books Inc., Dulles, Virginia.

Bartlett, I.S. (Editor). 1918. *History of Wyoming: Volume I.* The S.J. Clarke Publishing Company, Chicago, Illinois.

Bartlett, I.S. (Editor). 1918. *History of Wyoming. Volume II*. The S.J. Clarke Publishing Company, Chicago, Illinois.

Beard, F.B. (Editor). 1935. *Wyoming from Territorial Days to the Present*. Chicago: American Historical Society, Chicago, Illinois.

Bowman, M.W. 2009. *The Bedford Triangle: US Undercover Operations from England in World War Two*. The History Press Ltd., Stroud, Gloucestershire, United Kingdom.

Burns, R.H., Gillespie, A.S., and Richardson, W.G. 1955. *Wyoming's Pioneer Ranches*. Top of the World Press, Laramie, Wyoming.

Buys, C.J. 2004. *A Quick History of Leadville*. Western Reflections Publishing Company, Montrose, Colorado.

Carlton, C. 1992. *The Experience of the British Civil Wars*. Routledge Publishers, London, United Kingdom.

Cawthorne, N. 2011. *The Story of the SS: Hitler's Infamous Legions of Death*. Arcturus Publishing Ltd., London, United Kingdom.

Celis, P. 2003. *Runways to Victory: Belgian Airfields and Allied Tactical Fighter Operations 1944–1945*. Marhav S.A., Luxembourg.

Chamblin, T.S. (Editor). 1970. *The Historical Encyclopedia of Wyoming*. Historical Institute, Cheyenne, Wyoming.

Churchill, W.S. 1951. *The Second World War: Volumes 1–6*. Houghton Mifflin Company, New York.

Collins, M., and King, M. 2011. *Voices of the Bulge: Untold Stories from Veterans of the Battle of the Bulge*. Zenith Press, Minneapolis, Minnesota.

Davis, W.C. 2010. *The American Frontier: Pioneers, Settlers, and Cowboys 1800–1899*. Salamander Books, University of Oklahoma Press, Norman, Oklahoma.

Drake, F.S. 1878. *The Town of Roxbury: Its Memorable Persons and Places, Its History and Antiquities, with Numerous Illustrations of Its Old Landmarks and Noted Personages*. Published by the

Author, 131 Warren Street, Boston. *Out of Print—available through the Boston Public Library. Also available at:* http://openlibrary.org/books/OL7057823M/The_town_of_Roxbury

Fox, B., and Poulet, C. 2012. *Wyoming from the Air: Where the Eagle Soars*. CMP Publishing, Dubois, Wyoming.

Fraser, A. 1973. *Cromwell: Our Chief of Men*. Wedenfield and Nicholson, London, United Kingdom.

Fraser, A. 2001. *Cromwell: The Lord Protector*. Grove Press, New York.

Frederick, S. 2010. *Daisy in the Sky*. November. http://www.conscript-heroes.com/escapelines/EEIE-Articles/Art-10-Frederick.htm

Hastings. M. 2011. *Inferno: The World at War, 1939–1945*. Vintage Books, Random, House, New York.

Haythornthwaite, P. 1983. *The English Civil War 1642–1652: An Illustrated Military History*. Brockhampton Press, Leicester, Leicestershire, United Kingdom.

Hendrickson, G.O. (Editor). 1977. *Peopling the High Plains: Wyoming's European Heritage*. Wyoming State Archives and Historical Department, Cheyenne, Wyoming.

Higham, R.D.S., and Williams, C. 2004. *Flying American Aircraft of WWII 1939–1945, Volume 1*. Stackpole Books, Mechanicsburg, Pennsylvania.

Kershaw, A. 2004. *The Longest Winter: The Battle of the Bulge and the Epic Story of WW II's Most Decorated Platoon*. Da Capo Press, Perseus Books Group, Cambridge, Massachusetts.

Larson, T.A. 1965. *History of Wyoming*. University of Nebraska Press, Lincoln, Nebraska.

Maurer, M. 1961. *Air Force Combat Units of World War II*. US Government Printing Office, Washington, DC.

Miller, D.C. 1977. *Ghost Towns of Wyoming*. Village Books, Medford, Oregon.

Milliken, Robert C., and Milliken, Zella F. 1946–2012 *Family Archives*, Laramie Wyoming.

Mombeek, E. 2001. *Defenders of the Reich: Jagdgeschwader 1. Volume One 1939–1942*. Classic Publications Ltd., Crowborough, East Sussex, United Kingdom.

Mombeek, E. 2001. *Defenders of the Reich: Jagdgeschwader 1. Volume Two 1943*. Classic Publications Ltd., Crowborough, East Sussex, United Kingdom.

Mombeek, E. 2001. *Defenders of the Reich: Jagdgeschwader 1. Volume Three 1944–1945*. Classic Publications Ltd., Crowborough, East Sussex, United Kingdom.

Morgan, R., and Powers, R. 2001. *The Man Who Flew the Memphis Belle: Memoir of a WWII Bomber Pilot*. Dutton-Penguin Putnam Inc., New York.

Moulton, C. 1997. *The Grand Encampment: Settling the High Country*. High Plains Press, Glendo, Wyoming.

Moulton, C. 2010. *Following Calamity Jane: From Cheyenne, Wyoming, to Virginia City, Montana*. True West Magazine: Preserving the American West. Cave Creek, Arizona.

Moser, J.F., and Baron, G.R. 2009. *A Fighter Pilot in Buchenwald*. Edens Vail Media and All Clear Publishing LLC, Bellingham, Washington.

Oleson, J.A. 2007. *In Their Own Words. True Stories and Adventures of the American Fighter Ace*. iUniverse Inc., Lincoln Nebraska.

Peterson, C. 2007. *Images of America: Laramie*. Arcadia Publishing, Chicago, Illinois.

Rea, T. *The Rock Springs Massacre*. http://www.wyohistory.org/ essays/rock-springs-massacre. Accessed March 24, 2013.

Rust, K.C., Letzer, G.J., Grygier, J.J., and Groh, R. 1967. *The 9th Air Force in World War II*. Aero Publishers, Fallbrook, California.

Schrijvers, P. 2001. *The Crash of Ruin: American Combat Soldiers in Europe during World War II*. NYU Press, New York. Page 79-80.

Shelton, V.E. 2006. *Swat's Story—World War II Fighter Pilot Ace: Reminiscences of Robert C. Milliken*. Modern Printing Co., Laramie, Wyoming.

Slocombe, R. 2010. *British Posters of the Second World War*. Imperial War Museum, London, United Kingdom.

Swindt, K. 1978. *429th Fighter Squadron: The Retail Gang: European Theater, World War II*. Heritage Publications, Sacramento, California.

The Northern California Friends of the American Fighter Aces Association. *P-38 Lightning Aces* (DVD). 2009. Aerospace Museum of California (formerly McClellan AFB), North Highlands, Sacramento County, California.

Thybony, S., Rosenberg, R.G., and Rosenberg, E.M. 2001. *The Medicine Bows: Wyoming's Mountain Country*. Caxton Press, Caldwell, Idaho.

Tillet, P. 2014. *Tentative History of In/Exfiltrations into/from France during WW II 1940 to 1945* (Parachutes, Plane, & Sea Landings). http://www.plan-sussex-1944.net/anglais/pdf/ infiltrations_into_france.pdf

Tillitt, M.H. 1944. "Army–Navy Pay Tops Most Civilians' Unmarried Private's Income Equivalent to $3,600 Salary". Barron's National Business and Financial Weekly, April 24.

University of Wyoming Bulletin and Catalog. "Announcements for the Academic Year 1944–1945. Volume XLI, No. 1".

US WW2 Military Records. "Pilots Shot Down July 6, 1944". http://forum.armyairforces.com/Pilots-shot-down-July-6th-1944-m179656.aspx

Weidel, N. 2001. *Sheepwagon: Home on the Range*. High Plains Press, Glendo, Wyoming.

White, D. 2008. *Bitter Ocean: The Battle of the Atlantic, 1939–1945*. Simon & Schuster, New York.

Yenne, B. 2009. *Aces High: The Heroic Saga of the Two Top-Scoring American Aces of World War II*. Berkley Caliber, Berkley Publishing Group, New York.

Young, P., and Holmes, R. 1974. *The English Civil War: A Military History of the Three Civil Wars 1642–1651*. Eyre Methuen, York, Yorkshire, United Kingdom.

Also:

The Lost Airmen of Buchenwald. 2012. Documentary Film. The Military Channel, DirecTV. Note: "The Military Channel" has been remained "The American Heroes Channel."

A documentary film that chronicles the little-known story of the rigors and threats of death faced by Allied airmen who were imprisoned at Buchenwald Concentration Camp during the latter part of World War II.
http://www.lostairmen.com/
http://jonathanturley.org/2013/04/21/kirby-cowan-the-airmen-of-buchenwald-and-the-klb-club-a-cautionary-tale/

ABOUT THE AUTHOR

Dr. James G. Speight earned his B.Sc. and PhD degrees from the University of Manchester, England; he also holds a DSc (Geological Sciences) and a PhD (Petroleum Engineering). In addition to being the author of more than sixty technical books on fossil fuel science and engineering, biomass science and technology, environmental sciences, and business, he has published three novels and is currently working on a fourth.

His hobbies are *history* and *languages*, and being a soccer referee for almost twenty years, he has an avid liking for soccer.

This is an American story as told to me during many conversations that I had over a four-year period with Robert Carl Milliken (Bob). The book is important because it tells of men and women who stood up to be counted when their country called – people whose deeds are fading into history and soon may be forgotten. The book incorporates the early history of Wyoming by starting with the first arrival of Bob's family in the Wyoming Territory before Statehood was conferred and follows the events which led Bob to his actions as a World War II Fighter Ace (he flew 68 combat missions). For the reader, I have also placed Bob's life in the perspective of the parallel actions that occurred in the Western United States and then during World War II in the European and Pacific Theaters.

The book will serve as a reminder for those readers who are not familiar with the events of World War II but who will appreciate and understand events outside of their own experience. In addition, it will help the families of World War II veterans to remember with pride the men and women who answered the call of their country.

And last but definitely not least, there is also Zella's story – the young woman who Bob married on August 25 1946 and who bore four children, three daughters and one son. Zella's family history is also interesting – the family can be traced back to 1617 in England and she is a descendent of one of the two regicide judges who authorized the execution of King Charles I of England after he was deposed by the forces of Oliver Cromwell during the English Civil War (1642-1649). Furthermore, this book is not only a tribute to Bob and Zella but also to Zella's brother Bobby (Master Sergeant Robert Lewis Bell) who saw action on many missions as the belly gunner in a B-24 bomber and who researched the history of the Bell family in considerable detail.

authorHOUSE®

ISBN 978-1-4969-6423-6

52395

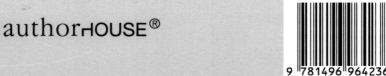